GENDER AND NEWSROOM CULTURES

Identities at Work

THE HAMPTON PRESS COMMUNICATION SERIES

WOMEN, CULTURE AND MASS COMMUNICATION
Karen Ross and Marjan de Bruin, Series Editors

Gender and Newsroom Cultures:
  Identities at Work
    Marjan de Bruin and Karen Ross (eds.)

forthcoming

Women/Advertising/Representation:
  Extending Beyond Familiar Paradigms
    Sue Abel, Anita Nowak, and Marjan de Bruin (eds.)

Commercializing Women:
  Images of Asian Women in the Media
    Katherine T. Frith and Kavita Karan

GENDER AND NEWSROOM CULTURES

Identities at Work

edited by

Marjan de Bruin
University of the West Indies

Karen Ross
Coventry University (U.K.)

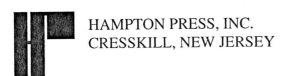

HAMPTON PRESS, INC.
CRESSKILL, NEW JERSEY

Printed in the United States of America

Library of Congress Cataloging-in-Publication Data

Gender and newsroom cultures : identities at work / edited by Marjan de Bruin, Karen Ross.
    p. cm. — (The Hampton Press communication series)
  ISBN 1-57273-588-0 — ISBN 1-57273-589-9
 1. Women in journalism. 2. Sex role in the work environment. I. Bruin, Marjan de.
II. Ross, Karen, 1957 III. Series.

PN4784.W7G46 2004
070.4'082–dc22

                                             2004054002

Hampton Press, Inc.
23 Broadway
Cresskill, NJ 07626

Contents

Introduction: Beyond the Body Count   vii
Marjan de Bruin and Karen Ross

1 Organizational, Professional and Gender Identities—Overlapping,
   Coinciding and Contradicting Realities in Caribbean Media Practices   1
   Marjan de Bruin

2 Gender, Occupational Knowledge and Control Over Work in the
   Newspaper Newsroom   17
   Wilson Lowrey

3 Gender Stereotyping in the Production of News   45
   *Juana Gallego, Elvira Altés, María José Cantón,
      María Eugenia Melús and Jaume Soriano*

4 Feminine and Feminist Values in Communication Professions:
   Exceptional Skills and Expertise or "Friendliness Trap?"   67
   Romy Fröhlich

5 Gender-Typing in the Newsroom: The Feminization of Swedish
   Television News Production, 1958-2000   81
   Monika Djerf-Pierre and Monica Löfgren-Nilsson

6 Hanging in There: Women, Gender and Newsroom Cultures
   in Africa   107
   Aida Opoku-Mensah

7 Organizational Factors in the Radio Newsroom: Cause for Hope
   or Despair?   121
   Aliza Lavie

8 Sex at Work: Gender Politics and Newsroom Culture   145
   Karen Ross

9 The Gender (Dis)Advantage in Indian Print Media   163
   Ammu Joseph

10 Gender in the Newsroom: Canadian Experiences   181
    Gertrude J. Robinson

11 Coping with Journalism: Gendered Newsroom Culture   197
    Margareta Melin-Higgins

12 Shifting Sites: Feminist, Gay and Lesbian News Activism in the   223
    U.S. Context
    Carolyn M. Byerly

13 Does Gender Matter in the Newsroom? Some Remarks on
    Gendered Discourse and Estonian Journalist Culture   243
    Barbi Pilvri

Contributors   255
Author Index   259
Subject Index   267

INTRODUCTION

Beyond the Body Count

Marjan de Bruin
Karen Ross

Not too long ago, researchers writing about gender and (journalistic) profession-alism in the newsroom focused primarily on the presence of female journalists in media organizations (e.g., Beasley, 1993; Gallagher, 1995; Gallagher & Quindoza-Santiago, 1994). The underlying, sometimes implicit, assumption was, once women in the newsroom reached a "critical mass," they would influ-ence story selection, handling, and reporting approaches (Mills, 1997). Gradually, however, academic discourse has begun to move beyond this "body count" and started to focus on gender and professional ideology, and gender and journalistic culture. Concentrating only—or mainly—on the proportion of women in the newsroom had proved to be too narrow a focus. The rigidity—or flexibility—of the journalistic culture in the midst of which women journalists worked could not be left out if one was to explain their opportunities or obsta-cles (Zilliacus-Tikkanen, 1997). Some authors argued that masculinity, as cur-rently defined by Western societies, accorded so much better with journalism's values (van Zoonen, 1998), or, that professional values were subordinate to the "social and cultural expectations of the macho newsroom that women are expected to work within" (Skidmore, 1998, p. 208). Others suggested that jour-nalism's values—constructed by male decision makers—had been made to fit masculine values (de Bruin, 2000).

Newsroom interaction between women and men journalists has also entered the discussion, suggesting that the male journalist preferred to view his female colleague in terms of her gender before accepting her as a profession-al—sending the message that journalism and femininity didn't really go togeth-er (Steiner, 1998). "Newsroom culture" and "journalistic culture"—more specifically, gendered professional practices in the newsroom—became the focus of attention (Allan, 1998, 1999; Carter, Branston, & Allan, 1998; Creedon, 1993; de Bruin, 2000; Kitzinger, 1998; Steiner, 1998; Skidmore, 1998; van Zoonen, 1998; Weaver, 1997).

In trying to capture gender and professionalism as variables in media production, "gender orientation in journalism" (van Zoonen, 1998, pp. 35, 36) or
"gendered professionalism" (Skidmore, 1998, p. 208) became the catch phrases.
Authors began to recognize the "gendered realities of journalism" (Allan,
1999), which expressed themselves in steps routinely taken in the news production: story selection, story assignment, source selection, editing, and, according
to some, in actual writing style and story approach.

But it is only over the last few years that media studies have paid, in any
systematic way, more attention to the dynamics between gender and the (media)
organization (Allan, 1999; Carter et al., 1998; Ross, 2001). A similar void existed in organizational communications studies and in organizational studies in
general. Influenced by feminist research, women in organizations had been a
study topic in these fields since the 1980s, but the behavior of women and men
was seen as determined by their positions, reflecting the patriarchal society that
structured apparently "gender-neutral" organizations. It was not until the early
to mid-1990s that the focus began to shift to a consideration of the dynamics
between gender and organizational structures and practices, and their role in
reproducing gender inequality.

After the mid-1990s, a steady stream of publications in organizational studies began to break away only from looking at the organization as a gender-neutral "no one's land" (e.g., Alvesson & Billing, 1997; Ashforth & Johnson, 2001;
Bartel & Dutton, 2001; Gherardi, 1995; Halford, Savage, & Witz, 1997;
Whetten & Godfrey, 1998). Rather than viewing gender as "a fixed attribute
imported into workplace organizations" (Witz & Savage, 1992, p. 26), this new
research began to focus on gender as a relational quality expressed in specific
social practices. The emergence of this interpretive perspective, as a new
approach, shifted researchers' interests "away from controlling organizational
outcomes to understanding the process of organizing and the role of discourse
in that process" (Fine, 1993, p. 126).

Gender and Newsroom Culture: Identities at Work seeks to continue this
trend. The authors in this volume interpret behavior of female and male journalists in media organizations as the result of practices and interaction in a culture in
which gender is a major "given." They choose the analysis of gendered symbols,
values, meanings, and significations as the key to understanding relationships in
organizations, rather than power differences based on organizational rank.

The contributions that we have brought together represent a variety of
approaches and very different realities. We made a deliberate effort to include
voices that are heard less often in international academic debate, yet that represent a majority of the world's realities. Sometimes, the absence of these voices
can be explained by their lack of resources to set and execute their own research
agenda and instead have to work with an agenda driven by the interests of external funding agencies or by better resourced communications scholars.
Sometimes, the same limited resources make research undertakings much more
modest and therefore out of sync with an international debate dominated by

numbers and large-scale projects. We recognize that smaller, qualitative projects with high-quality and richly textured testimonies will contribute to our understanding of the different contexts and realities of which most of us ignorant, which we are *not* confronted with. Therefore, this book contains a mix of methods and approaches, a mix of small and large numbers, a mix of cultures and different priorities that we hope will provide some original food for thought.

THE CHAPTERS

Marjan de Bruin (chapter 1) explores the concepts of *gender, organizational*, and *professional identities*. Her basic assumption is that people assume multiple identities to serve different functions, depending on circumstances and interests. She demonstrates some of the complex dynamics between these multiple identities through the preliminary analysis of 20 in-depth qualitative interviews with journalists in Caribbean newsrooms. Her analysis shows the strategies these journalists developed to minimize or inflate the socially accepted meanings attached to certain identities. Other strategies are aimed at claiming certain identities and ignoring others, again depending on the incentives coming with these shifts.

Newsroom practices involve occupational subgroups, such as editors, designers, and photographers. They compete in daily negotiations on the shaping of media output. How does gender influence the degree to which design experts (as opposed to text editors) influence the planning and final decision making for news presentation? And how does gender interact with other predictors of occupational control, such as occupational and technological knowledge, occupational cohesiveness, centrality to the work process, and organizational structure? If the impact of gender differs from one subspecialty to another, then we may need to talk in a less generalized way about gender as an influencing factor in news production. Wilson Lowrey (chapter 2) focuses on the interactions between the various subgroups and concludes convincingly that gender plays a role in newsroom decision making about content. For his study, Lowrey selected design managers and international news editors as interview respondents in a survey. His survey included 233 U.S.-based newspapers.

One strategy that can be seen in the social practices of journalists in newsrooms is gender stereotyping and sex-typing in structural arrangements. This process of gender stereotyping in the newsroom is the main focus of five Spanish researchers (Juana Gallego, Elvira Altés, María José Cantón, María Eugenia Melús, Jaume Soriano) in chapter 3. Through participant observation in four national Spanish newspapers and one news agency, these researchers identified how often the perpetuation of gender stereotypes took place in ways that were implicit, difficult to distinguish, embodied in rituals, and as part of professional and organizational routines. The researchers took several dimensions into account: organizational culture, journalistic culture, the sociocultural context, and the personal dimension of the individual journalist. The editorial meetings, as one of the crucial decision-making moments in the production process of print journalism, received special attention. Their analysis of findings provides insight into the gendered patterns of journalistic treatment of certain issues—inclusion of certain topics, rejection of others—and the dynamics that lead to these varying decisions.

One of the popular images of women in the media and communication industry is the stereotype of women as "better communicators." A questionable image, Romy Fröhlich contends in chapter 4, and a dangerous myth as well, because it imports the "mothering" role from home into the workplace. In Fröhlich's secondary analysis she indicates how, with an assumption of exceptional communication skills, women frequently and increasingly choose the professions that are deemed "appropriate" for their gender. The same gender-based expectations may trigger a corresponding demand by employers, which in turn reinforce those gender stereotypes. In the professional labor market, a re-codification takes place, whereby the higher "value" placed on men compensates for their supposed entry-level disadvantage (of being poorer communicators than women).

Monika Djerf-Pierre and Monica Löfgren-Nilsson (chapter 5) studied the changing social organization of the news department and its working conditions in Swedish broadcasting (TV) over a period of almost 50 years, combining quantitative content analysis with a survey. They chose to study the gender patterns of these news organizations at three analytical levels. The first level is the structural, and deals with basic sex-typing within organizations in terms of work tasks, assignments, and positions. The second level is the symbolic (i.e., the construction of symbols and notions of gender). The third analytical level is the relational and deals with the interaction between women and men within an organization.

The examination of the positions of men and women in newsrooms and the division of roles, responsibilities, benefits, rights, power, and privilege in African countries is a serious challenge. There is a dearth of information and research on these topics, writes Aida Opoku-Mensah in chapter 6, and experiences have so far not been documented in any systematic way. The sociocultural factors that inhibit women in their professional lives as journalists have rarely been discussed in relation to the power dynamics which exist in newsrooms across the continent. Opoku-Mensah undertook what she calls, "a very modest study" and interviewed a number of male and female journalists. Through their testimonies, this chapter explores the persistence of the male–female divide and its translation into sociolegal and sociocultural media practice that produces a culture of discrimination and bias, characterized by inequity and inequality in all aspects of media work.

The working environment as a potential influence on structuring the patterns of reasoning and behavior of professionals in the newsroom is Aliza

Lavie's point of departure in chapter 7. Her main focus is whether and in what ways the work environment could have such an impact, through an analysis of the social practices of (radio) professionals. What are the organizational factors that influence, or create, gender-based differences in perceptions, attitudes, and professional practice among female and male editors? Assuming that work environments reproduce the patterns of gender relationships prevalent in the wider society, Lavie expects that the radio newsroom work environment, through its implicit social practices, positions female and male editors differently. Her study focused on male and female news editors in two national public radio stations in Israel—*The Voice of Israel* and *IDF* (Israel Defense Forces) Radio. These are substantively different Israeli news organizations in terms of their organizational practice and gender bias, structured by differences in formal job description, occupational history, and professional specialization and Lavie argues that these structural differences have a specific impact on how women and men practitioners experience working life in each newsroom environment.

What do women working as news journalists think about their work? Do they believe that their gender is an important aspect of their professional practice or is gender entirely subordinate to profession? As part of a larger study of women, politics, and news, Karen Ross (chapter 8) undertook a small-scale study in order to gain a preliminary understanding of the significance of gender in the practice of journalism in Britain, from a female practitioner perspective. Her research suggests that gender is important in the newsroom but that its impact is often felt in negative ways. Ross challenges us to ask some questions of principle: Is identification with and loyalty to the profession a stronger force than other personal variables such as gender, ethnicity, or sexuality? If journalists operate as an "interpretive community" can dissenting voices still speak from inside that community? Moreover, how can this notion of "community" accommodate what we know to be structural inequalities in women's experiences and career prospects within media industries?

These questions are not only relevant in Britain. Ammu Joseph (chapter 9), writing about Indian women journalists, recognizes the influence of other identities (class, caste, creed, race, and ethnicity) on women's access to and experiences in the profession, their interactions with its structures, and individuals within it. These experiences, in turn, are bound to determine the perceptions of women journalists and the way they are perceived and treated both within the profession and in the wider society. Joseph interviewed more than 200 Indian women journalists working in English and various Indian languages and noticed a dichotomy in their self-perception: Despite the fact that many of them have been publicly recognized for their excellent work, the category "woman" continues to connote inferiority. On the other hand, many women in the profession made it clear to Joseph that women possess certain inherent qualities that enhance their contribution to media in a number of ways.

More proactive newsroom strategies form a major focus of several other chapters. Gertrude Robinson (chapter 10) provides examples from Canadian newsroom practices, illustrating how women have developed different strategies for building their professional careers. They use a range of understandings of how to perform their work roles in the heterosexual newsroom culture. She describes three types of systemic biases in this culture: the masculinist notions about what constitutes a professional career; the so-called "professional climate" and a third set of factors relating to societal norms that expect females to act out a "passive" rather than an "active" professional role. Robinson's analysis is based on a national comparison of Canadian journalists of both sexes.

In looking at journalistic culture as a power struggle between the dominant culture and oppositional cultures, Margareta Melin-Higgins (chapter 11) explores the variety of strategies that male journalists apply to confirm and maintain the dominant (male) journalist culture. However, the women in her study appear to have some very clear and outspoken tactics for coping with this hegemony. Based on observations and thematic interviews of 35 British journalists conducted in 1992 and again—with the same journalists—in 1998, this chapter explores how female journalists seem to have more fragmented identities as journalists, but at the same time seem to be much more convinced of their identities as journalists and their approach to journalism than their male colleagues.

When notions of gender and sex-typing in the newsroom change, these changes usually take place against the background of a normative notion of assumed heterosexuality. Carolyn Byerly (chapter 12) is, in her words "specifically concerned with the gains and the hindrances that women and sexual minorities have encountered in their efforts to establish a more powerful relationship to news over the years." This relationship has always been the site of struggles to include new and different voices and Byerly presents an overview of strategies used in this struggle and places them in the historical context of the U.S. media industry. Initially only communicating and advocating through alternative media, the gay press "clearly contributed to the construction of both a political identity and cohesive cultural community strong enough for gays and lesbians to begin to challenge homophobia." This community has become stronger and more influential through campaigns led by advocacy groups, to open up the media industry as a whole, as well as campaigns within mainstream news organizations. Byerly takes us through these shifting sites of struggle, in which interests cross race, ethnic, national, and sexual orientation lines.

Estonia is another country in which, for different reasons, there is little documented research on gender in the newsroom. Journalists do not identify themselves very often by gender, explains Barbi Pilvri (chapter 13) in a personal commentary. Women journalists do not have any special network and there is no women's section in the union of journalists. Pilvri's explanation for this absence of gender-consciousness is, it seems to her, a general fatigue about the position of the Soviet working woman burdened with social and state duties who does not have any time or energy to enjoy a private life, family, and children. A career in the 1990s seemed to be old-fashioned and somehow Soviet-labeled because since the 1950s, it was expected that women would work and have careers. Therefore, not to work, to stay home and care for the family, was regarded as "modern" as images of the Western "housewife" were uncritically absorbed.

In this book we share experiences across countries and cultures: North America, northern Europe, southern Europe, eastern Europe, Africa, India, the Middle East, and the Caribbean. However, we are aware that vast areas are still underrepresented. Our wish list contained many more countries from these underrepresented areas—the pan-African continent, Asia, Latin America—but we ran into communication problems (language and separated networks) and the relative lack of indigenous research. This book is the first in Hampton Press' new series, *Gender, Media and Culture*. In forthcoming books in the series, we will keep trying to restore this imbalance.

REFERENCES

Allan, S. (1998). (En)gendering the truth politics of news discourse. In C. Carter, G. Branston, & S. Allan (Eds.), *News, gender and power* (pp. 121–137). London & New York: Routledge.

Allan, S. (1999). *News culture*. Buckingham, UK: Open University Press.

Alvesson, M., & Billing, Y. (1997). *Understanding gender and organizations*. Thousand Oaks, CA, London, New Delhi: Sage.

Ashforth, B., & Johnson, S. (2001). Which hat to wear? The relative salience of multiple identities in organizational contexts. In M. Hogg & D. Terry (Eds.), *Social identity processes in organizational contexts* (pp. 31–48). Philadelphia: Psychology Press, Taylor and Francis Group.

Bartel, C., & Dutton, J (2001). Ambiguous organizational memberships: Constructing organizational identities in interactions with Others. In M. Hogg & D. Terry (Eds.), *Social identity processes in organizational contexts* (pp.115–130). Philadelphia: Psychology Press, Taylor and Francis Group.

Beasley, M. H. (1993). Newspapers—Is there a new majority defining the news? In P. J. Creedon (Ed.), *Women in mass communication* (2nd ed., pp. 118–133). Thousand Oaks, CA: Sage.

Carter, C., Branston G., & Allan, S. (1998). *News, gender and power*. London: Routledge.

Creedon, P. (Ed.). (1993). *Women in mass communication* (2nd ed.). Thousand Oaks, CA: Sage.

de Bruin, M. (2000). Gender, organizational and professional identities in journalism, *Journalism—Theory, Practice and Criticism, 1*(2), 239–260.

Fine, M. (1993). New voices in organizational communication: A feminist commentary and critique. In S. Perlmutter Bowen & N. Wyatt (Eds.), *Transforming visions: Feminist critiques in communication studies* (pp. 125–166). Cresskill, NJ: Hampton Press.

Gallagher, M., & Quindoza-Santiago, L. (Eds.). (1994). *Women empowering communication: A resource book on women and the globalisation of media.* London: WACC; Manila: Isis International and New York: Methuen.

Gallagher, M. with von Euler, M. (1995). An unfinished story: Gender patterns in media employment. In *Reports and Papers on Mass Communication* (Vol. 110). Paris: UNESCO.

Gherardi, S. (1995). *Gender, symbolism and organizational cultures.* London: Sage.

Halford, S., Savage, M., & Witz, A. (1997). *Gender, careers and organizations: Current developments in banking, nursing and local government.* London: MacMillan.

Kitzinger, J. (1998). The gender-politics of news production: Silenced voices and false memories. In C. Carter, G. Branston, & S. Allan (Eds.), *News, gender and power* (pp. 186–203). London, UK: Routledge.

Mills, K. (1997). What difference do women journalists make? In P. Norris (Ed.), *Women, media and politics* (pp. 41–55). New York & Oxford: Oxford University Press.

Ross, K. (2001). Women at work: Journalism as en-gendered practice. *Journalism Studies,* 2(4) 531–544.

Skidmore, P. (1998). Gender and the agenda: News reporting of child sexual abuse. In C. Carter, G. Branston, & S. Allan (Eds.), *News, gender and power* (pp. 204–218). London & New York: Routledge.

Steiner, L. (1998). Newsroom accounts of power at work. In C. Carter, G. Branston, & S. Allan (Eds.), *News, gender and power* (pp. 145–159). London & New York: Routledge.

van Zoonen, L. (1998). One of the girls?: The changing gender of journalism. In C. Carter, G. Branston, & S. Allan (Eds.), *News, gender and power* (pp. 33–46). London & New York: Routledge.

Weaver, D. (1997). Women as journalists. In P. Norris (Ed.), *Women, media and politics* (pp. 21–40). New York & Oxford: Oxford University Press.

Weaver, D., & Wilhoit, G. (1996). *The American journalist in the 1990s: U.S. news people at the end of an era.* Mahwah, NJ: Erlbaum.

Whetten A., & Godfrey, P. (Eds.). (1998). *Identity in organizations, building theory through conversations.* Thousand Oaks, CA, London, Delhi: Sage.

Witz, A., & Savage, M. (1992). Theoretical introduction: The gender of organizations. In M. Savage & A. Witz (Eds.), *Gender and bureaucracy* (pp. 3–62). Oxford: Blackwell.

Zilliacus-Tikkanen, H. (1997). *Journalistikens essens i ett konsperspektiv, Runddradions Jamstalldhetskommitte*: Stockholm. (English Summary), pp. 151-164.

1

Organizational, Professional, and Gender Identities—Overlapping, Coinciding and Contradicting Realities in Caribbean Media Practices

Marjan de Bruin

In media organizations, men and women working as journalists are commonly expected to be guided by professional values while, simultaneously, fulfilling the demands of the organization that employs them. In analyzing the influences on their production, at least three factors or variables may be seen as crucial: gender, professional standards, and the (media) organization itself. Each has been the subject of discussion and study, but the intersection of these areas remained implicit or described only partially.

Various authors over the last few years have begun to discuss gender and media production by defining and looking at the gendered substructures in media organizations (Allan, 1998; Carter, Branston, & Allan, 1998; de Bruin, 1998, 1999; Kitzinger, 1998; Skidmore, 1998; Steiner, 1998; van Zoonen, 1998a). Earlier studies (e.g., Gallagher, 1995) on the division of labor in media organizations into "male" and "female" areas, or on vertical segregation—both examples of gendered substructures—presented these realities more as labor profiles of the organization than as processes taking place within the organizational culture. The focus mainly had been on employment patterns and less on cultural interpretations of everyday work in which relations were structured according to—often implicit—notions of what was "feminine" or "masculine."

The descriptions of practices and discourses in the various case studies and essays just mentioned actually prepare new ground for distinguishing—certainly at the conceptual level—gender, organizational and professional identity, and identification as useful concepts. I am aware of the many other identities (e.g.,

1

based on categories such as class, rural/urban, ethnicity, territory, etc.) that could be mentioned in addition to the three categories just singled out. Masculinity and femininity and what is considered to be the norm in the relationships between women and men are anchored in these different life experiences that form the bedrock for behavior. But, I feel that this focus in my analysis, at this point, will help to clarify the usefulness of the core concepts with which I am working.

In this chapter, I first introduce the theoretical orientation that I prefer: Core concepts and approaches used in my analysis are inspired by social identity theory, social constructionism and cultural studies. This discussion is followed by a further exploration of the concepts mentioned earlier: gender, organizational and professional identity, and identification. I focus on the interplay between these identities and identifications by presenting some preliminary findings from a qualitative analysis of 20 in-depth interviews with female and male journalists working in newsrooms in Caribbean media (Jamaica and Trinidad & Tobago). The complete analysis of this material is in progress.

SOCIAL IDENTITIES

Gender, organizational, and professional identities are social identities that can be regarded as personal as well as social constructs. They depend on commonly shared stereotypes, but they are also idiosyncratic (Crisp & Hewstone, 2000; Deaux, 2000). They are not fixed and static, but may be seen as processes. In fact, Hall (1996) urged us to look at identities as "more a process of becoming than of being" (p. 4). For this reason, some authors prefer to speak about identification instead of identity (Hall, 1996; Van Dijk, 1998). In this chapter, I use both concepts: *Identification* is used when I intend to refer explicitly to the process of identifying.

People may take on multiple social identities to serve different functions. These identities may change priority in everyday life according to circumstances and interests; they are subject to negotiation, they overlap, they flow or spill over.

The different identities we adopt may also be seen as different identity orientations, with specific loci of self-definition, motivated by different interests: personal, relational, and collective identity orientations (Brickson & Brewer, 2001).

The basic idea of social identity theory is "that (of) a social category . . . within which one falls, and to which one feels one belongs, provides a definition of who one is in terms of the defining characteristics of the category—a self-definition that is part of the self-concept" (Hogg & Terry, 2001, p. 3). Social identities are descriptive, prescriptive, and evaluative. This means they may be seen as providing a psychological framework that defines who we are, how we are supposed to feel, think, and act and in doing so, making it possible for us to live as "we" differing from "the other(s)" (Hogg & Terry, 2001, p. 3). People may actively strive for certain social identities, by claiming membership of particular social categories. In this claiming, it may be useful to assume the characteristics associated with the prototypical group member—a process of "self-stereotyping" (Deaux, 2000, p. 5)—for example, by taking on particular professional identities. Claiming can only be successful if others are willing to affirm or confirm this claim, described as "granting membership" (Bartel & Dutton, 2001, p. 124).

When identities—especially those based on more visible categories as for example, gender identity—are being imposed on someone, some authors emphasize that, although "it is difficult to wholly deny category membership" (Deaux, 2000, p. 9), people may still develop strategies to minimize the socially accepted meaning attached to certain social identities. They may develop the skills of shifting one category to a lower position in their personal "identity hierarchy" while stressing other identities instead. This shifting of identities might also be seen in situations where certain identities seem to conflict with each other. An example of such a shift may be seen where certain U.S. journalists judged their organization's product to be too influential in the formation of public opinion and stated their belief that this influence should be less (Weaver, 1998). One could interpret this distancing of self from the organization's output as an attempt to separate professional identity from an increasingly hegemonic organizational identity (de Bruin, 2000, p. 231).

A third dynamic relates to identities that are the result of passive acquisition, where people happen to have taken them on, almost incidentally, en passant. This may apply to organizational identity—it may come with the job. In general, people fit themselves into and, at the same time are fitted into, social categories. They "take the cue for their identity from the conduct of others, but they make the active effort to influence this conduct to begin with. There is a complex mixture of proaction and reaction" (Weick, 1995, p. 23).

Some identities, or maybe most of them, even if carrying a label representing a category that suggests a clearly defined meaning, may involve vast differences in content and connotation. This idiosyncratic nature means that understanding their functions and dynamics needs to be done through trying to see "from within."

Gender Identity

Gender identity is an example of a concept that takes many different forms and carries many different meanings. To avoid getting tangled up in epistemological questions when defining gender identity, I refer to the distinction by Lorber, quoted in Ferree, Lorber, and Hess (1999, p. 6), between "the concepts of biological sex (which refers to either genetic or morphological characteristics), sexuality (which refers to desire and orientation), and gender (which refers to social status and identity)"—the latter also described as a specific social version of men and women (Alvesson & Billing, 1997). Of course, distinguishing between sex and gender at a conceptual level does not reflect any such separation in everyday life. Glick and Fiske, (1999) maintain that sex is the primary category by which we automatically classify others and that "this automatic process leads to the nonconscious activation of gender stereotypes" (p. 366). Gender identity would refer to identification with a social category associated with cultural models and notions of masculinity and/or femininity, seen as "traits or forms of subjectivities (orientations in thinking, feeling and valuing) that are present in all persons . . . although to different degrees" (Alvesson & Billing, 1997, p. 85)—qualities to which both sexes have access rather than being the exclusive property of men or women (Marshall, 1993). In other words, in how a subject is socially constructed, social practice may carry more weight than biology does (Alvesson & Billing, 1997, p. 218).

The ideosyncratic nature of gender identities implies that we cannot speak of a single feminine–masculine polarity but need to recognize different versions of, multiple, "femininities" and "masculinities." The construction of these different versions—sometimes referred to as "doing gender" or "gendering"—in (media) organizations is maintained by the members of the organization through their functioning within organizational structures, cultures, and practices.

Organizational Identity

In the debate on gender and production in media organizations, van Zoonen is one of the few authors who mentions "organizational identity" although without much elaboration. She contends that organizational identity "reflects the individual styles and preferences of the communicator and the structural imperatives of the media organisation" (van Zoonen, 1998b, p. 137). Organizational identity is positioned as "more or less coterminous with agency" whereby agency "refers to what journalists do within the structural constraints posed by the organization of the profession and is thus always embedded in organizational routines and pressures" (pp. 128, 137). I prefer to explore a more precise definition of *organizational identity*, which captures several dimensions, as that which members believe to be central, enduring, and distinctive about their organization: It is the collectively constructed and continuously renegotiated understanding among the members of an organization of "who-we-are" (Albert & Whetten, 1985, cited in Whetten & Godfrey, 1998, p. 35) and it is "the aspect of culturally embedded sensemaking that is self-focused" (p. 56). It defines who we are in relation to the larger social system to which we belong.

In quoting Albert & Whetten's definition, I have ignored one aspect of their argument with which I do not agree. They describe the understanding among the members of an organization of "who-we-are" as a "shared" understanding. This "shared understanding" may be the highest common factor of employee identification in the context of hegemonic organizational culture, but the highest common factor may not, in fact, be very high. Or it may be common only among certain groups in the organization. This focus corresponds with the understanding that "the salience of an identity to an individual in an organizational context is determined by the subjective importance and situational relevance" (Ashforth, 2001, cited in Ashforth & Johnson, 2001, p. 32). This reality, in my view, allows fragmentation in meaning and meaning structures, which weakens the argument of shared understanding as a condition for organizational identity.

Although some researchers emphasize "beliefs" as central in organizational identification (Pratt, 1998), others focus on the "cognitive connection between the definition of the organization and the definition a person applies to her-or himself" (Dutton, Dukerich, & Harquail, 1994, p. 242). I feel more comfortable with a definition that includes the emotional component—feelings, loyalty, belonging—in addition to values and beliefs. I certainly see organizational identity as a relational and comparative concept (de Bruin, 2000). Organizational identity is not constructed in a single, linear process, but through many processes within the context of an organizational culture. It can shape the organization's interpretation of issues and actions over time (Dutton & Dukerich, 1991). It can also trigger emotional responses from the members of the organization, for instance when the organization's actions are perceived as consistent or inconsistent with organizational identity.

Closely connected with organizational identity are the concepts of *reputation*—how the larger environment defines the organizational identity—and *image*—insiders' assessments of what outsiders think of the organization (Dutton & Dukerich, 1991). Image projection (how I want outsiders to define/perceive me) and image interpretation (how I believe outsiders define/perceive me) are dynamics affecting my claim of social identity. The importance of the latter—image interpretation—can be found in Weaver and Wilhoit's (1996) survey findings among journalists. How journalists believe outsiders see their organization—in this case, whether the media organization is seen as successful or not—is still "one of the most important predictors of job well-being" for U.S. journalists (p. 110). In Taiwan, the rating of journalists' news organization (and subsequent belief of how outsiders see them—image interpretation) is the second most important predictor of job satisfaction among them (Lo, 1998). Organizational identification can also lead to negative effects. In Algeria, a majority of Algerian journalists rated their news organizations as doing a fair or poor job—image interpretation—and a substantial proportion of the same group also expressed a low level of job satisfaction (Kirat, 1998).

Professional Identity

Recent discussions in organizational theory and social psychology underline the fact that organizational boundaries often cannot be seen simply as separating members from nonmembers, but are becoming more and more porous. Yet, it seems safe to say that organizational identity in media production is connected to a cultural and spatial "territory"—in this case the organization—and carried by the members who form part of the organization as long as they belong to it. *Professional identity*, however, stretches across organizations. It refers to a wider frame of reference—an ideology—not so much carried by the members of a clearly identifiable organization, but rather by a virtual community. Moving out of a particular organization does not usually imply an ending of the professional identity.

Most of the earlier studies of professional journalists discuss professionalism as an identification with a certain set of beliefs concerning the functions of the media and the role of journalists. For McLeod and Hawley in the 1960s, a professional, in defining his (sic) job, will emphasize certain characteristics: the job is unique and delivers an essential service, it demands "intellectual activity" and it includes a broad range of autonomy. The professional journalists will also exhibit "distinctive patterns of cognitive judgement and differing specific attitudes" (McLeod & Hawley, 1964, p. 538). Other authors add to this the broader social obligations that come with being a professional as well as the view that professional culture is transmitted through a long period of socialization (Johnstone, Slawski, & Bowman, 1972/1973; McLeod & Rush, 1969; Menanteau-Horta, 1967).

But what professional identity contained and meant remained uncertain. Here too, we see vast differences in content and connotation. Values, supposed to be crucial to the profession, were continuously under scrutiny—objectivity versus subjectivity; detachment versus advocacy; observer versus watchdog. Professional identity reflected many different, sometimes conflicting orientations—even within the same organization or medium (Burns, 1964/1972). These conflicting orientations did not seem to weaken the idea of a professional basis of journalism, of "a professional identity."

Recent research on professional roles, functions, values, and reporting practices among professional journalists show similar pluralistic role perceptions. Journalists in the 1990s from six regions of the world agreed generally on the relative importance of only one or two professional roles: getting information to the public quickly, and the importance of providing access for the public to express opinions (Weaver, 1998). Apart from those two roles, the rankings show extreme variations. It now appears that what may have been true in the 1970s may still be true in 2003, that there are occupational segments organized around alternative professional identities, while other elements of the professional ideology are commonly shared (Johnstone et al., 1972/1973).

IDENTITIES AT WORK

The interplay between gender, professional, and organizational identities—or the processes that constitute them: identifications—is complex with overlapping, coinciding, and contradictory positions and locations. The construction of gender identity may be seen as a force shaping and maintaining work structures, but also a consequence of established positions. An example of the former may be when, at the level of everyday work, cultural interpretations of what is "feminine" or "masculine" play a crucial role in the structuring of this work into what are considered to be typical male and female "beats." The influence of organizational structures on gender identity and identification is clear when positions of power are not available for women. The underrepresentation of women in senior positions "may highlight for women their limited mobility and reinforce their lower status as women [which in turn] helps to shape the meaning and significance women attach to being female" in the organization (Ely, 1994, pp. 205, 207). In those cases, it may not suit a woman to align with or identify strongly with "female" and "femininity" in that organization.

Dynamics between organizational and professional identities are at least as complex. Perhaps in the 1970s, the journalist working in a media organization could still be described as a professional with "dual citizenship"—committed to the methods and goals of both the organization and the profession (Sigelman, 1973). This possibility seems to have changed drastically. In recent times, organizational interests intrude more often, and less apologetically—emphasizing the concern for profit over quality and emphasizing the need to compete. In many newsrooms the relationship between organizational identity (what is taken by journalists to be central to the organization) and professional identity (what they see as central to their profession) has become more and more a source of serious conflict. In the United States, journalists consider "the ascendance of a corporate culture" (organizational constraints of editorial control, time–space limits, inadequate staffing) as one of the main causes of diminishing professional autonomy (Weaver, 1998; Weaver & Wilhoit, 1996)—a development that I interpret as organizational interests deforming journalists' professional identity.

Trying to understand these dynamics implies paying attention to the cultural interpretations of everyday work, in which relations are structured according to notions that are usually taken for granted and applied automatically. There is hardly any time or mental space in the routines of news production to question what is understood to be "feminine" or "masculine"; to be newsworthy or to be stale news; to be the appropriate responses to the expectations embedded in organizational structures and culture. People in the newsroom are expected to simply work and act, and in doing so—in the midst of cultural definitions, expectations, and values—their interactions and behavior contribute to creating and maintaining social identities, which, in turn, are reflected in subjective orientations. Exploring journalists' experiences in the newsroom, their perceptions of the relationships and interactions of which they form part and in the midst of which they work, could bring us closer to an understanding of identities at work.

There are several ways to try to view the subjectivities that constitute the working life of men and women journalists. The method I preferred was qualitative, in-depth interviewing outside of the newsroom. I had the feeling that interviewing on the spot would be skewed by the presence of influential others, by the witnessing of colleagues, and by the visibility of ongoing work. My aim was to collect stories, accounts, and narratives that would present me with experiences in newsroom production through the eyes of (a selection of) professionals. The data from these interviews should be considered as descriptions of perceptions and not as descriptions of facts. It is not important whether their statements are true or false: The texts provide an insight into how interactions with journalists at work are perceived.

The interviews were open-ended, in-depth, with a minimal structure. The interviewers had been given a short list of keywords—indicating topic areas, which, if necessary could be used as a checklist. Interviewees were practicing journalists in the Caribbean—10 women and 10 men. Most of them work in the print media, some work in broadcasting. Most of them received a form of (educational) training and have at least a first degree. The majority was under 30 years of age and had been in the profession between 4 and 8 years, although a few were older and more senior. The full analysis of the interviews is in progress and I, therefore, simply present here some of the interim findings. They intend to explore the usefulness of the core concepts with which I am working.

Because I share the view that interviews can be seen "as negotiated accomplishments of both interviewers and respondents . . . shaped by the contexts and situations in which they take place" and that interviewers are "active participants in interactions with respondents" (Fontana & Frey, 2001, p. 663), the choice of interviewers and locations of interviews was made after careful consideration. Given the fact that the interviews were open-ended and in-depth yet would be expected to cover certain specific aspects, although with as little direction as possible, experience in interviewing was a first consideration in the selection of interviewers. Other considerations were gender, nationality, status, ethnicity, and familiarity with the field. The interviews were conducted by two professional journalists, neither of whom were employed (full time) by any of the media organizations in the Caribbean: One was a woman in her early 30s, whereas the man was much older. The majority of male interviewees were interviewed by the man, the majority of female interviewees by the woman. All interviews (face-to-face) lasted for about 90 minutes, were recorded and took place outside the workplace—full confidentiality was assured.

SHARING WORK IN PROGRESS

My interpretation of the journalists' narratives focused on processes of identification: the claiming of identities; the handling of what seemed to be imposed identities; the coping with conflicting identities; the shifting of identities; the preference for certain identities; the assertion, rejection, or denial of others. In short, I focused on recognizing indications for identities at work.

Gender relations are seen by all interviewees as a steering force in patterning newsroom interactions, even when work is the issue. For both sexes, however, this recognition seems to lead to different experiences, a different reality, although taking place in the same work environment. An example illustrating this is sexual harassment as part of newsroom culture—mentioned by all female interviewees, but redefined by most male interviewees.

Women journalists describe this harassment as coming in many shapes and forms. For newcomers it seems a rite of passage—part of what "everybody" is expecting to happen and it is up to the individual to resist. *"When you're the new kid on the block . . . everybody is trying to see who first is gonna get to sleep with this person."* Those who have been on the job for a while speak about harassment as a fact of life, with which they have learned to live. They recognize it in different behaviors and see it happen in many ways, subtly or directly; through body language or verbally; serving many different purposes and interests. Talking about their male colleagues' behavior:

"The way some of them look at me."

"Somebody saying that they'd like to go to bed with you or to perform some specific sexual act."

"People used to touch me."

"Every now and then somebody still strip your clothes off with their eyes."

"He'll come to you . . . and he'll laugh and he'll play in your hair."

"His front part just rub on your bottom, sort of casually, but he did it in such a way, as if you don't stop it right then, he's going to do it again."

Male colleagues (and in fact, some of the very males to whom the women referred) defined the same situations differently. They wouldn't want to use the word harassment:

"I don't know if it's sexual harassment per se, touching on their shoulder and so on and so on . . . you could call it that if you wish."

"People tend to have good relationships and sometimes they tend to run jokes which might be accepted."

"You run a joke and stuff like that, but nothing that could be called harassment!"

These different definitions of newsroom reality did not seem to ever have been a topic of discussion among the journalists involved. Women simply developed their responses, their strategies. Several of them mentioned that even the possibility of harassment made them feel "forced" to keep their distance from male colleagues: *"I keep a certain distance, I am pleasant to them, I might talk to them, but I don't encourage them to be too familiar, cause I can see . . . that they would like the opportunity."* Avoiding closeness is avoiding trouble—that's how you do it if you want to rebuff and yet not spoil working relationships:

> *"You'll tell him 'don't do that' [playing with her hair, MdB] and he will realize 'she is resisting'."*
> *"I loudly said that I did not like it, and that stopped."*
> *"You glare at them, they'll stop."*
> *"I tell them that I don't want nobody, but I do it in a nice and polite way and don't offend anybody."*
> *"From the beginning I made my position clear—I'm a Christian."*

Employing these strategies seems to come as second nature, as something that is learned pretty quickly. The deal is understood by all parties involved. If women are firm and decisive, if they draw the boundaries seriously, they will win the negotiations:

> *"If you say you don't like that, and 'I don't want you to do that', then ... he will stop."*
> *"If you are clear and assert that you do not want this kind of behavior ... then it must stop—it must!"*
> *"They will see that they're not getting anywhere."*
> *"When you are serious, I think they quietly respect you for that."*

Confirmed by a male colleague: *"but the ones who don't like it you don't really mess around with them."*

At the same time, however, women applying these strategies feel they have the worst of it. They feel locked into a situation they cannot change. Whoever would want to complain about the game or the rules it is played by, expects the gender of those in power to be a stronger force than formal organizational rules. Male solidarity will close the ranks and triumph over fairness to the—female—worker: *"You can't do something about it. They are all friends, so if you report it your are gonna get fired."*

In many instances for the women in the newsroom, keeping their distance also meant removing themselves from centers of power and influence—organizational power, leading to economic power. This position of formal powerlessness, however, did not seem to necessarily imply occupying a position of subordination. When gender identity seemed to be the dominant category in structuring the work relations, work interactions were perceived as power challenges. In some instances, the identification with gender frames implied a challenge of power in more informal ways. Suspensions received for falling out of line became something of which to be proud.

Female journalists are aware of their lack of power but at the same time they are unwilling to "beg" or negotiate with male editors if this would lessen the distance they decided to keep: *"A big reason why I don't say anything about the subsistence, is that I don't want to be that close to that editor for that length of time."* This is an example where these "underground" strategies affect organizational arrangements, sometimes to the detriment of the women in the newsroom. Several women at this point demonstrated a shift in priorities—the disadvantages they suffered were placed second to a higher, professional goal—*"As long as it's to get the job done, even though I'm not getting reimbursed [for expensed incurred] I go ahead and do it anyway."* A similar emphasis on professional contribution appeared when avoiding conflicts with male colleagues may seem a lack of female assertiveness: *"I console myself with the fact that OK he needs me. He needs my contribution. I have a lot to offer, that's why he minds when I am not around."*

This persistent attitude, together with the appeal to professional distance and aloofness, and a strong pushing of traditional journalistic values, sometimes seemed to be used as a strategy to avoid dealing with male colleagues in sexual terms—professional identification offering the way out of a stalemate caused by the powerful overlap of gender inequality and organizational inequality.

This change in identities' priorities occurred quite often. Some women journalists who lacked status in the newsroom emphasized the prestige they enjoy from the audience, the readers of their paper: *"I'll get the praise from outside if it boils down to that."* Image interpretation (how I believe outsiders see me), as part of organizational identity, comes to their rescue when their gender identity does not seem to offer sufficient incentive. Or, they emphasized the professional benefits they enjoyed in a job—working on a special publication for which they were paid less than their male colleagues, or sometimes received no payment at all: *"I get to show my stuff, my work. I can do it my way."* In underlining this professional interest they are stressing their professional identity and shifting their gender identity to a lower position. Some women, speaking about the lack of professional praise from within the newsroom, refused to see this as gender discrimination. Instead they preferred to interpret it as an informal organizational precautionary measure: *"My editor would know that I did a good job, but it would kill him to tell you it's good. Suppose I should [then] ask for a pay increase or something!"* They demonstrate what could be interpreted as shifts of priorities in their "identity hierarchy"—minimizing their gender identity and stressing professional and organizational identities instead. These shifts certainly guaranteed them greater social benefits (status), allowed them to ignore the more painful experience of discrimination in payment and praise and enabled them to create their own niches of independent gratification.

Sometimes it seems women deliberately played up particular gender identities. Some of the female interviewees, in telling their stories of newsroom reali-

ties, were asserting their gender identity in traditional terms, appealing to familiar discourse. One of them described herself as the go-between, the caretaker, the
harmony bringer, the "mother of the desk." Her emphasis on traditional female
characteristics—which she felt her male colleagues expected her to have—
seemed to match her perception of how her male co-workers looked at her:
"They wonder [talking about low salary] *how come you still manage to wear
such nice clothes, suits?"* As a professional she felt undervalued: *"You would be
the last to be considered for assignments. When it comes to big stuff, nobody
remembers you. You don't think sex has a lot to do with that?"* The same inter-
viewee, in turn, extended this low esteem to her female colleagues—referring to
a female editor: *"She is never asked to come in* [editorial meetings], *because it
doesn't really matter."* She described the female professionals who were working with her the same way she herself felt seen through the eyes of the men:
What can a woman contribute. Who listens to a woman? Yet she is the one who
complained, more than any other of her interviewed colleagues, about sexual
harassment in the newsroom and cited examples of the connection between
harassment, organizational power, and economic power: *"If you are friendly
with the ones in power . . . you will be asked 'where do you live? who pays your
rent?' And underneath that, the suggestion, 'I can do all these things for you'."*

Here it seems as if using traditional feminine characteristics as points of
identification also provoked an emphasis on asserting this identity by others. In
choosing to play up gender identity, professional identity was shifted to a lower
position in the hierarchy. Although it may have been a more desired attachment
it also could have represented potential conflicts in a less familiar territory.
And, at least, living gender is what women have been trained for all their lives.

None of the women in the male-directed organizations had much hope of
upward mobility: *"For promotions? Be male first. It is not experience, it's not
qualifications, it's the boys club." "Somebody has to resign or die."* Where the
prospects for women to climb the organizational ladder are dim, it doesn't serve
women's interest to identify strongly with other women in the organization.
Effects in behavior and interaction are then almost predictable. If it is not attractive to be associated with women as a category, there is not much else left other
than to fight for yourself and by yourself—to "engage in personal self-enhanc-
ing strategies," which threaten solidarity, cooperation, and support among and
between women (Ely, 1994). But what was described by some of the interviewees as "back-biting" was seen by all them as something that typically happens
among women: *"a female thing . . . sometimes females are the ones that hold
each other down."* Some sought for a psychological explanation, where the
need for appreciation coming from a male dominated environment was seen as
the major drive: *"the competition and rivalry. It maybe a matter of wanting to
fit into the environment, wanting to feel appreciated."* But no one imagined it
could be related to the organization's lack of opportunity for women: Large differences in status and power between men and women can negatively affect
work relationships among women (Ely, 1994). This organizational feature,

which could be seen as a result of systematic discrimination at all levels of the organization (Baxter & Wright, 2000), is very likely to affect solidarity and gender identification.

Depending on the dominant newsroom culture, inside the organization it may be risky to show vulnerability, express doubt or uncertainty because of being a woman, as several women stated: *"If you say you can't go there or you can't do this, because you are a woman, . . . or if you are afraid that something will happen to you, then you will never get the [big] story."* On the other hand, helplessness as a prototypical feminine tactic—outside the newsroom—was sometimes recognized as being helpful: *"If I'm at Parliament, and I miss something, and I ask any one of the guys, I'll get it, but I don't know if they're that friendly when it's one of my male colleagues."*

Outside the office—on assignment, or attending a seminar—other points of identification seem to become more viable. Not only was helplessness allowed, but also the backbiting gave way to enjoying each other's company. Independently of each other, all female journalists of one particular newsroom mentioned the satisfaction they got from sharing a day of training outside of the working environment.

DISCUSSION

I have tried to explore the usefulness of the concept of *social identities* when discussing gender—and other—identities in newsroom relationships. The basic assumption in this exercise was the view that people take on multiple identities to serve different functions, depending on circumstances and interests. As a consequence, in our efforts to understand gender relations in the newsroom, we also need to focus on the interactions and behaviors that create and maintain the social construction of identities.

The examples given here detail some clearly developed strategies to minimize or inflate the socially accepted meanings attached to certain identities. Other strategies focused on the shifting of identities—claiming certain identities and ignoring others. Depending on circumstances and incentives gender identity could seen to be shifted to a lower position in the personal identity hierarchy. (Over)identification with a traditional male work ethos and professional values—which, of course, in the male-led newsrooms, are undisputed—seemed to be instrumental in avoiding gender tensions and polarization. Emphasizing professional identity and playing down gender identity in certain instances seemed to have been a self-determined choice diminishing the potential for gender tension that comes with gender relations—professional identity used as a shield of protection. Choosing these positions also focuses a slightly different light on the view that sees traditional (male) journalistic culture competing with gender by excluding feminist values (Zilliacus-Tikkanen, 1997).

The claiming of certain professional identities, "self-stereotyping," is only one side of the coin. It can only work successfully if others are willing to affirm or confirm this claim. In organizations where gender is still a steering force in newsroom interactions and often coincides with organizational power, this may lead to conflicting situations: Where professional exchange seems appropriate, gender can still be an obstacle.

For men, strategies emphasizing gender identities were seen to serve organizational identities, demonstrating how their use of sexuality was to establish a hierarchy "that separates them (men) from women and keeps women 'in their place'" (Martin & Collinson, 1999, p. 295).

In many media organizations, the limited options for women to rise through the ranks may make organizational identity the least attractive psychological frame with which to identify. This potential lack of organizational identity by itself may contribute to the marginalizing of women in the organization. Also contributing to this marginalization may be the tendency of women to stay away from potential gender conflicts by "keeping distance." Because gender and power in media organizations often go together, given the male-dominated decision-making structures, keeping distance may imply moving away from mainstream decision making, and thus sustaining the limited mobility. Gender identity brings trouble, and organizational identity offers no promises.

Of course, this analysis so far had to avoid the question of class identity, which in strongly class-stratified societies like Jamaica is a very important condition, influencing dynamics of multiple identities. This aspect will be the next important area of new research.

REFERENCES

Allan, S. (1998). (En)gendering the truth politics of news discourse. In C. Carter, G. Branston, & S. Allan (Eds.), *News, gender & power* (pp. 121-137). London & New York: Routledge.

Alvesson, M., & Billing, Y. (1997). *Understanding gender & organizations.* Thousand Oaks, CA: London, New Delhi: Sage.

Ashforth, B., & Johnson, S. (2001). Which hat to wear? The relative salience of multiple identities in organizational contexts. In M. Hogg & D. Terry (Eds.), *Social identity processes in organizational contexts* (pp. 31-48). Philadelphia: Psychology Press, Taylor & Francis Group.

Bartel, C., & Dutton, J. (2001). Ambiguous organizational memberships: constructing organizational identities in interactions with others. In M. Hogg & D. Terry (Eds.), *Social identity processes in organizational contexts* (pp. 115-130). Philadelphia: Psychology Press, Taylor & Francis Group.

Baxter, J., & Wright., E. (2000). The glass ceiling hypotheses, a comparative study of the United States, Sweden & Australia. *Gender & Society, 14*(2), 275-294.

Brickson, S., & Brewer, M. (2001). Identity orientation & intergroup relations in organizations. In M. Hogg & D. Terry (Eds.), *Social identity processes in organizational contexts* (pp. 49-66). Philadelphia: Psychology Press, Taylor & Francis Group.

Burns, T. (1972). Commitment and career in the BBC. In D. McQuail (Ed.), *Sociology of mass communications* (pp. 281-310). Harmondsworth: Penguin. (Original work published 1964)

Carter, C., Branston, G., & Allan, S. (1998). *News, gender & power*. London: Routledge.

Crisp, R., & Hewstone, M. (2000). Multiple categorization & social identity. In D. Capozza & R. Brown (Eds.), *Social identity processes; Trends in theory & research* (pp. 149-166). Thousand Oaks, CA, London, New Delhi: Sage.

Deaux, K. (2000). Models, meanings & motivations. In D. Capozza & R. Brown (Eds.), *Social identity processes: Trends in theory & research* (pp. 1-14). Thousand Oaks, CA, London, New Delhi: Sage.

de Bruin, M. (1998, July). *Gender in Caribbean media, beyond the body count*. Paper presented at the 21st Scientific Conference & General Assembly of the International Association for Media & Communication Research, University of Strathclyde, Glasgow.

de Bruin, M. (1999). Gender, media production & output. *Media Development, XLVI*(2), 50-54.

de Bruin, M. (2000). Gender, organizational & professional identities in journalism. *Journalism–Theory, Practice & Criticism, 1*(2), 239-260.

Dutton, J., & Dukerich, J. (1991). Keeping an eye on the mirror: Image & identity in organizational adaptation. *Academy of Management Journal, 34*(3), 517-554.

Dutton, J., Dukerich, J., & Harquail, C. (1994). Organizational images & member identification. *Administrative Science Quarterly, 39*, 239-263.

Ely, R. (1994). The effects of organizational demographics & social identity on relationships among professional women. *Administrative Science Quarterly, 39*; 203-238.

Ferree, M., Lorber, J., & Hess, B. (Eds.) *Revisioning gender*. Thousand Oaks, CA, London, New Delhi: Sage.

Fontana, A., & Frey, J. (2000). The interview: From structured questions to negotiated text. In N. Denzin & Y. Lincoln (Eds.), *Handbook of qualitative research* (pp. 645-672). Thousand Oaks, CA, London, New Delhi: Sage.

Gallagher, M., with von Euler, M. (1995). *An unfinished story: Gender patterns in media employment*. Paris: UNESCO.

Glick, P., & Fiske, S. (1999). Gender, power dynamics, & social interaction. In M. Ferree, J. Lorber, & B. Hess (Eds.), *Revisioning gender* (pp. 365-398). Thousand Oaks, CA, London, New Delhi: Sage.

Hall, S. (1996). Introduction: Who needs "identity"? In S. Hall & P. du Gay (Eds.), *Questions of cultural identity* (pp. 1-17). London: Sage.

Hogg, M., & Terry, D. (2001). Social identity theory & organizational processes. In M. Hogg & D. Terry (Eds.), *Social identity processes in organizational contexts* (pp. 1-12). Philadelphia: Psychology Press, Taylor & Francis Group.

Johnstone, J., Slawski, E., & Bowman. W. (1972/1973). The professional values of American newsmen. *Public Opinion Quarterly, XXVI*(1), 522-540.

Kirat, M. (1998). Algerian journalists & their world. In D. Weaver (Ed.), *The global journalist: News people around the world* (pp. 323-348). Cresskill, NJ: Hampton Press.

Kitzinger, J. (1998). The gender-politics of news production: Silenced voices & false memories. In C. Carter, G. Branston, & S. Allan (Eds.), *News, gender & power* (pp. 186-203). London: Routledge.

Lo, V. (1998). The new Taiwan journalist: A sociological profile. In D. Weaver (Ed.), *The global journalist: News people around the world* (pp. 71-88). Cresskill, NJ: Hampton Press.

Marshall, J. (1993). Organizational communication from a feminist perspective. In S. Deetz (Ed.), *Communication yearbook* (Vol. 16). Newbury, CA: Sage.

Martin, P. & Collinson, D. (1999). Gender & sexuality in organizations. In M. Ferree, J. Lorber & B. Hess (Eds.), *Revisioning gender* (pp. 285-310). Thousand Oaks, CA, London, New Delhi: Sage.

McLeod, J., & Hawley, S., Jr. (1964). Professionalization among newsmen. *Journalism Quarterly, 41*, 529-539.

McLeod J., & Rush, R. (1969). Professionalization of Latin American & U.S. journalists. *Journalism Quarterly, 46*(3), 583-590.

Menanteau-Horta, D. (1967). Professionalism of journalists in Santiago de Chile. *Journalism Quarterly, 44*(4), 715-723.

Pratt, M. (1998). To be or not to be? Central questions in organizational identification. In D. Whetten & P. Godfrey (Eds.), *Identity in organizations: Building theory through conversations* (pp. 171-207). Thousand Oaks, CA, London, New Delhi: Sage.

Sigelman, L. (1973). Reporting the news: An organizational analysis. *American Journal of Sociology, 79*(1), 132-151.

Skidmore, P. (1998). Gender & the agenda: News reporting of child sexual abuse. In C. Carter, G. Branston, & S. Allan (Eds.), *News, gender & power* (pp. 204-218). London & New York: Routledge.

Steiner, L. (1998). Newsroom accounts of power at work. In C. Carter, G. Branston, & S. Allan (Eds.), *News, gender & power* (pp. 145-159). London & New York: Routledge.

van Dijk, T. (1998). *Ideology: A multidisciplinary approach.* London, Thousand Oaks, CA, New Delhi: Sage.

van Zoonen, L. (1998a). One of the girls?: The changing gender of journalism. In C. Carter, G. Branston, & S. Allan (Eds.), *News, gender & power* (pp. 33-46). London & New York: Routledge.

van Zoonen, L. (1998b). A professional, unreliable, heroic marionette (M/F): Structure, agency & subjectivity in contemporary journalism. *European Journal of Cultural Studies, 1*(1), 123-143.

Weaver, D. (Ed.). (1998). *The global journalist: News people around the world.* Cresskill, NJ: Hampton Press.

Weaver, D. & Wilhoit, G. (1996). *The American journalist in the 1990s: US news people at the end of an era.* Mahwah, NJ: Erlbaum.

Weick, K. (1995). *Sensemaking in organizations.* London, Thousand Oaks, CA, New Delhi: Sage.

Whetten, D. & Godfrey, P. (Eds.). (1998). *Identity in organizations: Building theory through conversations.* Thousand Oaks, CA, London, New Delhi: Sage.

Zilliacus-Tikkanen, H. (1997). *Journalistikens essens i ett könsperspektiv* [The essence of journalism in a gender perspective] (English Summary, pp. 151-164). Stockholm: Runddradions Jamstalldhetskommitte.

2

Gender, Occupational Knowledge, and Control Over Work in the Newspaper Newsroom

Wilson Lowrey

Since the 1980s, the gap between the numbers of men and women working in journalism and in journalism management has narrowed (ASNE, 2000; Becker, Kosicki, Prine, & Lowrey, 2000; Stone, 1997; Weaver and Wilhoit, 1996). Relative to male journalists, women journalists report greater gains in degree of work autonomy, promotion expegctations, and to a lesser degree, in salaries (Becker et al., 2000; Weaver & Wilhoit, 1996). However, the broad assessments in many of these studies may obscure the complexity of the way gender shapes decision making in news work. Most studies of news work take a wide view of journalism, conceptualizing it as a singular occupation that is synonymous with newsgathering (with maybe a side glance at editing). Yet, news work is made up of a host of subspecialties. Among them are reporting, content editing, copyediting, page design, photography, illustration, and reference/ archiving. These subspecialties are to some degree occupationally unique, and therefore, the impact of gender may differ from one subspecialty to another.

Newsroom subspecialties—or subgroups—have trappings of occupational structure. They have their own professional organizations, conferences, publications, and to some degree their own college curricula.[1] Subgroups compete for control over decision making, and their relative influence varies from newsroom to newsroom (Lowrey, 2000). Also, certain subgroups may consistently have less influence in relation to other subgroups, regardless of which newsroom they work in. There are a number of factors that explain these differences. This chapter seeks to determine whether gender is one of these factors, and if it is, how important gender is to the ability of a subgroup to control decision making over its work area.

The occupational subgroup of page designers receives special scrutiny in this chapter. Page designers are a good case for this study because the degree to which they control their work varies widely across newsrooms. Designers are relative newcomers to newsrooms, and they have encroached into editors' traditional jurisdiction over the work of news presentation,[2] which involves the juxtaposition and sizing of stories, headlines and art, and the selection of visual images.

There is evidence in the trade and academic literature of conflict and competition between "visual journalists"—designers, photographers, and artists—on the one hand, and "word journalists"—editors and reporters—on the other. Visual journalists say editors too often make decisions on space without consulting them (Gentry & Zang, 1989) or provide insufficient page material for effective design (Kohorst, 1999), that reporters and editors do not give them full professional status as journalists (Gentry & Zang, 1989; Moses, 2000) and that their opinions go largely unheeded (Lowrey, 2002; Moses, 2000; Sines, 2000; Wilson, 2001). Editors, on the other hand, have complained that "page

---

[1]Designers and news artists have the Society for News Design, the membership of which grew from 200 at its inception to almost 3,000 in 2002. More than 2,000 photojournalists are members of the National Press Photographers Association, and copyeditors formed the American Copy Editors Society in 1997, with a present membership of more than 1,500. These organizations also have student chapters. Most college–level journalism programs offer photojournalism courses, and many offer sequences (Smith & Mendelson, 1996). A growing number of schools are planning visual communication sequences and new media sequences as well (Becker, Kosicki et al., 2000).

[2] Presentation work is defined here as the tasks involved in constructing the visual context for newspaper information. These tasks include juxtaposing news elements, such as stories, headlines, and art; sizing news elements; and selecting visually symbolic elements such as photos and graphics. Page designers are defined as the workers whose primary responsibility is the performance of these tasks. As other studies have noted (Auman, 1995; Wanta & Danner, 1997), not all papers call these workers "page designers," and in smaller papers especially, such workers may be considered desk workers or layout editors. It is expected, however, that almost all papers with more than 50,000 circulation will have designers or a close equivalent.

designers are running amok" (Hansen, Neuzil, & Ward, 1998, p. 811) and news decisions are too often shaped by visual considerations (Ryan, 1997; Underwood, Giffard, & Stamm, 1994). The work of news presentation has apparently become a contested work area, with editors assuming greater authority over it in some newsrooms, and designers assuming greater authority in others. Because of this variability in control, the effects of factors like gender should also vary and therefore should be easier to see.

It is also assumed that the outcome of these competitions among subgroups should have an impact on the shape of the news product. Each group is expert in a different knowledge area (although knowledge areas do overlap), and it is expected that the winners of these competitions should push their symbolic content to the forefront. In the present case, when design experts have greater influence over presentation work, the result should be a greater emphasis on visual display in newspaper pages. Such an outcome would also have implications for audiences. And studies show that the final presentation of news content has an important effect on reader attention to the news and on the way news is interpreted.[3]

AIMS OF THE CHAPTER

This chapter asks several research questions in an attempt to better understand the relationship between gender and control over work among subgroups in newsrooms:

1. How much do gender composition of the design subgroup and gender of the design director explain the degree to which designers control decision making about presentation?

2. It is expected that occupational–level factors such as degree of specialized knowledge should also help explain designer control, as well as factors that have to do with organizational resources and size. Does gender still have an impact when accounting for these other variables?

---

[3]Research shows that variability in news design and image juxtaposition affects interpretation of news content (e.g., Culbertson, 1969; Middlestadt & Barnhurst, 1999; Pasternack & Utt, 1986; Wanta, 1988). Studies show that images create more memorable impressions on readers and aid recall (David, 1998; Stevenson & Griffin, 1994, 1996; Stark & Hollander, 1990). Studies also show that readers "scan" rather than read stories in detail (Garcia & Stark, 1991), and that graphics and photos attract readers (Garcia & Stark, 1991; Kelly, 1989; Lott, 1994).

3. Finally, does gender moderate the relationship between other predictors and control? For example, is possessing specialized design knowledge more important to women than to men in their efforts to control presentation work?

METHODOLOGY

To answer these questions, data were drawn from a national telephone survey of design managers and international news editors at all daily U.S. newspapers with an average weekday circulation of more than 50,000. The survey was conducted from January to April 2000. The sample, taken from a 1999 *Editor and Publisher* database, included 233 newspapers. The survey measured degree of designer control over presentation work as well as predictors of control. The dependent variable, Designer Control over Work, is defined here as authority over all stages of a work process, including early context setting and control over final decision making. Control is conceptualized as existing in degrees because no designer will have complete control over design work. More dominant authority resides at higher levels of management, should managers choose to exercise this authority. The question then, is not *whether* designers control their work, but *to what degree* they control their work, and why this degree of control varies across news organizations. The word *influence* is used interchangeably with the word *control* in this chapter. These terms are considered conceptually identical given the incremental nature of the concept of control in this chapter.

Survey data included the gender of the design directors and editors, but data for gender composition of design subgroups at each paper were collected from a database created by the Society for News Design, the major professional organization for news designers and graphic artists. These data were less complete than survey data, consisting of 184 papers. Finally, the *Editor & Publisher* database was used to gather data on circulation size and number of pages printed. Measures for predictors of control and for degree of control itself are shown in Table 2.1.

Design managers and international news editors were selected as interview respondents in the survey. Design managers were chosen as respondents because they could provide a perspective on the work process and the actions of the staff and would be able to provide information about structure and department rules. It was decided to also interview international news editors because, although they are players in the presentation process, they are not deeply involved with the design work of the paper. It was expected that the convergence of these two viewpoints would bolster the validity of the data. Responses from design directors and editors were not substantially different, and this finding increased the believability of the design director findings. Responses from design directors and editors were aggregated.[4] Ultimately, completed surveys were obtained from 459 of the 466 respondents, for a rate of 98.5% percent.[5]

TABLE 2.1

Variable Measures and Alpha Correlations For Scaled Variables

VARIABLES	MEASURES
Dependent variable	
Degree of Control over presentation	Degree of influence designers have over the assignment of photos*
	Degree of influence designers have over the planning of news projects*
Work by design subgroup	
Cronbach's α = .69	Degree of control designers have over page layout*
	Degree of control designers have over the selection of images*
	Degree of control designers have over the content of headlines*
	Degree of control designers have over the final length of stories*

---

[4]Findings from survey measures for each of the dependent and independent variables were standardized and scaled. Where data from a design director were missing, the finding from the corresponding editor survey was substituted, and vice versa. Prior to creating scaled indices, factor analyses and bivariate correlations were conducted for each set of measures in order to more thoroughly identify which measures held together empirically. The Cronbach's alpha for measures of the dependent variable, Degree of Control over Presentation Work, was .69, which is very close to the conventional level of acceptability, .70. Scales were also created for several of the independent variables (measures and alphas for all variables are presented in Table 2.1). Correlations among these measures and the alphas for the scales were low for many of the independent variables. It was decided however to keep all measures in the indices, because this way the independent variables represented a wide array of conceptual dimensions. This method of conceptual sampling produces low intercorrelation among measures for the scaled variable, but it is likely to increase content validity.

[5]Because these return rates are so close to 100%, inference to the larger population was deemed unnecessary. The sample, in effect, becomes a census, and there are no significance tests.

TABLE 2.1 *(Continued)*

Variable Measures and Alpha Correlations For Scaled Variables

VARIABLES	MEASURES

Independent Variables

Gender composition	Percentage of males in designer subgroups (from SND database)
Gender of design director	Measure taken from survey (1 = female, 2 = male)

Occupational–Level Predictors

Journalism knowledge	Degree to which designers read stories they lay out
(Degree of exposure to journalism knowledge) *Cronbach's* α = .61	Degree to which paper tries to hire designers with journalism background
	Degree to which design director thinks journalism background is important for designers to have
	Does design director have journalism education?
	Do designers have journalism education?
	Number of professional journalism workshops attended within last year
	Number of professional journalism organizations of which director is member
Art Knowledge	Degree to which paper tries to hire designers with art background
(Degree of exposure to graphic design knowledge)	Degree to which design director thinks art background is important for designers to have
Cronbach's α = .56	Does design director have art education?
	Do designers have art education?
	Number of professional graphic design organizations of which design director is member
Degree of Cohesiveness	How close are designers' workstations to one another?
Cronbach's α = .24	Do designers all report to the same manager?
	How often do designers socialize with one another outside of work hours?

TABLE 2.1 *(Continued)*

Variable Measures and Alpha Correlations For Scaled Variables

VARIABLES	MEASURES
Degree of Centrality	How often photographers discuss work with designers
	How often photo editors discuss work with designers
Cronbach's α = .50	How often copy editors discuss work with designers*
	How often reporters discuss work with designers*
	Does newsroom have collaborative meetings on a regular basis?
	How close designers are stationed to photo editors in newsroom
Years experience	Average years of newspaper experience possessed by the design subgroup

Organizational–Level Predictors

Technological usability	Degree to which pagination system helps rather than hinders design work
(Degree to which technology aids design work)	Degree of difficulty using pagination system
Volume of work	Ratio between average daily amount of page space devoted to editorial content and number of both full–time and part-time designers
(Amount of resources in terms of time and staff)	
Access to top management	Ratio of number of hierarchical positions between design director and top newsroom manager to overall number of positions in newsroom hierarchy.
Organizational size	Total average weekday circulation

*From both design director and international editor responses—no asterisk means only design director responses collected. All questions measuring the dependent variable, graphical control over presentation work, were asked of both design directors and international editors. Not all questions measuring the predictors were asked of editors, as it was assumed most would not be knowledgeable about details of designers and design work.

DISCUSSION

Analysis of this data show that gender does have a notable effect on the degree to which designers control work (see Table 2.2). Design staffs that are mostly male have more influence over project planning, image selection, headline writing, story length, and final layout decisions than do design staffs that are mostly female. Design staffs that have male directors have more influence in these areas as well, and they also have greater influence over photo assigning. The difference in degree of control by gender is especially strong in influence over news project planning and control over final layout. These are important categories. By having influence over early planning, a subgroup is able to shape the context within which decisions are made, thus potentially affecting all later decisions (Perrow, 1986). By having influence over final layout, designers can also affect all previous decisions.

Of course there are many factors that can affect how influential a newsroom subgroup is—gender is just one of these. In order to truly test the impact of gender on designer control, these other factors should be considered. For example, if we compare two design subgroups at two different newspapers, and we find that the subgroup composed of mostly males has more influence than the design staff composed of mostly females, we would be tempted to see this as evidence of gender discrimination. But perhaps the group composed of mostly males has more influence because their newsroom has more resources to

TABLE 2.2

Relationship of Gender and Control Over Work: Percent of Design Subgroups with "A Great Deal" or "Complete" Control Over Presentation Work

Measures of Degree of Control Over Work (Below)	Design Subgroups 50% or Less Male (*N* = 70)	Design Subgroups Over 50% Male (*N* = 114)	Design Subgroups with Female Director (*N* = 65)	Design Subgroups with Male Director (*N* = 164)
Influence planning of projects	61.4%	65.0%	52.3%	65.8%
Influence photo assignment	18.6	18.4	13.8	17.0
Control over layout	67.2	75.4	61.6	74.4
Control over image selection	42.8	53.5	47.7	48.8
Control over headlines	30.0	33.4	30.8	35.3
Control over story length	10.0	13.3	13.9	15.9
Average percent of all measures	38.3	43.2	36.7	42.9

devote to design, or because these designers have a more extensive knowledge base or more experience than the mostly female staff. These rival explanations need to be held constant in order to get a truer assessment of the impact of gender on designer control. This was accomplished using *regression analysis,* which makes it possible to test the impact of gender after these rival factors have been considered.

Rival explanations can be found at both the level of the organization and the level of the subgroup. Subgroups perform their work within news organizations, and of course their work is shaped by organizational factors. But subgroups are more than just interconnected parts of a larger newsroom machine, which is how they are typically portrayed in studies of the division of labor in newsrooms. In these studies, the differentiation of newsroom tasks is viewed as mostly beneficial for the news organization (Russial, 1998; Salcetti, 1995; Solomon, 1995). Yet these subgroups may also be seen as distinct *occupational* entities with their own knowledge bases.[6] As occupational subgroups they have their own agendas, and they use their specialized knowledge to compete for control over areas of work (Abbott, 1988; Light, 1988; Simpson, 1985; Westley, 1984). In organizations, these subgroups vie for legitimacy and for the right to define the norms and values of the workplace (Bloor & Dawson, 1994; Trice, 1993; Van Maanen & Barley, 1984).

At the subgroup level, degree of control rises and falls according to factors that are intrinsic to the subgroup and come into play during daily staff interaction. These factors are the degree and nature of specialized knowledge possessed by a subgroup, the degree to which a subgroup is integrated and involved with other subgroups, and the cohesiveness of a subgroup.

At the organizational level, subgroups are viewed as divisions of labor in an organization. Each subgroup performs a task that is functional for the organization, and their control over work rises and falls depending on the needs of the organization. Organizational structure, size, and resources shape the needs of organizations and should therefore shape subgroup control.

---

[6]An occupation can be said to exist when its members claim the right to perform a distinctive set of tasks, and there is a consensus that certain individuals are expected to perform these tasks and to exercise degrees of control over how they are done (Child & Fulk, 1982; Hughes, 1958; Trice, 1993). Copyediting, designing, reporting, and photography are all considered to be occupations in this study. This study does not address whether an occupation qualifies as a profession or not, which Hughes (1958) called "a false question" and Abbott (1988) called "uninteresting." This question has occupied the bulk of the writings on the professional status of journalism and journalists (Gerald, 1963; Merrill, 1986; Nayman, 1973; Singletary, 1982). It is assumed in this study that all occupations attempt to assert control over work areas, and some are more successful than others. This success can be attributed to a variety of factors, and it is the rise and fall of these factors that are most interesting.

Rival explanations for subgroup control are explained here (see Table 2.1 for the measures of these explanatory variables).

Explanations at the Subgroup Level

Specialized Knowledge. For designers specialized knowledge includes knowledge of journalism and knowledge of art (Auman, 1995; Hilliard, 1989; Wanta & Danner, 1997). Knowledge here is a social factor. It is measured by a subgroup's exposure to the social structures that provide the occupation's knowledge base, such as school curricula, professional training, and daily job experience.

Degree of Centrality is the degree to which designers discuss work with other subgroups that are key to the presentation process. When designers are more involved with the different facets of the presentation process, they are likely to better understand the overall process and thereby be able to reduce uncertainty for the newsroom (Pfeffer, 1981). They are also more able to influence the decision making of other subgroups that are important players in the presentation work process (copyeditors, photographers, reporters).

Degree Of Cohesiveness within the Occupational Subgroup. Groups that are more cohesive are more likely to have unified goals and be more politically effective in newsroom negotiation (Perrow, 1986; Van Maanen & Barley, 1984).

The Average Years of Experience of a Subgroup. Design staffs with more years of newspaper experience should also have more influence than staffs with less experience (Trice, 1993; Van Maanen & Barley, 1984). Years of experience make work processes more predictable, and experienced staff gain clout by reducing uncertainty for the organization.

Explanations at the Organizational Level

Availability of Organizational Resources. Organizational resources include *volume of work* and *technological usability.* Design subgroups with greater staff resources (more designers per pages to be designed) will have a lower work volume and therefore more time to negotiate decision making with other subgroups. They should be able to produce design work that is more highly valued by the organization. Design subgroups with easier–to–use pagination systems (pagination systems allow page composition on computer screens) should also be better able to create valued output and should have more time to negotiate decision making (Perrow, 1986; Pfeffer, 1981).

Access to Top Management. Design directors who are higher up the management ladder should have better access to top newsroom decision makers. This should benefit the design staff (Perrow, 1986).

Organizational Size. In larger newsrooms, work is more specialized, and tasks overlap less. Increased specialization can lead to minority subgroups (i.e., less powerful subgroups, such as the design staff) having higher levels of expertise and more organizational clout. In smaller newsrooms, minority subgroups are less distinct and have less clout. Also, large organizations should have more resources for a wider variety of newsroom tasks, thus potentially strengthening minority subgroups such as designers.

REGRESSION RESULTS AND DISCUSSION

Results from the regression analysis show that the factor of gender is more important than most of the other predictors (see Table 2.3). When controlling for all these rival explanations, both the gender composition of the design subgroup and the gender of the design director were better predictors of the degree to which designers controlled decision making than any of the organizational level predictors. Gender composition was a stronger predictor than all factors except for degree of journalism knowledge and degree of centrality. Gender of design director was a stronger determinant than all but degree of centrality, degrees of journalism and art knowledge, and years of experience.

This appears to be evidence of discrimination on the basis of gender. Being male holds up as an important explanation for subgroup control even in the face of these rival explanations. But how does discrimination work in this case? And what is the relationship with the other important predictors, centrality, and specialized knowledge?

There is a logical connection among the key predictors—centrality, occupational knowledge, and staff gender composition. All three factors play a role in reducing uncertainty for decision makers. Key decision makers in newsrooms are most likely to be male news editors, and designers have the most authority when they are able to seamlessly integrate with the larger newsroom in a way that is most normal and predictable for these male editors. Therefore, the more influential designers are those who are mostly male and who discuss work in terms of journalism knowledge, not graphic arts knowledge.

Kanter (1977) attributes gender inequity in the workplace in part to this desire by managers to reduce uncertainty in daily contacts with work colleagues. Kanter calls this behavior homosocial. Male managers exhibiting *homosocial* behavior tend to view negotiation with women as wrought with uncertainty, while they feel more sure–footed and familiar in negotiations with men. According to Kanter, because much important decision making at the manageri-

TABLE 2.3

Regression of Degree of Control Over Presentation Work by the Design Subgroup on Gender Composition of Design Subgroup (Percent Male), Gender Of Director, Organizationa Level Predictors, and Occupational Level Predictors

Independent Variables	Regression Model Without Gender Variables (N=228)	Regression Model With Gender and Director's Gender (N=228)
	$R^2 = .228$	$R^2 = .327$
Organizational Predictors		
Volume of work	−.015*	−.098
Technological usability	.041	−.069
Access to top management	.044	−.098
Organizational size	−.023	−.032
Occupational Predictors		
Journalism knowledge	.294	.361
Art knowledge	.108	.206
Degree of centrality	.310	.309
Degree of cohesiveness	.051	.091
Years experience	.096	.180
Gender composition (percent male)	—	.219
Gender of design Director	—	.133

*Standardized Beta Coefficients

al level takes place in informal settings (e.g., a male manager may walk into another male manager's office and discuss strategies prior to formal meetings), opportunities to influence decision making often bypass female managers. It may be that mostly female design subgroups suffer loss of influence because male decision makers in other subgroups informally exclude women in key discussions about presentation.

Why should levels of occupational knowledge and centrality have such a strong impact on how much influence a subgroup has? Occupational knowledge, according to studies of occupational competition, is considered highly valuable to occupations seeking to control their work. Knowledge—especially knowledge that is abstract and theoretical in nature—allows an occupation to "redefine its problems and tasks, defend them from interlopers and seize new problems" (Abbott, 1988, p. 9). In contrast, work that is routine and rule–bound is more easily performed by other occupations and is susceptible to jurisdictional takeover (Abbott, 1988; Child & Fulk, 1982; Jamous & Peloille, 1970; Nilson, 1979; Simpson, 1985).

The importance of centrality in this study likely reflects the benefits gained from sharing specialized knowledge, or from using arguments based on this knowledge in negotiations. It may also reflect advantages gained from coalition building. Prior case study research has shown that design staffs knowledgeable about the news and about news judgment were more effective in negotiations with editors over page space and design configuration than those with less knowledge. These design subgroups also tended to collaborate more with the photography subgroups during early stages of project planning. With the help of allies, designers were more successful in setting the premises that constrain later decisions (Lowrey, 2002).

In the quest for control, why should the possession of occupational knowledge and the ability to use it in negotiation with others be more important attributes than being male? Literature on gender effects in work organizations offers some insight. Managers place great importance on ensuring that employees with specialized skills and knowledge are rewarded with ample pay, autonomy, and a bright future. They do this because they fear the high costs and uncertainty of staff turnover (Bielby & Baron, 1986). On the one hand, this may mean managers will relegate women to lesser skilled roles because managers fear women will leave for family reasons. Such positions have less authority and do not pay as well (Bielby & Baron, 1986). On the other hand, women who demonstrate high levels of knowledge and skill are in a stronger position to fight this banishment to lesser skilled positions. They are in a better position to demand higher pay and greater authority.

Tam (1997) argued that inequity in salary and autonomy between men and women in the workplace is due to the fact that fewer women than men have obtained the specialized knowledge necessary for success in the workplace. Gender inequity in the workplace is not due mainly to discrimination in the workplace but is a result of inequality in training. Tam acknowledged that this may point to gender discrimination earlier in the occupational process. Similarly, others have argued that women have been blocked from receiving the knowledge and skills necessary for success in the workplace (e.g., Polachek, 1981).

Findings here, although clearly demonstrating the importance of knowledge and training, do not support Tam's argument. First, the effects of both gender composition and gender of director register strongly as predictors of degree of designer control. They do not disappear when level of specialized knowledge is controlled. Second, gender composition is a more important factor than either art knowledge or years of experience. This is an eye–opening finding, indicating that extensive experience and art expertise in a design staff may not carry much weight if that staff is mostly female.

Also, in schools that train future workers of journalism and mass communication, women dominate enrollment numbers at both undergraduate and graduate levels. More women than men obtain media internships, and a higher number of graduates of these schools are women. On average, female graduates also have a slightly higher grade point average than male graduates (Becker, Kosicki, Lowrey, Prine, & Punathambekar, 2000). Clearly, something other than insufficient training or lack of specialized knowledge must account for the finding that mostly female design staffs have less control over their work than mostly male staffs.

Perhaps the way design work is perceived in the newsroom changes when the gender composition of the design subgroup changes. Although this is speculative, it could be that design subgroups are particularly susceptible to the devaluing effects of gender composition. According to the devaluation hypothesis, work areas dominated by females become undervalued relative to mixed–gender or male–dominated occupations (Reid, 1998), and no economic factors (such as training inequity) can account for this devaluation (Maume, 1999). A rise in the percentage of female workers in an occupation may trigger unequal treatment, and this inequity stems from a culture of discrimination against "women's work" (Steinberg, 1990; Stover, 1994; Tam, 1997). Wajcman (1991) said, "The introduction of female labor is usually accompanied by a downgrading of the skill content and a consequent fall in pay for the job. . . . Skill definitions are saturated with gender bias" (pp. 36, 37).

Certain technical skills are undervalued because they are seen as stemming from women's natural aptitude rather than having been earned (Grayson, 1993; Steinberg, 1990; Wajcman, 1991). For example, work involving client relations and the manipulation of complex phone systems may be devalued if performed by women because of the stereotype that women are innately nurturing, which brings forth patience and cordiality (England, Herbert, Kilbourne, Reid, & Megdal, 1994). At least one case study has suggested positions within graphic design may be divided by gender, with male design students embracing new computer technologies more easily than female design students (Clegg, Mayfield, & Trayhurn, 1999).

The regression analysis indicates specialized journalism and art knowledge bolster designer influence, but do these knowledge areas benefit women in the same way they benefit men? In other words, is the impact of specialized knowledge on control over work different for subgroups that are mostly male than for subgroups that are mostly female? And does this impact differ for subgroups that have male directors rather than female directors? If differences were found, it could mean that the perceived nature of design work and the perceived nature of the knowledge required to do design work change, depending on whether men or women are doing the work. Furthermore, it may suggest design work is particularly devalued when conducted by women. To explore answers to these questions, design subgroups were put into two categories. In one category each design subgroup was composed of more than 50% men, and in the other, each subgroup was less than 50% male. For each category, degree of control over presentation work by these subgroups was correlated with degree of journalism knowledge and then with degree of art knowledge. Results for the two categories were compared. The same procedure was followed for a comparison of design subgroups with male directors versus subgroups with female directors (see Table 2.4).

Results show that the effects of journalism and art knowledge on designer control do work differently for women and men. Art knowledge is of little consequence for either mostly male subgroups or mostly female subgroups, but for design subgroups with female directors, art knowledge weakens designer control somewhat.

The effect of journalism knowledge on ability to control work is substantially different for men than for women. Men are more likely to wield influence with or without high levels of this knowledge. Journalism knowledge was also more important to subgroups with female directors than subgroups with male directors. These findings suggest a double standard is at work. Design subgroups that are mostly male have a lower hurdle to jump on their way to greater control over work than do mostly female subgroups. Several individual measures of journalism knowledge proved to be especially important for increasing women's control over design work, including the reading of stories prior to layout, design director's estimation of the importance of journalism knowledge, and emphasis placed by the organization on hiring designers with journalism backgrounds.

These findings lend support to the devaluation hypothesis. It seems design work conducted by mostly male subgroups or with a male director is effective

TABLE 2.4

Correlations of Specialized Knowledge and Control Over Work by Gender Composition and Gender of Director

	Degree of Control Over Work (Design Subgroups That Are Over 50% Men)	Degree of Control Over Work (Design Subgroups That Are 50% or Less Men)	Degree of Control Over Work (Design Subgroups With Male Director)	Degree of Control Over Work (Design Groups With Female Director)
Degree of journalism knowledge	.254* (N = 106)	.323 (N = 67)	.220 (N = 154)	.393 (N = 61)
Degree of art knowledge	−.022 (N = 108)	−.022 (N = 66)	−.023 (N = 155)	−.178 (N = 62)

*Pearson Product–Moment Correlation Coefficients

enough on its own terms, but for mostly female subgroups or for subgroups with female directors, it is more important that design work have a newsy, or journalistic orientation. This is speculative, but these findings imply that design work conducted by women looks like graphic design to the rest of the newsroom, but design work conducted by men looks more like journalism. This would explain why women must possess a greater understanding of news content and news judgment than their male counterparts when negotiating for control in the wider newsroom. As noted, design staff orientation toward art knowledge weakens control by design subgroups with women directors more than it did subgroups with male directors.

Graphic design is traditionally connected with "soft news" and subjectivity, and having a staff composed largely of females may compound this perception.[7] Historically, specialized design work has been identified with women's content in the newspaper. Graphic arts as a suboccupation initially entered the newsroom by way of advertising and "soft news" sections like the women's pages. As Nerone and Barnhurst (1995) suggested, "These sections were ghettoes partitioned by the journalist's ideology of the public mission of the newspaper. . . . One senses that 'serious' journalists came to shun the sections more and more over time, and this may be what allowed the sections to become centers for design innovation" (p. 30). Photography entered the newspapers the same way, initially only appearing in soft news sections such as women's and society pages (Zelizer, 1995).

Textbooks and trade articles alike condemn the notion of art for art's sake and stress that design must follow content.[8] Graphic designers are expected to shed orientation toward the subjectivity of the arts and adopt a more serious journalistic orientation. Historically, women news workers have also been called on to eschew emotionalism and subjectivity—qualities defined as both "feminine" and nonjournalistic by the male–dominated newsroom. Histories of women in journalism suggest women journalists were relegated to sections of the paper that dealt with soft news (Brennen, 1995; Guenin, 1975; Streitmatter,

---

[7]This is not to imply that most designers and design directors are female. On the contrary, more than two thirds of the design directors interviewed were men, and roughly 60% of staff designers were men, according to the Society for News Design database.

[8]Textbooks and trade articles acknowledge a conflict between art norms and journalism norms in the occupations of visual journalism, and typically advocate adopting the latter. The following statements are examples: "The great visual journalist is . . . someone who knows that visual impact matters, but journalism matters more (Moses, 1999, p. 14); "Good design . . . emphasizes information and communication over art (Garcia, 1993, p. 34); "All too often, particularly at newspapers, illustration serves as a lazy journalist's way out" (Meyer, 1997, p. 264). News managers often try to turn artists into journalists (Lowrey, 2000; Wanta & Danner, 1997), even as they lament the difficulty inherent in melding the two occupations (Utt & Pasternack, 2000; Lowrey, 2000).

1998), and for them to be taken seriously in the male dominated newsroom they were expected to shed their "feminine selves" (Lumsden, 1995).

Literature also indicates that work performed by women is likely to be seen as *routine* work that requires less specialized training than "men's work." This perception results in lower pay, fewer promotion opportunities and less autonomy (Bielby & Baron, 1986; Reid, 1998; Steinberg, 1990; Tam, 1997; Wajcman, 1991). Male managers may even steer women toward routine positions with short promotion ladders so that men are free to compete among themselves for positions offering higher autonomy and pay (Maume, 1999; Reskin, 1988). An analysis was conducted here to see if the degree to which editors and design directors viewed design work as routine correlated with the gender composition of the design subgroup. A strong correlation would be further evidence that design work was devalued when performed by women. Results of this analysis do not lend support to the devaluation hypothesis—the gender composition of the design staff did *not* appear to alter respondents' views on how routine design work was. Clearly, gender matters to the ability of designers to influence decision making about news presentation, and there is evidence in this study of a relationship between the perceived value of the work of design and the work of women. However, neither gender composition nor director gender appear to make nondesigners believe design work is more routine or easier to perform.

ORGANIZATIONAL INFLUENCES, GENDER, AND CONTROL OVER WORK

To this point the study has taken an occupational perspective, focusing on the relationships between specialized knowledge, centrality, and gender as predictors of control over work. It is important to note, however, that news work takes place within the walls of work organizations. The classic studies on news construction place special emphasis on the importance of organizational constraints on decision making in newsrooms (e.g., Roshco, 1975; Shoemaker & Reese, 1996; Sigal, 1973; Tuchman, 1978), and this perspective is evident in news construction research today (e.g., Becker, Lowrey, Claussen, & Anderson, 2000; Demers, 1998; Shoemaker, Eichholz, Kim, & Wrigley, 2001). In this framework, subgroups in the newsroom reflect a division of labor that serves managerial needs for efficiency. A subgroup's specialized knowledge serves the purpose of accomplishing work for the organization (Fishman, 1982; Tuchman, 1978). Professional knowledge is in essence knowledge of work routines, and subgroups control their work only to the extent that organizational management allows this control. In this framework, subgroups are only a product of the organization and its needs, and the relationship between gender and control over work would be explained by organizational factors.

Findings from the regression analysis seem to contradict this perspective, as organizational factors have little impact on the degree of control designers have over their work. Organizational resources, organizational size, and position of the design manager on the managerial ladder matter less than most occupational subgroup factors. Of course, through hiring guidelines, the news organization may have an impact on subgroup–level factors like degree of a design staff's journalism knowledge. Such guidelines would not, however, spell out how designers use this knowledge in negotiation with other subgroups.

It seems most surprising that organizational size has little impact on designer control. This factor has proved one of the more important factors affecting changes in organizational decision making because it so fundamentally alters availability or resources and the way work is structured (Hall, 1999; Perrow, 1986). As organizations grow in size, skills tend to become more specialized, while in smaller organizations workers are more likely to wear several hats (Blau, 1970; Hall, 1999). This has been noted in analyses of newsrooms as well (Becker et al., 2000; Epstein, 1973; Russial, 1998; Sigal, 1973).

Because of its theoretical importance to the nature of subgroups and the division of labor, the impact of organizational size was tested again. An analysis was performed to see if organizational size would moderate the relationship between gender and designer control over work. In other words, would gender be as strong a predictor in smaller newsrooms as in larger newsrooms? If size changed the relationship, it would be evidence that subgroup control was not all about agency but that structure played a role too. To find out, all newspapers in the survey were sorted into three groups, by circulation size. The first group included all papers in the sample with average weekday circulations from 50,000 to 75,000. The second group included all papers over 75,000 but under 150,000 circulation, and the third group included all papers over 150,000 circulation. Gender composition of design subgroups and gender of design director were correlated with degree of designer control over presentation work for papers in each of the three size categories.

Findings from this analysis are mixed (see Table 2.5). Generally, as organizational size increased, so did the impact of gender composition and gender of director on control, but the relationships were not straightforward. For example, the impact of gender composition on degree of control is higher in mid–sized newsrooms than in large newsrooms, and the impact of director's gender was less in mid–sized newsrooms than in smaller newsrooms.

The most dramatic result from this analysis is the strength of the factor of centrality in mid–sized organizations. The frequency with which designers discuss work with members of other key subgroups—photo staff, reporters, and copyeditors in particular—is by far the most important explainer of designer control. It is telling that as newsroom size changes, the fluctuation in importance of centrality mirrors the fluctuation in the importance of design staff gender composition. Where informal discussion among subgroups is most important to designer control, so is the degree of "maleness" of the staff composition.

TABLE 2.5

Regression of Degree of Control Over Presentation Work on Predictors by Organizational Size

Independent variables	Degree of Control Over Work (small newspapers, 50,000 to 75,000 circulation) (N = 79)	Degree of Control Over Work (mid-sized newspapers, 75,000 to 150,000 circulation) (N = 73)	Degree of Control Over Work (large newspapers, over 150,000 circulation) (N = 78)
	$R^2 = .404$	$R^2 = .542$	$R^2 = .444$
Organizational Predictors			
Volume of work	−.099*	−.023	−.237
Technological usability	−.123	−.159	.128
Access to top management	.012	−.258	−.211
Occupational Predictors			
Journalism knowledge	.574	.355	.289
Art knowledge	.281	.154	.262
Degree of centrality	.143	.704	.346
Degree of cohesiveness	.162	−.109	.160
Years experience	.153	−.104	.034
Gender composition	.182	.337	.224
Gender of design director	.088	−.028	.192

---

*Standardized Beta Coefficients

Journalism knowledge is also an important factor in mid–sized newsrooms. As noted earlier, women may be excluded from informal discussion by the homosocial behavior of male managers who seek the predictable and familiar (i.e., discussion with other males with a journalism orientation).

Why should these three factors have such a strong effect in mid–sized newsrooms? It may be that in larger newsrooms control over work becomes more bureaucratic, and managerial rules and policies dictate decision making to a greater degree. Subgroup negotiations at the staff level may not have as much impact in more bureaucratic newsrooms. In smaller newsrooms, subgroup roles overlap, and individual subgroups may not be as distinct, thus putting control in the hands of a few overarching managers. In such a setting, negotiation among subgroups is likely less prevalent and less relevant. So the environment of mid–sized newsrooms may be "just right" for subgroup interaction. These newsrooms offer the right mix of informality and degree of task specialization. However, it may be "just wrong" for the ability of mostly female design subgroups to influence decision making.

In smaller newsrooms, neither gender of design director nor gender composition of the subgroup has much of an effect on the ability of the subgroup to control work. This finding may be due in part to the likelihood that in smaller organizations tasks collapse, and designers are also editors. Because of this, in smaller newsrooms, design work may be identified less with graphic design (as it is in larger newsrooms), and it may avoid the stigma associated with soft, subjective news. Design work, therefore, benefits from the status accorded editing work in newsrooms, and it may be less necessary that designers be male for them to have influence. There are also a fewer number of job types in smaller organizations, which makes it more difficult to segregate work areas according to gender by creating "female" jobs and "male" jobs (Bielby & Baron, 1986).

The collapsing of tasks might also explain why the extent of a design staff's journalism knowledge is much more important to designer control in smaller newsrooms than in larger newsrooms. Designers in small newsrooms are more likely to edit copy and are therefore more likely to have a journalism background than an art background. The editing role traditionally confers authority, which in part explains the relationship between journalism knowledge and control. However, journalism knowledge is still important in medium–sized and larger newsrooms, and so the collapsing of tasks does not explain its effect entirely.

It appears then that organizational size, although not a strongly determining factor, does alter the importance of gender to designer control in subtle and various ways. Differences in structure and in the way labor is divided have an effect on the factors that shape subgroups' abilities to control their work.

FINAL THOUGHTS

Results from this study make it clear that design subgroups made up of mostly women are received less favorably than mostly male design subgroups. Gender of the design director has a similar effect. These effects hold up even when considering rival explanations. In short, findings suggest strong evidence of discrimination based on gender operating in newsrooms at the subgroup level. Gender, however, is not the dominant explanation for designer control, and its effects vary depending on rival explanations and on organizational size.

The fact that degree of journalism knowledge and degree of centrality were the strongest predictors of subgroup control, regardless of gender, suggests discrimination on the basis of gender is not impossible to overcome. Training, skills and knowledge (which women appear to be getting, given enrollment figures from journalism schools), and the ability to use this knowledge in negotiation on staff and management levels can increase the influence of women and men alike. A relevant example comes from the work of high school craft teachers. Paechter and Head (1996) depicted an episode at a particular school where course curriculum was being changed from a hand–tool workshop format to a computer graphics approach. During the transition, newly hired women (many from art teaching backgrounds) were better able to adapt to the required knowledge and to establish effective alliances. Male teachers tended to cling to the older approach. Ultimately, female teachers gained influence at the expense of male teachers, despite the fact that men were more well established in the school's hierarchy.

However, if the concepts of *satisficing* and *homosocial behavior* have validity, women may have an uphill battle achieving influence through negotiation with other staff in male–dominated newsrooms. Women may have to be more knowledgeable then men in negotiations. The fact that specialized journalism knowledge is highly important to the ability of mostly female groups to wield influence, and not as important to mostly male groups, indicates that knowledge of news and news judgment is more *expected* of men. There are lower expectations for females in newsrooms (similar to findings that female sports journalists feel they are not expected to know as much as male sports journalists, Miller & Miller, 1995). Seemingly then, design groups that are mostly made up of women are penalized more harshly for a *lack* of journalism knowledge and background than are mostly male design subgroups with a similar lack.

At the same time, degree of art knowledge was no more helpful to mostly female subgroups than it was for mostly male subgroups. In fact, art knowledge decreased the control of designer subgroups that have female directors. It may be that the perception that designers work somewhat outside the mainstream norms of journalism undercuts the efforts of the design director in negotiations with other managers—especially when the design director is female and especially in larger newsrooms. In larger newsrooms, design subgroups are more likely to include staffers with specialized art backgrounds rather than journalism backgrounds. Conversely, in smaller newsrooms designers are more likely to perform text–editing duties, and design directors are more likely to be editors.

In effect, homosocial behavior on the part of male managers may exclude not only women, but also artists. Perhaps women who are associated with art are excluded most severely. Negotiating informally with designers, with their foreign occupational knowledge base and unique occupational culture, may be just as uncomfortable to traditional news editors as negotiating informally with women. The fact that a design group's director is female may actually feed the impression that design work is less serious, or less journalistic. And the fact that the female manager is associated with design work may feed the impression that women journalists are not to be taken as seriously as male journalists.

Although findings here suggest this correlation, more research should be done to discern a direct relationship between the perception of visual journalism and the perception of women in the newsroom. Trade and academic literature suggest that both women and visual journalists have had their journalistic legitimacy questioned, and it is evident from the historical literature that both visual journalists and women were segregated into the same soft news sections of the paper. This study does not compare different types of subgroups. It would be interesting to see in future research if gender composition or gender of subgroup director matters as much to the influence of copyediting or reporting subgroups. Perhaps because these subgroups are more closely identified with the dominant professional culture and knowledge base in the newsroom (journalism), the effects of gender would prove less important.

Findings in this study, based on data from survey measures, suggest possible ways variables interact, but case–study or in–depth interview research could help strengthen these assumptions. Newsroom observation could add validity to the perceptions of control by design directors and editors. Observation could verify that designers use specialized knowledge in negotiation with other subgroups, and that the outcome of these negotiations affects how much control they have over decision making. Interview and observation research could also help validate that largely female subgroups and nonjournalistic subcultures are devalued by other newsroom staff and management.

This study sheds light on the complex nature of occupational influence and the role gender and specialized knowledge play in this influence. Occupations and their work can mean different things in different organizational settings, and the control over work by occupations varies across organizations. Gender effects may work differently depending on the nature of a subgroup and its work area. This idea is intriguing and deserves more attention in the media research. Undoubtedly, as this study makes clear, gender plays a role in newsroom decision making about content. Just how gender works on decision-making—as newsroom and subgroup conditions change—remains to be fully understood.

REFERENCES

Abbott, A. (1988). *The system of professions: An essay on the division of expert labor.* Chicago: University of Chicago Press.

American Society of Newspaper Editors. (2000). *ASNE's 2000 newsroom census: Minority journalists make small gains in daily newspapers.* URL (consulted

November 2001: http://www.asne.org/kiosk/diversity/2000 Survey/2000Census Report.html)

Auman, A. (1995). Seeing the big picture: The integrated editor of the 1990s. *Newspaper Research Journal, 16*(1), 35-47.

Becker, L., Kosicki, G., Lowrey, W., Prine, J., & Punathambekar, A. (2000). 1999 Annual survey of Journalism & Mass Communication Enrollments. Retrieved Feb. 2, 2003. http://www.grady.uga.edu/annualsurveys/ Enrollment99/ENR99JE.htm

Becker, L. B., Kosicki, G., Prine, J., & Lowrey, W. (2000). 1999 Annual survey of journalism and mass communication graduates. Paper presented at the annual convention for the Association for Education in Journalism and Mass Communication, Phoenix, AZ.

Becker, L. B., Lowrey, W., Claussen D. A., & Anderson, W. B. (2000). Why does the beat go on? An examination of the beat structure in the newsroom. *Newspaper Research Journal, 21*(4), 2-16.

Bielby, W. T., & Baron, J. N. (1986). Men and women at work: Sex segregation and statistical discrimination. *American Journal of Sociology, 91*(4), 759-799.

Blau, P. M. (1970). A formal theory of differentiation in organizations. *American Sociological Review, 35*(2), 201-218.

Bloor, G., & Dawson, P. (1994). Understanding professional culture in organizational context. *Organization Studies, 15*(2), 275-295.

Brennen, B. (1995). Cultural discourse of journalists: The material conditions of newsroom labor. In B. Brennen & H. Hardt (Eds.), *Picturing the past: Media, history and photography* (pp. 75-109). Urbana: University of Illinois Press.

Child, J., & Fulk, J. (1982). Maintenance of occupational control: The case of professions. *Work and Occupations, 9*(2), 155-192.

Clegg, S., Mayfield, W., & Trayhurn, D. (1999). Disciplinary discourses: A case study of gender in information technology and design courses. *Gender and Education, 11*(1), 43-55.

Culbertson, H. M. (1969). The effect of art work on perceived writer stand. *Journalism Quarterly, 46*(2), 294-301.

David, P. (1998). News concreteness and visual–verbal association. *Human Communication Research, 25*(2), 180-203.

Demers, D. K. (1998). Structural pluralism, corporate newspaper structure and news source perceptions: Another test of the editorial vigor hypothesis. *Journalism and Mass Communication Quarterly, 75*(3), 572-592.

England, P., Herbert, M. S., Kilbourne, B. S., Reid, L. L., & Megdal, L. M. (1994). The gendered valuation of occupations and skills: Earnings in 1980 census occupations. *Social Forces, 73*(1), 65-99.

Epstein, E. J. (1973). *News from nowhere: Television and the news.* New York: Random House.

Fishman, M. (1982). News and non-events: Making the visible invisible. In J. Ettema & D. C. Whitney (Eds.), *Individuals in mass media organizations: Creativity and constraint* (pp. 219-240). Beverly Hills: Sage.

Garcia, M. R. (1993). *Contemporary newspaper design.* Englewood Cliffs, NJ: Prentice-Hall.

Garcia, M. R., & Stark, P. (1991). *Eyes on the news.* St. Petersburg, FL: The Poynter Institute.

Gentry, J. K., & Zang, B. (1989). Characteristics of graphics managers at metropolitan dailies. *Newspaper Research Journal, 10*(4), 85-95.

Gerald, E. J. (1963). *The social responsibility of the press.* Minneapolis: University of Minnesota Press.

Grayson, J. P. (1993). Skill, autonomy and technological change in Canada. *Work and Occupations, 20*(1), 23-45.

Guenin, Z. B. (1975). Women's pages in American newspapers: Missing out on contemporary content? *Journalism Quarterly, 52*(1), 66-69.

Hall, R. H. (1999). *Organizations: Structures, processes and outcomes* (7th ed.). Upper Saddle River, NJ: Prentice Hall.

Hansen, K. A., Neuzil, M., & Ward, J. (1998). Newsroom topic teams: Journalists' assessments of effects on news routines and newspaper quality. *Journalism and Mass Communication Quarterly, 75*(4), 803-821.

Hilliard, R. D. (1989). The graphics explosion: Questions remain about roles. *Journalism Quarterly, 66*(1), 192-194.

Hughes, E. C. (1958). *Men and their work.* Glencoe, IL: The Free Press.

Jamous, H., & Peloille, B. (1970). Changes in the French university–hospital system. In J. A. Jackson (Ed.), *Professions and professionalization* (pp. 109-152). Cambridge: Cambridge University Press.

Kanter, R. M. (1977). *Men and women of the corporation.* New York: Basic Books.

Kelly, J. D. (1989). The data–ink ratio and accuracy of newspaper graphics. *Journalism Quarterly, 66*(3), 632-639.

Kohorst, E. (1999, Fall). Designers are people to be reckoned with. *Design: Publication of The Society for News Design, 4.*

Light, D. W. (1988). Turf battles and the theory of professional dominance. *Research in the Sociology of Health Care, 7,* 203-225.

Lott, P. (1994, August). *Informational graphics: Are non-lead visual displays beneficial to the reader?* Paper presented at the annual convention of the Association for Education in Journalism and Mass Communication. Atlanta, GA.

Lowrey, W. (2002, Winter). The influential designer: Explaining variability in control over news presentation work. *Visual Communication Quarterly, 9*(1), 4-13.

Lumsden, L. (1995). "You're a tough guy, Mary—and a first-rate newspaperman": Gender and women journalists in the 1920s and 1930s. *Journalism and Mass Communication Quarterly, 72*(4), 913-921.

Maume, D. J., Jr. (1999). Occupational segregation and the career mobility of white men and women. *Social Forces, 77*(4), 1433-1459.

Merrill, J. (1986). Journalistic professionalization: Danger to freedom and pluralism. *Journal of Mass Media Ethics, 1*(2), 56-60.

Meyer, E. (1997). *Designing infographics. Theory, creative techniques and practical solutions.* Indianapolis: Hayden Books.

Middlestadt, S. E., & Barnhurst, K. G. (1999). The influence of layout on the perceived tone of news articles. *Journalism and Mass Communication Quarterly, 76*(2), 264-276.

Miller, P., & Miller, R. (1995). The invisible woman: Female sports journalists in the workplace. *Journalism and Mass Communication Quarterly, 72*(4), 883-889.

Moses, M. (1999, Fall). Readers consume what they see. *Poynter Report:* pp. 14-17.

Moses, M. (2000). Consumer mentality. *The American Editor, 808,* 6-7.

Nayman, O. B. (1973). Professional orientation of journalists: An introduction to communicator analysis studies. *Gazette, 14*, 195-212.

Nerone, J., & Barnhurst, K. G. (1995). Visual mapping and cultural authority: Design changes in U.S. newspapers 1920-1940. *Journal of Communication, 45*(1), 9-42.

Nilson, L. B. (1979). An application of the occupational "uncertainty principle" to the professions. *Social Problems, 26*(5), 570-581.

Paechter, C., & Head, J. (1996). Power and gender in the staffroom. *British Educational Research Journal, 22*(1), 57-69.

Pasternack, S., & Utt, S. H. (1986). Subject perception of newspaper characteristics based on front page design. *Newspaper Research Journal, 7*(3), 29-35.

Perrow, C. (1986). *Complex organizations: A critical essay* (3rd ed.). New York: Random House.

Pfeffer, J. (1981). *Power in organizations*. Marshfield, MA: Pitman.

Polachek, S. (1981). Occupational self-selection: A human capital approach to sex differences in occupational structure. *Review of Economics and Statistics, 63*(1), 60-69.

Reid, L. L. (1998). Devaluing women and minorities: The effects of race/ethnic and sex composition of occupations on wage levels. *Work and Occupations, 25*(4), 511-536.

Reskin, B. (1988). Bringing the men back in: Sex differentiation and the devaluation of women's work. *Gender and Society, 2*, 58-81.

Roshco, B. (1975). *Newsmaking*. Chicago: The University of Chicago Press.

Russial, J. (1998). Goodbye copy desks, hello trouble? *Newspaper Research Journal, 19*(2), 2-17.

Ryan, B. (1997). Main areas of accomplishment, biggest points of lingering concern. URL (consulted November 2001: http://209.241.184.41/Research/copy/ce11.html)

Salcetti, M. (1995). The emergence of the reporter: Mechanization and devaluation of editorial workers. In H. Hardt & B. Brennan (Eds.), *News workers* (pp. 48-74). Minneapolis: University of Minnesota Press.

Shoemaker, P. J., Eichholz, M., Kim, E., & Wrigley, B. (2001). Individual and routine forces in gatekeeping. *Journalism & Mass Communication Quarterly, 78*(2), 233-246.

Shoemaker, P. J., & Reese, S. D. (1996). *Mediating the message: Theories of influence on mass media content*. White Plains, NY: Longman.

Sigal, L. V. (1973). *Reporters and officials: The organization and politics of newsmaking*. Lexington, MA: D.C. Heath.

Simpson, R. L. (1985). Social control of occupations and work. *Annual Review of Sociology, 11*, 415-436.

Sines, S. (2000, February). From darkroom to newsroom. *News Photographer, 55*.

Singletary, M. W. (1982). Commentary: Are journalists professionals? *Newspaper Research Journal, 3*(2), 75-87.

Smith, C. Z., & Mendelson, A. (1996). Visual communication education: Cause for concern or bright future? *Journalism and Mass Communication Educator, 51*(3), 66-73.

Solomon, W. S. (1995). The site of newsroom labor: The division of editorial practices. In H. Hardt & B. Brennan (Eds.), *News workers* (pp. 110-134). Minneapolis: University of Minnesota Press.

Stark, P., & Hollander, B. (1990, August). *Information graphics: Do they help readers understand news events?* Paper presented at the annual convention of the Association for Education in Journalism and Mass Communication, Minneapolis, MN.

Steinberg, R. J. (1990). Social construction of skill: Gender, power and comparable worth. *Work and Occupations, 17*(4), 449-482.

Stevenson, R., & Griffin, J. (1996, July). The influence of statistical graphics on newspaper reader recall. *News Photographer, 51*(7), 9-11.

Stover, D. L. (1994). The horizontal distribution of female managers within organizations. *Work and Occupations, 21*(4), 385-402.

Streitmatter, R. (1998). Transforming the women's pages. *Journalism History, 24*(2), 72-81.

Tam, T. (1997). Sex segregation and occupational gender inequality in the United States: Devaluation or specialized training? *American Journal of Sociology, 102*(6), 1652-1692.

Trice, H. M. (1993). *Occupational subcultures in the workplace.* Ithaca, NY: ILR Press.

Tuchman, G. (1978). *Making the news: A study in the construction of reality.* New York: The Free Press.

Underwood, D. C., Giffard, A., & Stamm, K. (1994). Computers and editing: Pagination's impact on the newsroom. *Newspaper Research Journal, 15*(2), 116-127.

Utt, S. H., & Pasternack, S. (2000). Update on infographics in American newspapers. *Newspaper Research Journal, 21*(2), 55-66.

Van Maanen, J., & Barley, S. R. (1984). Occupational communities: Culture and control in organizations. *Research in Organizational Behavior, 6*, 287-365.

Wajcman, J. (1991). Patriarchy, technology and conception of skill. *Work and Occupations, 18*(1), 29-45.

Wanta, W. (1988). The effects of dominant photographs: An agenda–setting experiment. *Journalism Quarterly, 65*(1), 107-111.

Wanta, W., & Danner, L. (1997). The designers' toolbox: Newsroom experience and ideal characteristics of newspaper designers. *Visual Communication Quarterly, 6*, 8-9, 14.

Weaver, D. H., & Wilhoit, G. C. (1996). *The American journalist in the 1990s: U.S. news people at the end of an era.* Mahwah, NJ: Erlbaum.

Westley, M. (1984). The nursing role in general hospitals: An organizational analysis. In A. Wipper (Ed.), *The sociology of work* (pp. 266-279). Ottawa: Carleton University Press.

Wilson, B. (2001, January). Whither thou goest? APME report on photo/graphics/design in 21st century. *News Photographer, 57*, 16.

Zelizer, B. (1995). Journalism's "last" stand: Wirephoto and the discourse of resistance. *Journal of Communication, 45*(1), 78-92.

3

Gender Stereotyping in the Production of News

Juana Gallego, Elvira Altés, María José Cantón, María Eugenia Melús, and Jaume Soriano

Since the 1970s, many research projects have been conducted to determine how the media have dealt with gender, especially the female gender. The progressive introduction of women into the working world and the weakening of certain patterns of behavior as exclusive of a single gender have stirred the consciences of male and female researchers to determine how this trend has been reflected by mass media. The many studies conducted on this subject have demonstrated the limited consideration by the media of structural changes such as the one described.

It is true that the number of women in the newsrooms of newspapers, television, and radio stations has increased notably in recent years. It is also true that the output produced by the editorial departments reflects images of women that are different from those that prevailed in the 1970s, for example. Both kinds of change, that is, in the newsroom itself as well as to the output, suggest two lines of inquiry, which have been used to approach the empirical study of gender and mass communication. First, there are studies concerned with measuring the gradual integration of women into the production structures of the media; second, there is a significant number of content-analytical studies that argue that women are underrepresented in this symbolic universe and portrayed mostly stereotypically.

These lines of research are clearly informed by critical perspectives and behind some of these studies one finds pressure groups, collectives, associations, and so on, which are associated with feminist and or women's movements, and which use the conclusions of such projects as arguments to support their claims before official bodies, communications business people, and professional associations. Our motivation in this chapter is not very different from those others, although perhaps it is necessary to add a certain indignation at the lack of sensitivity shown by Spanish media toward complaints about the ways in which women are represented in the media. These complaints come up against a professionalism that uses journalistic convention and tradition as their excuse not to change. We have also observed that this virtually incontrovertible approach by the profession convinces colleagues who are journalists to justify these actions at a time when the number of women working on Spanish newspapers is increasing.

All this leads us to seek arguments beyond newspaper content: It is not a matter of continuing further along the path already traveled—because we believe in the strength of the content analysis performed up until now—but rather of adopting a new perspective. As researchers, we are looking for another point of view even if this means also changing the subject of the study from content to the organizations. We also seek to provoke change as a consequence of the research, in order to challenge the arguments relating to gender differences where they perpetuate discriminatory representations in the media.

FROM STEREOTYPES TO STEREOTYPING

In Spain, women represent 34% of the active labor force. Just over one quarter (27.9%) of sole traders are women, and 16.5% of companies are owned by women; more than half (54.8%) of the students studying for vocational and professional awards are women as well as 63.9% of students following other kinds of programs. Additionally, women hold 42% of the jobs in the public sector. Nevertheless, women write only 11.5% of stories published in the major Spanish newspapers. Looking at content of stories, women feature as the objects and subjects of news stories in the same newspapers in less than 12% of all stories (Gallego, 1998). Besides the quantitative research, some important qualitative studies have shown the complex ways in which media discourse is en-gendered (Bach, 1999; Fagoaga, 1993). These studies not only identify the underrepresentation of women mentioned previously, but also show the importance of this phenomenon because it is located within the communicative process itself.

Most previous studies on news have focused on the employment rates and ratios and the situation of women who work in newspapers, radio and/or tele vision, which have tended to suggest the limited presence of women in the newsrooms (Gallego & del Río, 1993; Lünenborg, 1996; Zilliacus-Tikkanen, 1997). Although some studies maintain that changes in media output are only possible (and evident) when a sufficient number of women reach the highest levels of the organizations (Fagoaga, 1993), others consider that there is no correlation between the gender of those who hold decision-making posts and the types of output, but rather that the decisions on content are based primarily on economic need (Baehr, 1996).

Feminist studies have focused on the position, experiences, and point of view of individual women media professionals. van Zoonen defined several different levels of en-gendered structure to be found in the production of media: work (Creedon, 1989; Gallagher, 1981; van Zoonen, 1988), organization (Farley, 1978; Smith, 1976), and professional routines and habits. The gender structure is expressed in specific posts, tasks, experiences, values, and so on, of the women media professionals. Moreover, van Zoonen questioned whether this gendered structure affects the process of coding news items and how this occurs. We agree that it is not suitable to approach the debate only in terms of whether a larger number of female journalists would improve news contents.

This debate on the level of participation of women in news organizations serves as the background for our research, which is based on the premise that the gender of those who make decisions on media contents is a factor in the final selection but not the sole nor the most important one. It is also based on the assumption that men dominate the news production process in Spain's print media and that the professional culture that has developed as a result is due to the stereotypes that are often used by the press in the representation of women. In this context, we believe that a close look at the production process, especially oriented toward gender issues, could be used to identify the existence of gender stereotyping. The objective of this research is to identify and analyze the mechanisms of (male) professional common sense and to analyze how it works so that it could be transformed.

THE RESEARCH PROCESS

The aim of this research was to consider journalism culture and the relation between news and gender from within news organizations. Our project was oriented toward conducting sociocritical research using a method that tends to avoid being too intrusive. This type of approach requires an understanding (*Verstehen*) approach to the values and meanings of the group studied, a scrupulous respect for the context and a reflexive and critical position by the researcher. Therefore, we used participant observation as the main instrument of data collection. As a parallel process, we also conducted several formal and informal interviews with members of the various organizations studied, and combined this data with those derived from the participation observation phase (Bericat, 1998). With a team of four people, we were able to be ambitious in the range of the organizations we could study. Each of the researchers was responsible for monitoring the work conducted at each of the sample sites: four newspapers (*El País, La Vanguardia, El Periódico de Catalunya,* and *Avui*) and a news agency (Agencia EFE).[1]

The fieldwork was undertaken between June 1998 and May 1999. During this period, we spent 124 person days in media organizations. We all began the research at the same time for 1 week in order to jointly consider any issues as they arose and to consider future contingencies. We also agreed to pay special attention to the decisions made at different levels (from the writers to the editorial meeting) and the professional routines in some of the sections that we considered to be the most important (Society, Politics, Culture, and Economy). Other than that, the rest of the fieldwork was conducted on an individual basis. Each researcher planned her own schedule of visits to the newsroom, interviewed and spoke with the members of the organization considered to be suitable, and observed those areas that were considered to be relevant based on our subject of study.

A specific characteristic of the fieldwork was the "mask" through which we developed our relationships with newsroom staff. Although the senior members of each organization were aware of all of the details of our subject of study, most were only informed of our interest in the news production process in general and not about the gender focus. Where, as often occurs in studies of this type of organization, we were subject to restrictions of access to some areas or documents, we do not believe that such prohibitions changed the results we obtained.

Based on the data collected, each researcher exchanged her fieldnotes with the other members of the team to comment on the problems and findings. All the researchers agreed that the fieldwork was a process that involved more than simply collecting data, but that could in fact be considered as a life experience. Subsequently, each of the researchers prepared a monographic report based on a model designed by the team to achieve formal uniformity. Nevertheless, this did not extend to the contents because each newspaper has a specific structure, history, and operation. This common framework was to be used for the analysis of

---

[1]*El País* was founded after the dictatorship, in 1976, in Madrid. It is considered the Spanish reference newspaper. Ideologically, it is related to the left wing. La Vanguardia was founded in 1881 in Barcelona; it is the oldest newspaper in Spain. It is seen as a conservative and traditional newspaper and read mostly in Catalonia. *El Periódico* was founded in Barcelona in 1978; it is considered as a popular and progressive newspaper; its area of influence is Catalonia. *Avui* was also founded in Barcelona in 1976 and it is a Catalan newspaper, written in Catalan and just distributed in Catalonia; it is a nationalist journal.

the data collected within the following limits: methodological particularities, context (historical background, geographical area and demographic characteristics, social environment), areas of interest in the production of news (general description of the production process, description of editorial meetings, description of sections, and development of news), and partial conclusions.

Anticipating the criticism of lack of rigor leveled against qualitative research by those pursuing a more positivist approach, we decided to test our data for credibility and to triangulate our findings as techniques to maximize the validity of the data collected. In relation to credibility, by combining the ongoing observation of working practices at the newspapers surveyed with the regular meetings held by the researchers throughout the fieldwork, we were able to maximize the data's credibility as a whole, beyond the validity of each individual observation. Moreover, the triangulation of the data (Denzin, 1978) from the five different contexts allowed us to achieve a high degree of validity for the data as a whole.

OUR FINDINGS

In reviewing the reports from each of the newspapers observed, one finds multiple realities despite organizational similarities. The differences between the environments, climates, and values suggest a cautious approach to be taken in arriving at results that may give the impression that they represent a homogeneous whole. Each newspaper was developed in a specific sociohistorical context and with human capital that provide a model of the dominant social relations. We find ourselves, for example, with a newspaper that has been publishing for 100 years (*La Vanguardia*) and another that has become a reference for the profession (*El País*); another very popular newspaper (*El Periódico*) and finally an example of an everyday nationalist press (*Avui*). The news agency was an office established at the end of the Civil War, which has evolved from the controlled, censored communication that prevailed during the Franco era to the more tolerant environment of the democratic period. Therefore, from the historical point of view, three of the newspapers (*El País, El Periódico de Catalunya,* and *Avui*) began their operations in a sociopolitical context marked by the Spanish political transition toward a stable democracy and by the tough social negotiation of the new spaces of freedom that this transition placed in the hands of the citizens. These historical circumstances play a role in determining the publishing projects of each of the newspapers and affect the values that each journalist assimilates in order to fit into the organization, as well as informing the image that the audience forms of the newspaper. The routine customs and practices that have developed over time and influence the attitudes and behavior of the journalists, validate the existing production structures and, moreover, make it more difficult to implement possible transformations or changes.

Along with the aforementioned historical peculiarities, each publication presents an immediate reality that is shaped by an organizational order that is quite different in each case. Three of the newspapers studied (*El País, La Vanguardia,* and *El Periódico de Catalunya*) have some of the largest newsrooms in Spain.[2] They have complex organizational structures with a wide range of different intermediate professional categories and posts between the executive director, the director, and the writing staff. The organization is structured with a maze of section heads, head writers, area coordinators, subdirectors, and assistant directors set up by the publication based on their publishing interests and practices, as a form of recognition or disdain toward their journalists, or simply in accordance with historical inertia and growth.

In all cases, female journalists represent 20% to 40% of the newsroom, whereas their presence in the aforementioned maze of senior positions depends on the power of the post. The figures compiled in our project simply reaffirm the data in this matter already reported by previous studies in Spain and other European countries.

This situation represents a context in which men dominate: averaging across the four newspapers, women accounted for only 13.4% of senior editorial staff working in news sections. Women are located on the periphery of decisionmaking, often in positions such as weekend editors (*El País*), publishing, photography, and computer graphics (*La Vanguardia*), acting in a subordinate manner as secretaries or assistants to the section heads (*El Periódico de Catalunya*), or in documentation and as correspondents (*Avui*), which is often as far as they are able to progress in their professional career. About 45% of women work in the Society, Culture, and Entertainment sections, compared to the more male-dominated Sports, Politics, or Economy sections. This situation is not experienced as a sign of discrimination in any of the newspapers. The fact that there are no "women's networks" (Melin-Higgins & Djerf Pierre, 1998) in which new strategies could be developed to influence, change, or establish a different sort of operational dynamics, may further prohibit changes in attitude and practice.

Many of the journalists we observed seem to overcome their contradictory existence of the desire for professional recognition despite being women, by

---

[2]*El País* has 197 journalists and distributes 435,000 issues; *La Vanguardia* employs 228 journalists and has a circulation of 205,126 issues; *El Periódico* has 150 journalists and a circulation of 217,607; finally, *Avui* has 107 journalists and distributes 31,840 issues. These figures were for employees as of 1999. As for circulation statistics, these figures are taken from the Oficina de Justificación de la Difusión, 2000. There are two other major newspaper in Spain, edited in Madrid, but with nationwide circulation: *ABC* (293,000 issues) and *El Mundo* (285,000 issues), which have not been studied in this research due to budget restrictions.

denying in some sense that they are women at all and adopting the strategy of being one of them (Melin-Higgins & Djerf Pierre, 1998). This involves internalizing a specific set of assumptions, one of which is precisely that a publication that reflects the course of events in the public sphere and that fails to take into account half of the population (based on the public/masculine and private/feminine principle) is unproblematic. Another assumption could be to consider that the professional approach is to inform from a distance, avoiding ideological or personal involvement. A third assumption is thinking that the objective (male) approach to events is the professional one and that being a woman and defending women's issues is a subjective (female) approach and unprofessional culture. The most important aspect of these realities is what topics are deemed newsworthy and the fact that they are assumed to be gender-neutral. A final assumption is that those who deal with hard news issues do so because they are considered to be good professionals, not because they are men.

Along with this series of values shared by the dominant professional culture in the newspapers studied, there are some aspects that distinguish each of the publications, such as the sense of social responsibility associated with working for a major newspaper like *El País*; a policy of laisser faire, laisser passer that prevails in *La Vanguardia* and leads to valuing comfort, individualism, and limited interest for joint projects; an industrial concept of the production of news that attempts to attract the attention of buyers (*El Periódico de Catalunya*); and an attitude of ideological cohesion that makes it possible to understand the resistant spirit of nationalism with which the contents of *Avui* are emphasized. In the case of the EFE Press Agency office, the hierarchical centralization leads to ideological and professional subordination, as well as constant questioning—from a simple geographical point of view—of the importance of each story as news. These assumptions and professional and organizational values make it difficult to pursue professional autonomy and independence among both women and men journalists, and make it difficult to propose subjects related to gender and to approach news from a gender perspective. For example, regardless of sex, journalists find it very difficult to promote issues related to gender because, according to journalistic doxa (Melin-Higgins, 2001), they would be considered by their colleagues as unprofessional.

THE PRODUCTION PROCESS

In all the newspapers studied, we found a series of general factors that influence the preparation of the product. The space set aside for news is determined by the advertising; the reality is the way in which each newspapers fragments or organizes reality, that is to say, each newspaper organizes reality by means of their stable sections; more time and attention is dedicated to how news is transmitted (in terms of length or space of the news, genre, approach, point of view) rather than to the contents of what is reported (social processes, people's activities, scenarios, etc.); and the selection of news is based on a series of items or categories that establish what is newsworthy, what is assumed, and what is never questioned, by the professional culture. In some publications, the political alignment (*El País, Avui*) is considered to be significant, whereas in others it seems that business objectives (*La Vanguardia, El Periódico de Catalunya*) or productivity (Agencia EFE) are more important, although this does not mean they have no ideological bias.

In all the newspapers, factors such as the existing news channels and the work carried out by their competitors play a key role in the production process. Our observations indicate that the press agencies and the press offices of companies and institutions supply much of the content of newspaper stories. Nevertheless, as we can see on a daily basis in the Agencia EFE, the origin of such material is not always attributed. The original sources package the information in such a way that media can easily understand its content. Also, each newspaper tries to offer news that is not too different from what the other newspapers publish. Newspapers consider it a success if their stories coincide with those published by their competitors. In all the newsrooms, the stories known as "own subjects" (exclusives) are highly valued because of the distinction they are accorded by the readership and the professionalism with which they are imbued. Most of these exclusives are developed from information coming from journalists' personal sources, complemented by data from other respectable news channels until they finally become exemplary illustrations of professional practice and signs of distinction within the profession. The exclusives are usually the product of the journalist's professional autonomy and the profile and characteristics of the publication. Many stories with a gender perspective are developed through this particular strategy.

At this point, it is worth presenting some typologies that have arisen from the research, which were useful in the analysis of fieldnotes and that we also used in our quantitative study. These typologies or analysis categories are a graded series from no attention to gender aspects at one end, to some discussion of gender differences in relation to the topic, at the other. Briefly, we distinguish the following categories:

1. Topics with no gender references: issues that are stated in the forthcoming events list or whose main title at the newspaper is written without any reference to a human being.

2. Topics with male presence: when a man or a group of men appear in the statement of the topic or the main title of the news. This can happen in different ways:

   • Male generic: using a male noun to point to a group formed not only by men but also by women. This way, the female presence vanishes behind male nouns. This is not an issue in English, but is for the languages that come from Latin.

- Proper noun: news with main headlines containing the name or surname of one or more men.

- Common noun: news with main headlines referring to one or more men without specifying their identity. For instance the judge, the doctors, and the kids.

3. Topics with female presence: when a woman or a group of women appear in the main headline of the news. This can also happen in different ways:

- Female generic: using a female noun to point to a group formed not only by women but also by men. This is a rare procedure in the Spanish language. For example, housewives, nurses or babysitters.

- Proper noun: news with main headlines containing the name or surname of one or more women.

- Common noun: news with main headlines referring to one or more women without specifying their identity.

4. Topics with mixed presence: topics or news whose main title presents the presence both of a man and a woman or a mixed group.

5. Topics that affect especially women as a group or men as a group, that is to say, topics that have gender connotations per se. Here we've considered two possibilities of presenting this kind of topics:

- Sex component: news that explicitly considers specific social facts related to gender. This news refers to individual cases. For instance the story of a rape or a case of domestic violence.

- Gender component: these news stories have an implicit gender component. It is left to the audience to discover this. The stories refer to groups, not to individual cases.

6. Topics with gender perspective: these topics are developed as news giving meaning to gender differences; the different social positions of men and women in society are pointed out. It must exist a comparison between genders, either explicit or implicit.

Having said this, we believe that the way in which women are portrayed in the sample newspapers and agency, is not simply related to the authority (or lack there of) of women journalists. In order to understand gender stereotyping amongst the editorial staff we have taken into account the consideration granted to gender issues, that is, those subjects that affect women as a group or men as a group and issues that pay special attention to their different roles in society, within the editorial staff groups. For example, we have observed that subjects with a specific gender reference, or even stories from a gender perspective (according to our own definition given earlier) may be introduced by women and men.

Every morning, the observers in three of the four newspapers (*La Vanguardia, El Periódico de Catalunya*, and *El País*) had access to what is known as the futures, futures list, forthcoming events list, or assignment book, which is a list that deals with news stories that can be planned in advance. The assignment book is a list of issues organized by sections, which may be published the following day as news. Each section proposes its forecast of topics to the editorial meeting for comments, discussion, and final decision making (in or out). At this point, some subjects may be eliminated and, therefore, not published. It is also possible to introduce changes in the way some information is to be dealt with. In this game of inclusion and exclusion of news, the assignment book is the ground on which the daily match is played. Regardless of whether or not gender-related subjects enter the ground, they are always situated in the grey periphery on the edges of inclusion and exclusion. When they do appear in the futures list, gender subjects are proposed before the editorial meeting.

Based on the quantitative analysis of the assignment book, we highlight the general results regarding the degree of fulfillment of such forecasts and especially the classification of subjects based on gender-related content. The index of fulfillment of these forecasts is slightly more than 71%. In other words, 29% of the news published each day can be attributed to unforeseen events or last minute events. In absolute figures, this means that of the 4,541 items included in the assignment books of the three newspapers during the periods studied, 3,237 were published. This data confirm the importance of the news forecasts in defining the agenda of the media and, by extension, the relevance of studying them. The way in which gender is dealt with must be described in greater detail. Nearly half of the subjects included in the forthcoming events list (42.8%) did not focus on either women or men, 47.6% were associated with men, and only 4.9% were focused on women; 4.7% focused on women and men. The subjects with a gender component included in the assignment book represent 1.5% of the total items, whereas those with a gender perspective account for 0.6%. Despite the limited presence of such items, the latter seem to have gained a firm foothold in the newsrooms' agenda if one considers that they are the type of news item included in assignment book that are most frequently accepted for publication: 83% of them were published, in comparison to 66% of those with a gender component. We think this high percentage of publication of items with a gender perspective is due to the fact that they have already passed through a very strict control. However, we can't forget that, globally, presence in the assignment book of items with gender perspective is 0.6%.

Finally, it should be mentioned that the news forecasts of the newspapers in which there is a visible female presence are located entirely in a specific group of sections: Communications, People, Culture, Entertainment, and Society. The Agencia EFE has also allowed its forecasts to be compared with the unforeseen stories. Of the 1,423 news stories analyzed, only 27.7% were included in the assignment book and the remaining 72.3% were news stories based on unforeseen events, unannounced actions, and statements. This balance reflected the outputs we would expect from a news agency. Looking at news coming from the assignment book (52.1%) as well as the unplanned news (57.1%), most of the stories included some reference to gender, although men were mentioned in 80% of cases, whereas the references to women accounted for 8.2%. In the other categories, 3.1% of news included an (implicit) sex and gender component (e.g., abortion news, prostitution, or maternity) and 2.5% of stories had an explicit gender perspective (e.g., stories focused on gender differences such as "men earn much money than women").

The editorial meetings have been given special attention in our research. The analysis of the observation phase of the study confirms the importance of the editorial meeting in determining the way in which gender is or is not incorporated into the *process* of journalism. Despite the different structure of the editorial meetings in each of the newspapers and the agency studied (hierarchical representations, exhibition of prestige, or instances of control) and their diverse configuration, they all represent a crucial moment in the process of news production. In all of the editorial meetings we observed, it was clear that they had the symbolic function of representing the power and authority of the senior members of the organization, as well as the practical function of filtering and determining content. For both aspects of this daily ritual, it was repeatedly observed that the dominant point of view in the media was male, regardless of how many women attended meetings as senior editors. This male point of view refers especially to a vision of life (therefore, also of information) where public and private spheres are completely separated and the relevant things are the ones that take place in the public arena.

Observing the dynamics of participation in the editorial meetings, the managing editor usually exercised final control in the meeting and often played different roles at different times (moderator, giving opinions, establishing conclusions, instructing others, or imposing criteria), although the degree of authoritarianism displayed by editors differed. The group of journalists and editors whose status allowed them to participate in these meetings—the senior editors—were already familiar with the ritual and adapted their participation and the content of their news proposals to the circumstances by particular actions such as agreements between the head writers not to mention certain issues, so that the contents were not be debated and no fissures would be evident in their sections nor among themselves (*El País*). Another strategy was to contextualise the drama of the news with comments on trivial events that served as a counterpoint to the drama. Another was to ignore aspects that were not understandable or shared, or were external to group experiences (such as the news on the law of abortion or aggression against and ill-treatment of women (*La Vanguardia*), or else the mechanical reading of the proposals with a brief explanation (*El Periódico de Catalunya*), or simply limiting the participation as much as possible and therefore excluding many of the subjects from the debate. There was also the journalistic propensity in meetings to simply accept the newsworthiness of many of the subjects to be published without question (*Avui*).

This review of how gender features in the contents of the different news sections confirms that the everyday practice of Spanish newspapers is to concentrate the stories with a female focus in the Society, Culture, Entertainment, and People sections. This strategy then services to exclude such stories and foci from all the other sections considered to be hard, important and necessary. The consideration of soft content, which some authors have presented only as a series of requirements regarding content (van Zoonen, 1988), is also a powerful tool for stereotyping that occurs in all newspaper sections. Content with hard profiles are concentrated in sections such as Politics or Economics, whereas those with soft profiles are usually confined to Society or Culture. In the daily practice, there are few cases in which journalists recognize stereotyping processes, and when they are asked about the approach to some of the news in which women are ignored, they indicate the partiality of their sources, or point to a general interest that takes no account of gender differences among audiences, or say that story's point of view is already established when it comes to them. Therefore, although each section displays certain organizational peculiarities, specific forms of relating to the sources and specific values when judging the news that differentiate the sections from each other, overall, the degree of hardness of topics and stories to be dealt with, is a key principle for the editorial staff as a whole.

Nevertheless, there are practices and situations, which lead to content in which gender stereotypes are not so evident. Some journalists avoid the issue of stereotyping by introducing corrections during the preparation of the news or selecting other information in which more attention is granted to the invisible gender. In *Avui*'s newsroom, for example, this is known as being more sensitive toward some subjects and it is considered that women are more sensitive toward gender subjects (confusing the social construct of gender with the biological label of female). In *La Vanguardia*, although most of the journalists state that they write for an undefined audience, the heads of the book supplement operate on the explicit understanding that the cultural consumption index of women is higher than that of men. This is the only newspaper supplement in which the characteristics of the audience are so overtly taken into account, where it is considered that there are men and women behind the concept of *reader* and that women and men have different behaviors. In *El Periódico de Catalunya*, a neutral reader and undifferentiated audience is envisioned. Finally, in *El País*, the assistant director for the Sunday newspaper promoted a page with the heading "Women," which was able to normalize the introduction of news, subjects, interviews, and information that would be of interest to women.

THE MECHANISMS OF GENDER STEREOTYPING

In organizing our data on the different mechanisms for perpetuating gender stereotypes, we identified an organizational dimension, an aspect related to journalistic culture, another aspect concerned with the sociocultural context and, finally, the individual–personal dimension. We elaborate our analysis of the data under these four headings, in the sections following.

Organizational Mechanisms

Media organizations, organized as individual companies, all have their hierarchies, practices, processes, and work routines, which more or less prohibit the use of alternative approaches to events and the use of different perspectives. Such structures reject the fragmentation of reality as a source of concern and media organizations are based on an unequal distribution of power between women and men in a number of ways.

The Editorial Meeting. Traditionally, the editorial meeting acts as a filter that plays an important role in determining whether or not a subject is considered newsworthy. Present-day news production is still based on this foundation, which was developed as a professional tool for planning, sharing, discussing, and organizing the everyday work of the staff. A series of interactions take place in the meeting, some of them practical and other symbolic, such as the ways and order of presenting the forecast issues to the other senior editors; who the spokesperson is in terms of prestige and personal character inside the newsroom; the attention paid by those present to the spokesperson; the specific degree of importance given to the different topics; the ironic comments on specific topics; informal comments on other subjects, jokes, and so on. These interactions are highly significant and revealing and have specific effects on the final shape of news discourse. Although the real utility of the editorial meeting in informing the process of news production seemed to us to be ambiguous, a more obvious function was to provide a forum through which to play out the power struggles among and between staff.

Because of the structure and format of editorial meetings, gender remains outside the editorial meeting room. This applies both to the sense of physical presence of women and men media workers as well as in terms of the value judgments made about particular topics. First of all, this means that journalists (both men and women, but especially women) consider themselves as gender-neutral "professionals." They believe they can act as if questions related to their sex could not interfere in their work. Furthermore, we believe that gender remains outside the editorial meeting room because journalists think news is just neutral facts that they pick up from an objective reality that is outside the newsroom. So they ignore the gendered aspect of all kinds of human activity. The concept of gender does not exist in the mental scheme of journalists, nor in the journalistic culture in which they are immersed. Of course, this process extends vertically through the hierarchical structure, and also occurs on the lower levels of the pyramid: so it can be observed, for example, within the sections, although in this case there is a less highly institutionalized ritual (such as the editorial meetings), but rather an interpersonal relationship between the section heads and the male and female staff writers.

Systematic Fragmentation in News Gathering. To provide news in a system with a high level of complexity, the generalist newspapers introduce divisions, which in fact do not exist in the real world. They divide areas of social, political, and economic reality that do not have an independent existence, into categories in order to parcel out the work of the newsroom. This fragmentation is not considered to be a source of concern and acts as a powerful mechanism for annihilating gender-related topics. From the start, the first major division of the social space is established by granting a privileged position to actions conducted in the public sphere, whereas coverage of actions in the private sphere only occurs when these acquire a public dimension (violation of laws, exemplary achievements) or, in more modern times, when attention is granted to those private actions that are made public for reasons of entertainment.

Women as Decision Makers. The presence of women in positions of responsibility (from subeditors to editor-in-chief) ranges from 11.5% in *La Vanguardia*, 12% in *El Periódico de Catalunya*, 16.5% in *El País*, 20% in *Avui*, and up to 33.3% in Agencia EFE. Their underrepresentation as decision makers means that alternatives to stereotyped information about women are limited. During our observation sessions, we were able to confirm that there are very few (13.4%) women working as senior editors in the newsrooms of our sample newspapers. Women rarely hold executive posts and even those who do gain entrance to the elite sector have less responsibility within the hierarchical pyramid and feel less involved in the business structure. During the formal and informal interviews held with several journalists it was evident that, with a few exceptions, women do not seek to hold positions of power as frequently as their male colleagues. In fact, some of the women we talked to told us that they had rejected offers to hold more senior positions because they prefer to enjoy a more relaxed personal life than they would have if they had accepted positions with greater responsibility. Older female journalists, as well as their younger counterparts, agree on the importance of reconciling their private life and their professional activity. However, none of the male journalists we interviewed found it problematic to conciliate these two aspects of life.

Mechanisms Based on Professional Culture

One of the crucial aspects of the culture of journalism is the value judgments that are based on the classification of news; the influence of the other media as reference points that verify their own decisions on contents; an undifferentiated and neutral image of the audience; and the discrediting of gender differentiation as a basis for factual interpretation. We make this point because journalists approach every event with a supposedly "neutral" point of view, without taking into account any kind of gender considerations. Including the significance of gender in news production would be seen as a distortion or deviation from the allegedly objective approach to reality claimed by journalists.

Classification of News. In the newspapers studied, and certainly in nearly all of the major newsrooms, there are some sections that merit greater professional consideration than others. Politics, International, and Economy are considered to be hard sections, whereas Society and Culture are considered soft. This general perception affects content and story preparation. For example, not many years ago, the number of reported incidents of domestic violence and other acts of violence against women was relatively low and therefore quite different from the scale that exists today. When these facts are placed in an official context and made public by institutional channels (policy, Women's Institute, social welfare, etc.) the media will naturally report them, especially if they can provide statistics (figures on formal complaints filed, assassinations, number of women killed each year, comparison with previous years, etc.). The classification of the news favors the subjects considered to be hard and contributes to the stereotyping of contents. Some journalists consider that making the news harder is precisely what their job entails. The task of transferring the information from the periphery of the soft sections to the front page or to the central role of the hard sections is the daily aspiration of many members of the editorial staff.

Influence of Other Media. During our observation sessions, we realized that these newspapers consider other media to be of key importance. This self-referential impulse acts as a circular flow that perpetuates a static journalistic culture. It is a mechanism that not only provides the confirmation of self-importance but also significantly reduces the number of subjects or events considered to be newsworthy. In other words, it reduces the news market, because all the media then speak about the same subjects.

Legitimized Ideologies. A key foundation that supports the culture of journalism is the belief that news production is not based on ideology. Rather, it is seen as an objective reflection of an external reality that is somehow given, and the journalist merely transmits this reality. Nevertheless, this line of reasoning clashes with the explicit recognition of the limits experienced by journalists when undertaking their own job. It is paradoxical that, although they argue that their task involves reflecting reality, journalists nonetheless acknowledge that one must "accept what you can and cannot do" within the newsroom in order to enjoy a broad degree of personal autonomy. In other words, in order to enjoy a certain amount of freedom, first one must internalize the model and style of the newspaper one works for, that is, assimilate its ideology and philosophy. Therefore, it seems that there are some ideologies considered to be legitimate, acceptable, and defensible—such as nationalism, Catholicism, leftwing or conservative tendencies, confessional orientation—as well as perspectives that should be rejected because they are apparently considered unacceptable and distorting—such as feminism.

In the newsroom, this leads to the stereotyping of gender perspectives as an illegitimate lens through which to interpret current events and daily life, in both public and private spheres. Frequently, this involves offering a newsworthy item from a perspective that, rather than resorting to a possible interpretation in terms of a conflicting relationship between the sexes, opts for a political interpretation. For example, in our observation sessions, we were able to identify how the subject of abortion was more frequently considered from a political perspective (votes cast on such issues, reactions of different parties to the extension of the fourth condition of abortion, etc.) than as a problem that arises due to differences between the social positions held by men and women within the context of a tense relationship between the sexes. Another similar theme is the law on unmarried couples, in which emphasis is placed on the description of the applicable legal regulations rather than on the underlying social situation that it reveals.

Audience Without Gender. A key element in the nexus of beliefs and assumptions that journalist culture is based on is the idea that there is no specific profile that characterizes the audience. It seems that neither women nor men consider that the reader has specific characteristics, forms part of a specific geographical, political and/or cultural milieu or (of course) is a person of a certain sex who has been socialized into a gender role. The statements made by journalists often pointed out that they do not write for anybody in particular, for example "I never think of the readers." In some cases, they revealed that they have "an idea in terms of the possible cultural level" or a notion based on their own self-image. However, none of them associated the vague image of a model reader whom they are addressing with a woman. There were no cases in which they suggested that the reader was female. Journalists of both sexes repeatedly stated that "I never consider whether the readers are men or women." (Except for those responsible for the Cultural Supplement of *La Vanguardia*.)

Contextual Mechanisms

The mechanisms deriving from the sociocultural context just outlined refer to important determining factors for journalistic production such as the worldview of the dominant gender, a morality that judges the behavior and attitudes of each gender differently and the acceptance of minority group differences that contrast with the nonacceptance of a majority group difference such as that of gender.

Accepting "Male" Values. Our society forms part of a context that we could refer to as androcentric or male-centered (Bourdieu, 2000). Therefore, in the field of journalism we find that women have been included in a professional culture that is dominated by a masculine worldview (Melin-Higgins, 2001; van Zoonen, 1994). In the newsroom, the most important events to cover (in fact, almost all the events covered) take place in the public sphere and there is a separation of rationality from emotionality, as if human behavior could be guided by rationality alone. Women journalists go through primary gender socialization and when they begin to work in the media, we argue that they undergo a secondary "male" socialization process. Therefore, their inclusion in this professional sector involves suppressing, denying, avoiding, or rejecting the nondominant values, in other words, those of their primary socialization.

Many professional women solve this contradiction with statements such as "First of all, I am a professional." In other words, they attempt to avoid belonging to a gender, or they believe that the constellation of values with which they were brought up and educated does not influence the work they perform: Instead they have accepted the values of the dominant gender. On the other hand, men find it difficult to accept the need to incorporate the values seen as belonging to "women" such as rendering important the interrelationship between public and private life, the recognition of the relevance of the emotional part of human subjects and trying to establish a balance with their rational part, their interest in people, their capacity to feel empathy, and so on. This is because they are not familiar with them, do not share them and, from their view, these values appear to lack prestige in the same way as the entire constellation of female values lacks prestige in the society. They find that dealing with subjects that involve different gender situations and aspects that are extremely foreign to them are uncomfortable, disturbing, bothersome, and confusing. At times, they introduce humorous elements in order to come to terms with such items, or evade them by claiming that they are redundant, as in "we already said that yesterday, or a few days ago, etc." At other times, both male and female professionals avoid proposing these subjects so as not to be labeled as "feminists."

Stereotyping. The members of the newsroom transfer to their professional daily routine, stereotypes and behavior patterns that belong or come from an androcentric sociocultural context. Therefore, in their daily negotiation with current affairs, they judge actions and behavior of men and women differently and stereotype them. They consider male activities such as political negotiation, economic achievements, sporting success, as the more serious and relevant ones, while female activities are undervalued. We find a paradigmatic example in the report of most female sports, which are systematically ignored by the media. The reason for the need to resort to stereotypes can be explained by the fact that all journalists share the desire for their discourse to reflect the cultural patterns that allow them to gain a wider audience. As far as women are concerned, the description of their physical appearance is frequently mentioned when the move beyond the private dimension they usually occupy, into the public gaze. Another example of this is the familiar, domestic treatment granted to women by journalistic discourse, in comparison to the social status associated with men.

Minority Status. It seems that newsrooms are using the model of minority status which is found more widely in society, as their framework for understanding and reporting on difference, rather than acknowledging the gender-related contradictions that can be found at all levels of social relations. Therefore, the approach to gender conflicts is similar to that granted to other groups and women become another minority group, like immigrants, people with disabilities, young people and so on.

Personal–Individual Mechanisms

Finally, there are the mechanisms that we believe can be attributed to the personal characteristics of individual journalists in the transmission of gender stereotypes, which are related to the personal involvement of the individuals with contemporary topics that involve gender and the special level of sensitivity or subjectivity of the journalist towards some issues rather than others.

Personal Involvement. On several occasions, we observed how personal involvement with a particular issue was the factor that led to the disclosure of certain events in journalistic discourse. This may be a journalist who observes the endless construction work on his or her street, who repeatedly arrives late for work due to heavy traffic, has a problem at his or her daughter's school, or is overwhelmed by the passivity of the administration toward a claim being made. Moreover, a feeling of guilt for an action, a feeling that one has in a relationship with a colleague or a problem with others may lead to the consideration of such a subject as news. In order to do this, the situation must be generalized to a broader context, where the journalist's specific experience is replaced by the testimonies offered by other sources that allow it to be considered professionally acceptable for the individual journalist as well as for the senior staff who must give approval. Such situations demonstrate the perceptiveness and cleverness of individual journalists and if they can obtain the data or statements that could legitimate the situation that first prompted them to action, which may be a personal or private issue, then their intervention has been worthwhile. Thus, because the editorial staff do not usually have a definite position or a clear concept regarding gender subjects, the mechanisms through which it is most likely that a male or female journalist can introduce subjects or themes with a gender perspective occur on the individual level.

Social Beliefs. There is also a mechanism similar to that just described that is based more on a social belief or concern than a personal problem. In such situations, journalists are allowed to disclose their social concerns in accordance with their own personal values as long as they comply with the assumptions that form the basis of the journalistic profession (objective reality, distance from the facts, nonrecognition of ideological preferences) and remain within those boundaries. This mechanism allows the different social groups (and the sources, in general) to identify the professionals who are most likely to portray their claims or problems. This is a possible point of entry for gender-related subjects or themes that would otherwise not be given coverage.

CONCLUSION

The structural factors (due to the business organization), group factors (due to the journalistic culture), sociocultural factors (due to the context), and the individual factors (subjective) are not unrelated to one another, but on the contrary, form a dense pattern whereby it is difficult to distinguish the causes and the consequences of each of these factors affecting the production of the news discourse.

After more than 3 years studying this subject, the first conclusion we can offer is our verification that the routine discourse, as we know it today, is a discourse that does not consider gender issues in its assumptions and approach. Therefore, no interpretation is made of the different social positions held by men and women in society because this is not deemed newsworthy or important. This question exists in the general environment of the newsroom as well as in the minds of women and men. It remains as a nonexplicit ideological subtext, which is uncomfortable and difficult to place. The journalistic treatment of gender issues follows a pattern that ranges from completely denying or asserting indifference to gender through to acknowledging its existence and allowing gendered themes to be included in sections where it is possible to show and/or express concern for gender. Due to the relative invisibility of gender—in some cases, it is more a denial than a lack of knowledge, in others it is contempt, or indifference—gender issues are approached intuitively, by approximation, based on the impulses or inclinations of each member of the newsroom and the degree of boldness or cleverness of the professionals in discovering new areas of news that are under- or unexplored. The different positions adopted by the sampled newspapers regarding gender issues are almost always implicit rather than overt and none of the approaches is exclusive to a specific form of media:

All of them may include a variety of stances, or even contradictory approaches in the same issue of the newspaper, because there is no overall position for the newspaper, nor guidelines on such subject, nor even awareness of whether or not such positioning is possible.

Nevertheless, our aim here is that of encouraging reflection on the existence of gender, the differences due to this fact, and the subsequent adoption of a progressive approach to subjects with a gender perspective, which would be the professional expression of the recognition of gender difference. Adopting a gender perspective does not necessarily suggest feminist journalism (which would be the politico-ideological expression of gender difference), but rather journalism based on the evidence of the difference due to gender and granting a meaning and a place in the news discourse to this difference, which it lacks at present.

The inclusion of a gender perspective may be applied to hard information as well as soft information, to international subjects and sports, as well as to the cultural and political spheres. This recognition would eliminate the development observed in other countries where female journalists tend to cover soft topics, whereas male journalists dominate hard sections (van Zoonen, 1994; Zilliacus-Tikkanen, 1997). Accepting the differences between women and men and formulating a journalistic discourse based on difference is not easy: nor is it easy to accept that gender differences continue to exist, regardless of the extent to which the evolution of society and education have accommodated women and men's perspectives equally. However, the recognition of gender difference and the professional practice to which it leads—the inclusion of a gender perspective—would make visible the presence of women in different social environments and, as a result, make them feel represented in a discourse which, with a few exceptions, currently excludes them.

REFERENCES

Bach, M. (1999). *El sexe de la notícia. Reflexions sobre el gènere a la informació i recomanacions d'estil* [The sex of news: Thoughts about gender in information and recommendations of style]. Barcelona: Icaria

Baehr, H. (1996). *Women in television.* London: University of Westminster Press.

Bericat, E. (1998). *La integración de los métodos cuantitativo y cualitativo en la investigación social* [The integration of quantitative and qualitative methods in social research]. Barcelona: Ariel.

Bourdieu, P. (2000). *La dominación masculina.* Barcelona: Angrama.

Creedon, P., (Ed.). (1989). *Women in mass communication: Challenging gender values.* Beverly Hills, CA: Sage.

Denzin, N. K. (1978). *The research act: A theoretical introduction to sociological methods.* New York: McGraw-Hill.

Fagoaga, C. (1993). Género, sexo y élites en los medios informativos [Gender, sex and elites in mass media]. In F. Ortega (Ed.), *La flotante identidad sexual. La construc-ción del género en la vida cotidiana de la juventud* (pp. 97-118). Madrid: Dirección General de la Mujer de la Comunidad de Madrid.

Farley, J. (1978). Women's magazines and the equal rights amendment: Friend or foe? *Journal of Communication, 28*(1), 187-192.

Gallagher, M. (1981). *Unequal opportunities: The case of women and the media.* Paris: Unesco.

Gallego, J. (1998). *Gènere i informació* [Gender and information]. Barcelona: Associació de Dones Periodistes.

Gallego, J., & Del Río, O. (1993). *El sostre de vidre Situació sòcio-professional de les dones periodistes a Catalunya* [The glass-ceiling. The professional situation of women journalists in Catalunya]. Barcelona: Institut Català de la Dona.

Lünenborg, M. (1996). *Journalistinnen in Europa: Eine International vergleichende Analyse zum Gendering im sozialen System Journalismus* [Journalists in Europe: An international comparative analysis about gender and journalism systems]. Opladen: Westdeutscher Verlag.

Melin-Higgins, M., & Djerf Pierre, M. (1998, July). *Networking in the newsroom. Journalist and gender cultures.* Paper presented at IAMCR conference, Glasgow, Scotland.

Melin-Higgins, M. (2001). *Coping with journalism. The place of gender in the news-room's culture.* Paper presented to the Seminar Gender Stereotype Construction in the Mass Media, Barcelona, Spain.

Smith, R. (1976). Sex and occupational roles in Fleet Street. In D.L. Barker & S. Allen (Eds.), *Dependence and exploitation in work and marriage* (pp. 70-87). London: Longman.

van Zoonen, L. (1988). Rethinking women and the news. *European Journal of Communication, 3*(1), 35-54.

van Zoonen, L. (1994). *Feminist media studies.* London: Sage.

Zilliacus-Tikkanen, H. (1997). *Journalistikensessens i ett könsperspectiv* [The essence of journalism from a gender perspective]. Helsinki: Yleisradio.

4

Feminine and Feminist Values in Communication Professions: Exceptional Skills and Expertise or "Friendliness Trap?"

Romy Fröhlich

Since the mid-1980s, the communications sector has expanded at an amazing rate in virtually all Western industrialized nations. Western Europe, North America, and Japan as well as some of the so-called Tiger States have made the transition from an industrial to an information society relatively rapidly. This process shows no signs of stopping and with it comes the demand for competent, trained communications and information experts. This development has made and continues to make strides at such a fast pace that the demands of the job market cannot adequately be met. Women have particularly benefited from the development of these newly created professional fields. In the face of increasingly high demand, they have been able to secure positions in certain fields within the communications sector, for example, journalism, advertising, and public relations that were, until recently, traditionally "men's professions." Particularly in North America and Europe, the number of women employed in these fields has increased substantially in the last few decades, although, for the most part, the trend across countries shows striking differences. But at any rate, international studies have provided convincing evidence to support the feminization of communications (see, e.g., Creedon; 1989; Fröhlich, 1991, 1992; Fröhlich & Lafky, in press; Gallagher, 1992, 1995; Savolainen & Zilliacus-Tikkanen, 1992; Schneider, Schönbach, & Stürzebecher, 1993a, 1993b; Weaver, 1998).

The clearest example of this feminization trend can be seen in the United States, where the transition from an industrial to an information society took place much earlier than anywhere else. Since the 1980s, around 60% of all students who majored in journalism and communications have been women and since the beginning of the 1990s, 66% of graduates are women (Creedon, 1993; Kosicki & Becker, 1992; Peterson, 1988). Apart from journalism and advertising, public relations in the United States has experienced the highest increase in female employees. By the end of the 1980s, four times as many women as men studied public relations, business communication, or organizational communication in the United States and 10 times as many female as male students are active in the *Public Relations Student Society of America* (PRSSA; Wright, Grunig, Springston, & Toth, 1991). It's no wonder then, that by 1998, approximately 66% of Americans employed in fields such as public relations and business communication were women (US Department of Commerce, 1998).

In Europe, Canada, and Japan there is a similar trend of growing numbers of women in the communications sector but at different rates in different countries (see Fröhlich & Lafky, in press). In Germany, for example, since the beginning of the 1990s, the majority of students in public relations, journalism, communications, and media studies are female. In the same country, two public broadcasting companies—the most common training ground for broadcast journalism—ARD[1] and ZDF[2]—have also experienced the gender switch within their training programs and both organizations have trained more women than men since the 1980s. This trend can also be seen in other media sectors in Germany (Weischenberg, Keuneke, Löffelholz, & Scholl, 1994).

But before we turn to the question of whether the high ratio of women to men in training has a *quantitative* effect on employment in the sector as a whole, let us first take a closer look at other possible reasons that could account for the sudden increase of women in media industries. Are we merely dealing here with a trend, that is, that women have simply taken the corporate world by storm in such a way that even the field of journalism has not been spared? But this is a weak argument. A comparison of employment figures of women in European journalism with the overall employment figures of women in the European labor force shows that the increasing number of women who have obtained high educational qualifications and who are working in the media sector is strikingly above average in terms of relevance of qualification to employment.[3] The question therefore remains: "What makes the field of communications so appealing to women?"

One reason could be that having good communication skills is a particular, socially dependent, and/or biologically determined trait that women possess

---

[1]*Arbeitsgemeinschaft der öffentlich-rechtlichen Rundfunkanstalten Deutschlands* (Working Group of the German Public Broadcasting Stations) founded in 1950 and thus Germany's oldest public broadcasting station.

[2]*Zweites Deutsches Fernsehen* (Second German Television) founded in 1963.

[3]Own calculations with help of statistics from the EU (see http://europa. eu.int/index_de.htm#) and figures from Fröhlich and Lafky (in press).

(cf. Aries, 1976; Capek, 1989; Foss, Foss, & Griffin, 1999; Hall, 1978, 1984; Reif, Newstrom, & Monczka, 1978; Sargent, 1981; Stier & Hall, 1984), which makes them especially suited for professions such as journalism and public relations. With these ideal qualities, we could argue, women can rise to challenges typically found in these professions. Obviously, these qualities cannot simply be learned during academic education or journalism training like writing skills or special public relations techniques. Rakow (1989a, 1989b) supported the argument that it is exactly those positive qualities that are attributed to women in Western culture and society, such as being able to establish and maintain intra- as well as interpersonal relationships at all levels (in both public and private situations), which comprise important prerequisites for a successful career in the field of professions like journalism or public relations. Van Zoonen (in press) wrote that *it is exactly the traditional cultural prescriptions of femininity—good looks, interest in other people, care and compassion—that the new market driven journalism seems to ask for.* Furthermore, Grunig, Toth, and Hon (2000) even juxtaposed values supposedly associated with the feminine gender, for example, cooperation, honesty or fairness, and morality, with the norms of public relations practice. In the fields of communication professions, "female" characteristics such as empathy, thoughtfulness, the need to reach consensus, a talent for dealing with people, and the ability to work in a team-oriented atmosphere, are all considered to be qualifications that could be used as career advantages in contrast to supposedly typical male characteristics such as cool rationality, competitiveness, aggression, and individualism (see Aldoory & Toth, 2001). In the case of public relations, for example, it has been argued that women's "natural" intuition and profound sense of ethical responsibility can potentially serve as catalysts for shaping the image of public relations as responsible, more efficient and more reputable (Bates, 1983; Grunig et al., 2000; Rakow, 1989b; Wakefield, 1993). Within this context, Aldoory (1998) outlined her "feminist model of leadership" in public relations and Grunig et al. (2000) even referred to a "revolution of the heart" (p. 63).

The emphasis placed on gender differences between men and women has traditionally functioned as a justification for the theory of male "superiority," especially in the job market. In attempting to explain the "female boom" in the communications sector, the rationale looks different for the first time. The new emphasis is that (presumed) gender differences between men and women are used to argue that women seem better suited to working in the sector than men. But, as popular and apparently plausible as this explanation seems, communications researchers have never scientifically examined such a claim. The question then is to find out what really lies behind the presumption that women are better communicators. I believe that as a result of the thesis that women are better communicators, more importance will be attached to gender as a social category and it will once again be linked to strict, culturally determined stereotypes. Women could be forced into a fixed corset—in this case the corset takes the

form of the ideal communicator—which will more than likely determine
our/their behavior. This could manifest as, for example, women journalists
being assigned to subjects that are "appropriate" for their gender and will be
expected to remain within the confines of these prescribed roles. Any attempt to
deviate from those roles will, in all probability, be prohibited, but I return to that
later.

FEMINIZATION OF COMMUNICATION
PROFESSIONS? NOT REALLY!

First of all, let us examine whether women really have made the successful
quantitative strides in communications professions such as journalism and public relations as the figures presented to us from the educational sector would
lead us to expect. Taking journalism as an example, despite the stable gender-
switch that has taken place in the last few years in journalism training, the profession clearly continues to be male-dominated, at least at senior levels, in the
majority of Western industrialized nations[4] (Gallagher, 1992, 1995) as well as
Japan (Kato et al., 1994; Reid, 1995). In Germany, for example, currently 75%
of all West German journalists are men (Schneider et al., 1993b) and in the
United States, men comprise around 65% of journalists (Weaver & Wilhoit,
1996). The only European country in which women journalists work in equal
numbers to men is Finland (Zilliakus-Tikkanen, in press). And there are several
eastern European countries where women make up the majority in the field of
journalism, for now at least. However, overall, despite the high percentage of
women who graduate from journalism programs, this trend has had no significant impact on the number of women actively employed in senior positions in
journalism, although, as indicated previously, there are considerable national
differences.

A similar, if no less dramatic picture, can be seen in the field of training in
public relations. For a number of years, a distinct gender-switch has taken place
in the public relations education and training sector throughout Europe and
North America. Depending on the country and its training system, the changing
proportion of female versus male trainees is anywhere from 51% to 90% (see
Fröhlich, 1992, 1994; Fröhlich & Holtz-Bacha, 2003). Looking at these statistics, it would seem that training for a profession does not necessarily lead to
employment in that profession and depends on the national situation. In

---

[4]For example, for Canada see Robinson and Saint-Jean (1998), for France see Neveu (in
press); for Israel see Limor and Caspi (1994) and Lachover (in press); for Sweden see
Löfgren-Nilsson (1993); for The Netherlands see van Zoonen (in press).

Germany, for instance, the female boom in the German Public Relations Society (*Deutsche Public Relations Gesellschaft*) has remained steady at 43% since the 1990s (Fröhlich, 2001). In the United States, opportunities for women look much better: About 60% of all public relations professionals are women. But comparing the gender-ratio in the public relations' training sector, where women have comprised 70% to 90% of the students for a number of years, with the number of women employed in public relations, especially in management positions, the differences are still striking. The number of women working in public relations is far less than one would expect based on women's presence as students undertaking public relations training.

Statistics from several different European countries (Fröhlich & Lafky, in press) show that at entry-level positions, the percentage of women in journalism and public relations is close to 50%. In the field of journalism in Germany, for example, 40% of all entry-level employees actively employed in this field for less than 5 years are women. In the United States, this proportion is 45%. When we look at women who have been employed in the profession for at least 10 years, the figure goes down to 21% in Germany and to 34% in the United States (Schneider et al., 1993a). This shows that the so-called feminization (more women in the sector) taking place in the field of communications is a relatively new trend but also suggests that women appear to leave the profession earlier than men. These findings lead one to question why the high number of women media graduates has not had a significant impact on the profession, why the numbers of women in training are not reflected in long-term employment figures, and why so many women leave the profession within the first 5 years?

DO WOMEN COMMUNICATE BETTER?

That women appear to abandon their journey to the top of the corporate ladder is a process that has been witnessed in other professions. In regions such as North America and Europe, the reasons behind women's "disappearing act" in communications professions are sufficiently well-known: starting a family, the associated responsibilities of raising children, "double shifts" in career and home (Gallagher, 1981; Lafky, 1991; Neveu, in press; Rakow, 1989a; Robinson, in press; van Zoonen, 1994); lack of support at home and from employers, discrimination through gender-role stereotyping, male–female interaction and/or social norms (Grunig, 1989), and greater control from management (Löfgren–Nilsson, 1993). However, I believe that these well-known reasons are not the only ones behind this development and I direct attention to other possible causes.

On the basis of the claim that women communicate better, public relations women and female journalists are expected to fulfill particular behavioral patterns and roles. This expectation is independent or even in contradiction to their personal skills, which poses a problem. Psychologist Dorothee Alfermann (1996) asked, rightly, in this context,

> if by using these gender differences as a basis for this reasoning, we actually support the tendency to categorize and direct our attention way too much towards those very differences instead of emphasizing the psychological similarities between men and women. (p. 93)

To date, there has been little international research conducted by communications scholars into the question of whether women actually are better communicators than their male counterparts because of their supposed gender-specific skills, which are appropriate for communications professions such as journalism and public relations.

The field of psychology has released a preponderance of studies that have attempted to explain in general—without focusing on a specific profession— whether there actually exist significant gender-related differences in behavior between women and men in the workplace and between them in general. Indeed, substantial evidence can be found to support the claim that women are well equipped with a series of socially determined skills that are precisely relevant for jobs in the communications field, which is why they appear to be better suited than men to those professions. For example, it has been shown that during verbal interactions, women read nonverbal signals better and more accurately than men but they express nonverbal communication differently, as well. Gender-specific differences expressed through nonverbal behavior allow women to appear more understanding, friendlier, and kinder as well as generally more sensitive in social situations than men. Women's nonverbal behavior also expresses more warmth and social approachability. They tend to send more nonverbal signals during verbal interaction, generally express more emotion, and are less distant and territorial than men (Hall, 1978, 1984; Stier & Hall, 1984).

There are also differences in verbal behavior between men and women. Men tend to interact in more task-oriented, direct, dominant, and hierarchical ways than women. Women tend to behave more cooperatively and are more supportive than men. They also tend to be more concerned about the social climate in social situations, strive for consensus more often than men during discussions, emphasize similarities more than differences, and give more compliments and positive assessments than men (cf. Aries, 1976, 1987). Overt gender-specific differences in verbal and nonverbal communication skills between men and women seem to have diminished since the 1980s (Collaer & Hines, 1995), whereas earlier studies suggested that, during verbal interaction, women, more than men, tended to be more consensus- and dialogue-oriented, more honest, sensitive, fair, loyal, tolerant, cooperative, and able to treat others on a more equal basis (Berryman-Fink, 1985; Reif et al., 1978; Sargent, 1981).

THE FRIENDLINESS TRAP:
A CAREER HEAD START PUT TO THE TEST

If women's specific communication skills are in fact the reason behind the ever-increasing number of women training for and entering the communications sector, it could be posited that women have been deliberately targeted by the industry over the past few years because of the particular communication skills they possess. This claim, however, is hard to prove and the fact that this argument is supported even by practitioners, employers, and/or chief executives within the communications sector as an explanation for the female boom (cf. Berryman-Fink, 1985; Christmas, 1997; Gallagher, in press) still does not make it more valid. It is undoubtedly true that worse things could happen to women working in public relations and journalism than to be casually regarded as being able to communicate better simply because of their friendly, polite, consensus-oriented behavior. However, gender-specific behavior is a result of gender-specific socialization as "girls" and "boys" and the different behavior patterns of men and women (e.g., in the workplace) is also related to the fact that men and women have different social positions in society and their personal interactive and communicative behavior reflects their socially prescribed status. Alfermann (1996) suggested the following:

> Women, the group having the lower social status, are expected to be more socially sensitive in comparison to people with a higher social status, because these are the tools that would enable them to survive and function in society. Thus, being able to read important non-verbal signals would be an important requirement enabling them to function in the world. People with a higher social status, on the other hand, can afford to misinterpret information without running the risk of being rejected. (p. 139)

It can be speculated, then, that this "reading" strategy becomes more prevalent, the more clearly defined are the differences in social positioning. Symbolic as well as actual characteristics (e.g., such as power or higher income) associated with different positions also play an important factor. The corporate world, with its own fixed hierarchical system and elitist practices, is one such context, as is the communications sector. I suggest that women's "exceptional" communication skills are nothing more than the learned (if not always fully conscious) use of particular behaviors and strategies, acquired during childhood socialization that positioned them as less important than boys/men. In adulthood, then, this learned behavior principally serves the purpose of maintaining a harmonious atmosphere during the communication process in order to achieve personal goals and to prosper within the given system. Research conducted by behavioral scientists refers to such behavior as "conciliatory gestures' (Alfermann, 1996).

Therefore, differences in verbal and nonverbal communication between men and women cannot be explained simply as the employment of different abilities. Women's cooperative behavior could be the result of their limited social power, whereas the hierarchical and direct behavior of men is a result of their greater dominance and status (Henley, 1977). However, if the status and hierarchy positions of women and men change, interactive and communicative behaviors can also change, independent of any supposedly fixed gender-specific skills. But this type of "metamorphosis" is usually judged negatively and even condemned as deviant. In extreme cases, it can turn out to be a "career killer" for men as well as for women, if they try and become more like members of the opposite sex.

Thus, it becomes clear that a vicious cycle emerges. That public relations and journalism require communication skills especially oriented toward consensus and dialogue allows women more access to communication professions at the *entry level* because of the very skills they possess. However, these skills do not have a significant influence on how long women remain in the profession or how far they will be able to advance: Women continue to drop out of media careers. Perhaps the very attributes that get women into the communications sector—sensitivity, caring, honesty, fairness or morality—are also associated with a lack of assertiveness, poor conflict management, and weak leadership skills (see, e.g., Cline, 1989). The result is that women fall into the "friendliness trap" without even realizing it. People who are constantly praised because of their particular skills would perhaps not consider that these same skills could prove to be a disadvantage at some later point in their career.

The image of women as "the better communicators" is a questionable stereotype and a dangerous myth because it imports the "mothering" role from home into the workplace (see also Robinson, in press). Moreover, the fact that the majority of women in public relations do not even work in those spheres where their supposedly exceptional communicative skills could be fully utilized (e.g., in strategic management roles requiring a lot of personal contact or team-building), further diminishes the credibility of the "women are better communicators" argument. Data from the United States indicate that the majority of women who work in the creative public relations industry carry out technical duties such as writing and editing, producing material for electronic media, composing speeches, conceptualizing advertising campaigns, and so on (Creedon, 1991; Toth & Grunig, 1993). These positions are often isolated with relatively limited client contact. At these positions, the likelihood of team-work is reduced, and contact with the general public is also limited. In contrast to this, men tend to be active in public relations management where the so-called feminine skills discussed earlier are most obviously required, with a lot of client contact and need to maintain good working relationships with clients and staff. In Germany, similar trends exist and the majority of leadership positions are held by men (Merten, 1997).

BACKSTAGE: BEHIND THE FACADE
THE MYTH LOSES ITS LUSTRE

As in other professions, women do not have the same chances as men in journalism and public relations, despite the rhetoric. Because of gender-role expectations, in our case the expectation that women communicate better, they frequently and increasingly choose those professions that are deemed appropriate for their gender. The same gender-based expectations may trigger a corresponding demand by employers, which in turn reinforces supposed gender-specific expectations. In the professional labor market, a re-codification takes place, whereby the higher value placed on men compensates for their supposed entry-level disadvantage (of being poorer communicators than women) and makes it easier for them to advance in a field in which they are naturally less qualified. In contrast, women's exceptional skills are utilized less because of the gender-based, vertical segregation that routinely takes place once they are working in the sector.

It is evident that the percentage of women employed in the communications sector has steadily and significantly increased within a relatively short time. Journalists, public relations professionals, and researchers may take this as evidence that women can now routinely and without obstruction pursue a professional media career. However, such a belief fails to recognize that women's careers have often turned out to be as short-lived as in other professions. Interpreting the female boom in the communications sector as resulting from equal opportunities in the sector is to continue to believe in a myth. We should prepare ourselves (and our female students) for the fact that the communications sector is still a locus for gender-based differentiation despite changes in role expectation. We have yet to achieve a real understanding of the development of the so-called "feminization" of communication through an appreciation of feminine and feminist values within journalism or public relations and the sector has, instead, created a new restricted gender stereotype.

REFERENCES

Aldoory, L. (1998). The language of leadership for female public relations professionals. *Journal of Public Relations Research, 10*, 73-101.

Aldoory, L., & Toth, E. L. (2001). Two feminists, six opinions: The complexities of feminism in communication scholarship today. In W. B. Gudykunst (Ed.), *Communication yearbook* (Vol. 24, pp. 345-361). Newbury Park, CA: Sage.

Alfermann, D. (1996). *Geschlechterrollen und geschlechtypisches Verhalten* [Gender roles and gender specific behaviour]. Stuttgart, Berlin, Köln: Kohlhammer.

Aries, E. (1976). Interaction patterns and themes of male, female, and mixed groups. *Small Group Behaviour, 7*(1), 7-18.

Aries, E. (1987). Gender and communication. In P. Shaver & C. Hendrick (Eds.), *Sex and gender* (pp. 149-176). Newbury Park, CA: Sage.

Bates, D. (1983). A concern: Will women inherit the profession? *Public Relations Journal, 7*, 6-7.

Berryman-Fink, C. (1985). Male and female managers' views of communication skills and training needs of women in management. *Public Personnel Management, 14*, 307-313.

Capek, M. E. S. (Ed.). (1989). *A woman's thesaurus: An index of language used to describe and locate information by and about women.* New York: Harper & Row.

Cline, C. G. (1989). Public relations. The $1 million penalty for being a woman. In P. J. Creedon (Ed.), *Women in mass communication. Challenging gender values* (pp. 263-275). Newbury Park, CA, London, New Delhi: Sage.

Christmas, L. (1997). *Chaps of both sexes? Women decision-makers in newspapers: Do they make a difference?* London: The BT Forum.

Collaer, M. L., & Hines, M. (1995). Human behavioural sex differences: A role for gonadal hormones during early development? *Psychological Bulletin, 118*(1), 55-107.

Creedon, P. J. (Ed.). (1989). *Women in mass communication: Challenging gender values.* Newbury Park, CA, London, New Delhi: Sage.

Creedon, P. J. (1991). Public relations and women's work: Toward a feminist analysis of public relations roles. *Public Relations Research Annual, 3*(1), 67-84.

Creedon, P. J. (Ed.). (1993). *Women in mass communication* (2nd ed.). Newbury Park, CA, London, New Delhi: Sage.

Foss, K. A., Foss, S. K., & Griffin, C. L. (1999). *Feminist rhetorical theories.* Thousand Oaks, CA: Sage.

Fröhlich, R. (1991). Gender switch. Zur Feminisierung der Kommunikationsberufe in den USA und Deutschland [Gender switch. About the feminization of communication professions in the United States and Germany]. *Medium, 22*(1), 70-73.

Fröhlich, R. (1992). Einleitung: Frauen und Medien—Nur ein Thema "en vogue"? [Introduction: Women and media—Only an issue "in vogue"?] In R. Fröhlich (Ed.), *Der andere Blick. Aktuelles zur Massenkommunikation aus weiblicher Sicht* (pp. 9-24). Bochum: Universitätsverlag Dr. N. Brochmeyer.

Fröhlich, R. (1994). Einstieg und Aufstieg mit Tücken. Das Beispiel Public Relations [Entrance and promotion with malice. The public relations case]. In M.-L. Angerer & J. Dorer (Eds.), *Gender und Medien. Theoretische Ansätze, empirische Befunde und Praxis der Massenkommunikation: Ein Textbuch zur Einführung* (pp. 94-101). Wien: Braumüller.

Fröhlich, R. (2001). Die Feminisierung der PR—Zwischen Boom und Stagnation [The feminization of PR—Between boom and stagnation]. In P. Leitolf (Ed.), *Lexikon der Public Relations* (pp. 111-114). München: Oldenbourg.

Fröhlich, R., & Holtz-Bacha, C. (Eds.). (2003.) *Journalism education in Europe and North America. A structural comparison.* Cresskill, NJ: Hampton Press.

Fröhlich, R., & Lafky, S. (in press). *Women journalists in the western world: Equal opportunities and what surveys tell us.* Cresskill, NJ: Hampton Press.

Gallagher, M. (1981). *Unequal opportunities. The case of women and the media.* Paris: UNESCO.

Gallagher, M. (1992). Women and men in the media. *Communication Research Trends, 12*(1), 1-36.

Gallagher, M. (1995) *An unfinished story: Gender patterns in media employment.* Paris: UNESCO.

Gallegher, M. (in press). At the millenium. Shitfing patterns in gender, culture and journalism. In R. Fröhlich & S. Lafky (Eds.), *Women journalists in the western world: What surveys tell us.* Cresskill, NJ: Hampton Press.

Grunig, L. S. (1989). The "glass ceiling" effect on mass communication students. In P. J. Creedon (Ed.), *Women in mass communication. Challenging gender values* (pp. 125-147). Newbury Park, CA, London, New Delhi: Sage.

Grunig, L. A., Toth, E. L., & Hon, L. C. (2000). Feminist values in public relations. *Journal of Public Relations Research, 12*(1), 49-68.

Hall, J. A. (1978). Gender effects in decoding nonverbal cues. *Psychological Bulletin, 85*(12), 845-857.

Hall, J. A. (1984). *Nonverbal sex differences: Communication accuracy and expressive style.* Baltimore, MD: John Hopkins University Press.

Henley, N. (1977). *Body politics. Power, sex, and nonverbal communication.* Englewood Cliffs: Prentice-Hall. (German edition: *Körperstrategien. Geschlecht, Macht und nonverbale Kommunikation.* Frankfurt: Fischer, 1988)

Kato, H., Inoue, T., Iwasaki, C., Kodama, M., Suzuki, M., & Muramatsu, Y. (1994). *Report on women in mass media.* Tokyo: Japan Study Committee on Women and the Media.

Kosicki, G. M., & Becker, L. B. (1992). Annual census and analysis of enrollment and graduation. *Journalism Educator, 47*(3), 61-70.

Lachover, E. (in press). Women journalists in the Israeli press. In R. Fröhlich & S. Lafky (Eds.), *Women journalists in the western world: What surveys tell us.* Cresskill, NJ: Hampton Press.

Lafky, S. (1991). Women journalists. In D. H. Weaver & G. C. Wilhoit (Eds.), *The American journalist: A portrait of U.S. news people an their work* (2nd ed., pp. 160-181). Bloomington: Indiana University Press.

Lafky, S. (1993). The progress of women and people of colour in the U.S. journalistic workforce. A long, slow journey. In P. J. Creedon (Ed.), *Women in mass communication* (2nd ed., pp. 87-103). Newbury Park, CA. London, New Delhi: Sage.

Limor, Y., & Caspi, D. (1994). The feminization of the Israeli journalism. *Kesher, 15*(1), 37-45.

Löfgren Nilsson, M. (1993). *Klimat och kön* [Climate and gender]. Göteborg: Department of Journalism and Mass Communication, Göteborg University.

Merten, K. (1997). PR als Beruf. Auforderungsprofile und Trends für die PR-Ausbildung [Public relations as a profession. Requirements and trends for PR education]. *pr magazin,* 1, 43-50.

Neveu, E. (in press). Female journalists in France. In R. Fröhlich & S. Lafky (Eds.), *Women journalists in the western world: What surveys tell us.* Cresskill, NJ: Hampton Press.

Peterson, P. V. (1988). Journalism and mass communication enrollment levelled off in '87. *Journalism Educator, 43*(1), 4-10.

Rakow, L. F. (1989a). A bridge to the future: Re-visioning gender in communication. In P. J. Creedon (Ed.), *Women in mass communication: Challenging gender values* (pp. 299-312). Newbury Park, CA: Sage.

Rakow, L. F. (1989b). From the feminization of public relations to the promise of feminism. In E. L. Toth & C. G. Cline (Eds.), *Beyond the velvet ghetto* (pp. 287-298). San Francisco: IABC Research Foundation.

Reid, T. R. (1995, May 31). Japan. The land of the rising daughter. *Washington Post,* (Style section), p. 1.

Reif, W. E., Newstrom, J.W., & Monczka, R. M. (1978). Exploding some myths about women managers. In B. A. Snead (Ed), *Women in management* (pp. 11-23). Englewood Cliffs, NJ: Prentice-Hall.

Robinson, G. J. (in press). Theorizing the impact of gender in Canadian journalism. In R. Fröhlich & S. Lafky (Eds.), *Women journalists in the western world: What surveys tell us.* Cresskill, NJ: Hampton Press.

Robinson, G. J., & Saint-Jean, A. (1998). Canadian women journalists: The "other half" of the equation. In D. Weaver (Ed.), *The global journalist: News people around the world* (pp. 351-372). Cresskill, NJ: Hampton Press.

Sargent, A. G. (1981). *The androgenous manager.* New York: Amacom.

Savolainen, T., & Zilliacus-Tikkanen, H. (1992). *Women in Finnish broadcasting* (Publication of the Finnish National Commission for Unesco No 61). Helsinki: Finnish National Commission for Unesco.

Schneider, B., Schönbach, K., & Stürzebecher, D. (1993a). Journalisten im vereinigten Deutschland. Strukturen, Arbeitsweisen und Einstellungen im Ost-West-Vergleich [Journalists in reunificated Germany. An East-West comparison of structures, working methods and attitudes]. *Publizistik, 38*(4), 353-382.

Schneider, B., Schönbach, K., & Stürzebecher, D. (1993b). Westdeutsche Journalisten im Vergleich: jung, professionell und mit Spaß an der Arbeit [West German journalists: Young, professional and with fun at work]. *Publizistik, 38*(1), 5-30.

Stier, D. S., & Hall, J. A. (1984). Gender differences in touch: An empirical and theoretical review. *Journal of Personality and Social Psychology, 47*(4), 440-459.

Toth, E. L., & Grunig, L. A. (1993). The missing story of women in public relations. *Journal of Public Relations Research, 5,* 153-176.

U.S. Department of Commerce. (1998). *Statistical abstract of the United States, 1998: The national data book* (117th ed.). Washington, DC: U.S. Government Printing Office.

van Zoonen, L. (1994). *Feminist media studies.* London: Sage.

van Zoonen, L. (in press). Women in serious and popular journalism. In R. Fröhlich & S. Lafky (Eds.), *Women journalists in the western world: Equal opportunities and what surveys tell us.* Cresskill, NJ: Hampton Press.

Wakefield, G. (1993). Trouble, trouble, trouble… . *PR Update, 4,* 4.

Weaver, D. H. (Ed.). (1998). *The global journalist. News people around the world.* Cresskill, NJ: Hampton Press.

Weaver, D. H., & Wilhoit, G. C. (1996). *The American journalist in the 1990s. U.S. news people at the end of an era.* Mahwah, NJ: Erlbaum.

Weischenberg, S., Keuneke, S., Löffelholz, M., & Scholl, A. (1994). *Frauen im Journalismus. Gutachten über die Geschlechterverhältnisse bei den Medien in Deutschland im Auftrag der Industriegewerkschaft Medien* [Women in journalism.

Report on gender representation in the media in Germany. By order of the Industriegewerkschaft Medien]. Stuttgart, Germany: IG Medien, Fachgruppe Journalismus (dju/SWJV).

Wright, D. K., Grunig, L. A., Springston, J. K., & Toth, E. L. (1991). *Under the glass ceiling: An analysis of gender issues in American public relations.* New York: The PRSA Foundation.

Zilliacus-Tikkanen, H. (in press). Female journalists in Finland. In R. Fröhlich & S. Lafky (Eds.), *Women journalists in the western world: Equal opportunities and what surveys tell us.* Cresskill, NJ: Hampton Press.

5

Gender-Typing in the Newsroom: The Feminization of Swedish Television News Production, 1958–2000

Monika Djerf-Pierre
Monica Löfgren-Nilsson

One of the most important issues for feminist media research is to understand the changing place of women in the public sphere, and what has propelled these changes. Since the 1980s, the number of women in journalism has increased in most Western countries (Spears, Seydegart, & Gallagher, 2000). In Sweden, for example, the proportion of female journalists doubled in the 1960s and has continued to rise. Female journalists now constitute 47% of the entire Swedish journalist corps. Along with the growth in numbers of female journalists, both in Sweden and in many other parts of the Western world, was a hope that more women would affect media output. Research in the area seems, to a certain extent, to have been caught up in a feeling of optimism of how women would improve media output and the image of women in the media. In most Western countries, the increasing number of women in journalism seems to have run parallel to significant changes in the news genre. *Tabloidization, infotainment, commercialization*, and *popularization* are concepts frequently employed to describe the new style of journalism. But the changes of the news are also frequently described in gendered terms. The key concept used in this discussion is *feminization*. Based on the assumption that news was established as a male genre, the argument now is that news in the 1990s and 2000s became more feminine in form and content. In many European countries, the feminization of news also seemed to coincide with the introduction and/or expansion of commercial television. This shift, as well as changes in the news genre, led researchers to advance the theory that it is commercialization—or rather market-driven journalism—that has caused a feminization of the news (Hartley, 1998; Holland, 1998; van Zoonen, 1998b). This is one attempt to address the notoriously tricky question about cause and effect in media research: Is it true, as van Zoonen (1998a) suggested, that the changing news genre opened up journalism to women, or is it rather that the increasing number of women has changed the forms and content of the news?

In this chapter, we discuss the nature and the possible causes and effects of the feminization of Swedish television news. In the analysis presented here, we apply a historical perspective to the changes in news and news production from the beginning of broadcasting in the mid-1950s until the early 2000s. We begin with a discussion of some of the theoretical issues concerning gender and journalism, particularly what feminization and concepts such as *male* and *female* mean in a journalistic context. Second, we look at the actual numbers of female journalists reporting stories in the news, and the positions that women have held in the newsrooms over various periods. We also discuss how assignments and positions have been defined in gendered terms within the news departments, the differences in the topic areas covered by female and male journalists, and the power relations between men and women in the newsrooms. In the concluding section of the chapter, we draw some empirical conclusions on the causes and effects of feminization in Swedish television.

The chapter is based on the first findings from the research project "Women in the Journalist Culture," a project that seeks to analyze the role and the conditions of women reporters in television news from a historical perspective. The first and most important source of data used in this chapter is collected from within this project. It is a quantitative analysis of 7,700 news stories from 1958 to 2000. The sample included 8 weeks of news broadcast material for each of the following years: 1958 (only 4 weeks), 1960, 1965, 1968,[1] 1970, 1975, 1980, 1985, 1990, 1995, and 2000 (only 4 weeks). The study included newscasts of *Aktuellt* (SVT1—on air from 1958–2000), *Rapport* (SVT2—on air from 1969–2000), and *Nyheterna* (TV4—on air from 1992).[2] The second set of data (mainly documents and interviews with journalists) has been collected within the framework of the project "Mirror, Watch-Dog, Interpreter: News and Current Affairs Programming in Swedish Radio and Television during the 20th Century" (Djerf-Pierre & Weibull, 2001). Some of the empirical findings presented here have previously been published in Djerf-Pierre (2000) and in Djerf-Pierre & Weibull (2001), while some are the outcome of secondary analysis of previously collected data from a gender perspective.

---

[1]The odd year 1968 is included because we wanted to include the last year of *Aktuellt* and the single channel system, before the start of the second television channel in 1969, in the analysis.

[2]The project will also be empirically based on documentary analysis and interviews and further analyses of the newsrooms will be conducted.

THE GENDERED PRACTICE OF NEWS

One of the basic preconditions for change in journalism that could result from an increased number of women in the sector would be that female journalists have a different perspective and work method than their male colleagues. Feminist media research usually assumes that such differences exist, although there is no common or shared view on what constitutes them or how such differences are expressed. Journalists themselves also seem to believe that there are differences between male and female journalism. In a newly conducted study, a representative sample of Swedish journalists were asked to respond to a series of statements concerning if and how the increasing number of female journalists have changed news journalism.[3] According to the journalists, the greatest change brought about by women is the broadening of experience in the newsrooms. The journalists unanimously agreed that this had led to different judgments on the evaluation of potential stories and reports as well as new news angles. These results correspond with the views of Canadian and American journalists about the role of women in the profession (Gallagher, 1994; Robinson & Saint-Jean, 1998). On a number of points, however, the journalists were not unanimous. Opinions diverged, for example, on the issue of whether journalism has become more active and professional as a result of the increase in the number of women in journalism. There were also significant gender differences in the opinions: Female journalists generally assigned greater importance to all the changes mentioned compared to their male counterparts.

Defining Feminization

For most feminist media research, the point of departure has also been that journalism is dominated by male values but that the news genre lately has become more "feminine." Any such implication or conclusion must challenge definitions of *male* and *female* in journalism. Various definitions have been suggested, focused on different aspects of news and news work such as differences in news selection (or assignments to different types of work or stories), angles applied, ethics, professional values, and organizational strategies (Creedon, 1989; Gallagher, 1994; Löfgren-Nilsson, 1994, 1999; Melin-Higgins, 1995, 1996; Savolainen, 1992; van Zoonen, 1998a, 1998b; Zilliacus-Tikkanen, 1997). We summarize these suggestions here and comment on each of them.

---

[3]Löfgren-Nilsson (2000). The study was conducted in 1999 and the representative sample was drawn among members of Swedish Association of Journalists (Svenska journalistförbundet, SJF). Approximately 95% of the Swedish journalists belong to SJF, of which 47% are women.

Male and Female Dimensions in Journalism

The following lists male and female dimensions in journalism.

Male	Female
Hard news	Soft news
Public sphere/macro-level	Private sphere/micro-level
Male sources and perspectives	Female sources and perspectives
Distance/neutrality	Intimacy/empathy
Detachment	Audience orientation
News hounds	Pedagogues
Professional ethics	Personal ethics
Competition/individualism	Cooperation/collective
Hierarchical and formal organization	Horizontal and informal organization

The first gendered aspect of the news—and probably the most intensely debated issue—deals with the topics and issues covered (i.e., the news selection). Here, the distinction is usually made between soft and hard news, although opinions differ on how *soft* and *hard* should be defined. The label *soft news* is often used when referring to news about social and consumer issues, health care, education, child care, the environment, and housing. But sometimes, human interest, culture, and entertainment are included in soft news. Hard news, on the other hand, usually refers to politics, business news, union issues, and war, but sometimes also to technology, science, crime, and sports news. The different definitions of soft and hard news seem to derive from two different logics: importance and taste or pleasure. The first logic is derived from the view that women and men have different beliefs about what are important (and therefore newsworthy) public issues. Hard news includes issues believed to be important to men because they relate to spheres in which men dominate such as politics, the economy, and business. Soft news includes issues related to social spheres, such as health care, education, child care, where women traditionally dominate and where they are defined as consumers (consumer news). The second logic assumes that women and men are interested in and derive pleasure from different subjects and topics. These gender divisions also draw on gender differences found in other areas of popular culture, such as women's and men's magazines. Topics such as sports, pornography, science, and crime derive from a *male* logic and personal relations, human interest, fashion, and home-making are guided by a *female* logic. Thus, when we talk about soft and hard news in the following paragraphs, we use the first logic just discussed.

Female journalism is also associated with a personal engagement and empathy for the people covered in the news, trying to respond to the interests of the audiences and prioritizing female sources and perspectives. Male journalism, on the other hand, is seen to be neutral, distancing and impartial, detached from the audience. But behind this seemingly neutral relationship and detachment hides a male norm and a male worldview that generates male biases and male sources in the news. Female journalism, on the other hand, is supposed to prioritize female sources and perspectives.

Female journalism is seen as placing greater emphasis on the bigger picture and on context, whereas male journalism reports on isolated incidents and facts. Whereas male journalism is seen to be about hunting down news and immediately presenting it (news hounds), female journalism is seen as gathering information and presenting it in a pedagogical way after first providing a basis for understanding (pedagogues). Female journalism strives to concretize and illustrate the consequences of events on the everyday lives of the individual(s), that is, the micro-level of society, whereas male journalism is supposed to neutrally report the facts and to focus on the macro-level of society. Female journalism is also supposed to combine personal identity and professional identity, involving working with "the whole person", assuming a personal and moral responsibility as well as a professional ethical approach. Male journalism is seen to apply a purely professional approach—to report the news without regard for the consequences.

The aspects discussed so far highlight differences in journalistic culture and can be complemented by a consideration of the organizational principles of journalism. These apsects of female journalism have received little attention, but there are a couple of ways in which female organizational principles might be defined. Female journalism could be said to be associated with nonhierarchical editorial structures and with informal leadership rather than hierarchies and formal leaders. Cooperation is prioritized over competition, and collective responsibility is more important than individualism.

STEREOTYPES AND DICHOTOMIZATION

There are two major problems with the ways in which female and male journalism has been defined and analyzed so far. First of all, research on feminization—at least most of the empirical research—has focused on the character of the journalistic product (i.e., the form and content of news). We believe that media research needs to pay more attention to the questions of power in the newsroomwhen discussing feminization.[4] Because the position of women in any

---

[4]Recent studies dealing with the question of power in the newsrooms are conducted by Egsmose (1993), Löfgren-Nilsson (1999), Melin-Higgins and Djerf-Pierre (1998), and Steiner (1998).

social field is essentially a matter of social power, in society at large as well as in journalism, we argue that research on the possible feminization of news should also include studies on the process of making news: the working conditions and power relations within the newsroom. If we are to talk about a feminization of journalism we should not just refer to a change in the form, style, and content. We must also include the organizational principles of journalism and the issue of status and power.

Second, the dichotomization of news into two different types—*male* and *female*—is problematic for several reasons. First of all, it focuses on familiar stereotypes between men and women but certain topics, areas of specialization, assignments, and positions then tend to be defined as *appropriate* for male and female journalists. This, in turn, may create expectations for real working women and men, often encouraging, if not forcing, them to stay in their "proper place." Because the definitions are based on traditional notions about male and female qualities, they might be perpetuating traditional values rather than contributing to positive change.

The most important problem, however, is that the definitions are highly normative and may have very little to do with the actual journalistic practices of real women and men. When analyzing the gendered practice of news production from a historical perspective, the theoretical concepts of *male* and *female* journalism are particularly problematic in this respect. The character of what is said to be female journalism bears a strong resemblance to what was presented as a female ideal within the women's movement in the 1970s and early 1980s. We believe that assuming that *one* female ideal and *one* male ideal have been dominant in the television news departments at all times is a difficult position to hold. The dichotomization in terms of female and male journalism does not account for the possibility of different femininities and masculinities that have been—and still are—produced and expressed in journalism, both in the newsrooms and in news output.

Our view is that we need to develop dialectical, rather than dichotomized thinking about gender (Mörtberg, 1997; Sandstig, 2001). When gender is linked to other social and cultural factors—class and ethnicity, for example—it will allow us to think in terms of *multiple* masculinities and femininities. In research on masculinity, several studies deal with the relationship between gender, class, and ethnicity and discuss different masculinities (Brodd & Kaufman, 1994; Connell, 1995; Kimmel, 1996). Here, the relationships between men and women *have* been analyzed, but also the power relations between men and the internalized hierarchies that follow from them. Within the research on gender and organizations, and within feminist media studies, a considerable effort has also been made to analyze relations between men, women, and hierarchies. However, theories and empirical studies that highlight hierarchies among women are rare (Hagemann & Åmark, 1999). The recognition of the existence of multiple femininities and masculinities suggests the need to give attention (both theoretically and empirically) to hierarchies and power relations, both between and within the social categories of men and women. Research on feminization should highlight the cultural notions of masculinity and femininity, recognize the possibility of multiple masculinities and femininities in the newsrooms as well as the internal hierarchies and power relations that follow from them. Furthermore, masculinity and femininity should be considered as concepts that give meaning to each other and should be studied in their historical context. To be able to do this in our own research on gender and news, we have developed closer links with theoretical perspectives on organization and gender, such as Acker (1990), Gherardi (1995), Alvesson and Billing (1997), Sundin (1998) & L. Abrahamsson (2000).

The first aspect of our analysis is its cultural perspective on organizations, where *culture* is defined as "a set of meaning, ideas, and symbols that are shared by the members of a collective and that have evolved over time" (Alvesson & Billing, 1997, p. 103). The assumption is that "the ideas, the definitions of reality and the meanings which are shared in common by a collective . . . are a central—perhaps even the central—feature of organizations" (pp. 104–105). We also believe that all organizations are gendered, albeit in different ways. If we are to understand how news organizations are gendered we need to study how collective ideals and meanings about gender are produced and how gender symbolism works in the newsrooms. Also, the gender patterns of the news organizations must be studied from different analytical levels (Acker, 1990).

The first analytical level is the structural, and deals with basic gender-typing within organizations in terms of work tasks, assignments, and positions. On a structural level, "body counting" and dichotomization is often necessary (i.e., how different types of work tasks and positions are assigned to men and women, respectively). The second analytical level is the symbolic, (i.e., the construction of symbols and notions of gender that relate to the first level of basic gender-typing).

> While sex-typing only means that some jobs are defined as suitable for men or women respectively, gender symbolism refers to the cultural logic behind such form of masculinity or femininity, either vaguely or in shape of more specific ideas about what the work involves and the kind of qualities typically possessed by "man" or "woman." (Alvesson & Billing, 1997, p. 90)

Needless to say, the first and second levels do not have to be in total congruence. The third analytical level is the relational (i.e., the interaction between women and men within an organization). This level raises questions about how and under which conditions interaction is to be undertaken and thereby addresses questions of power.[5]

---

[5]Acker (1990) also referred to a fourth and a fifth level, dealing with individual identity and organizational identity.

The gendered processes on these three analytical levels are linked to each other and they often lead to patterns of segregation and hierarcization. These patterns of horizontal and vertical gender differentiation can be referred to as the *gender order* of an organization (L. Abrahamsson, 2000; Sundin, 1998).[6] Our research strategy is to understand the gendered nature of news by analyzing how news organizations are gendered on different levels (i.e., to study the gender order of news departments). The focus is on the structural level, but we also discuss some important aspects of the symbolic and relational levels.

THE PLACE OR WOMEN IN THE NEWS

Swedish public service television was for many decades one of the most stable public service monopolies in the world. From the beginning of regular broadcasting in 1956, the broadcasting company Sveriges Radio (SR) enjoyed a monopoly on providing television programs to the Swedish public. Public service television expanded from one channel, TV1 (or SVT1), to two channels, TV2 (or SVT2), in 1969. In 1992, after 65 years of uninterrupted monopoly for the public service company, TV4, a privately owned, terrestrially distributed commercial Swedish channel with nationwide reach began broadcasting.[7] During the five decades in which television news has been broadcast, both the genre of news and news organizations have changed. Also the gender order of the newsrooms has changed considerably over time. In this analysis, we have identified three distinct periods, each one characterized by a specific gender order. In the following section we characterize these periods and relate the gender order to the particular context of news production during each period: the organization of television and the news department, the development of the news genre, and characteristics of the journalist culture.[8]

One of a Kind, 1958–1965

The first news magazine on Swedish television, *Aktuellt*, started in 1958 and provided news and news commentary on weekday evenings. The early *Aktuellt* contained no political news at all, and only few news items on the economy.

---

[6]Both Sundin and Abrahamsson depart from Hirdman's (1990) theories of the gender system of society.

[7]TV4 started out as a satellite channel in 1990, but began terrestrial transmissions in 1992.

[8]The journalistic culture here refers to the professional ideals, values, and rules that dominate within the news organization at a given point in time.

Sensational news (accidents and crime), human interest, culture, and entertainment made up more than 60% of the news stories. During the early years, stories about Iceland's fish industry were presented alongside interviews with famous entertainers. Reporting took its cue from the classic questions of journalism: where, when, and how something happened. Questions about why, with what consequences, or in what context were of secondary interest and little was offered in terms of background, commentary, or analysis.

The dominant approach to news reporting among members of *Aktuellt's* newsdesk was to mirror events, with strict observance of factuality and impartiality in the reporting: it was the heyday of the objectivist approach in Swedish television journalism (Djerf-Pierre & Weibull, 2001). News selection and the prioritization of the visual aspects of news were highly influenced by the tabloid press. Indeed, the first chief editor of the program was recruited from Sweden's largest tabloid paper, *Expressen*. It is, however, important to note that this objectivity was a radical idea at the time. The new journalistic ambition—that marked both public service radio and television—was to show the world "as it is" in an unprejudiced and unbiased way. It was in sharp contrast to the educational approach that had been the dominant approach during the early period of radio broadcasting in the 1920s through 1940s. Compared to earlier decades, when journalism was supposed to educate and work to achieve higher cultural and moral standards among the public and where the paternalistic approach to the audience was quite strong, the realistic approach became more dominant during the 1950s. Paradoxically perhaps, the monopoly-based, public service broadcaster of the 1950s was very much aware of its audience and made substantive efforts to provide material they believed would attract large numbers of viewers (Djerf-Pierre & Weibull, 2001). This new approach also increased attention to the issues and topics that could attract female viewers. The basic motivation for recruiting a female journalist was to cater to the interests and needs of the female audience.

Men dominated the news department and there was a notable absence of female reporters during the first years of broadcasting. The first and only female reporter hired on a permanent basis during this period was recruited in 1960. The numbers of stories produced by women amounted to about 14% in 1958, a figure that subsequently declined to about 7% (see Table 5.1). We argue that one of the reasons for this decline could be the attitude toward women's professionalism that dominated the newsroom at the time. During the early years, the news department employed two female and one male news anchor, recruited for their nice appearance, their ability to read the news telegrams clearly, and to present facts in a balanced way. They were not considered "real" journalists, and were not allowed to write their own voice-over comments to the news they presented. Thus, they mostly read what other reporters had written for them, but because the format of news during these years was based on short clips of film with studio-based commentaries, some of these comments were read by the female anchors.

TABLE 5.1

Topics in Stories Covered by Female and Male Reporters in Public Service (*Aktuellt* in SVT1 and *Rapport* in SVT2) and Commercial (*Nyheterna* in TV4) Newscasts 1958-2000 (percent)

| | Public Service (SVT1 and SVT2) | | | | | | | | | Commercial (TV4) | | |
| | 1958-1965 | | | 1968-1980 | | | 1985-2000 | | | 1995-2000 | | |
	Female	Male	Diff	Female	Male	Diff	Female	Male	Diff	Female	Male	Diff
War and International	0	17	-17	8	21	-15	18	21	-3	15	20	-5
Economy and Labor Market	3	6	-3	20	18	+2	14	11	+3	7	4	+3
Politics	5	8	-3	14	17	-3	15	18	-3	12	17	-5
Social and Consumer Issues	6	6	0	16	6	+10	13	9	+4	14	10	+4
Accidents and Crime	13	10	+3	7	6	+1	10	11	-1	15	19	-4
Environment and Energy	2	1	+1	10	5	+5	4	5	-1	2	2	0

Business News	5	7	-2	4	9	-5	7	8	-1	9	7	+2
Culture and Human Interest	48	13	+35	10	4	+6	9	6	+3	17	7	+10
Sport	6	11	-4	1	7	-6	2	3	-1	3	8	-5
Other	12	21	-9	10	7	+3	8	8	0	6	6	0
Sum	100	100		100	100		100	100		100	100	
Number of stories	62	631		348	2496		1191	2605		2283	6	9

Note. War and international issues include international policy, negotiations, the European Union, and diplomacy. Politics is narrowly defined in this study; it only includes stories on the political parties and the workings of parliamentary politics. If a story is about the social democratic party's policy on health care is categorized as social issues. Economy includes labor market, taxes, unemployment, interest rates, and so on. Social issues include immigration, education, health care, care of the elderly, housing, and child care. Culture includes both "high culture," such as opera or literature, and "popular culture," entertainment and the media. *Aktuellt* was broadcast 1958–2000, *Rapport* 1969–2000, and *Nyheterna* 1992–2000.

In 1962, the management of *Aktuellt* decided that the news anchors should be professional journalists. The two female anchors were transferred to other assignments and replaced by an all-male "professional" team. At the same time, the number of women appearing in the news decreased. Reporters from other departments were frequently used as additional staff. From the outset, Swedish television had a special division for women's programs—the Home and family section—which produced programs aimed at the female audience. Here, the section's staff was all-female with a female editor, and they were occasionally employed by *Aktuellt* to produce news from a female perspective. As the news department grew, the need for assistance from the home and family section declined. Additionally, the journalistic culture changed in the middle of the 1960s and the principles for news selection became more focused on hard news. This also brought about less attention to news from the female sphere, as well as culture and human interest stories.

The first and only female reporter appointed on a full-time basis in the news department at *Aktuellt* was Ingrid Schrewelius, who was employed as a general reporter in 1960. Although the management of the news department realized the need for a female reporter, they had difficulties accepting a female voice. At first, Schrewelius was not allowed to use her own voice in the stories she produced, but had to ask one of her male colleagues to act as the speaker. Schrewelius' ambition was to get into foreign or political reporting but she was not allowed to cover serious matters, only culture, human interest, and news regarding activities in the "female" sphere. Foreign policy, war, the economy, employment, politics, and sports were all male areas. Instead, the first female reporter at *Aktuellt* found her own, alternative space within the newsroom through the introduction of fashion reporting and she made this topic into her special "beat." The news department provided a very narrowly defined space for women: Of all the news stories produced by women in the first period of newscasting surveyed, almost 50% were in the fields of human interest or culture (see Table 5.1). However, these were not regarded as high status areas and the stories making the headlines—the stories placed first in the program— were usually accidents and crime stories (see Table 5.2). High status areas, and areas where specialist reporters where required were politics and international news.

The social organization of the news department and its working conditions were marked by scarcity of resources: the number of staff was small (only 14 reporters and editors in 1960), and consequently reporter workloads were heavy: Working late and unsocial hours was routine. At a time when day-care centers or any other organized form of child care was nonexistent, it was almost impossible to have a family, unless one was a man with a wife at home to take care of the children. Social relations between reporters were common as work and leisure time merged into each other. To work as a television reporter at this time was not really a profession, it was a way of life.

TABLE 5.2

The Placement of Different Categories of News Stories in Newscasts in Public Service (Aktuellt in SVT1 and Rapport in SVT2) and Commercial (Nyheterna in TV4) Television 1958-2000 (percent)

| | Public Service (SVT1 and SVT2) | | | | | | Commercial (TV4) | |
| | 1958-1965 | | 1968-1980 | | 1985-2000 | | 1995-2000 | |
	First	Last	First	Last	First	Last	First	Last
War and International	12	10	17	7	22	3	14	5
Economy and Labor Market	6	2	30	6	17	4	4	2
Politics	6	2	14	8	18	10	20	2
Social and Consumer Issues	6	6	3	6	10	6	11	5
Accidents and Crime	35	4	12	2	16	8	42	7
Environment and Energy	0	0	6	5	1	5	0	4
Business News	2	0	9	6	8	5	5	5
Culture and Human Interest	7	26	1	14	2	34	0	47
Sport	3	32	2	36	2	15	1	17
Other	23	18	6	10	4	10	3	6
Sum	100	100	100	100	100	100	100	100
Number of Stories	95	95	378	378	388	388	85	85

Note. See footnote to Table 5.1.

The first female reporters' experiences of working in the news department were somewhat contradictory. On the one hand, as was experienced by Schrewelius, they were excluded from certain assignments and positions and generally given low status areas. But on the other hand, there were so few women that they felt special and unique. Some of the female reporters who entered broadcasting in the 1960s even felt that they had an advantage in their work by being women: Sources often gave the female journalists special attention and to be interviewed by a woman was obviously an interesting novelty.

The gender order that existed within the news department was based on a notion of gender as sex-stereotyped biology and the horizontal and vertical gender differentiation was very strong. There were believed to be "natural" differences between men and women, where men would be assigned to "male" tasks and positions and women to "female" tasks and positions. For example, women generally were recruited as secretaries and script girls, whereas the men were employed as reporters and editors: The positions and news areas given to men were associated with higher status and power. In the 1950s, expectations of female reporters were that they would support and complement male reporters' coverage of important news, with light-weight, or entertaining news stories and news of interest to women. Although female topics had their place in the news, they were considered less important. Such an environment was seen as the natural order of things and there was an absence of conflict around gender issues. This was probably because for the pioneer women, it was hard enough work just to fit in. To question the gender order of the newsroom or to challenge the journalistic culture was probably unthinkable at this time.

Fighting for Air: 1965–1985

After a heated debate about whether Sweden should allow commercial television, the noncommercial alternative won out and Sweden opted to accept a second public service channel, TV2, which began broadcasting in December 1969. TV2 was supposed to compete with TV1, to create an internal competition within the existing public service monopoly and the new station had its own news program, *Rapport*. In the 1970s, when *Rapport* first aired, the news genre changed dramatically: It became more critical about the dominant social institutions and important news (defined as the economy, politics, and foreign affairs by the newsroom) took precedence over interesting news (defined as accidents, crime, entertainment, popular culture, and human interest).[9] Primarily hard news reporting, but also coverage of social issues and the environment, increased during this period in both *Aktuellt* and *Rapport*, whereas sensational

---

[9]This was also the case in many other Nordic and European countries, such as Norway, Denmark, and the Netherlands (van Zoonen, 1998a).

news, human interest, culture, and science stories became much less visible. The objective approach was replaced by a new watchdog ideal, which included critical scrutiny and journalists adopted the mantle of the "Fourth Estate." By means of pedagogical explanations, news reporting sought primarily to document the causes and consequences of social problems. News programs now prioritized in-depth reportage, commentary, and studio discussions.

At both *Aktuellt* and *Rapport*, the distinct focus on hard news met more and more criticism, particularly from the female reporters who realized that social areas and issues important to women were not given appropriate attention in the news. The places and positions usually occupied by women in society—such as in education, health care, care of the elderly, and child care—rarely made the headlines. The criticism was taken seriously, particularly at *Aktuellt*, and in the late 1970s and early 1980s, the news editors tried to change the news selection criteria and give more time to soft news. Still, even though soft news got more attention, it was not considered an important news area. The most prestigious news categories were—even more than in the late 1950s—politics, the labor market, the economy, and international politics (see Table 5.2).

The start of TV2 also brought about the largest recruitment drive ever undertaken by Swedish media and the company recruited 260 journalists to work for the new channel (Engblom, 1998). The professional requirements for news reporters became more rigorous and many of the newly recruited journalists had an academic degree and/or had attended journalism school. The news desks witnessed a growing number of female reporters and producers. At *Rapport* in 1973, there where 23 male reporters, anchors, and editors and 5 female reporters. The newsroom of *Aktuellt* in 1973 comprised 26 male reporters, anchors, and editors and 4 female reporters. In both newsrooms, the specialist reporters in the economic, foreign affairs, and political divisions were all men. Similarly, newsroom managers and almost all of the other specialist reporters were men. For the first time, however, a woman headed the political division at *Rapport*. Her name was Christina Jutterström and she was the first female newsroom manager ever appointed in Swedish television.

Despite male dominance in the late 1960s and early 1970s, female reporters working in television nonetheless managed to find a new space for women in the news. Novel specialist areas and beats were introduced, all of which were in soft news areas such as environmental reporting, housing, and consumer issues and female reporters were usually assigned to these positions. A few women sometimes also covered foreign affairs, politics, and the labor market and there were a few female foreign correspondents.

The 1970s in Sweden was also a time of a radicalization of politics, which included a demand for equality and democratization in the labor market. This movement also made a great impact on public service industries. Serious attempts were made to level out the decision-making processes and to break down the barriers between editors, producers, and other staff members. Employees were encouraged to engage in democratic participation, and the company policy was to improve the working conditions for lower level workers and management. All this provided more opportunities for women and some female secretaries and script girls worked their way up to becoming producers.

Still, there were few female news reporters. In 1970, only 10% of the stories in *Aktuellt* and 15% in *Rapport* were made by women. In 1975, the number of female reporters in news programs decreased but by 1980, the proportion of news stories made by women had increased again to a little less than 20% (see Fig. 5.1). There were significant gender differences regarding story assignments throughout the 1970s, with female reporters often assigned to social and consumer news, whereas men almost exclusively covered foreign affairs and politics. In 1975, the gender differences in the coverage of topics such as war and international news and politics (male dominance), and social/consumer issues and environmental news (female dominance) was particularly strong. Five years later, in 1980, gender differences in story assignments started to go down and in 1985 it had almost disappeared; both male and female reporters where assigned to, or chose to cover, the same type of stories.

The gender order in the newsrooms also changed in the 1970s. By the middle of that decade, there were significant gender-based conflicts in the newsrooms. Discussions on gender issues started cautiously in the 1960s, but the level of attention and the heat in the discussion grew significantly in the early 1970s. The year 1975 marked the starting point for organized gender equality campaigns within the public sector (U. Abrahamsson, 1991). New gender-equality policies were introduced and activism toward equality in journalism began to yield results and with three main strategies employed. First, women should enter previously male-dominated news areas and should receive the same status as men and shift news content. The so-called "soft news" would increase in visibility and receive equal status to hard news. Second, the proportion of female sources in stories should increase, thus increasing the number of women portrayed in and reported on, in news stories. Finally, gender stereotyping in the media would be identified and challenged.

The allocation of positions and gender equality in daily management, for example project leaders who head tasks according to traditional gender roles, was also put on the agenda at this time, as shown by the following quote from a female journalist, June Carlsson, in the employee newsletter *Antennen* in 1976:

> The editorial leadership at the news program Aktuellt consists of men. Program directors and other editorial chiefs are men, foreign and domestic reporters are men. Are there then no female reporters at Aktuellt? Of course—secretaries, script girls, producers and five female reporters. And what do they do? Well, they deal with medicine, the environment, housing, family, social and children's issues. Just like at home, one might say. Issues that don't have the same status as foreign policy, the labor market and business. (Carlsson, 1976, p. 76)

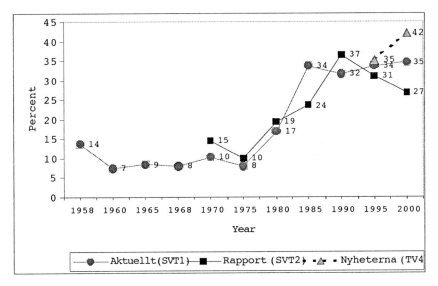

FIGURE 5.1 News stories covered by female reporters in Aktuellt (SVTV1), Rapport (SVTV2), and Nyheterna (TV4) newscasts 1958–2000 (percent of news stories)

The gender-based struggles in the 1970s resulted in several conflicts over the appointment of new male editors and reporters. The women also demanded more female anchors and a change in the content and profile of the news programs with more attention to soft news. Female networking became more common. The fight for gender equality, however, was not always led and campaigned on by women only. Some of the male newsroom managers actively supported the struggles and actively worked for gender equality, although there were significant differences in the gender order within the two newsrooms (U. Abrahamsson, Boëthius, & Modig, 1983). At *Aktuellt*, equality and gender issues were primarily issues put forward by the managing editors and directors who were all men: Female reporters showed less interest in "feminizing" the news. At *Rapport*, there were more explicit gender conflicts and the newsroom management were less interested in and supportive of gender issues and as result, there seem to have been a higher incidence of women's networking for mutual support at *Rapport*. One reason for the higher saliency of these issues at *Aktuellt* was that it had to be able to compete with the more successful (in terms of audience share) *Rapport*. The management stated in the 1980s that this was essential, not only as an expression of an active equality philosophy, but also for purely competitive reasons. Half the potential audience consisted of women and *Aktuellt* was determined to reach the female audience. As a result, a number of female reporters were recruited and therefore news stories produced by women were significantly more common in *Aktuellt* than in *Rapport* in 1985 (see Fig.

5.1). This clearly illustrates a conclusion drawn from Swedish equality work: Without interest and support from management, changes are not likely to occur (Baude, 1998; Höök, 2001).

Besides increasing the number of female reporters and placing soft news on the news agenda, one of the specific goals for gender equality work was to increase the proportion of female sources. For instance, at *Aktuellt*, special lists containing female sources were compiled. In the early days of *Aktuellt*, only 10% interview subjects were women, but that proportion began to increase slightly in the 1970s, although it had reached no more than 15% by 1985 despite efforts made to improve the news in this respect. It was a politically radical time with gender issues connected to class issues and an awareness of the social cleavages and injustices that existed both in the news and in the newsrooms. The subordination of women, both by "class" society and "patriarchy," were now on the political agenda and the conflicts around these issues grew. Gender equality received a lot of attention, albeit sporadically, but it was also a site of conflict. Female reporters now comprised a large enough group to challenge the existing gender order and journalistic culture, although the fight for gender equality was not always an easy one. Many reporters, both men and women, bore witness to the tough climate of discussion and harsh attitudes toward female reporters that sometimes surfaced in the debate, particularly at *Rapport*. Some newly recruited female reporters experienced severe problems with both the climate of discussion and the attitude of some the newsroom managers.

In the 1970s, the expectations of women in the news department had changed significantly compared to the 1950s. Female reporters were now (supposed) to be the ordinary woman's representative in the newsroom, reporting on issues of political importance to women. It was no longer only human interest, culture, entertainment, and accidents that were assigned to the female reporters. The new gender order was founded on a somewhat contradictory notion of gender: It departed from a constructivist perspective but it was contradictory in the way it highlighted the similarity of the sexes, while at the same time emphasizing the importance of the unique female experience and life worlds.

Almost Equal?: From 1985 Onward

In the 1980s, technological developments in the area of communications, especially satellite and cable television, made an increasing number of foreign TV channels available to the Swedish public and external competition had become a fact of life for the SVT. The political breakthrough for commercial radio and television came in the early 1990s and in 1992, a new terrestrial commercial TV channel was set up. In contrast to the license-financed public service channels, advertising revenues financed TV4 and the new commercial channel was also the beneficiary of state concessions on some of the rules that apply to SVT, the public service broadcaster.

The format of *Nyheterna* initially differed in many respects from the formats used in the other two media. For example, the news selection seemed to favor somewhat lighter news stories that were often short and up-beat, high-paced style where the presentation was less formal and individual reporters were encouraged to give the newscasts a personal touch. SVT2's *Rapport* displayed the most standardized format and remained the program with the highest ratings. Meanwhile, *Aktuellt's* news desk experimented with format and styles of presentation and carried longer stories and reportage. With regard to staff, the two SVT news desks were each significantly larger than that of TV4 and many of the reporters at TV4 were recruited from the public service media such as *Rapport*, *Aktuellt*, or *Dagens Eko* (the public service radio newscast).

The journalist culture continued to change in both public service and commercial television and in the late 1980s and early 1990s, there were signs of popularization of the news, although not as significant as in other countries. New narrative strategies were introduced, particularly in TV4's *Nyheterna*. Popular narrative techniques aimed to make news more interesting in the eyes of the viewer and to increase the perceived relevance and/or entertainment value of the story. Visualizations and narrative configurations were carefully crafted and news stories were cast in contexts and language styles that related to viewers' everyday experiences, inviting identification. Furthermore, reporting increasingly acknowledged the pleasure dimensions of the news in order to stimulate viewers' interest and involvement. This feature was most evident in TV4, where "News you can use" was initially used as a slogan.[10] From the mid-1980s, there were also signs of change toward a softer news profile in the news, manifested primarily in an increasing emphasis on social issues and by the 1990s, the popularization of news also implied a greater prioritization of sport (in some media such as TV4) and crime reports (all news media).

When TV4 began its news broadcasting in 1992, one explicit goal was to target the female audience and the news department recruited several female reporters. The first news staff of the channel comprised 23 male and 14 female reporters, anchors, and editors. At *Rapport* and *Aktuellt*, the proportion of women was also about one third in the 1990s. In addition, the proportion of the news stories that were produced by female journalists in the main newscasts of the two public service channels and the commercial channel TV4 during the first half of the 1990s was about one third (see Fig. 5.1). In 2000, the proportion of female reporters had increased to 42% in *Nyheterna*, whereas *Aktuellt* and particularly *Rapport* lagged behind the commercial channel.

---

[10]The popularization of the news did, however, not continue in the second half of the 1990s. *Nyheterna* in TV4 even changed in the opposite direction toward a more traditional news profile and style. The result was, as in many other European countries, convergence rather than differentiation (Brants, 1998).

For a long time, the place of women in news organizations remained at junior positions, but by the 1990s it became more common for female journalists to occupy senior executive positions such as news director and chief editor. In 1988, the first female chief editor Ewonne Winblad, was appointed at *Rapport*, and public service organizations were much more successful in recruiting women as managers than TV4. SVT generally also had a much higher rate of senior women managers than other media including the local and metropolitan press (Petersson, Hermausson, Micheletti, & Westholm, 1996). Two recent women recruits to senior positions are Maria Curman who became director of Swedish Television in 2000 but was forced to resign in spring 2001, and Christina Jutterström who replaced her in summer 2001.

Gender differences in newsrooms continued to narrow during the 1990s. In 1995, there were no apparent signs of gender differences in story assignments in public service television newscasts (see Table 5.3), although by 2000, gender differences had again begun to surface in SVT, particularly in the social issues area where once again this beat became women's territory while men worked in the political news domain.

Interestingly enough, *Nyheterna* changed in the opposite direction: In 1995, women were assigned to the traditional female areas of social and consumer issues, culture and human interest more often than men but by 2000, gender differentiation at TV4 had almost disappeared. There are many possible reasons for this difference between SVT and TV4. One important factor was probably the heavy political and financial pressure on the public service company during the latter half of the 1990s. The news department in particular was subject to frequent reorganizations and suffered from a lack of financial resources. In this situation traditional ways of working and thinking again took precedence—in time of crisis, gender issues came second. The news media professionals at TV4 on the other hand, were working in a financially successful and profitable channel and in an expanding news organization. Also being a commercial channel, the news department at TV4 was forced to be continuously attentive to the ratings of the news program, and to try to reach the female part of the audience.

The gender order of the newsroom during the 1990s was founded on a notion of gender that presupposed the similarity of the sexes. A consensus about the importance of gender issues had been established and the expectations of gender equality in the news were very high both within newsrooms and in society. This was particularly evident for the public service sector, where the promotion of gender equality was believed to be one of the important tasks for a company working in the service of the public. When our research on the decline of female reporters and sources in public service news was presented at a seminar for journalists in 2000, it received a lot of attention and caused intense discussions within the public service sector. Some time after publication of our report, management of one of the news organizations changed and one consequence was the appointment of women into several management positions.

TABLE 5.3

Topics in Stories Covered by Female and Male Reporters in Public Service (Aktuellt in SVT1 and Rapport in SVT2) and Commercial (Nyheterna in TV4) Newscasts 1995 and 2000 (percent)

| | Public Service (SVT1 and SVT2) | | | | | | Commercial (TV4) | | | | | |
| | 1995 | | | 2000 | | | 1995 | | | 2000 | | |
	Female	Male	Diff	Female	Male	Diff	Female	Male	Diff	Female	Male	Diff
War and International	19	21	-2	23	27	-4	10	15	-5	19	27	-8
Economy and Labor Market	7	10	-3	9	8	+1	11	7	+3	3	1	+2
Politics	16	16	0	9	19	-10	10	17	-7	14	17	-3
Social and Consumer Issues	12	9	+3	22	9	+13	17	10	+7	10	10	0
Accidents and Crime	16	16	0	11	14	-3	13	19	-5	18	18	0
Environment and Energy	5	4	+1	3	2	+1	2	4	-2	3	1	+2
Business News	6	6	0	3	10	-7	12	10	+2	6	3	+3
Culture and Human Interest	9	6	+3	10	3	+7	17	5	+12	17	9	+8
Sport	4	3	+1	1	0	+1	3	6	-3	3	10	-7
Other	6	9	-3	9	8	+1	5	7	-2	7	4	+3
Sum	100	100		100	100		100	100		100	100	
Number of Stories	373	783		151	345		110	206		118	163	

Note. See footnote to Table 5.1.

The relationship between men and women in the newsroom was much more consensual in the 1990s than it had been in the 1970s. Gender issues sometimes still caused controversy but conflicts were much less common than during previous years. The importance of the unique female experience was now a less important argument for hiring female reporters and instead, gender equality was seen as a question of good human resource management. The dominant notion of gender presupposed no difference in working conditions and professional requirements for men and women but in the real world, this was not always necessarily the case. In our study, women working in television newsrooms in 2000 differed both socially and professionally from their male counterparts (Djerf-Pierre, 2001). For example, they were much younger, were better qualified (having usually attended both journalism school and achieved a college degree), and had a higher social class background. Also, although the proportion of female reporters had doubled between 1975 and 1980, and doubled again between 1980 and 1990, there seemed to be a finite space for advancement, the classic glass ceiling: During the 1990s and into 2000, the space for women in the news, both as reporters and as interviewees, remained at about 30% and no more.

CONCLUSION

In this chapter we discussed the gender order of newsrooms in Swedish television from the start of broadcasting until the 2000s. We showed that there have been significant changes in the gendered aspects of the news since the start of television in 1956. The number of female reporters and editors has increased considerably over time. It is also clear that the increase in numbers of women in television journalism started long before the introduction of commercial television and before signs of popularization were seen in the news in the public service channels. The biggest advances for women in journalism occurred between 1980 and 1985 whereas the popularization of the news started, we would argue, in the late 1980s and commercial television did not appear until 1992. We have also shown that gender-typing in the newsroom has decreased over the period, although a backlash can be noted in SVT in 2000. It is interesting to see that the supposedly female news area—soft news—was not a feminine area at all during the first years of television. It became so in the 1970s, almost two decades later. And during the 1970s, there was evidence that women were not simply assigned to these issues routinely and against their will but that it was sometimes a result of active choices by female journalists to cover news stories that they deemed important.

Has television news journalism then—as is often presupposed by feminist researchers—been a male culture steered by male values and norms with conditions that have severely limited the progress of female journalism? Our research suggests that it would be a mistake to believe that women have always been actively excluded from television news journalism and that media scholars should be careful in making general statements about the gendered character of news, particularly when describing journalism as male. News journalism in the 2000s is, first and foremost, heterogeneous and consists of several genres and media that differ either in terms of the journalistic values that underlie production or in terms of other editorial relationships. It is still unclear if and how commercialization will affect the gendered nature of news and news production, and whether the consumer orientation of news journalism will empower female journalists and benefit female news consumers in the long run.

One possible negative consequence could be that news journalism will once again become fragmented in terms of gender and status (i.e., that those differences that, to a certain extent have been successfully overcome in Swedish television will reappear). The risk exists that commercial logic will coincide with the separation of gender, emphasizing the differences rather than the similarities, both human and journalistic. Second, there is a problem with describing changes in the genre of news in terms of feminization when it is evident that, as the Swedish case suggests, different gender orders and journalist cultures produce and support different femininities and masculinities in different newsrooms at different times. It is also clear that the gender order of the newsrooms during the three periods studied were founded on very different notions of gender, from the essentialist view in the 1950s, where the different genders were supposed to exist in complementary harmony, to the constructivist perspective in the 1970s, where patriarchy was challenged and the relation between men and women was seen as one of conflict, subordination, and domination.

In our view, media studies has also so far been too mediacentric in its attempt to explain and understand the gendered nature of the news. Researchers have given too much attention to intramedia processes, and rarely addressed the fundamental issues of status, prestige and power in society, issues that entail change in the gender order within and outside the media.[11] Neither have they given much attention to the importance of the active strategies of real men and women in journalism seeking to change the existing gender order. As this analysis shows, the expansion of women into television journalism in Sweden started within the public service monopoly. The trend continued even though the news showed only limited signs of popularization, so there is obviously the possibility for feminization without commercialization.

What, then, makes the difference for women in the news? Our conclusion is that the place for women in the news is formed at the nexus of three interacting forces and structures, all of which need to be considered when trying to understand the changing gender of journalism. The first is the combination of social,

---

[11]Compare Nordberg (1993) and Steiner (1998).

economic, political, and cultural forces of the existing gender system in different societies and time periods. This highlights the need for more comparative research if we are to understand the gender processes working in the news. The second factor is the journalist culture within the news organizations. A previous study of the changes in the journalist culture in Swedish television news came to the conclusion that there have been three different journalist ideals that have dominated Swedish television news: objectivism (1956–1965), critical scrutiny (1965–1985), and popularization (1985–). These phases correspond neatly with the phases we have identified in our analysis of the gendered order of the news across differing time periods. This implies the need for an historical perspectives to be taken when asking questions about gender and journalism, because different journalist cultures tend to support different gender orders and news organizations, like any other, are always gendered, but in different ways.

The third and final factor relates to the active strategies of individuals and/or groups of women and men trying to change or reproduce the existing structure of power in journalism. The feminization of the news in Swedish television that started in the 1970s was more a result of active work toward gender equality, social, and professional democratization than of a changing news genre. The continuing interest in gender issues in Swedish television in the past few years has also stemmed from a combination of active inputs from female and male journalists working for a gender equality in combination with other, more general patterns of change in journalism, culture, and society.

REFERENCES

Abrahamsson, L. (2000). *Att återställa ordningen. Könsmönster och förändring i arbetsorganisationer* [To re-establish order: gender patterns and change in work organizations]. Umeå: Boréa bokförlag.

Abrahamsson, U. (1991). Hälften vunnet?—anteckningar från 10 års jämställdhetsarbete i Sveriges Radio koncernen [Half won?—notes from 10 years of gender equality work in the public service broadcasting corporation]. In U. Carlsson (Ed.), *Medier, människor, samhälle* (pp. 93-110). Göteborg: Nordicom.

Abrahamsson, U., Boëthius, G., and Modig, M. (1983). *Nyheter för kvinnor och män?* [News for women and men?] Stockholm: Sveriges Radio, Publik och Programforskningsavdelningen.

Acker, J. (1990). Hierarchies, jobs, bodies: A theory of gendered organizations. *Gender and Society* 4(2), 139-158.

Alvesson, M., & Billing, Y. (1997), *Understanding gender and organizations*. London: Sage.

Baude, A. (1998). *Genus i praktiken: på hans eller hennes villkor?* [Gender in practice: On his or her terms?] Vällingby: Jämställdhetsarbetares förening.

Brants, K. (1998). Who's afraid of infotainment? *European Journal of Communication, 13*(3), 315-335.

Brodd, H., & Kaufman, M. (Eds.). (1994). *Theorizing masculinities*. London: Sage.
Carlsson, J. (1976). Män, män och män [Men, men and men]. *Antennen, 2, 76*.
Connell, R. W. (1995). *Masculinities*. Berkeley: University of California Press.
Creedon, P. (Ed.). (1989). *Women in mass communication: Challenging gender values*. London: Sage.
Djerf-Pierre, M. (2000). Squaring the circle: Public service and commercial news on Swedish television 1956-99. *Journalism Studies, 1*(2), 239-260.
Djerf-Pierre, M. (2001). Olika medier—samma journalister? [Different media?—Different journalists?]. *JMG-granskaren*, 2-3, 10-11.
Djerf-Pierre, M., & Weibull, L. (2001). *Spegla, Granska, Tolka: Aktualitetsjournalistik i svensk radio och TV under 1900-talet* [Mirror, watch-dog, interpreter. News and current affairs journalism in Swedish radio and television in the 1900s]. Stockholm: Prisma.
Egsmose, L. (1993). *Medvind og modvind i TV. Karrieremuligheder for kvindelige medieprofessionelle i Danmark og England* [Opportunities and restraints in television. Career possibilities for women media professionals in Denmark and England]. In U. Carlsson (Ed.), *Nordisk forskning om kvinnor och medier* (pp. 201-227). Göteborg: Nordicom.
Engblom, L-Å. (1998). *Radio-och TV-folket* [Radio and television people]. Stockholm: Stiftelsen Etermedierna i Sverige.
Gallagher, M. (1994, August). *Women in the media—Making a difference*. Paper presented at the Beijing Conference.
Gherardi, S. (1995). *Gender, symbolism and organizational cultures*. London: Sage.
Hagemann, G., & Åmark, K. (1999). Fra "husmorskontrakt" til "likestillingskonstrakt." Yvonne Hirdmans genusteori [From a "housewife contract" to a "gender equality contract." Yvonne Hirdman's gender theory]. In F. Engelstad (Ed.), *Om makt: Teori og kritikk* (pp. 174-206). Oslo: Gyldendal.
Hartley, J. (1998). Juvenation. News, girls and power. In C. Carter, G. Branston, & S. Allan (Eds.), *News, gender and power* (pp. 47-70). London & New York: Routledge.
Hirdman, Y. (1990). Genussystemet [The gender system]. In *Demokrati och makt i Sverige* (pp. 73-116). Government Commission Report, SOU 1990:44. Stockholm: Fritzes.
Holland, P. (1998). The politics of the smile. "Soft news" and the sexualisation of the popular press. In C. Carter, G. Branston, & S. Allan (Eds.), *News, gender and power* (pp. 17-32). London & New York: Routledge.
Höök, P. (2001). *Stridspiloter i kjolar: om ledarskapsutveckling och jämställdhet* [Fighter pilots in wide skirts: On leadership development and gender equality]. Stockholm: Ekonomiska forskningsinstitutet vid Handelshögskolan.
Kimmel, M. (1996). *Manhood in America*. New York: The Free Press.
Löfgren-Nilsson, M. (1994). En dag på redaktionen—kvinnors och mäns arbete [A day in the newsroom—women and men at work]. In S. A. Nohrstedt (Ed.), *En nyhetsdag* (pp. 89-106). Högskolan i Örebro: Göteborgs universitet and Mitthögskolan i Sundsvall.
Löfgren-Nilsson, M. (1999). *På Bladet, Kuriren och Allehanda. Ideal och organiseringsprinciper i den redaktionella vardagen* [The star, the gazette and the examiner. Ideals and organizational principles in the newsroom culture]. Göteborg: Institutionen för journalistik och masskommunikation, Göteborgs Universitet.

Löfgren-Nilsson, M. (2000). Att göra skillnad—Kvinnors villkor och betydelse i svensk nyhetsjournalistik [Making a difference—women's place in the news 1958-2000]. In G. Jarlbro & A. Näslund Dahlgren (Ed.), *Kvinnor och medier* (pp. 7-20). Stockholm: Stiftelsen institutet för mediestudier.

Melin-Higgins, M. (1995). Female educators and male craftsmen. The professional ideal among Swedish journalists. *The Nordicom Review, 1*, 153-171.

Melin-Higgins, M. (1996). Bloodhounds or bloodbitches. Female ideals and catch 22. In *Kjønn i Media* (pp. 100-120). Oslo: Sekretariatet for kvinneforskning.

Melin-Higgins, M., & Djerf-Pierre, M. (1998, July). *Networking in newsrooms: Journalist and gender cultures.* Paper presented at IAMCR, Glasgow, UK.

Mörtberg, C. (1997). *"Det beror på att man är kvinna..." Gränsvandrerskor formas och formar informationsteknologi* ["That depends on being a woman..." Women border crossers being formed by and forming information technology]. Luleå: Institutionen för arbetsvetenskap, Luleå tekniska universitet

Nordberg, K. (1993). Bakslag och barrikader. Historia och kön i medieforskningen [Backlashes and barricades. History and gender in media research]. In U. Carlsson (Ed.), *Nordisk forskning om kvinnor och medier* (pp. 201-227). Göteborg: Nordicom.

Petersson, O., Hermansson, J., Micheletti, M., & Westholm, A. (1996). *Demokrati och ledarskap* [Democracy and leadership]. Stockholm: SNS.

Robinson, G., & Saint-Jean, A. (1998). Canadian women journalists: The "other half" of the equation. In D. H. Weaver (Ed.), *The global journalist. News people around the world* (pp. 351-372). NJ: Hampton Press.

Sandstig, G. (2001). *Organisation och kön* [Organization and gender]. Göteborg: Institutionen för journalistik och masskommunikation, Göteborgs Universitet.

Savolainen, T. (1992). The representation of women and women issues. In T. Savolainen & H. Zilliacus-Tikkanen (Eds.), *Women in Finnish broadcasting* (pp. 24-38). Helsinki: Publications of the Finnish National Commission for Unesco.

Spears, G., Seydegart, K., & Gallagher, M. (2000). *Who makes the news? Global media monitoring project 2000.* London: The World Association for Christian Communication.

Steiner, L. (1998). Newsroom accounts for power at work. In C. Carter, G. Branston, & S. Allan (Eds.), *News, gender and power* (pp. 145-159). London & New York: Routledge.

Sundin, E. (1998). Genus i organisationer [Gender in organizations]. In B. Czarniawska (Ed.), *Organisationsteori på svenska* (pp. 233-256). Malmö: Liber.

van Zoonen, L. (1998a). One of the girls? The changing gender of journalism. In C. Carter, G. Branston , & S. Allan (Eds.), *News, gender and power* (pp. 47-70). London & New York: Routledge.

van Zoonen, L. (1998b). A professional, unreliable, heroic marionette (M/F). Structure, agency and subjectivity in contemporary journalisms. *European Journal of Cultural Studies, 1*(1), 123-143.

Zilliacus-Tikkanen, H. (1997). *Journalistikens essens i ett könsperspektiv* [The essence of journalism from a gender perspective]. Helsingfors: Rundradions jämställdhetskommitté.

6

Hanging in There: Women, Gender, and Newsroom Cultures in Africa

Aida Opoku-Mensah

Undertaking gender analyses in the African continent is a relatively new concept that began in 1994 when it became clear that development strategies had not adequately addressed women's access to and control over economic resources, and had failed to account for women's contributions to national economies (UNECA, 1998). Subsequently, gender analyses became a useful tool for different groups, particularly those working in civil society, although it is still a relatively new concept in the media and communication field. However, material on employment patterns in most parts of the continent is easily available. For example, in 1995 UNESCO showed how, on average, women account for only 8.4% of the most senior jobs in broadcast media management and 14.1% in the print media (AGI, 2000). Another study undertaken by the Federation of African Media Women of the Southern Africa Development Community (Opoku-Mensah & Makunike-Sibanda, 1999) on employment patterns of 37 media organizations in Malawi, Mozambique, Namibia, Swaziland, Tanzania, Zambia, and Zimbabwe, indicated that the majority of these institutions hire men for decision-making positions (e.g., editor/general manager). When women reach promotion, they usually rise up to the level of deputy editor. In addition, although 54% of responding organizations said they had at least one female on their management board, most had an average ratio of five men to two women. Forty-three percent had no female board member and 40% of organizations said they had both male and female on their boards, but again the average ratio was six men to two women.

WOMEN, GENDER, AND THE MEDIA IN AFRICA: CONSTRUCTING A FRAMEWORK

However, beyond the numbers, certain questions arise. How are social and traditional norms replicated in newsrooms and how do they define the power relations between female and male media workers? Are women free to pursue a career in journalism in the same way as men? Are women free to cover the same stories as men? These questions are useful in trying to determine the relationships that currently exist in newsrooms as well as determine how women journalists themselves feel about their roles and responsibilities.

It is against this background that this chapter focuses on women, gender, and newsroom cultures in Africa, examining and assessing the complexities that surround gender roles and responsibilities in societies. There are no real definitions of what constitutes gender relations within the context of African newsrooms because this is still an underdeveloped area of research. Consequently, any attempts at building knowledge based on research from multiple perspectives on the complex and multiple experiences of women in African media will contribute to the development of gender, women, and media studies that are currently underdeveloped in Africa. However, the University of Cape Town's African Gender Institute (AGI) supports indigenous studies that produce knowledge of gender relations in African contexts. AGI is creating a rich knowledge base on women's experiences, and on the complexity of gender relations with regard to production and reproduction.[1] This chapter attempts to capture the experiences of women journalists, relating these experiences to media operation and production. It intends to analyze the implications of "gendered" media and how this process of gendering becomes an aspect of social production that also recognizes men's experiences.

The examination of the relative positions of men and women in newsrooms and the division of roles, responsibilities, benefits, rights, power, and privilege have so far been anecdotal and have not been documented in any systematic way. The sociocultural factors that inhibit women in their professional lives as journalists have often not been discussed in relation to the power dynamics that exist in newsrooms across the continent. Through the testimonies of both women and men, journalists themselves, this chapter examines the persistence of the male–female divide and its translation into sociolegal and sociocultural media practice that produces a culture of discrimination and bias, characterized by inequity and inequality in all aspects of media work. This chapter concludes with recommendations for a paradigm shift in the field of journalism and the need to mainstream gender in media operations and institutions, in order to promote greater diversity.

---

[1]www.uct.ac.za.org/agi/newslet/voll/agiestab.htm

WOMEN IN THE AFRICAN MEDIA: IMAGES, VOICES, AND TEXTS

To understand the exact nature of relationships between men and women in newsrooms, it is important to understand the wider relationship between women and the media itself. The media's pervasive nature, and their impact on societies have far-reaching effects in supporting or undermining women' status in society. In a Nigerian study focusing on women from the northern and pre-dominantly Muslim city of Kano, Imam (1992) examined the images of women as presented in the broadcast media, which led her to the following conclusion:

> the media generally produce sexists images of women, presenting negative stereotypes and under-representing women. Both television and radio pro-grammes under-represented female characters and women's viewpoints. They present dominantly negative images of women, and put forward ideo-logical themes sanctioning women's control and subordination. In short, they broadcast significantly conservative ideologies which carry the mes-sage that women should acquiesce to men, strengthening and maintaining relations of gender subordination. (p. 83)

Imam's observation stems from socialist feminist thinking that locates the reproduction of gender and patriarchal values of the media within an ideological framework advanced by neo-Marxists such as Althusser and Gramsci. An illus-tration of this ideological construct can be seen in the following observation by a Nigerian female journalist:

> There had existed the erroneous impression that women in the arts, theatre, broadcasting and mass media are too assertive and wayward, not the right material for marriage, home-making and motherhood. To the African men-tality, this was abhorrent, and parents were known to have dissuaded their daughters from pursuing careers in the media. This attitude contributed to the small number of women in the early days of broadcasting, and may also have resulted in the slow pace of their advancement to managerial posi-tions, even though such ideas have changed with time. (Nwanko, 1996, p. 83)

Again, the role of women as seen by society is entrenched in patriarchal beliefs that restrict women to domesticity and to their reproductive roles. Such attitudes and beliefs are what has led to the need for mainstreaming gender in the media so as to create better perceptions of women's roles, positions, and conditions in society. Three leading UN agencies—UNDP, UNIFEM, and UNICEF—have been at the forefront of developing gender frameworks as ways to encourage countries to integrate gender awareness into their processes, institutions and practices, including the media. An evaluation of these frameworks, and their impact on African countries would serve as a useful resource for gender and media analysts alike.

According to the African Women's Media Center (AWMC), a study conducted by Margaret Gallagher in 1996 revealed that women appeared in just 19% of all news. In a 1999 online discussion sponsored by the United Nations Development Program, one journalist referred to the persistent negative representations of women in the media in her own country, Malawi. She noted that although more stories about women could be found in Malawian newspapers by 1997, these stories were seldom found on the front page. When they did occur on the front page, they focused on women as victims of rape or battering, or as recipients of government awards: however, stories about prostitution or rape treated these incidents as serious problems.[2]

NEWSROOM CULTURE IN AFRICA: FIGHTING A MIND SET?

There is a dearth of information and research on media and gender issues in Africa. I conducted a very modest study to verify the general belief that, in journalism, women often work in "hostile" working environments. Open-ended interviews with African media practitioners were conducted over a 4-week period with an equal number of women and men journalists ($N = 8$), on their experiences of working in newsrooms in five African countries (Ghana, Kenya, Zimbabwe, Lesotho, and Zambia). Additionally, an interview was conducted with a leading African communication scholar, Professor Alfred Opubor who is based in Harare, Zimababwe. (Opubor's immediate response to this interview was: "Where *are* the women in the newsrooms of Africa? Are they present? What positions do they hold? If they occupy junior positions and the culture of the newsrooms are hierarchical and undemocratic with an overlay of the cultural practices of the larger society, gender relations in the newsroom may be unhealthy.") Invitations to participate in the study were sent by e-mail to journalists in other countries (Nigeria, Uganda, Tanzania, Senegal, and South Africa) but generated a nil response.

Although the interviews generated rich qualitative data based on the perceptions of individual journalists toward issues of gender, women, and the media in Africa, this methodology is by no means the only effective or practical

---

[2]http://www.ecu.edu/african/sersas/Robins400.html)

way of originating data. However, as stated earlier, given the paucity of information on this subject on the African continent, this method certainly generated interesting insights into how some African journalists think about gender, women, and media. Given the scale of this exploring research it is not possible to make any precise and authoritative assessments on how women fare in African newsrooms, even though other research (Made, 2000) confirms the marginalization of female journalists in the African media. Certainly, the thoughts and feelings of journalists interviewed in the study could be the basis for further research and studies.

Codified and documented data on how attitudes hamper women's professional development, are not readily available, but the few women who are working in newsrooms report they are often confronted with a mindset based on the current social and traditional norms that prevail in many African societies. This mindset results in stereotypical attitudes that hamper women's professional development. Conversations with both male and female media practitioners mention the existence of the perception that women are the weaker sex, are poor performers, and lack depth.

WHAT MALE COLLEAGUES THINK AND SAY: THE SOCIOCULTURAL BAGGAGE

Despite the unavailability of detailed research on male attitudes toward female colleagues in newsrooms, the exploring interviews indicated that male reporters harbour stereotypical notions of women in general that derive from the wider society. They form the basis for male journalists' perceptions of female colleagues. In many African societies, there are clear demarcations when it comes to employment as the following comment from one of the interviewees makes clear: "Journalism was considered a male preserve and to this day the majority of African journalists are men" (Kwesi Gyan Appenteng, Editor, *African Topics* magazine in London).

A similar opinion was found in the interview with Pelekelo Liswaniso, a former news editor of the Zambia *Daily Mail* newspaper. Liswaniso stated the following:

> Editors treat stories on merit despite the sex of the authors. However, there is that salient compromise to strengthen the copy written by a female journalist because of the long-standing belief that their copy could be "weak." A prolific writer is usually a man and their stories are easily used for publication.

Statements like these reinforce stereotypical images of women reporters as incapable, infirm, and technically inferior to their male counterpart in newsrooms. Women are seen as capable of certain topics only. "Women shy away from political issues," said Blay-Kabral Amihere, a journalist, newspaper publisher, and diplomat. "They are comfortable with female topics—fashion, entertainment, and these days health issues." And, "Most of the leading writers on health, population etc. are women," observed another respondent. These opinions and observations by leading and senior male professionals may indicate perhaps one of the reasons why the content of African news stories does not reflect gender diversity. Female journalists fail to impact on the way news is produced, and in the words of Liswaniso "their ideas, aspirations, frustrations, fears, anxieties, vision and feelings are not adequately and effectively articulated in their stories, as compared to the interests of the men folk."

Some women journalists also seem to have accepted these notions as journalistic norms. During a media training program carried out several years ago for a group of men and women journalist in Africa, most participants claimed that they did not seek out women as sources of information because "women do not know anything about difficult topics like economics and technology" and, referring to women in rural areas, "they are illiterate" (Made, 2000, p. 2).

Jennifer Makunike-Sibanda, a journalist, and former controller of the Zimbabwe Broadcasting Corporation (ZBC), confirmed this notion and said: "In most cases women reporters made no difference to news reporting whatsoever and tended to behave like their male counterparts. Consequently, the news reports that came out of ZBC were either negative, reinforcing stereotypes, or gender blind. There were hardly any news reports to talk about which were engendered. The definition of news was seen as having a male perspective."

Many female media practitioners have consistently lamented the lack of women-centered reporting in the media. As they began to realize they can make a difference outside the mainstream media, they formed women's media associations in almost every country in Africa. In various African countries, there are numerous media projects run by women and for women, constituting interesting and innovative communication models. The Tanzania Media Women's Association (TAMWA) was formed by women from various media institutions in Tanzania who decided to get together and address the women's issues that their employers ignored. They produced radio programs targeted at women that achieved instant popularity (Alloo, 1995). TAMWA became one of the most innovative and energetic civil society groups in Tanzania. Many countries in Africa have similar organizations that can use media to advance the cause of women media professionals as well as women in the wider society. It is through such organizations that advocacy in promoting gender programs in media institutions can be achieved. It is also through such institutions that women can obtain formal or informal media training that is otherwise very difficult to access.

GENDER ROLES IN NEWSROOMS: UNEQUAL PARTNERSHIP?

In Africa, gender relations and interactions in newsrooms are shaped by societal and culturally defined roles witnessed in public and private spaces. Men dominate in newsrooms and are almost always in positions of authority as editors, managers, specialist, and staff reporters. Table 6.1 shows how poorly women feature in senior positions in the top three media organizations in Swaziland.

Women mostly hold lower positions compared to their male counterparts and are mainly reporters and/or feature writers usually accountable to male managers. In the three media organizations surveyed in Malawi (the *Nation* publications, the *Daily Times*, and the Malawi Broadcasting Corporation) 83.3% of senior reporters were men and only 16.6% were women. A survey on gender distribution and employment patterns conducted among 13 media organizations in Zimbabwe showed that men accounted for 79% of senior reporters, compared to 21% of women (Opoku-Mensah & Makunike-Sibanda 1999). In Mozambique, the contrast is even worse, where men constitute 98.6% of senior reporters (Opoku-Mensah & Makunike-Sibanda 1999).

Although there are virtually no reliable statistics and research available, anecdotal evidence suggests that male journalists most usually cover politics, economy, sports, agriculture and any specialized area such as trade, finance, or technology. Women are usually given issues such as health, education, lifestyle/social issues, and technology, which by many journalists are not considered as "hard-hitting." Some media employers have gender preferences for certain positions. In Tanzania, for example, the heads of media organizations who were surveyed reported no gender bias when it came to hiring producers, engineers and technical staff. But several less senior managers said they did

TABLE 6.1

Gender Profile of Senior Positions in Three Media Organizations in Swaziland

Category	Men	Women
General Manager	3	0
Deputy Managing Director	1	0
Board of Management	5	1
Board of Governors	7	1
Total	16	2

Note. From Opoku-Mensah and Makunike-Sibanda (1999).

have a gender preference for recruiting to these positions. Their reasons were that most women were either not qualified or did not perform as well as their male counterparts (Opoku-Mensah & Makunike-Sibanda, 1999). Although there is a minority of women who have broken "male" beats, these topics are still seen as male preserves used to climb the career ladder. The division of labor in newsrooms more or less relegates women to what is seen as their "place" as the following interviews illustrate:

> My experience in the newsroom was that some men exhibited a somewhat oppressive attitude toward their female colleagues, which undermined the self-confidence of women journalists. For example, attention would be given to a man's news idea and help given to polish up the concept, where-as a woman's idea would not be given much attention. When a woman is ambitious and sets professional goals for herself and starts to shine or suc-ceed, they simply conclude that you are sleeping your way to the top! You can't win as a woman working in an African newsroom. (*Etambuyu Anamela Gundersen, a former reporter and news reader for the Zambia National Broadcasting Corporation [ZNBC], currently based in Oslo, Norway, pursuing further studies in media*)

> The male reporter who is always in the company of high-level sources—politicians, economists, business leaders, policymakers, etc.—or who is the one always seen to be asking questions or talking in meetings, press confer-ences, is "viewed" as the one with the guts or stamina needed to make it in the profession. (*Patricia Made, director-general of the InterPress Service [IPS] based in Harare, Zimbabwe*)

Three out of five women journalists interviewed for this chapter have left the field of journalism and have either gone into civil society work or are pursu-ing further studies.

NEWSROOMS AS POLITICAL SPACES

The newsroom in many cases is also a political battleground where reporters compete for territory, power, and superiority. Thus, the strategic nature of news production constitutes a working context that is almost invariably defined by men, a context that men want to protect and maintain. This notion is reflected in the political space of the wider society, which is almost exclusively the preserve of men. According to Kwesi Gyan Appenteng, a Ghanaian journalist and editor, men prefer political reporting because it is macho and goes hand in hand with access to powerful political figures. Male journalists often tend to dominate this area of reporting. Consequently, gender equity is markedly absent in most

newsrooms because women have very little political clout. This view is supported by Gyan Appenteng, when he says, "Journalism in Africa is closely related
to control of the political space, which is again a male preserve. Taken together,
these conditions dictate the power structure in the newsroom as well."
Appenteng's statement is an interesting illustration of the theoretical notion that
perceives gender as an inherently unequal aspect of social relations, derived
from an unequal distribution of power (Marcelle, 2000).

Consequently, women are often marginalized in the newsroom and their
small number makes this easy: Few of the male respondents to this study had
any experience working for a female editor, although one man said: "I have a
limited experience of female editors in my own personal working life, but I
used to have a woman as my deputy at one newspaper and I don't think she did
her work differently from how a good male editor would have been required to
work." All the women in this study complained that even when they do hold
senior positions in the newsroom, they have a hard time getting men to take
instructions from them, a view that is replicated in other situations relating to
women and authority in Africa.

ACCESS TO RESOURCES

Another way of considering gender inequality in the newsroom is to look at
women and men's differential access to resources such as training and benefits.
From personal experience of newsroom environments, I would suggest that in
most newsrooms in Africa, men benefit more from training opportunities (for
both short- and long-term studies) than their female counterparts. Most media
establishments use the marital status of staff as the determining factors in ascertaining whether they deserve or are due for training. Many male editors appear
to believe that if a woman journalist is unmarried, she is not mature enough to
benefit from training. If she is married, she must think of her family first.

Part of the broader issue of gender inequality is women's poor access to
new technologies that further endangers their chances for participation in
employment or political networking (Robins, 2000). The current newsroom culture could potentially damage women's selfconfidence and downplay their contribution to journalism over time, especially given the advent of the information
revolution where media practice is becoming more computer-dependent. Huyer
(1999) found that "men are crowding out women's access to training in the new
technologies" (np).

Domestic circumstances can become a major stumbling block to women's
advancement in their journalism careers. During an Internet training workshop
for media practitioners organised by the Panos Institute's Southern Africa
regional office held in Lusaka, Zambia in 1997, only 5 out of 30 journalists
were women (Fagbemi & Ohiri-Aniche 1997). In fact, Panos had to make a

strong case to convince editors to send women reporters at all. Male editors' immediate reaction was that "if it is technology then we have to send a man." Other benefits that men receive over women include higher wages and access to other facilities such as loans for cars or even mortgages. Women's family responsibilities are often used against them: They are hardly ever assigned to work abroad—they have families and cannot be seen to leave them behind. This is not an issue when it comes to assigning the same trips to married men and in fact this then becomes a prestigious move for the male journalist.

SEXUAL HARASSMENT

Another factor that often characterizes and shapes working relations in African newsrooms is the rarely discussed problem of sexual harassment. This is often a sensitive and difficult issue for women to deal with. Many female journalists simply keep quiet about this for fear of reprisals from male colleagues and the media organisation. Consequently, evidence on the prevalence and nature of sexual harassment is often anecdotal and difficult to obtain, even though it is known that violence against women more generally is becoming more and more evident in African societies.

THE IMPACT OF DISCRIMINATION ON WOMEN JOURNALISTS

Being in a male-dominated environment also has certain cultural implications for both single and married women. Because of the social opprobrium that would be heaped on them by other members of society, their families, and partners if they fraternized with men, women often isolate themselves from their (male) colleagues. Men, however, will huddle together in the newsroom, go to lunch together to discuss stories, pick up news tips, and go off to bars after work. Women journalists and even those who become editors often find that they must work on their own and/or create different strategies for developing sources and staying in touch with what's going on.

> Women journalists are often very competent writers, editors, but how they project themselves is often the criterion used to determine whether journalists will make it in the profession and be promoted. A woman in a newsroom in Africa will not project herself in the same way [as a man] for fear that she will be viewed as 'too forward' or "aggressive," and, even "a loose woman" because she is always in the company of men. These are not viewed as "acceptable" characteristics or patterns of behaviour for a woman

journalist in Africa. So, while a woman may be quite competent and capable in her work, she will not project this openly in a style that suggests "tough, hard-hitting journalist". This attitude undermines right form the start the relationship between men and women in the newsroom, with some women making the sacrifice of wanting to stay back and stay in her place to survive. (Made, 2000, p. 3)

Although figures are scarce, many women tend to leave the profession because they carry the burden of cultural and social expectations, dictating certain behavior and patterns of socializing with men, which often conflict with their professional work as journalists. As a result, they often come across as shy and not tough enough to handle the work, when in fact they are only acting out in the newsroom the same social behavior required of them elsewhere in society—be it in the home or other public institutions. According to Gyan Appenteng, "male journalists usually stayed late and then went out for a drink while the women went home earlier to take care of their families. These conventions therefore determined the networks that were formed and operated at work."

The information age is creating different outlets for media women, providing them with opportunities for better and more effective networking. An example of this is a team of international women journalists who will help launch the "Virtual Newsroom", a pioneering project linking women journalists and activists in four African countries (Zimababwe, Ghana, Kenya, and Uganda). The women will work remotely for 1 year, using British Council offices and specially adapted hardware and software donated by IBM. The aim of this project is to increase the impact of journalists writing on issues of particular importance to Africa.

CONCLUSIONS

A media environment, which allows women equal opportunities to men, requires a paradigm shift in Africa's media culture. This will take time and can only happen if and when those who control the news media are ready and willing to share power with their female counterparts—if they are willing to work together to their mutual benefit. This shift has to be comprehensive, involving the structures, content and operations of media establishments, all of which need to be engendered.

In the short to medium term, gender-awareness training for news reporters should be introduced as widely as possible. Most journalists (both male and female) in Africa have not been trained to incorporate gender perspectives into their reporting. Yet, it is often taken for granted that journalists are able to cover issues affecting women in a sensitive and subtle way. Such a change can only be achieved by exposing journalists to gender perspectives and encouraging them, over time, to appreciate this new way of thinking. The Africa Bureau of InterPress Service (IPS), which is a global news agency committed to development information, has introduced a series of gender training programmes for news media staff in Southern Africa. A manual has been produced on gender violence which was launched in June 2000 with UNIFEM in New York at the Beijing+5 Review Meeting. IPS also runs workshops for radio journalists on gender and human rights, as well as a news bulletin on the same issue, distributed to development practitioners and decision makers throughout Africa. Such strategies should be supported by other media institutions in Africa, and an evaluation on the impact of such training for reporters would contribute important data to this debate.

Incorporating gender perspectives into journalism practice—investigating how men and women affect and are affected by economic, political, social, legal and cultural events and processes—would also encourage better working relationships between women and men reporters. Media organizations should be encouraged to develop gender policies to assist them in mainstreaming gender into their structures and operations. One way this can be done is by "gender profiling" of media organisations: assessing whether they have gender policies, whether there is gender equity in recruitment, promotions, and so on. In this way, gender does not just become an aspect of reporting but an integral part of media institutions themselves. Mainstreaming gender in media and journalism courses, particularly in publications would also prove useful in the long run.

AFRICA GENDER AND MEDIA INITIATIVE

This initiative advocates the fair representation of women and increased coverage of gender issues in the mainstream media in Africa, and consists of three partners: Inter Press Service, a global development news agency, The African Women and Child Feature Service, based in Nairobi, and Gender Links, a Southern African Organization committed to giving effect to the Southern African Development Community (SADC) Declaration on Gender and Development.

This is a laudable initiative and one that others must follow. As Ms Thenjiwe Mtintso, Chairperson of the Gender Links Board says: *"Gender in media is an uncharted path—exciting but also frightening. Frightening because when you dare to challenge the lion in its den, you are likely to encounter extreme difficulties."*

The debate on gender relations in African newsrooms as advanced in this chapter, is part of a wider media and gender discourse that is still in its infancy in Africa. However, the more experiences that are shared and recorded, the more knowledge in this area will be advanced which, in turn, could generate useful theories in this particular field. It is hoped that various groups interested in this area of work will undertake much needed research and develop studies that can shed more light on women's experiences within media establishments and tease out men's experiences in order to provide a greater understanding of gender dynamics.

REFERENCES

AGI/ (2000). Building knowledge for gender equity in African contexts. Cape Town, South Africa: African Gender Institute/University of Cape Town. URL (consulted August 2001): www.uct.ac.sa/org/agi/newslet/vol1/agiestab.htm.

Alloo, F. (1995). Using IT as a mobilising force: The case of the Tanzania Media Women's Association (TAMWA). In S. Mitter & S. Rowbotham (Eds.), *Women encounter technology* (pp. 303-313). London: Routledge/UNU.

AWMC. (2000). *Women meeting the challenge: A handbook for media leadership.* African Women's Media Centre (AWMC). URL (consulted August 2001): www.awmc.com/Leaders/obstacle.htm.

Fagbemi, A.O., & Ohiri-Aniche, C. (Eds.). (1997). *National gender training manual: Module 1.* Lagos: UNDP/UNIFEM/UNICEF.

Gallagher, M. (1996). Cited in IWMF (2001, *[Leading] in a different language: Will women change the news media?]* New York, IWMF.

Huyer, S. (1999). Supporting women's use of information technologies for sustainable development. IDRC, URL (consulted November 2001): http://www.idrc.ca/index.html).

Imam, A. (1992). *Women and the mass media in Africa.* Paris: UNESCO.

IWMF. (2001). Leading in a different language: Will women change the news media? International Women's Media Foundation (IWMF). URL (consulted August 2001): www.iwmf.org/resources/lr.htm.

Made, P. (2000). Gender and the media: Tapping into a voice that has been silenced. In F. Banda (Ed.), *Signposts on the superhighway: African gender.* Lusaka: Panos Southern Africa.

Marcelle, G. M. (2000). *Transforming information and communication technologies for gender equality* (Gender in Development Monograph Series #9). New York: UNDP.

Nwanko, N. (1996). *Gender equality in Nigerian politics.* Lagos: Deutchetz Publishers.

Opoku-Mensah, A., & Makunike-Sibanda, J. (Eds.). (1999). *Study on employment patterns in media organisation in the Southern Africa region.* Harare: Friedrich Ebert Stiftung/UNESCO/Federation of African Media Women-SADC.

Robins, M. B. (2000). *Africa's women/Africa's women journalists: Critical perspectives on internet initiatives.* West Carolina University, USA. URL (consulted November 2001): www.ecu.edu/african/sersas/Robins400.html#REF8.

UNECA (1998). *Gender responsive development in Africa: Compendium of good practice.* Addis Ababa: United Nations Economic Commission for Africa.

7

Organizational Factors in the Radio Newsroom: Cause for Hope or Despair?

Aliza Lavie

The study of gender and media focuses on two central questions: First, whether gender[1] affects media products (i.e., can differences be identified in the content of the products of male and female media professionals holding similar positions?). Second, what is the cause and source of these differences or the absence thereof? Some researchers (e.g., van Zoonen, 1994; Weaver & Wilhoit, 1996) have claimed that even if biological differentiation dictates separate patterns of reasoning and functioning, socialization processes obliterate such gender-based differences as women adopt conventionally accepted patterns of reasoning and behavior in the workplace (van Zoonen, 1994). Hitherto, the discussion of these issues has been essentially theoretical and the few empirical studies that have been conducted, are unable to provide conclusive answers to either approach.

This chapter focuses on the second aforementioned question and specifically, on the differential effect of the work environment (the radio newsroom) on patterns of reasoning, and behavior of men and women employed in public radio newsrooms in Israel. The main claim is that work environments reproduce the patterns of gender relationships such as are prevalent in the wider society, impacting women's perceptions of their image, their professional abilities and their experience with gender-based discrimination. In other words, through the

---

[1]The definition of the term *sex* is anchored in the biological distinction between male and female, originating in their chromosomal differences. In contrast, gender expresses the sociocultural meaning ascribed to the biological categories of male and female. The definitions of male and female, in terms of gender, are products of the social environment.

social practices of professionals, the work environment structures the patterns of reasoning and behavior of men and women otherwise. This chapter is based on findings of a study conducted among a population of male and female news editors in two national public radio stations in Israel—The Voice of Israel and Israel Defense Forces (IDF) Radio, which indicate a gender effect.[2]

Pauline Fredrick, seen by some as a pioneer in radio journalism by women in the United States, began her work on the NBC radio station in 1939, by interviewing the Czechoslovak ambassador's wife, immediately following the Nazi invasion of Czechoslovakia (Bliss, 1991). Returning to the United States after having covered numerous and diverse topics overseas and gaining considerable professional experience and expertise, Fredrick discovered that being a radio journalist in her own homeland was not an easy option. Although she was offered full-time employment, her job included covering such topics as how to catch a husband or how to select the best nylon stocking.[3] After many battles, she eventually won the coveted position of journalist for UN affairs, which she filled for 21 years, with marked success and many achievements (Hosley & Yamada, 1987).

Struggles, disappointments, discrimination, rejections, audacity, defeats, and victories were all a part of Fredrick's (and probably other women's) professional life. In many ways, her story is similar to that of women in more recent times, who have attempted to enter the workplace generally and the field of journalism in particular. In the five decades since Fredrick attained her own professional success, many women have secured journalistic positions in the press and broadcast media in most of the world, although few hold senior positions.

An intriguing question has concerned many researchers worldwide: Is there evidence of distinct patterns of work and media products between male and female journalists? In other words, is gender implicated in the nature of journalistic practice and its products? This chapter focuses on work practices in Israel, with the primary claim that such a gender effect, which can be found in the work environment of newsrooms of public national radio stations, is confirmed by both objective and subjective data. The findings indicate that, through its

---

[2]This chapter is based on findings of a doctoral thesis that focused on the investigation of the claim, *inter alia*, that women's entry into media organizations is expected to change the structuring of the media agenda and affect traditional media products. The dissertation was completed under the guidance of Professor S. Leiman-Wiltzig and Dr. D. Goren of the Department of Political Studies (Public Communication Progarm) at Bar-Ilan University, Israel. I also wish to express my gratitude to my colleague, Dr. Yehiel Limor of Tel-Aviv University, for his helpful comments.

[3]Bliss (1991) used the category "women's news" to explain the prevalent theory regarding the division of news items into categories appropriate for coverage by women and men.

implicit social practices, the radio newsroom work environment positions female and male editors differently. Moreover, findings suggest that the existing process of information selection and rating reinforces the influence of male editors who, by virtue of their predominance in senior positions, have the authority to influence the media agenda and the treatment of these issues.

Radio's unique nature as a continuous, portable and highly accessible medium accounts for its dominance over other media, in terms of the speed at which issues are placed on the public agenda, its ability to track such issues continuously over time and contribute to the assimilation of relevant information by its listeners. In Israel, radio attracts particularly high ratings and plays a uniquely important part in the leisure activities of the population (Katz, Yanovzki, & Yalin, 2000), reflecting its special position in shaping the public news agenda. However, in contrast to other media, such as the press or television, radio has not been afforded sufficient research attention, either in Israel or worldwide and this paper aims to make a contribution to this small but growing literature.

BACKGROUND

The distinction between men and women is, arguably, a product of social construction (Acker, 1990), mediated by normative social contexts, rather than an inevitable and fixed biological given. Lorber (1994) suggested we should examine gender as a "social institution" that utilizes legal, scientific, and social value systems as ways by which to legitimize gender differences and gender-based segmentation also signifies power relations (Scott, 1990). Gender not only reflects human reasoning and behavior, but also creates an unequal stratification of power, wealth, and rights in society. Adopting the spirit of Rakow's (1986) approach, this chapter explores the ways (if any) in which the work environment informs the working identity of men and women, rather than focusing on specific attributes as reflections of gender-based divisions. The examination of the structure of organizations highlights a process of segregation in the labor market, by which occupations are not equally accessible by different social groups. A gender-based division of the workplace is one of many social practices that constitute arenas where gender-reproducing power relations are constructed and perpetuated (Gam & Pringle, 1983).

Researchers identify occupational segregation in occupations in which the ratio of men and women deviates from their respective ratios in the labor market. Employing this definition, occupations may be classified as *feminine, masculine,* or *mixed.*[4] For example, women are overrepresented in the service sector

---

[4]Definitions of *feminine, masculine* and *mixed* occupations are based on calculations by Cohen, Bachar, and Raijwan (1987).

and in clerical, semi-professional occupations, which may thus be classified as female occupations. The underrepresentation of women in managerial, industrial and political occupations is also well-documented (e.g., Charles, 1992; Herzog, 1994; Izraeli, 1997; Marini & Brinton, 1984; Oppenheimer, 1970).

In Israel in the late 1950s, women constituted only 9.3% of all journalists on Israel's four largest, leading daily newspapers (*Yediot Aharonot, Ma'ariv, Ha'aretz,* and *Jerusalem Post*), although they constituted 27% of the entire Israeli labor market (Kop, 2000). Four decades later, this figure blossomed to 37% in some of these newspapers (Caspi & Limor, 1999), although still falling short of women's 46% share of the labor market (Kop, 2000). Ostensibly, journalism has undergone a fundamental transformation, from a masculine profession to one in which feminization has gained some ground. Yet, although an awareness of segregation has led to various local attempts to rectify the imbalance,[5] the entry of women into senior positions is taking place at an extremely slow rate. Consequently, despite indications of feminization and progress, women remain underrepresented in senior editorial and managerial positions in the world of Israeli journalism (Lachover, 2000), compared to their relative presence in the field. For example, in the Israeli Public Broadcasting Authority, the percentage of women holding a position as section head is about half of that of men. Male dominance is also prevalent among department heads (80%) and division heads (90%) (Liran-Alper, 2000). Recent figures from studies elsewhere in the West also indicate hierarchical segregation (i.e., that women remain inadequately represented in senior and key positions in the world of the media in general, Beasley, 1993; Limor & Caspi, 1994; van Zoonen, 1988) and in news, in particular (Beasley, 1997; Gallagher, 1992; Oring, 1995; Walsh-Childers, 1996).

Additionally, organizations may also reflect gender-based functional segregation, which is created when men and women perform identical functional roles and tasks although they are formally assigned different titles and job descriptions. Functional segregation in the workplace channels men and women into different roles, specific types of roles and, consequently, to receive differential rewards and entitlements, develop different career paths and, in most cases, enjoy distinct levels of autonomy and responsibility (Bielby & Baron,

---

[5]For example, in the United States, a law on equal opportunities in the workplace was passed in 1972. A U.S. Supreme Court ruling expanded this concept by supporting affirmative actions for various minorities (including women and Blacks). A similar trend has also been evident in Israel in recent years: In 1992, an equal opportunities in the workplace was passed, while in 1994, the Supreme Court rules that the appointment of directors in public corporations requires a balance of sexes (The Women's Lobby in Israel vs. the State of Israel and others, 453-94/4, section 5, page 01). This ruling led to a large increase in the proportion of female directors in this sector. Additionally, the Supreme Court recently instructed the Air Force to accept women as pilot trainees during their military service.

1986; Reskin, 1988). Evidence of this structural compartmentalization may justify rethinking of an assessment of feminization, which is based on segregation definitions developed in the late 1970s.[6] Such an assessment based exclusively on women's presence in the labor market, is a partial, albeit essential, reflection of the feminization process in work environments. An in-depth examination of women's status requires that we delve beneath the surface, to identify and assess the less visible elements of gender-based segregation (i.e., hierarchical and functional segregation). Indeed, the most powerful instrument in preserving the hegemony of gender ideology is the fact of its invisibility (Gramsci, 1971).

METHODOLOGY

The aim of this chapter was to examine if and how the work environment, through the social practices of radio professionals, structures the patterns of reasoning and behavior of men and women differently and how patterns of gender behavior that are prevalent in the wider society are reproduced in newsrooms, influencing women's perceptions of their image, professional abilities, and their experience of gender-based discrimination. Focusing on an examination of gender in the radio newsroom is directly related to the significance of the medium as a social technology and the extensive role it plays in the leisure activities of the Israeli public (Katz et al., 2000). According to Israeli Advertisers' Association figures (1997), newscasts attract especially high audiences in Israel. Newscasts and current events programs on IDF Radio and The Voice of Israel attract ratings of 18.7% and 24% and are ranked higher than other program categories. Radio's popularity stems not only from the availability and accessibility of the medium, but also reflects a constant high demand on the part of the Israeli population for newscasts and up-to-date information, especially in light of the precarious national security situation that has blighted the country in recent years.

Three main models of radio stations operate in Israel: public national channels, regional radio stations and illegal ("pirate") radio stations (Limor, 1998). The first group of stations includes the two leading national radio stations: The Voice of Israel and IDF Radio. The Voice of Israel is part of the Public Broadcasting Authority whose operations are based on the Broadcasting Authority Act. In contrast, as a station owned by the army, IDF Radio is subject to the Broadcasting Authority Act 1965 Section 48(b) and additionally to General Staff provisions and regulations.

---

[6]The number of male managers in the Israeli labour force is five times the number of female managers. In the 20-year period from 1975 to 1995, the proportion of women in the labor market rose by 10% (from 33% to 43%), whereas the proportion of female managers increased by 12%, from 7% to 19% (Izraeli, 1997).

The global feminization process experienced in the media generally has not skipped over radio news broadcasting in Israel, which affords us an opportunity to examine the effect of gender from two different perspectives. First, women's organizational status compared to that of men; second, the subjects' subjective perceptions of their respective organizational status and power. To this end, two particular radio stations were chosen as the focus of this study: The Voice of Israel and IDF Radio. Within those organizations, the group of male and female editors of news programs and newscasts were selected as the sample base. The population of editors included media professionals performing editorial tasks in newscasts and current event programs production.

Preliminary observations of newscasts and current affairs program production at The Voice of Israel and IDF Radio in this study indicated a certain fluidity in employees' job descriptions. In some cases, news broadcasters held the official title of "editor," whereas editors in practice worked under the official job description of "producer."[7] Consequently, included in the study population were employees who were active participants in the editorial process, whether or not their official title was "editor" or "producer." Thus, inclusion in the study population was based on a functional rather than an official job description and encompassed the majority (approximately 80%) of professionals actively involved in the editorial processes of newscast and current events program production between January 1997 and January 1999. As such, the study population may be confidently considered to be representative of the total population of female and male editors of these programs on The Voice of Israel and IDF Radio.

Data collection was conducted in three phases: observations, a questionnaire-based survey, and in-depth interviews of female and male editors at the two radio stations. Sixty observations of the news-making process, in which the author was a passive observer, were conducted between September 1997 and September 1998 in the newsrooms of both ratio stations. Each observation tracked the production of a single newscast, from preproduction to the postbroadcast summary meeting. Fifty questionnaires were distributed, of which 41 were completed and returned by January 1998.[8] Individual interviews were conducted in two stages: both during the observation stage (1997-1998) and subsequent to the preliminary analysis of the questionnaires (2000-2001). A specific questionnaire comprising open and closed questions in four sections was

---

[7]No single instance existed of a male editor who held an official title of "producer."

[8]The population of editors is comprised of 41 subjects. Ten additional editors from both radio stations refused to complete the questionnaire, or provided extremely incomplete responses that necessitated their elimination from the sample. Consequently, the present study sample comprises approximately 80% of the total population of news and current events editors at both radio stations.

designed for this study, informed by my earlier work on agenda setting by female and male editors in the Israeli press (Lavie, 1997) with the aim of tapping into the subjects' professional behaviors, their cultural world and perceptions of subjects' own self-image and professional competency.[9] Based on initial observations of subjects' hesitation to disclose personal data, and in light of the fact that the type of variables examined in this study is most effectively gleaned from subjects' direct declarative statements rather than mediated and indirect information, the questionnaires were anonymous and included no material that could identify the respondents.

To obtain demographic data, the first section of the questionnaire elicited information on personal and work-related details (gender, age, education, origin, family status, number of children; tenure, frequency of editing, salary). The second section of the questionnaire focused on professional attributes, including work habits, professional status, self-concept, daily news media consumption habits, level of satisfaction in present place of employment, and continuity of journalistic work (over time and in previous positions).[10] In addition, subjects ranked simulated headlines according to their perceived newsworthiness. Of the questionnaire respondents, 23 were male and 18 were female (see Table 7.1).

TABLE 7.1

Study Population of Editors by Gender and Organization

	Women (N = 18)	Men (N = 23)	Total (N = 41)
The Voice of Israel	19 (38.4%)	16 (61.5%)	26 (63.4%)
IDF Radio	8 (53.3%)	7 (46.7%)	15 (36.6%)

---

[9]The questionnaire was comprised of four sections, the responses to two of which are analyzed and presented here.

[10]Questions referred to present job description, previous job description, news journalism practices, and advocacy of newsworthy items. Subjects articulated their personal opinions to open-ended questions.

FINDINGS

Gender and Decision Making

This chapter discusses the findings relating to the following four variables, based on all three methods of data collection: formal job description, occupational history, professional specialization and self-image, in terms of evidence of a gender difference

Table 7.2 below indicates that at The Voice of Israel, 75% of the men engaged in news-related decision making, compared to 30% of the women, held the job description of editor. Almost half (40%) of the women engaged in news-related decision making held the job description of producer, a lesser position in the organizational hierarchy. The numerous observations conducted at The Voice of Israel indicated a consistent routine, in which women, who held the formal title of producer, were engaged in editorial practice. This is evidenced by the following statement of a female editor at The Voice of Israel: "I am defined as a producer, but in practice, I function as an editor as well. For example, this evening, I am supposed to edit the midnight newscast. Now that you mention it, I think that I really don't know why I am not defined as an editor on the work schedule!" (personal interview, female producer/editor, The Voice of Israel, February 12, 2001).

Although radio news production is mainly a team effort, men and women participating in this effort play significantly different roles, as a result of differences in their formal positions within the organizational hierarchy, creating different social and material rewards. The most important activity in the newsroom is journalistic practice, whereas the more organizational aspects of the job—important in themselves—are, by definition, more of a "housekeeping" nature (Izraeli, 1999). At the heart of news journalism are editors who select and classify news items, whereas producers coordinate administrative elements, which support news collection and production. The organizational structure at The Voice of Israel perpetuated different formal job descriptions despite their inconsistency with actual practice—to the detriment of women. A different picture comes to light from the IDF Radio data (see Table 7.3). Noteworthy is the fact that no woman at IDF Radio held the title of "producer" while performing editorial tasks. At this station, no gender-based effect was found in the correlation between formal and practical engagement. The assignment of different roles to individuals performing similar tasks was not found to be gender-based. Women and men held the same job descriptions and formal titles and filled the same roles in practice.

TABLE 7.2

Role Definitions: The Voice of Israel

Role	Women	Men	Total
Editor	3 (30%)	12 (75%)	15 (58%)
Presenter	1 (10%)	1 (6.3%)	2 (7.7%)
Producer	4 (40%)	-	4 (15.4%)
Other	2 (20%)	3 (18.8%)	5 (12.2%)
Total	10 (100%)	16 (100%)	26 (100%)

TABLE 7.3

Role Definition: IDF Radio

Role	Women	Men	Total
Editor	2 (25%)	5 (71.4%)	7 (46.6%)
Presenter	2 (25%)	2 (28.5%)	4 (26.6%)
Producer	3 (37.5)	0	3 (20%)
Other	1 (12.5%)	0	1 (6.6%)
Total	8 (100%)	7 (100%)	15 (100%)

Career Patterns

In terms of occupational history, at The Voice of Israel, almost half (46.7%) of all male editors had reached their current position in the newsroom after previously working as field reporters, 33.3% had experience in editing prior to their present position, 6.7% were former anchormen, and 13.4% came to editing after a different experience or had no prior experience. At The Voice of Israel, only 30% of the female editors had previous experience as reporters, 40% of the female editors (yet not a single male editor!), attained their present position after working in production, 10% of the women noted previous experience in editing, whereas 20% had no prior experience. In contrast, at IDF Radio, no gender-based difference in the subjects' occupation history was indicated. One implication is that inequality is rooted in the structures, processes and formal job descriptions at The Voice of Israel (i.e., the deep-seated traditional structure dominated by masculine principles; Kanter, 1977). The traditional journalistic career path from reporter to editor is more clearly identified with males than with females, with the latter channelled to production jobs early in their careers.

An additional aspect examined was the prevalence of specialization in news coverage. No women, yet more than half (62.5%) of all male subjects at The Voice of Israel covered topics and areas that closely related to their formal education or other proven experience. Women generally covered random and incidental events. In contrast, the situation at IDF Radio indicated no gender effect in this dimension ("specialization") and "coverage of general events" was not unequally assigned to either gender.

Power and Influence

In addition to questions concerning their status at work, one section of the questionnaires and interviews was devoted to respondents' feelings as members of their organizations and their self-perception in terms of their influence on organizational conceptions of newsworthiness. The central question dealt with the respondents' ability to bring to broadcast an issue that they personally perceived to be interesting and newsworthy. At The Voice of Israel, a noteworthy difference was found between the perceived influence of male and female editors on the content of newscasts, in terms of item newsworthiness, while responses from the IDF Radio population did not indicate any gender-based differences in self-perception or perceived ability to influence the agenda. Among The Voice of Israel editors, one third of the male subjects and not a single female editor attested to their ability to broadcast items they perceived as newsworthy. The following testimony reflects the prevalent feeling of a female editor at The Voice of Israel: "If the issue is consistent with the conventional agenda, no problem exists, but if you want to promote other issues or inform the public of information about topics which you personally feel are important, you can for-get about doing that on the news. Or, you can try your luck on other programs" (personal interview, The Voice of Israel, February 14, 2001).

The subjects were also asked: "When you have an excellent idea for cover-age and a follow-up, how frequently are you successfully able to put it on the air?" Responses reinforced a gender-based discrepancy in subjects' profession-al-personal self-perception in terms of their success in putting issues on the air or placing issues on the media agenda. Whereas 81.8% of all male editors felt that they were "frequently" or "constantly" able to put issues on air, only 41.2% of the female editors believed they held a similar measure of power. The gen-der-based discrepancy was even more striking when subjects were compared in terms of their perceived "constant" influence: Whereas almost one third of the male editors felt that they were "constantly" able to put issues of their choice on air, only a single female editor, employed at The Voice of Israel, felt that she had a similar impact on the agenda. At IDF Radio, no gender effect was found in this regard.

Gender and Career Paths

Indirectly related to the above four variables under investigation was an inter-esting finding concerning subjects' experience of gender-based prejudice and discrimination at work. Whereas 60% of women at The Voice of Israel reported having witnessed nonpromotion due to gender, 81% of the men did not report having witnessed any similar phenomenon. The following testimonies of female editors at The Voice of Israel reflect the current situation at the radio station: "The feminization at The Voice of Israel is only superficial. Even when it appears that more women function as editors, journalists and professionals, all the managers are still men. Even when women are at the front line, they still function in a masculine institution, where men set the rules" (personal inter-view, female editor, The Voice of Israel, February 21, 2001). And again, "Everybody knows that radio professionals are underpaid. Managers try to pro-vide sources of supplementary income by referring employees to public speak-ing engagements, guest lectures, part-time jobs as course instructors or execu-tive positions at high profile radio stations. But, usually, the guys know about all this stuff ahead of us" (personal interview, female editor, The Voice of Israel, March 10, 2001). In contrast, interviewees at IDF Radio reflected no similar gender-effect differences. Both men and women reported having received an equal opportunity at IDF Radio (in terms of gender) and their career paths were not perceived to be influenced by their gender.

The findings presented here indicate a significant difference between staff at each of the two radio stations. While findings relating to The Voice of Israel point to a clear gender effect in all the areas under examination, findings relat-ing to IDF Radio indicate a general absence of a gender effect. The ostensible significant female presence in The Voice of Israel newsroom, which almost reflects women's representation in the wider workforce,[11] appears to suggest the successful feminization of the newsroom. However, a more meticulous and careful examination of organizational employment patterns still indicate professional segregation that is gender-determined (Izraeli, 1999; Reskin & Roos, 1990). The metaphor of a "glass ceiling" remains appropriate to describe the existing situation, at least in relation to senior editorial positions. An occupational analysis of newsroom employees at The Voice of Israel indicates that woman who are substantively engaged in news-related decision making, typically work under the professional definitions of "news producer." Moreover, consistent with the perspective of "queuing" theory,[12] in contrast to editorial positions perceived to be part of professional career development for men, women's promotion to editorial positions was more likely to be circumstantial and the result of the arbitrary needs of the organisation and, especially, a lack of suitable men to choose. Consequently, women and men receive differential rights and rewards, are diverted into different career paths and in some cases, attain different levels of autonomy and responsibility (Reskin & Roos, 1990).

However, the perspectives from interviewees at IDF Radio findings stood in contrast to the prominent gender-based effect indicated by the findings of The Voice of Israel population. The status and formal job descriptions of female and male editors at IDF Radio were not influenced by gender, a fact expressed by the similar numbers of men and women engaged in news-related activities, the similarity of their formal job descriptions and their previous professional experience. An examination of women's status in each of the elements of the new production process indicates the typicality of an egalitarian working environment.

Age Variables and Working Experience

In principle, it is possible to consider age differences as an important reason for any differences between the two populations of editors, including gender-based differences. Almost a complete generation divides the two populations: The

---

[11]Currently 43% of the labor force in Israel.

[12]Reskin and Roos (1990) conceptualized segregation of the labor market based on the Queue Theory. Using this metaphor, they explained that segregation is an outcome of two concurrent processes in the labor market: the first is the formation of a labor market queue that sorts workers based on their attractiveness for employers. At the head of this queue are white males. The second process is the formation of a professional queue, which arranges professions in terms of their attractiveness for employers. This queue is headed by professions to which the most prestige and income is attributed. In a process of accommodation, employers select workers from the highest possible position in the labor market queue, with the result that such workers receive the best possible jobs available to them.

average age of staff at The Voice of Israel is 47 compared to an average age of 28 at IDF Radio. Similarly, professional media experience was very different, with an average of 24 years at The Voice of Israel compared to only 8 years at IDF Radio. There were also significant differences in terms of individual specialization in news and current events in the organization, with an average of 13 years at The Voice of Israel compared to 2.5 years at IDF Radio. Most employees at The Voice of Israel began their employment in the media prior to second wave feminism in the mid-1970s, when the first efforts to use feminism as a social category bore fruit, a full decade after the United States (Aloni, 1976; Izraeli, 1984; Shelef et al., 1975). Consequently, it may be assumed that social developments since then have affected hierarchical structures and limited their propensity for perpetuation (Maor, 1997). IDF Radio employees entered the media in general and the area of current events and news in particular, after feminist ideologies had filtered through to various social strata and made their mark on social life. Nonetheless, as with other structural shifts, women's status in Israeli society and in the workplace was slow to change. So although the population of female and male editors at The Voice of Israel is different from their counterparts at IDF Radio, and the latter may have assimilated the values of gender equality more thoroughly during their own personal and professional development, the extent to which either radio station, at an organisation level, have seen a shift in culture, is a little less clearcut.

The Salience of Organization and Structure

Despite the simple appeal of the age variable—and although it provides a partial explanation—it cannot be considered as the exclusive source of the intergroup differences. The totality of findings that encompass objective organizational and subjective elements requires a more complex interpretation, in which the age variable is only one, and not necessarily the primary one. Rather, the findings suggest that organizational attributes may be more important factors in structuring gender differences. The significance of the organization on the practice of journalism and media products, compared to the effect of personal attributes (of which age is one) has been documented in a number of studies examining work in the newsroom. For example, in the study conducted by Dimmick and Coit (1982), of the nine factors ranked by impact on journalistic practice, "the organization" was placed fourth, whereas personal attributes were considered the least influential of all nine factors, ranked even lower than interorganizational factors that were ranked sixth. It is interesting to note that Breed (1955), in a much earlier study, identified the significance of interpersonal behavior and group dynamics in the consolidation of professional work patterns (de Bruin, 2000).

This may hint at the role of organizational policy in shaping professional decisions in the newsroom that were found in this study—see later. Later studies have also noted that journalists and journalistic practice are especially influenced by "factors in the organisational environment" (Weaver & Wilhoit, 1996, pp. 190-191), in their specific workplaces in general, and in the newsroom, in particular. Bergen (1991, cited by Weaver & Wilhoit, 1996), too, found that organizational factors such as income, seniority, type of media, nature of audience, ownership of media, and so on, affect journalists' work more than their own individual attributes such as age, gender, and education. The impact of organizational policy, especially in commercially oriented media organizations operating in a market economy, was also extensively discussed by other researchers exploring the political economy of media, such as Golding and Murdock (1991) and Herman and Chomsky (1988), who went so far as to define workers as the proletariat whose actions and reasoning are completely dictated by owners and managers.

DISCUSSION

The findings from this study suggest the need to identify the organizational factors that influence, or may create, gender-based differences in perceptions, attitudes, and professional practice among female and male editors involved in newscasts and current events programs. Although an integrated study of gender and organizational culture is not an easy task (Gherardi, 1995), we are encouraged to examine both formal and informal social practices (de Bruin, 2000), organizational history and tradition and the individuals employed in media organizations (Mitchell, 2000). The Voice of Israel and IDF Radio have different histories, traditions, and structures. To what extent are these differences in organisational provenance implicated in the perspectives of the stations' staffs? The Voice of Israel is part of a civilian umbrella organization, the Public Broadcasting Authority, whereas IDF Radio is a military organization, subject to the military authorities and the Ministry of Defence. These two different work environments are structured differently and have developed different patterns of work and behavior. A discussion of some organizational-based factors that may be part of the reason for gender-based differences in perspective and practice between The Voice of Israel and IDF Radio staff is set out next.

Organizational History

Although The Voice of Israel began its operations with the establishment of statehood in 1948, its roots are planted firmly in the British radio service, The Voice of Jerusalem, which had begun broadcasting some 14 years earlier. News and current affairs coverage were among its key features from its inception. IDF Radio began its own broadcasting in 1950, yet only after the October War of 1973 did it begin to broadcast non-military newscasts (Caspi & Limor, 1999;

Limor, 1974). The military radio continued to broadcast the news from within The Voice of Israel, but added its own programs late at night as well as half-hour news flashes during the day. The ties with The Voice of Israel were finally severed in the 1990s as IDF Radio began to provide its own independent news bulletins on the hour, opposite The Voice of Israel hourly broadcasts.

Work patterns and broadcast structure at The Voice of Israel, including the field of news coverage, are rooted in a traditional structure, the origins of which can be traced back to the BBC (Gil, 1965; Porat, 1961), like other public radio stations in the West and consistent with the prevalent norms of the settlement society in Israel at the time. The Voice of Israel stressed the collective at the expense of the individual. "The separation between public and private, which was taken for granted, and the undeniable primacy of the public sphere led to the denial and suppression of the individual's role and significance" (Bernstein, 1993, p. 89). In fact, the social communications platform that the young society developed was informed by different needs and values, but shared a common belief in what was private and what was public. In this setting, news patterns, manners of coverage, hierarchy of topics, and gendered practices became firmly established and gender based differences and discrimination were produced.

The development at IDF Radio was very different. The format of newscasts of an essentially civilian nature was shaped by editors and managers whose professional experience was not gained in the The Voice of Israel tradition. Most professionals employed in the IDF Radio news department were reservists who, in civilian life, were journalists and editors in the Israeli press. Without the influence of the BBC model, editors at IDF Radio attempted to formulate a unique broadcasting style, adopting professional norms that drew from broadcasting practice in the United States.[13]

The Workplace as a Reflection of Social Structure

The Voice of Israel began its broadcasts to a society in which egalitarian, socialist, and yet extremely "masculine" (Izraeli, 1984) values were prevalent. Men were primary breadwinners, whereas women were homemakers (Bernstein, 1983). Even when women worked outside the home, they were typically offered limited and predefined occupations (Gutkind, 1975). "Most

---

[13]One such editor was Dr.Yehiel Limor, former *Ma'ariv* journalist. As a reservist for a 6-month period following the October War, he was a member of a small team established to set up the news department at IDF Radio. "When we consolidated our work practices, we tried to compete with The Voice of Israel by constructing newscasts both similar and different from our competition. Inter alia, we imported broadcasting norms from the USA, which implied quicker, snappier and shorter broadcasts, with a more extensive use of inserts, i.e. sounds and images from the field" (personal interview, April 2, 2001).

women pioneers were the cleaners, seamstresses, teachers and nurses and not found among the farmer, construction workers and pavers of roads" (Bernstein, 1987, p. 9). Israeli society was reflected in the labor market that developed (Ofaz, 2000) and perpetuated inequality although, at the time, it was not perceived as such. Indeed, "in Israel, women required a number of decades to awake from the illusion of equality" (Herzog, 1999, p. 338). "Masculine" norms that characterized The Voice of Israel upon its establishment, remained in place over decades and inscribed patterns of work and thought. Moreover, The Voice of Israel is a rigidly bureaucratic organization, where many staff members have been in its employment for decades and the adoption of change is a slow and arduous process. In contrast, IDF is a younger organization, characterized by rapid turnover, less rigid patterns of work and thought, facilitating the penetration and adoption of new ideas and concepts. The social developments of the last two decades have, *inter alia*, undermined society's hierarchical structure (Maor, 1997) and consequently have had a greater impact on the work environment at the military radio station.

The following quotes from respondents in this study illustrate the awareness of male and female editors of gender-based discrimination at The Voice of Israel that is a result of their work environment's reproduction of social reality:

> Society has not gone through any change and certainly not feminisation. The change is superficial only, the money and power are in the hands of men and this is also true for The Voice of Israel. (editor, personal interview, February 20, 2001)

> The situation at The Voice of Israel reflects the reality of Israeli society. That is how it was and that is how it will be. This is the reality of Israeli society and not every revolution in America is appropriate for us. (editor, personal interview, January 4, 2001)

Structure of Employment

At The Voice of Israel, editorial and production staff working on news and current events are civilians who are tenured employees or employed on an individual contract basis. In contrast, news production at IDF Radio is in the hands of five groups: civilian IDF employees, reservists, young soldiers doing their mandatory military service, noncommissioned officers (NCOs), and civilian freelance employees. As a result of its structure of employment, the station has a high turnover rate, relatively low average age and high internal mobility, specifically, individuals move from production and writing positions to editing. In contrast, The Voice of Israel staff members tend to remain in their present place of employment for many years. Media professionals at this station envision lifetime employment at the station, usually until retirement, primarily due to the loss in pension rights that tenured employees experience when they leave the station. The result is a slow-moving career path.

The structure of employment at IDF Radio encourages a more relaxed style and works against the retention of rigid organizational traditions. Due to its reliance on the draft and the mobility of its staff, IDF Radio is regularly rejuvenated by new staff. Most soldiers leave the station at completion of their mandatory army service and many are tempted to join the commercial media sector. Such an organizational structure supports the rapid advancement of (young) individuals to relatively senior positions—as is typical of the entire military structure in Israel. This factor, among others, may also explain how young women and men soldiers joining the military station hold, or at least are affected by, more equalitarian values that are subsequently reflected in their professional performance.

Patterns of Recruitment

For generations, journalism and especially news coverage has been perceived as a typically male occupation that, in practice, was closed to women (Cramer, 1993; Markey, 1980; Turner, 1993; Vivan, 1991). For decades, the media in Israel have employed unsystematic recruitment processes (Caspi & Limor, 1999), primarily through friendship networks. As most journalists are men, it was highly likely that employees recommended other male friends, obstructing women's entry into the profession. Organizational culture grounded in male solidarity supports masculine power (Kanter, 1977). Although in the past, The Voice of Israel ran journalism training courses and recruited a small proportion of these trainees, most new recruits were and still are recruited through closed strategies, although recruitment for positions in news and current affairs is more complex. Civilian IDF employees are recruited through a process that is similar to that operating at The Voice of Israel while recruitment of soldiers is completely different. The hundreds of young applicants wishing to work at the station during their military service undergo gruelling anonymous tests, interviews with a panel and successful completion of a para-military course. This arduous process largely negates the affects of gender discrimination or bias.

PATHS OF PROMOTION

Patterns of recruitment and employment further affect differences in the career paths available at each organization. At The Voice of Israel, ad hoc recruitment and the use of friendship networks create a structured preference, not only privileging the entry of men into the organization, but also encouraging their promotion. However, as a national public broadcasting channel subject to ministerial authority, the political establishment have made attempts to intervene in the appointment process at The Voice of Israel from time to time (Caspi & Limor, 1999), providing further evidence of the ties between the local political and media elites. Unfortunately, these interventions further contributed to the over-representation of men and their professional advancement, and extended the old boys' network that already existed in Israel society to the media (Etzioni-Halevy, 1993). In contrast, the relatively limited term of employment of soldiers in their military service more or less restricts any promotion: the small minority who are offered continued employment at the stations, either as NCOs or IDF-employed civilians, are selected on the basis of their performance and proven professional abilities. As no gender bias was evident at the recruitment stage, further progression is also unlikely to be affected by gender bias. The recruitment of new employees to senior positions (evening news editors or editors of current affairs programs) from the general public, is also merit-based.

How, then, do the organizational factors discussed here explain why women at The Voice of Israel, a group that currently constitutes a considerable presence among newsroom decision makers, feel disadvantaged compared to men and why do they feel unable to bring about a significant change in sociorganizational norms, which have prevailed for decades? First, newsroom practices should be examined in light of "informal occupational socialization," as defined by Smith (1980). The news production process, as most media processes, is comprised of routine work that naturally impedes the adoption of innovations or transformations occurring outside professional practice. Thus, the newsroom develops its own "micro-culture" with its areas of coverage, norms, individual interests, sense of (male) camaraderie and obligations, which overshadow the involvement of women or the treatment of issues related to them (Reskin, 1988). This micro-culture additionally reinforces the power still concentrated in the hands of men (Skidmore, 1998) by relegating female decision making to specific areas or topics. This socioeconomic structure is also supported by the prevailing informal culture. The absence of consistent recruitment procedures and formal career paths and the existence of an "old boy network" (van Zoonen, 1994) implicitly encourages the use of personal contacts as routes to success (Smith, 1980). Finally, socioprofessional adaptation processes take place through a subtle system of rewards and benefits that reproduce professional socialization.

Second, women in radio news production today currently work within a framework of norms and values of newsmaking practice, anchored in the traditional nature of the organization. These are norms shaped by men and for men (Allan, 1998), at a time when women had little or no presence in the mass media, and when male interests dominated the organizational structures of authority (Kanter, 1977). The daily professional routine of the newsroom, the dominant gender-based politics, and the existence of news production rituals all strongly preserve this tradition, which has largely gone unchallenged. This everyday routine increases the chance that information deemed newsworthy, based on editorial consideration, is consistent with the dominant tradition, ensuring the coverage and promotion of such information.[14] The situation is different for female editors whose advocacy of topics they deem worthy may, in many cases, collapse in light of the dominant normative reality. Moreover, the pressurised nature of news production leaves little time for discussion or negotiation. Accommodation to an essentially male-focused value system enhances process efficiency. Moreover, the classification of news into predefined categories limits the range of areas covered (Tuchman, 1973), and consequently inhibits the penetration of "external" issues deemed newsworthy by women editors.

Third, after struggling to achieve a foothold in the decision-making structure, women may decide to adopt a strategy of conformity. Although the findings from this study suggest that women editors are very aware of discrimination and of their inferior position compared to their male counterparts, they hesitate to suggest new initiatives in the newsroom. After the persistent experience of frustration and disappointment, together with their frank recognition of men's "superior" status in the newsroom, women have reduced their news-related initiatives in order to avoid professional confrontations. Women are also not overly eager to cover issues on which there is no broad consensus of newsworthiness (van Zoonen, 1998) and recognize the impact of their decision making on the culture of the newsroom and their place within it. The situation of The Voice of Israel media professionals points to a problematic and vicious circle: Men's and women's perceptions of their status in the newsroom influence their status in practice and, subsequently, affects how they see themselves in their roles. Conventions and beliefs surrounding the marginalization of women affect behavioral norms through practices that shape hierarchies of power and status (Ridgeway, 1997). As a result, despite their notable presence in the newsroom at The Voice of Israel, women perceived a lack of organizational influence and power.

Noteworthy is the high level of job satisfaction reflected in the in-depth interviews with women editors at IDF Radio. Unique attributes of role perception and job satisfaction at IDF Radio may also contribute to the absence of gender bias at the station, as reflected in subjects' responses.[15] An individual's role-related behavior is a function of many independent variables, including social and individual perceptions and expectations (Cooley, 1922; Mead, 1934).

---

[14]In this context, it is worth noting that Galtung and Ruge (1973) indicated that when a specific area of interest penetrated the news pages, subsequent items relating to the same issue enjoyed advantageous ranking, relative to items from competing areas.

[15]Role theory research offers two basic approaches: sociologists such as Bibble and Thomas (1968) discussed structural factors and individual expectations, whereas psychologists concentrate on the individual fulfilling the role.

Role theory proposes that role expectations, defined as a collection of subjective beliefs, opinions, hypotheses, and information underlying the obligations and entitlements, tasks and undertakings that define individuals' behaviour in a specific role, are a central concept that bridges the individual and society (Sarbin & Allen, 1968). These researchers also note that social roles are shaped, in a reciprocal process, by the expectations of individuals and others in complementary roles. Expectations may explain the job satisfaction expressed by the female subjects in the present study, in the following manner: as they join what, for most of them in IDF, is a temporary work environment, they hold no aspirations for advancement to more senior positions over a lengthy employment period. "Whoever doesn't like the work, just moves on: after all, no one here has stock options or a pension," notes one female senior editor (personal interview, IDF Radio, March 13, 1997). Due to the subjects' minor investment in the work environment or in themselves as organizational members, the temporary nature of the job may facilitate the acceptance of prevailing norms on one hand and reduce the number of discriminatory experiences which typically come to light in career advancement attempts. As one female news editor and presenter noted: "the staff at the army station is young and naive, the level of idealism is high and so are the functional energies invested. Reality has not yet slapped these people in the face" (personal interview, IDF Radio, July 10, 2000).

High job satisfaction may underline the gender-neutral findings from the IDF Radio sample in another way. Job and workplace satisfaction may be conceptualized as the desire to continue employment in the same position and work environment (Porter & Streets, 1973). Military service at the IDF Radio station is in high demand by new recruits—an assignment at the station is a mark of success and an advantageous jumping-off point for a future in the media. A a former senior female editor remarks that, "The feeling is that the station is a home, a hothouse: there is no question of male and female" (personal interview, IDF Radio, December 16, 1997). Possibly, this sense of identification with IDF Radio (as well as the fact that most staff members belong to the same age stratum and share common experiences, desires and expectations) leads to an idealization of their experience that undermines perceptions of, or even discounts experiences of discrimination.

CONCLUSION

The civilian radio newsroom positions female and male editors differently through social practices, resulting in male dominance of the newsroom work environment and decision-making process. The selection and ranking of incoming information provides the opportunity to wield direct and meaningful impact on determination of newsworthiness, treatment of news items and, ultimately, on the media agenda.

In this study, two substantively different organizations were examined in terms of their organizational practice and gender bias, structured by differences in formal job description, occupational history and professional specialization of female and male editors. The age factor of media staff is one of the elements found to be important, which contributes to the formation of different organizational structures at each radio station. However, although it may have a differential gender-based impact on perceptions, attitudes, and behaviors, it is argued that age in itself is only one of several factors that are implicated in the development and perpetuation of an organization's culture.

In the next decade, the current editors at IDF Radio are destined to fill senior positions in the primary mass media in Israel—especially at daily newspapers, television, and The Voice of Israel—and hopefully carry with them the culture of IDF Radio. This process could effect change at a practical level—in terms of eliminating the glass ceiling effect—and on the subjective level by eliminating women's perceptions of their professional inferiority. Although many studies suggest that woman influence media outputs, this study highlights the need to expand the discussion of gender impact to an exploration of the working environment and routine professional norms that exist in media organizations, especially in news media, and their importance in perpetuating a male-focused status quo.

REFERENCES

Acker, J. (1990). Hierarchies, jobs, bodies: A theory of gendered organizations. *Gender & Society, 4*(2), 139-157.

Allan, S. (1998). (En)gendering the truth politics of news discourse. In C. Carter, G. Branston, & S. Allan (Eds.) *News, gender & power* (pp. 121-137). New York: Routledge.

Aloni, S. (1976). *Women as human beings.* Jerusalem: Mabat.

Beasley, M. (1993). Newspapers—Is there a new majority defining the news? In P. Creedon (Ed.), *Women in mass communication* (pp. 118-134). Newbury Park, CA: Sage.

Beasley, M. (1997). How can media coverage of women be improved? In P. Norris (Ed.), *Women, media and politics* (pp. 235-244). New York: Oxford University Press.

Bergen, L. A. (1991). *Testing the relative strength of individual and organizational characteristics in predicting content of journalists' best work.* Unpublished doctoral dissertation. Indiana University, Bloomington.

Bernstein, D. (1983). Women pioneers among the thorns: The status of women in the labor force during the settlement period. *Megamot, 1*(25), 7-19.

Bernstein, D. (1987). *Woman in the land of Israel: The aspiration for equality in the settlement period.* Tel Aviv: Hakibbutz Hame'uhad.

Bernstein, D. (1993). Between the woman-person and the woman at home—Woman and family among Jewish urban laborers in the settlement period. In A. Ram (Ed.), *Israeli society—critical aspects* (pp. 85-103). Tel Aviv: Brerorot.

Bibble, J., & Thomas, E. J. (1968). *Role theory—Concepts and research.* New York: John Wiley.

Bielby, W. T., & Baron, J.N. (1986). Men and women at work: Segmentation and statistical discrimination. *American Journal of Sociology, 91*(4), 759-775.

Bliss, E. (1991). *Now the news.* New York: Columbia University Press.

Breed, W. (1955). Social control in the newsroom: A function analysis. *Social Forces, 32,* 326-335.

Caspi, D., & Limor, Y. (1999). *The in/outsiders—the media in Israel.* Cresskill, NJ: Hampton Press.

Charles, M. (1992). Cross-national variation in occupational sex segregation. *American Sociological Review, 57*(4), 483-502.

Cohen, Y., Bachar, S., & Raijwan, R. (1987). Occupational sex segregation in Israel 1972-1983. *Israel Social Science Research, 51*(2), 97-107.

Cooley, Z. H. (1922). *Human nature and social order.* New York: Charles Scribner.

Cramer, J. A. (1993). Radio: A woman's place is on the air? In P. Creedon (Ed.), *Women in mass communication* (pp. 154-166). Newbury Park, CA: Sage.

de Bruin, M. (2000). Gender, organizational and professional in journalism. *Journalism Theory Practice & Criticism, 1*(2), 217-238.

Dimmick, J., & Coit, P. (1982). Levels of analysis in mass media decision making. *Communication Research, 9*(1), 3-32.

Etzioni-Halevy, H. (1993). *The elite conspiracy and democracy in Israel.* Tel Aviv: Hapoalim Press.

Gallagher, M. (1992). Women and men in the media. *Communication Research Trends, 12*(1), 1-14.

Galtung, J., & Ruge, M. (1973). Structuring and selecting news. In S. Cohen & J. Young (Eds.), *The manufacture of news* (pp. 62-67). London: Routledge.

Gam, A., & Pringle, R. (1983). *Gender at work.* Sydney: George Allen & Unwin.

Gherardi, S. (1995). *Gender symbolism and organization cultures.* London: Sage.

Gil, Z. (1965). From the voice of Jerusalem to the voice of Israel. In *The press yearbook* (pp. 295-307). Tel Aviv: The Press Association.

Golding, P., & Murdock, G. (1991). Culture, communication and political economy. In J. Curran & M. Gurevich (Eds.), *Mass media and society* (pp. 15-32). London: Edward Arnold.

Gutkind, N. (1975). "The Weaker Sex"—in the "Seventh Kingdom." In *The Journalism Almanac* (pp. 321-366). Tel Aviv: The Association of Journalists.

Gramsci, A. (1971). *Selection from the prison notebooks.* London: Lawrence & Wishart.

Herman, E., & Chomsky, N. (1988). *Manufacturing consent.* New York: Pantheon Books.

Herzog, H. (1994). *Realistic women—Women in local Israeli politics.* Jerusalem: Jerusalem Institute for Israeli Research.

Herzog, H. (1999). Women in politics and the politics of women. In D. Izraeli, A. Friedman, H. Dahan-Kalev, S. Fogel-Bijaoui, H. Herzog, M. Hasan, & H. Naveh, (Eds.), *Sex gender politics—Women in Israel* (pp. 307-356). Tel Aviv: Hakibbutz Hameuhad.

Hosley, D. H., & Yamada, G.K. (1987). *Hard news: Women in broadcast journalism.*Westport, CT: Greenwood Press.

Israeli Advertisers' Association (1997). *Media exposure survey—1997.*

Izraeli, D. (1979). Sex structure of occupations: The Israeli experience. *Sociology of Work and Occupations, 6*(4), 404-429.

Izraeli, D. (1984). The women's workers movement in Palestine, from inception to 1927. *Katedra, 32,* 109-140

Izraeli, D. (1997). Women managers in Israel. In A. Maor (Ed.), *Women—The rising power* (pp. 56-75). Tel Aviv: Hapoalim Press.

Izraeli, D. (1999). Genderization in the workplace. In D. Izraeli, A. Friedman, H. Dahan-Kalev, S. Fogel-Bijaoui, H. Herzog, M. Hasan, & H. Naveh (Eds.), *Sex gender politics—Women in Israel* (pp. 167-215). Tel Aviv: Hakibbutz Hameuhad.

Kanter, R. M. (1977). *Men and women of the corporation.* New York: Basic Books.

Katz, E., Yanovzki, Y., Haz, H., & Yalin, D. (Eds.). (2000). *Leisure culture in Israel.* Tel Aviv: The Open University.

Kop, Y. (Ed.) (2000). *Pluralism in Israel: From melting pot to "Jerusalem mixed."* Jerusalem: Center for Study of Social Policy in Israel, Maor-Wallach.

Lachover , E. (2000). Women journalists in the Israeli press. *Qesher, 28,* 63-74.

Lavie, A. (1997). *The agenda as shaped by female and male editors in Israel's print press.* Ramat Gan: Department of Political Studies (Communications Track), Bar-Ilan University, Israel.

Limor, Y. (1974). How the war integrated "Voice of Israel" and army radio broadcasts. In *The Journalism Almanac* (pp. 51-58). Tel Aviv: The Association of Journalists.

Limor, Y. (1998). *The pirate radio in Israel.* Jerusalem: The Hebrew University.

Limor, Y., & Caspi, D. (1994). The feminization of the Israeli Press. *Qesher, 15,* 37-45.

Liran-Alper, D. (2000). The future of media in communication in women's hand? The Committee for the Status of Women in the Israel Broadcasting Authority 1993-1998. *Patuach, 4,* 188-204.

Lorber, J. (1994). *Paradoxes of gender.* New Haven: CT: Yale University Press.

Maor, A. (Ed.). (1997). *Women—The growing force.* Tel Aviv: Hapoalim Press.

Marini M. M., & Brinton, M.C. (1984). Sex typing in occupational socialization. In B. Reskin & P. Roos (Eds.), *Sex segregation in the workplace* (pp. 192-239). Washington, DC: National Academy Press.

Markey, R. (1980). Women and labor 1800-1900. In E. Windschattle (Ed.), *Women, class and history* (pp. 85-97). Melbourne: Fontana.

Mead, G. H. M. (1934). *Self and society.* Chicago: University of Chicago Press.

Mitchell, C. (2000). *Women & radio.* London: Routledge

Ofaz, A. (2000). The question of woman and women's voice in pioneer society. *Katedra, 95,* 101-118.

Oppenheimer, V. K. (1970). *The female labor force in the U.S.A.* Berkeley: Berkeley Institute of International Studies, University of California.

Oring, S. (1995, June). Kissing the newsroom goodbye. *American Journalism Review,* 31-35.

Porat, L. (1961). *On the beginnings of the radio.* Jerusalem: Voice of Israel Archives.

Porter, L. W., & Streets, R.M. (1973). Organizational work: A personal factor in employment turnover and absenteeism. *Psychological Bulletin, 80*(2), 151-176.

Rakow, L. (1986). Rethinking gender research in communication. *Journal of Communication, 35*(4), 11-26.

Reskin, B. (1988). Bringing the men back in—Sex differentiation and the devaluation of women's work. *Gender and Society, 2*(1), 58-81.

Reskin, B., & Roos, R.M. (1990). *Job queues, gender queues*. Philadelphia: Temple University Press.

Ridgeway, C. L. (1997). Interaction and the conservation of gender inequality: Considering employment. *American Sociological Review, 62*(2), 218-235.

Sarbin, T. R., & Allen, V.L. (1968). Role theory. In G. Lindsey & E. Aronson (Eds.), *The handbook of social psychology* (pp. 488-567). Cambridge, MA: Addison-Wesley.

Scott, J. W. (1990). *The gender of modernism*. Bloomington: Indiana University Press.

Shelef, R., Sixs, S., Kaofman, S., Meir-Levy, H., & Vinberger, M. (Eds.). (1975). *Woman, women and femininity*. Tel Aviv: The Feminist Movement in Israel.

Skidmore, P. (1998). Gender and the agenda. In C. Carter, G. Branston, & S. Allan (Eds.), *News, gender & power* (pp. 204-218). New York: Routledge.

Smith, R. (1980). Images and equality—Women and the national press. In H. Christian (Ed.), *The sociology of journalism and the press* (pp. 76-93). London: Routledge & Kegan Paul.

Tuchman, G. (1973). Making news by doing work—Routinizing the unexpected. *American Journal of Sociology, 79*(1), 110-131.

Turner, G. (1993). Towards equity: The emerging role of women in Australian journalism. *Australian Studies in Journalism, 2*, 124-169.

van Zoonen, L. (1988). Rethinking women and the news. *European Journal of Communication, 3*(1), 35-53.

van Zoonen, L. (1994). *Feminist media studies*. London: Sage.

van Zoonen, L. (1998). One of the girls? The changing gender of journalism. In C. Carter, G. Branston, & S. Allan (Eds.), *News, gender and power* (pp. 33-46). New York: Routledge.

Vivan, J. (1991). *Media of mass communication*. Needham Heights, MA: Allyn and Bacon.

Walsh-Childers, K. J. (1996). Women journalists report discrimination in newsrooms. *Newspaper Research Journal, 17*(1-4), 68-87.

Weaver, D. H., & Wilhoit, G. C. (1996). *The American journalist in the 1990s*. Mahwah, NJ: Erlbaum.

8

Sex at Work: Gender Politics and Newsroom Culture

Karen Ross

THE SEXED NEWSROOM

Although a few studies of women news professionals have been conducted over the past two or three decades, especially in the United States, it was arguably during the 1990s that the topic became a more global issue of concern with media scholars worldwide, focusing on specifically gendered (and sometimes also color-coded) newsroom practices. Statistics on women's career profiles within media industries have been available in Europe and the United States for some time, especially via gender-oriented links to Web sites such as those of the United Nations and the European Commission. It is clear that although women are making more significant inroads into the sector in Western contexts, they still do not occupy senior positions in any great number. For example, in Lünenborg's (1996) study of nine European countries, women accounted for more than 25% of all reporter, subeditor and editor positions, but only comprised 12% of editorial executive posts. In Finland, the number of women working in media industries far outweighs men (Zilliacus-Tikkanen, 1997), although, this progress continues to be impeded by the still ubiquitous glass ceiling when the most senior positions are factored into the analysis. In the United States and Canada, the volume indicators are broadly the same with increasing numbers of women entering the industry, but too few achieving very senior positions within their particular domains.

Perhaps unsurprisingly, some scholars indicate that as women have begun to develop more significant roles as media professionals, so the median salaries of mainstream journalists have started to fall. Smith, Fredin, and Nardone

143

(1993) argue that, "It is . . . significant that the earnings of all reporters, in real dollars, have dropped as more and more women pursue successful careers in journalism." (p. 174). So the trade-off for women's success in the sector appears to have been a reduction in gross salaries. The new millennium would seem a good time to start monitoring the backlash that is certain to come in response to sectoral wage deflation, a problem that will almost certainly be laid at the door of women journalists. An interesting perspective on the twin peaks of women and journalism, and echoing the financial point made by Smith et al., was put forward by Creedon (1993). She argued that, on the one hand, increasing the number of women in the media will lead to a shift in news values, whereas at the same time, increasing the number of women in media occupations diminishes the status of the profession, the so-called "velvet ghetto" thesis. This phenomenon is well known as is its opposite, where the recent move of more men into a traditionally female profession such as nursing, is forcing wages to rise as men are unwilling to work for the poor pay generally associated with that profession: Their voices seem to carry a weight that the much greater number of women in nursing never managed.

But what do women working as news journalists think about their work? Do they believe that their sex is an important aspect of their professional practice or is gender entirely subordinate to profession? As part of a larger study of women, politics, and news, I undertook a small pilot project in order to gain a preliminary understanding of the significance of gender in the practice of journalism in Britain. Working with the campaign group, *Women in Journalism,* I surveyed members of the group via their regular newsletter in summer 1999 and received 22 completed replies.[1] Although these responses do not necessarily reflect the experiences of all women journalists, they nonetheless provide some interesting insights into working practices and beliefs among women media professionals in Britain.[2] As with other studies (Byerly & Warren, 1996; Robinson & Saint-Jean, 1997; Sieghart & Henry, 1998), women journalists in my study identified a number of concerns relating to the difficulties of trying to manage the work–home balance, especially among working mothers, but were con-

---

[1]An earlier version of this chapter was published in *Journalism Studies* (2002), 2(4), 531–544, and I am grateful to the publishers for allowing some of that material to be reproduced here. http://www.tandf.co.uk

[2]The broad demographics of my sample are that they comprised women between the ages of 26 and 70, with most respondents clustered around the 26 to 55 years age bands, nearly 75% were in full-time work, and there were equal numbers of salaried employees and freelancers. Of the 11 women in full-time salaried employment, 4 worked on magazines, 5 worked for a local newspaper, 1 worked for a national newspaper, and 1 worked jointly for a newspaper and magazine. Most women (91%) had been working as a journalist for more than 10 years, including 20% who had worked in the industry for more than 30 years.

cerned with the dominance, still, of a long-hours culture: For women considering having children in the future, the near impossibility of successfully combining family and career seem insurmountable problems (Lafky 1991, 1993; Ogan, Brown, & Weaver, 1979). Even women who do not have children identify these difficulties and believe that making workplaces more friendly toward working parents would be a positive way forward. The following comments are typical of those expressed.[3]

> More research needs to be done on wages for women with the findings acted upon. Flexible working conditions will help women maintain their careers. (Cara)
>
> Although I am not a mother, I see juggling home and family as the single most important issue affecting women journalists today. In my office, there are very few working mothers. The long hours culture must be stopped. (Amy)
>
> I don't feel being a woman has made any difference to me. However, I am divorced and never wanted children which is the main obstacle to any successful career, in journalism or elsewhere. (Jill)
>
> I think the biggest issue in my career is how to juggle my workload with the decision to start a family. Why should I give up my position, but the hours, at this rate, would be impossible with other responsibilities. (Sharon)
>
> Long hours culture makes life impossible. Many excellent journalists are being lost to the profession because of this. (Jackie)

Of course, there are ways round the "juggling" problem, if mothers are prepared to work as freelance journalists, as Sam points out, although there is the obvious problem of financial insecurity: "being a freelancer is an ideal job for women who wish to have a family and because of family experiences, you have a greater knowledge of everyday issues" (Sam). But this solution will not work for everyone and in any case, merely tries to make women's lives accommodate the male-ordered workplace rather than challenge the structure and culture that makes too many workplaces hostile to *all* working parents but especially mothers. "Part-time working is still greatly frowned upon by many regional newspapers. My attempts to get a workplace crèche going were ridiculed" (Sarah).

In work undertaken with women working on metropolitan newspapers in South Africa, Gillwald (1994) found that "few journalists, even those dissatisfied with discriminatory allocation of news stories, were aware of the 'male-centricity' of what they saw as standard journalistic practice—newsworthiness,

---

[3]All names have been changed.

readability, public interest" (p. 27). Some of the women in Gillwald's study were not only, apparently, gender blind but used the (too easy?) example of their own success as a means by which to refute the suggestion of sexism in the industry. This strategy of self-deception or, at best, a refusal to empathize with the lived experiences of other women was mirrored in the responses of some of the women in my study, neatly exemplifying internalized sexism by placing the blame for women's subordination squarely back in the hands of women themselves. The incorporation of women journalists into a largely male profession has the effect of "normalizing" what are essentially male-identified concerns and a male-directed agenda, so that acceptance of journalistic practice and convention is made on the basis of routinization, where male perspectives are constructed as unproblematic, uncontested, and, most importantly, apparently value-free.

Although some women undoubtedly do not experience sexism in their working lives, it is perhaps rather simplistic to believe that this must mean that no women ever experience such behaviour, reducing those very real experiences as being mere excuses for special pleading. This kind of playing the game by "male" rules results in what Phillips (1991) called *domesticated feminism*, striving for equality of opportunity within the existing structures of patriarchy rather than challenging the structures themselves. Fiona recognized this all too well: "Whilst the 'style' of journalism remains predominantly male determined, women joining journalism will simply continue to 'ape' men in approach and style." So, although the gains that women have made in media industries are to be applauded and celebrated, the underlying structural inequalities that persist in terms of access, culture, and real decision making still need to be identified and challenged.

In my study, respondents were asked what kinds of newsroom environments were the most empowering for women. Although some women mentioned generic qualities such as: "One in which ability and talent are recognized above all else" (Diana); or, "One where people get on with their jobs without politics" (Margaret), others pointed specifically to workplaces that do not discriminate against women. "One in which being a woman is not an issue. Journalist first, gender second" (Claire), "One in which gender is not an issue and women don't pander to men either by being macho or sexual" (Robyn). Diane does not believe that empowerment is a gender issue at all, claiming that "A woman can be empowered wherever she works. It is up to her to enable it," although this disavows the absolute experience and reality of many female journalists.

Evidence of sexual harassment, both overt and more subtle, has been revealed by several studies of women journalists during the 1990s. Research by Weaver (1992) revealed that between 40% and 60% of female journalists taking part in his study had directly experienced harassment. More than 50% of the women and slightly more than 25% of men who took part in Sieghart and Henry's (1998) study of British journalists said that they had either experienced and/or witnessed discrimination against women, with newspaper environments being more likely than magazines to produce discriminatory behaviors. In Walsh Childers, Chance, and Herzog's (1996) study of women journalists, the authors found that of the 227 participants in their study, 60 believe that sexual harassment is a problem for women in the industry, with 10% stating that they had personally experienced harassment. The kinds of harassment varied from degrading comments to sexual assault, and approximately 17% of the sample reported having experienced physical sexual harassment at least "sometimes."

In their study, Byerly and Warren (1996) cited the experience of one woman reporter who was regarded as having an aggressive reporting style, being given a jock strap as a leaving present by her male colleagues, with the words "sniff this for luck" written on the band. In my study, more than 75% of respondents stated that they had experienced discrimination in the newsroom. Some women spoke of an underlying "sense" of inadequacy, or of having to prove oneself as a woman as being examples of low-level, almost nonspecific harassment, viewing such behaviors as the price they have to pay to work in a male-ordered environment: "Part and parcel of traditional hierarchical operation" (Jenny); "Never specific incidents, simply overall men are considered more capable so I have to work harder to be noticed, not just on stories" (Elizabeth); "Previous editor [felt] threatened by women. Bullying and threatening behavior" (Sally). Other respondents described specific examples of blatant sexism, easily recognizing such behavior as harassment even as it pretended to be something altogether less sinister, like workplace banter (sexist comments) or the luck of the draw (allocation of news stories)

Offered a job which was later given to man. (Tina)

Was once "told off" for displaying emotions when I was a news editor. (Kate)

Headed an editorial desk which was "reorganised" when I got pregnant. (Sam)

Not taken seriously . . . lower wages . . . asked to do the photocopying. (Cara, Jo, Becky)

The kinds of "naturalistic" culture that pervades many newsrooms is one that masquerades as a neutral "professional journalism ethos" but is actually organized around a man-as-norm and woman-as-other structure. The consequences for women who choose to work in this male-ordered domain, then, are to either "beat the boys at their own game" by becoming more assertive and more macho, or else develop alternative ways of being a journalist, often by working in concert with other professionals who are on the "outside" of the "inner" circle by dint of the same or different reasons for exclusion—for example, journalists of color, self-identified gay and lesbian journalists, and so on. How women deal with the typical newsroom culture will of course depend on any number of personal, professional, and experiential factors and such strategies can include (following Melin-Higgins & Djerf-Pierre, 1998): *incorporation* (one of the boys), which requires women to take on so-called masculine approaches and values such as objectivity; *feminist*, where journalists make a conscious decision to provide an alternative voice, for example, writing on health in order to expose child abuse and rape; and *retreat*, where women choose to work as freelancers rather than continue to fight battles in the workplace. Women who choose incorporation do so for any number of reasons but mostly to avoid the sexism and low status associated with "women's work," but this can make them just as vulnerable to other kinds of sexist responses: "Several of the men [interviewees] (and women) talked of these (always successful) women in derogatory terms, e.g., 'so-and-so is a hard-bitten old hag' or 'so-and-so slept her way to her job with different editors'" (Melin-Higgins & Djerf-Pierre, 1998, p. 14).

Women in my study were asked to agree or disagree with a range of statements relating to gender and journalism. Table 8.1 provides their responses in aggregate form. What is particularly interesting from the results is the lack of consensus on most of the aspects of gendered journalism discussed except those that relate specifically to either the pursuit of a feminist practice or the potential games that women (might) play to achieve acceptance amongst their male peers, both of which were strongly denied. But on a number of crucial issues, such as differential chances of professional success, the male-oriented (and therefore exclusive) nature of the after-hours culture, the coverage of so-called women's issues, and the career opportunities for working mothers, there were significant disagreements among journalists, as the table demonstrates.

Most women who took part in the study believe that having more women in senior positions will provide a positive impact on the career prospects for other women. But there was rather more equivocation about the impact of more women in the industry to change the content of the news, that is, the news agenda itself. With such a small study, the findings can scarcely be extrapolated to the wider community of women journalists. However, they nonetheless demonstrate significant differences of opinion about how and in what ways women think of themselves as undertaking a different kind of journalism to male colleagues, making it difficult to see how the critical mass argument will ever be realized. Sharing the same sex is no guarantee of sharing perspectives, aims, and aspirations that work for change: Same gender does not map neatly into same politics.

I was also interested in identifying whether and in what ways women had been actively encouraged to write overly negative stories about women subjects. The women in my study were asked if they had ever covered a story about a woman that, in hindsight, they had felt troubled by. Some women had been involved in such stories: "Our paper has twice led on stories about mothers desperate for help for out-of-control children. I felt the treatment of 'the kids from

TABLE 8.1

Journalism as Practice and Policy: Strength of Agreement With Following Statements

Journalism — Practice and Policy	% Agree Strongly (1-3)	% Equivocal (4-7)	% Disagree Strongly (8-10)
Profession is still dominated by men	60	27	13
Women managers are more macho than male colleagues	23	41	36
Women and men have equal chance of professional success	41	9	50
It's hard to be a feminist in the newsroom	47	26	26
More senior women will impact positively on prospects for other women	59	32	9
Most men treat women colleagues as their equal	50	36	14
Women and men bring different perspectives to their work, so gender diversity is important	50	40	10
Motherhood is more important factor in career success than "only" gender	31	15	53
I try to do journalism from a feminist perspective	13	13	74
Covering women's issues in not highly regarded by senior staff	41	18	41
After hours pub culture makes it hard for women to gain "acceptance"	36	23	41
Women must adopt "macho" behaviours to get ahead	13	18	69
More women would make media output more women-friendly	41	36	22

Note. 1 = agree strongly, 10 = disagree strongly.

hell' was exploitative of the mothers" (Shirley); "an interview with Vanessa Redgrave. I took a particularly 'feminist' stance about a film she'd been in—*Wetherby*—and she clammed up. I reported it like that, making her look 'difficult.' It was journalistically 'cheap'" (Sally). Others clearly recognized the editorial push and were determined to try and subvert those intentions: "Sometimes women interviewers are encouraged by male editors to be bitchy about women interviewees but in my case, I made a point of being bitchy about men . . . but only when I could justify it!" (Sarah); "I decided early on that it's good to go to the limit to get a good story but never to exceed the boundary. I like to sleep nights" (Catherine). Jill's response to the question is interesting since she analyzes what she's done in terms of gender discrimination against *men* and feels guilty about it, rather than viewing her decision as one of trying to achieve an alternative view and perspective: "Last week, I commissioned a woman to write a piece about working hours when I already had another piece on the same subject written by a man. For some reason, I discounted the man's view, even though he was making the same points" (Jill).

In Melin-Higgins & Djerf-Pierre's (1998) study, women who actively chose to make a difference in their journalism tended to work in one of two ways: either to select a subject that they found interesting and then to actively work at that in their own way and with their own approach (although it is not completely clear from the study the extent of real choice available to those women), or else to work in woman-dominated media such as women's magazines or women's radio/TV shows.

Women in my study were asked if they had been prevented from covering certain stories or news events because of their sex. Some responses were unequivocal in their identification of specifically gender-based decisions, where the rationale for sending male reporters was overt, for example: "Sometimes a man is sent to interview a woman [who is perceived as] susceptible to male flattery but that happens less often these days" (Cheryl); or "At Reuters in the mid-1980s, there was a policy of not sending women to 'war zones' or difficult places like Africa. Even though I came from Africa, they were reluctant to send women to hot spots" (Claire). These examples suggest that things were bad before but better now. Pat observes the more difficult problem now of trying to get work accepted which adopts a different perspective: "I tried to get *The Independent* interested in feminist-oriented theater features; also, *The Guardian* [but the] style of writing has to be spiky, macho. Journalism is overwhelmingly still! male!" As with other comments that were responses to questions asked about discrimination, Diane seems unwilling to accept that sexism is being practised even as she identifies barriers to her own assignment interests: "I don't believe I have ever been prevented from covering a story because of my gender, other than that political editors on newspapers I have worked on have tended to be male and therefore I haven't been able to cover politics."

THE GENDERED JOURNALIST–
SEX AND PROFESSIONALISM

In some very significant ways, my work with women journalists suggests a somewhat equivocal stance on the salience of gender among journalists. Other studies also suggest that factors *other than* gender are often more reliable indicators of attitudes and values such as socioeconomic background and political values. Weaver (1997) found that there were few significant differences between women and men in terms of professional values and ethos. The variations that *did* emerge were associated more with culture than gender.

> This [finding] suggests that newsroom and community environments are stronger influences on journalists' professional values (and probably on the kind of news content they produce) than is gender, raising the question of whether news coverage is likely to change much as more women enter journalism and assume positions of increasing responsibility. (Weaver, 1997, p. 39)

However, within Weaver's work are contradictory findings, suggesting at the very least ambiguity and complexity in trying to characterize the experiences of women and men into neatly gendered and mutually exclusive boxes. So on the one hand, Weaver argued that gender seems a poor predictor of news content differences, but he also suggested that gender *can* have an influence in bringing new perspectives and ways of presenting news, in particular bringing a less formal tone to reports, the so-called feminizing of news: "Journalists, especially women, may be stepping out of the more conventional news beat systems and tapping ordinary people as sources more often" (p. 39). Thus, although gender may be ambiguous in terms of determining story content, there nonetheless seem to be some distinctions when considering subject, source, and tone that could be attributed to the sex of the journalist.

Reviewing the various studies that have tried to identify gendered differences, van Zoonen (1998) suggested that women journalists believe they do operate with a different set of beliefs and values, that they share a kind of "womanview" that can be contrasted with the perspectives of male colleagues in a number of important ways (e.g., that women are more interested in the news consumer, that they are more interested in story context and background, more interested in experiential elements than the end result, and are more likely to seek out female sources. "They also scorn the detachment and insensitivity in many of their male colleagues, believing they are hiding behind the idea of objectivity to exclude all compassion and humanity that one should bring to journalism" (van Zoonen, 1998, p. 36). As van Zoonen pointed out, although studies of journalists do indeed identify an appreciation of differences in tone, outlook, priority, and interest between women and men journalists, such differences reside in perceptions of self and other and relate to how women and men think about both their own practice and do not necessarily result in producing substantially different stories in terms of topic choice. If more women than men are assigned the fashion, lifestyle, cookery, education, or health beats, then it is hardly surprising that women journalists come to be seen (including by themselves!) to be good at and interested in lifestyle, background, and "soft" politics—the classic "chicken and egg" dilemma which I do not intend to try and resolve here, but merely to raise as an ongoing problematic.

> I make a particular point of not mentioning women's age or physical appearance unless essential to the story. I hope that, as a woman, I am able to empathise more with a female subject. (Jane)

> I am more likely to consider how the event has affected the woman in question's personal life. (Julie)

> I try to inject more personal memoir/emotion/anecdote. (Sarah)

Journalists were also asked if they adapted their interview style in response to whether they were interviewing a woman or a man. Most reported an unambiguous "no," as with the previous question: "No. It's a myth that one needs to differentiate" (Carol); "No. All interviews are unique" (Sam) But there were a number of "no, but . . . " comments that followed, for example, "No difference, although women in business can find it harder to relax than men during interviews" (Maureen); and "I try to approach them equally but my experience is that interviews with women tend to be more relaxed and informal" (Yvonne). However, women did recognize that male interviewees sometimes required different handling, as Karen pointed out, and they adopt styles that get the most out their subjects: "Men tend to say less and often need prompting" (Karen).

SEX AND MONEY

The deliberate efforts of newspapers to reinvigorate the tired formula of traditional print journalism by having shorter stories, more consumer features, and more photographs have been tried as part of a wider strategy to ward off an even more drastic decline in circulation figures, in particular trying to win back women news consumers. It is certainly the case that women journalists at least believe that women and men have different interests in terms of what they want from a newspaper or magazine, including that women are more in-depth readers, that they like human interest, health, and lifestyle features (Mills, 1997). In my study, Jane at least recognizes that there is a certain amount of gender stereotyping at play in the way in which the readership is considered, but argues that there is beginning to be a cross-over of interests (as does Helen) among women and men.

> Sport is more for men and possibly business. Health issues can be gender-specific but I like to think we care about each other. (Helen)

> Clearly there are the old demarcations, but much more "crossing over" and shared interests in lifestyle and culture issues. (Jane)

> I believe women's interests are wider. Men usually don't read human interest/health issues but women do read politics and sport. (Shirley)

> In my experience, men tend to be more "roaming" readers, reading widely in relation to their work, while women share increasingly similar interests, they tend to read more in depth. (Rosa)

> Women: family, domestic, health, fashion, relationships. Men: sport, leisure, film, work. Both: sex! (Cindy)

> Women are more interested in lifestyle, personality of people, and less in analysis which is often pompous. (Tina)

Although women in my study were clear that there are gender-specific interests among audiences and that these broadly conform to commonsense assumptions about women and men's particular topic preferences, there is a more ambiguous sense of women's role in perpetuating such perceptions, given that very few (in an admittedly small study), believe that their practice is significantly different as a consequence of their sex. There seems to be no real sense of the relationship between the context of news production (a largely sexist work environment) and the content of the news (where women are marginalized) among women journalists. Why not? Perhaps van Zoonen (1998) was right when she argued that it is not the active agency of women journalists themselves who have consciously engineered that feminized news shift but rather that the news industry itself has changed and is making the profession more friendly toward women. This assumes, of course, that *news professional* and *news consumer* are mutually exclusive categories and that the campaigning that has taken place in newsrooms since the 1980s has been ineffective except in those contexts where senior (male) managers decided that so-called women's ways of working were attractive to consumers. But this seems rather an odd argument—essentially the denial of women's active agency to want and be able to achieve change—to sustain, because it begs two questions: first, how and why is news changing (and who is responsible for "news" if not news producers, i.e., journalists and other news professionals?); and second, how can the industry be becoming more friendly toward women when women *already* work in significant numbers within the news sector, albeit mostly in junior or middle management roles?

Perhaps, for face-saving reasons, it is easier to rationalize a cultural shift on the grounds of changing consumer taste than admit that hitherto exclusionary practices not only operated to the detriment of women media workers, but also to profit margins, because the heavy "male" orientation of news media resulted in many potential (women) consumers declining to become readers, listeners, and viewers. Perhaps it is simply that "the public" has become less deferential toward the political process—and news is mostly about politics of some sort—less respectful of authority and less able or willing to concentrate on a single source for very long, given the myriad ways in which news can now be consumed. Thus, there may be a need for the media to adopt different forms of address, and particularly less formal modes and styles of communication. That these different modes, tones, and orientations are associated with women journalists' specific approaches and ways of working, says much about the connectedness of women to the ordinary public.

MYTHS AND REALITIES OF A GENDERED JOURNALISM

If we are to better understand the gender dynamics that take place in the newsroom by analyzing those particular contexts for their gender inflections, we must do more than simply look at staffing ratios and status positions, although this is, of course, important (de Bruin, 1998). Foss and Foss (1989) provided a useful framework within which to theorize the gendered nature of journalism by suggesting that any such theory should have four components:

1. It should have a comprehensive explanatory value that makes sense of what is a disparate set of research findings in the area.

2. It should acknowledge the differences between structure and agency and between hierarchy and practice.

3. It should acknowledge the importance of cultural and professional knowledge systems as they impact on the everyday life of journalists.

4. It should explore the specific meanings that people attach to their behavior (cited in Robinson & Saint-Jean, 2003).

If journalism, as a practice, is viewed as having its basis in a shared "culture," then it follows that members of that profession must operate as more or less a heterogeneous group inasmuch as their practice becomes routinized within certain agreed and accepted parameters. This idea of a journalistic culture can be regarded as a meta-theory, one that goes beyond individual media organizations: It is rather a set of practices, or even a professional framework that becomes the accepted way of doing things—developing and changing to be sure—but enjoying universal support for the legitimacy of its principles and practices (Melin-Higgins & Djerf-Pierre, 1998). But is identification with and loyalty to the profession a stronger force than other personal variables such as gender, ethnicity, or sexuality? If, as Zelizer (1993) suggested, journalists operate as an *interpretive community* because of their influence in agenda-setting, can dissenting voices still speak from *inside* that community (see, e.g., Bird & Dardenne, 1988; Eliasoph, 1988; Newcomb & Alley 1983; Reese, 1990; Turow, 1994).

Moreover, how can this notion of community accommodate what we know to be structural inequalities in women's experiences and career prospects within media industries? Robinson and Saint-Jean (2000) suggested that we can begin to unpack the gendered aspects of newsroom culture through a multilevel analysis that includes an understanding of the power of "classification" that assigns value to the categories *woman* and *man*; an understanding of structure that encourages women and men to act in expected ways and conform to "typical" and an understanding of the ideology that can influence management ethos and style. The journalist Kay Mills (1997) argued persuasively that increasing numbers of women journalists have had a real impact on process and structure in newsrooms, by forcing an expansion in the very conceptualization of what news *is*, in widening the scope of what issues, events, and stories are now regarded as newsworthy. Part of that widening out process has meant not just covering a more diverse range of issues but, as importantly, a wider choice of topics. Of course, those changes in content reflect not just the reality of women's presence in the newsroom in terms of simply being there but also their influence in forcing a change in tone and voice. Mills used a personal anecdote as illustration:

> In the early 1980s, when I was the lone woman on the editorial page staff at the *Los Angeles Times*, I constantly heard jokes or grumbling from male colleagues when I suggested that the paper run an editorial on a spousal rape case in Oregon or support actions to increase the number of women fire fighters and police officers. Today, there are four women writing editorials at the *Los Angeles Times* and they report in a much different climate. (p. 46)

But even Mills must admit that although the climate in newsrooms may well have changed to the point of accepting the legitimacy of the newsworthiness of stories that touch women's concerns, interest in actually covering those stories is still confined to women journalists. For example, coverage of women politicians is now a routine part of political and campaign reporting and arguably, women journalists were at the forefront of rendering those women visible, helping to, "bring women candidates into the mainstream of coverage" (Mills, 1997, p. 50). However, rather few male journalists are interested in making women politicians suitable subjects for story reports. It is not so much that men are overtly hostile to reporting on women-focused stories (although they *do* appear to be reluctant to feature stories that show men in a poor light, such as rape cases), but rather such stories are not a priority for them: Unlike their female colleagues, they do not live that reality every day. The most compelling reason to include more material of interest to women is commercial—trying to attract more women readers, listeners, and viewers to consume diverse news genres. Many media organizations are finally realizing that content is indeed gender-sensitive and that many women are simply not interested in much of what is offered in the name of "news" and "general interest," where "general" actually assumes a "male" norm. But progress is slow. Even in the early 1990s, the Knight-Ridder Women Readers' Task Force (1991) reported that, had the proportion of women readers of daily newspapers been maintained since 1970, then by the early 1990s, an additional 17 million readers would be buying newspapers regularly (cited in Mills, 1997, p. 53).

> Until recently everything important on the papers was done by men, and that was naturally enough reflected in the product. Then people woke up to the fact that 50% of readers were women . . . there started a trend toward the feminisation of newspapers. That's not necessarily downmarket at all. It doesn't mean triviality; it means a stronger sense of the human interest in a story. There was a curious sense of dryness in the old days. (Charles Moore, editor, *Daily Telegraph*, cited in *The Guardian*, 1996)

Although it is possible to identify where gender can make a difference in changing both culture and content, women's presence in newsrooms is often circumscribed by practices and processes that are deep-rooted and often fiercely defended and controlled. Van Zoonen (1998) argued that the belief that more women will lead to a different news agenda is predicated on two assumptions, both of which are highly contestable. First, journalists can indeed operate in ways that are outside the culture of the newsroom and second, women, by dint of their shared gender, will pursue a gendered/feminist news practice en bloc because gender is their principal form of personal/political identification. Although there has been a clear shift toward a more informal and personal style of news reporting with a human interest approach, so-called *soft journalism* that could represent a kind of feminization of news, such a shift has, arguably, been for commercial reasons rather than as a consequence of any determined action on the part of women journalists.

A study conducted by women members of the sector themselves on the impact of women decision makers (Christmas, 1997) argues that there has been a discernible expansion of topics now regarded as legitimately newsworthy and a change in the way in which issues are covered, as a consequence of women's incursions into decision-making positions:

> Women have helped to change the content of news pages. Material of particular interest to women, which used to be ignored . . . is now spread throughout the paper . . . even when women select the same news content as men, they write it in a different manner. (p. 52)

The enthusiasm of Mills and Christmas is to be applauded but most evidence, including my own presented here, suggests a deep ambivalence about gender as a driver for change. Gender *alone* will not make a difference in changing the culture of newsrooms or on the type of news produced. A journalist's sex is no guarantee that she or he will either embrace sentiments that privilege equality nor hold specific values and beliefs that promote a more equitable and nonoppressive practice: Some men may well be more sympathetic to the ideals (and realities) of inclusion than some women. In my study, 75% of the respondents disagreed profoundly with the statement: "I try to do journalism from a feminist perspective" whereas 50% agreed strongly with the statement: "Gender in journalism is important because women and men bring different perspectives to their work." Nearly 60% agreed strongly with the statement: "More women in senior positions will have a positive impact on the career prospects of women journalists," whereas only 40% agreed strongly with the statement: "More women in journalism would make media output more woman-friendly."

There are very different approaches to and perspectives on the salience of gender for women journalists, but the messages are very mixed and the hopes of some analysts, that getting more women into the industry would necessarily make a difference to both the workplace culture and to news content (Beasley, 1993; Gallagher, 1995), has proved to be a little more complicated than simple numbers. Research evidence that demonstrates significant change is, at best, equivocal about a specifically gendered journalism practice and at worst, suggests mass incorporation of women into the dominant (male) newsroom culture makes honorary men of everyone.

But there are indications, albeit tentative ones, that some journalists in the industry *are* actively campaigning for change *and* making a difference. For example, in Byerly and Warren's (1996) study of political activism in newsrooms, the majority of their "activist" respondents (women and men) reported identification with the values of feminism that were broadly defined as equal rights for women, so that seeking common cause with women's concerns was often a fundamental element in a wider strategy of inclusion for more marginalized staff groups. Interestingly, a number of respondents in their study suggested that the Anita Hill/Clarence Thomas debacle had prompted the setting up of women's caucuses within their newsrooms, such was the extent of outrage at the hearing and then the verdict.

The point about Byerly and Warren's work was that it focused on activists who tended to be either women, from minority ethnic backgrounds or else self-identified gays or lesbians. This suggests that the aspirations of feminism in terms of equality of opportunity and treatment are principles to which other disadvantaged groups subscribe because of the person-friendliness (rather than women-friendly) implied. Thus, the cause of gender equity in the newsroom could be usefully integrated into a wider workplace politics that strives for a merit-based environment, embracing diversity and recognizing the value of difference. But there needs to be both the recognition and the desire for change. Buying into the blame culture leads nowhere.

> Technology is freedom! It is possible to have it all with email and the internet, working from home, visiting the office. Women need to be confident enough to dictate their working conditions, not be a victim of them. (Stephanie)

> I feel strongly that women these days often blame their lack of initiative on "discrimination." The time for whinging has passed and it is up to us to fend for ourselves. (Caroline)

Although Stephanie is a little less derogatory than Caroline, the explicit message is very clear: Sisters must do it for themselves. Although this is a good slogan, its achievement must lie in the hands of *all* journalists, but especially senior women and men, and cannot simply rest with the least powerful: if history teaches us anything, it teaches us that.

> There is a[nother] problem we don't like to talk about. Not all women in power are our friends. The need to be "one of the boys" does exist. Some women are simply afraid to appear to tilt towards other women, afraid to be labelled feminist. As a result, they therefore fail to make their presence count. (Sanders, 1993, p. 171)

REFERENCES

Beasley, M. (1993). Newspapers—Is there a new majority defining the news? In P. Creedon (Ed.), *Women in communication* (2nd ed., pp. 118-134. Newbury Park, CA, London, New Delhi: Sage.

Bird, S. E., & Dardenne, R. W. (1988). Myth, chronicle and story: Exploring the narrative qualities of news. In J. Carey (Ed.), *Media, myths and narrative* (pp. 67-86). Newbury Park, CA: Sage.

Byerly, C. M., & Warren, C. A. (1996). At the margins of center: Organized protest in the newsroom. *Critical Studies in Mass Communication, 13*(1), 1-23.

Christmas, L. (1997). *Chaps of both sexes: Women decision-makers in newspapers—Do they make a difference?* London: Women in Journalism.

Creedon, P. (1993). The challenge of re-visioning gender values. In P. Creedon (Ed.), *Women in mass communication* (2nd ed., pp. 3-23). Newbury Park, CA, London, New Delhi: Sage.

de Bruin, M. (1998, July). *Gender in Caribbean media: Beyond the body count.* Paper presented to the 21st general assembly and scientific conference of the International Association for Media and Communication Research, Glasgow.

Eliasoph, N. (1988). Routines and the making of oppositional news. *Critical Studies in Mass Communication, 5,* 313-334.

Foss, K., & Foss, S. (1989). Incorporating the feminist perspective in communication scholarship: A research commentary. In K. Carter & C. Spitzack (Eds.), *Doing research on women's communication: Perspectives on theory and method* (pp. 65-91). Norwood, NJ: Ablex.

Gallagher, M. (1995). *An unfinished story: Gender patterns in media employment* (Reports and Papers in Mass Communication no. 110). Paris: UNESCO.

Gillwald, A. (1994). Women, democracy and media in South Africa. *Media Development, 2,* 27-32.

Lafky, S. (1991). Women journalists. In D. Weaver & G. C. Wilhoit (Eds.), *The American journalist: A portrait of U.S. news people and their work* (2nd ed., pp. 160-181). Bloomington: Indiana University Press.

Lafky, S. (1993). The progress of women and people of color in the U.S. journalistic workforce: A long, slow journey. In P. Creedon (Ed.), *Women in mass communication* (2nd ed., pp. 87-103). Newbury Park, CA, London, New Delhi: Sage.

Lünenborg, M. (1996). *Journalists in Europe: An international comparative study.* Wiesbaden: Westdeutscher Verlag.

Melin-Higgins, M., & Djerf-Pierre, M. (1998, July). *Networking in newsrooms: Journalist and gender cultures.* Paper presented at the 21st general assembly and scientific conference of the International Association for Media and Communication Research, Glasgow.

Mills, K. (1997). What difference do women journalists make? In P. Norris (Ed.), *Women, media and politics* (pp. 41-56). New York & Oxford: Oxford University Press.

Newcomb, H., & Alley, R. S. (1983). *The producer's medium.* New York: Oxford University Press.

Ogan, C. L., Brown, C. J., & Weaver, D.H. (1979). Characteristics of managers of selected U.S. daily newspapers. *Journalism Quarterly, 56*(4), 803-809.

Phillips, A. (1991). *Engendering democracy.* Cambridge: Polity Press.

Reese, S. D. (1990). The news paradigm and the ideology of objectivity: A socialist at the *Wall Street Journal. Criticial Studies in Mass Communication, 7,* 390-409.

Robinson, G. J., & Saint-Jean, A. (1997). *Women's participation in the Canadian news media: Progress since the 1970s.* Unpublished report, McGill University, Montreal.

Robinson, G. J., & Saint-Jean, A. (in press). Theorizing the impact of gender in Canadian journalism. In R. Fröhlich & S. Lafky (Eds.), *Women journalists in the western world: Equal opportunities and what surveys tell us.* Cresskill, NJ: Hampton Press.

Sanders, M. (1993). Television: The face of the network news is male. In P. Creedon (Ed.), *Women in mass communication* (2nd ed., pp. 167-171). Newbury Park, CA, London, New Delhi: Sage.

Sieghart, M. A., & Henry, G. (1998). *The cheaper sex: How women lose out in journalism.* London: Women in Journalism

Smith, C., Fredin, E. S., & Nardone, C. A. F. (1993). Television: The nature of sex discrimination in local television news shops. In P. Creedon (Ed.), *Women in mass communication* (2nd ed., pp. 171-182). Newbury Park, CA, London, New Delhi: Sage.

Turow, J. (1994). Hidden conflicts and journalistic norms: The case of self-coverage. *Journal of Communication, 44*(2), 29-46.

van Zoonen, L. (1998). One of the girls? The changing gender of journalism. In C. Carter, G. Branston, & S. Allan (Eds.), *News, gender and power* (pp. 33-46). London & New York: Routledge.

Walsh Childers, K., Chance, J., & Herzog, K. (1996). Sexual harassment of women journalists. *Journalism & Mass Communication Quarterly, 73*(3), 559-581.

Weaver, C. (1992, September). A secret no more. *Washington Journalism Review*, pp. 23-27.

Weaver, D. (1997). Women as journalists. In P. Norris (Ed.), *Women, media and politics* (pp. 21-40). New York and Oxford: Oxford University Press.

Zeilizer, B. (1993). Journalists as interpretive communities. *Critical Studies in Mass Communication, 10*(2), 219-237.

Zilliacus-Tikkanen, H. (1997). *The essence of journalism from a gender perspective.* Helsinki: Ylesradio Publications A1.

9

The Gender (Dis)advantage
in Indian Print Media

Ammu Joseph

*With rare exceptions, to be a woman in India is to be something less
than a slave, property of no worth beyond what she can cook, or
fetch, or carry, or can bring as a dowry to marriage.*

Voice-over during a segment on Indian women,
CBS 60 Minutes, June 2000

Media images of India and Indian women in many parts of the world often generate and reinforce unidimensional, monochromatic stereotypes that obscure the
magnitude, diversity, and complexity of the subcontinental nation, its multifari-
ous society, and its 1 billion plus citizens, male and female. Similarly, assumptions about the location and characteristics of the "First World" and the "Free
World" tend to blur significant differences between the countries and societies
spread over the rest of the globe and to blot out the existence elsewhere of rea-
sonably robust democratic institutions, including media that are as professional,
vibrant, and free—or unfree—as media anywhere else. I begin with this caveat
because the following discussion on gender, professionalism, and the media in
India will make sense only if such common, possibly subconscious, biases are
recognized and relinquished.

The focus of this chapter is on the Indian press and women working as
journalists within it. It is based on information and insights gained in the
process of researching and writing my recent book (Joseph, 2000) and during
subsequent workshops with women journalists in different parts of India to
explore the possibility of building a multipurpose, multilevel network of women

in journalism. The first section on the Indian press, and the history of women's participation in it, sets the stage for the subsequent discussion on gender and professionalism in media organizations in India, based on the experiences and opinions of women currently working as journalists. The second section provides a glimpse of the present situation of Indian women in print journalism. The third and final section presents the reflections and ruminations of Indian press women on various aspects of the interface between gender identity and professional identity.

BACKGROUND

The Indian press is two centuries old and widely regarded as the most pluralistic, least inhibited, and most assertive and independent in the developing world. In terms of both the number of newspapers published and total newspaper circulation, India is among the top four countries of the world, the others being Japan, the United States, and China (Ram, 2000). The print media sector in India currently comprises nearly 44,000 newspapers and periodicals with a total circulation of almost 127 million. Among these are approximately 5,000 dailies, 16,000 weeklies, 6,000 fortnightlies, and 12,000 monthlies. Newspapers and magazines are published in at least 100 languages and dialects, including English and the 18 "principal" languages enumerated in the Constitution of India. At least 41 publications that are still in circulation have been in existence for more than a century; the oldest existing Indian newspaper (the *Gujarati* daily paper, *Bombay Samachar)* was established in 1822 (*Manorama Yearbook,* 2001).

The Indian print media reach only 33.4% of the country's population of more than 1 billion (Indian Readership Survey [IRS], 2001), of whom 65% are literate (Census of India, 2001). Yet the Hindi newspaper, *Dainik Bhaskar,* which boasts the highest circulation among dailies, has more than 11 million readers. Close on its heels among the top 10 are dailies in other Indian languages: *Thanti* (Tamil) with more than 10 million readers, *Dainik Jagran* (Hindi) with 10 million readers, *Eenadu* (Telugu) with 9.8 million readers, and *Malayala Manorama* (Malayalam) with 6.8 million readers. The English-language daily with the highest circulation is *The Times of India* with 5.9 million readers. The English-language current affairs fortnightly, *India Today,* has a readership of 3.9 million, whereas the Hindi women's magazine, *Grihashobha,* boasts 3.7 million readers. According to the IRS (2001), there are 178 million readers in India, 46% of whom are located in rural areas. The heritage of the mainstream press in India is mostly liberal, thanks mainly to the role of the indigenous press—in English as well as Indian languages—during the country's struggle for freedom from colonial rule. The independence movement coincided with and partly paved the way for reform in many aspects of social and cultural life, including customs and practices inimical to women.

The adversarial role of the Fourth Estate vis-à-vis the foreign, imperial government gave way after Independence, in 1947, to a relationship between the press and the new, nationalist State that was characterized largely by complacency and compliance, if not complicity. This cozy relationship was severely tested in 1975, when former Prime Minister Indira Gandhi declared a state of internal emergency, suspending many democratic rights guaranteed by the Constitution and imposing press censorship for the first time in free India. The naivete of the assumption that a national government would automatically look after national interests was thereby exposed, albeit late in the day. Although the media as a whole failed to resist this short-lived imposition of censorship, the Emergency experience (1975-1977) shocked and galvanized both the press and civil society in India. It provoked a major shift in the media's perception of its role with respect to the State as well as society, leading to more, as well as better, coverage of events and issues concerning human rights and the condition of disadvantaged, marginalised social groups, including women. The post-Emergency period also witnessed the emergence of the contemporary women's movement in India, as a response to renewed and increased awareness about women's oppression and the need for emancipation, both within the country and globally. This was also the period when a large number of Indian women entered the field of journalism.

WOMEN'S PRESENCE IN THE INDIAN PRESS

There is little documented history of women's involvement in the Indian press and the accessible literature in English on the pioneers exists mainly in the form of casual reminiscences and feature articles that are woefully short on dates and other details and refer almost exclusively to Mumbai/Bombay and Delhi. However, the available information suggests that the pattern of Indian women's participation in the press was similar to that reported from many other parts of the world. A number of women across the country began contributing to the press in different languages from the late 19th century on. Many of these pioneers were extraordinary women who rose above personal tragedy, such as early widowhood (at a time when a man's death commonly signaled the end of normal life for his wife), to reach out to other women through writing and publishing. A number of them launched journals for women, encouraging female readers to seek further education and broaden their horizons.

Most women who entered the press during this early period belonged to relatively affluent and educated families influenced by the progressive ideas spread by the Independence movement and/or the various movements for religious and social reform sweeping across the country at the time. Many were therefore supported by their families in their creative and journalistic endeavors. Although women who worked alongside male relatives in family publications were shielded from social censure, several of those who branched out on their own did face criticism, especially if they appeared to be going against tradition and disseminating unconventional ideas about women's social and familial roles.

Women began entering the mainstream commercial press—as opposed to small journals published by individuals, families, or small collectives—in the period just before Independence, mainly in Mumbai (formerly Bombay) and Delhi. Many of them seem to have begun their careers in movie magazines, whereas others worked on women's magazines or women's pages. Only a handful gained entry into publications or pages devoted to current affairs and, even then, they were generally encouraged to write on matters of "feminine" interest.

There is, unfortunately, little data available on the number of women in journalism then or now and no significant effort has been made at any level so far to estimate the number of journalists in the country, let alone the percentage of women among them. Even within the press, the multiplicity of publications, representing different genres and languages, compounds the difficulties arising from the sheer size of the country and the huge numbers of people involved.[1]

If the women who entered the mainstream press in the 1940s and 1950s can be viewed as the first small wave of female journalists in the modern era, the next and bigger wave occurred in the 1960s and early 1970s. This was the period when a number of universities and other institutions within the country began to offer courses in journalism, opening up new vistas for women in search of nontraditional careers. A few women even ventured abroad for training in journalism. Those were the days before contemporary notions of women's liberation had taken root in India. Still, several of the obviously independent-minded women who joined the press during that period fought hard to escape the professional ghettos into which stray women in the media were customarily herded. A number of them managed to get into the coveted reporting stream, slowly making their way from flower shows to fires and, eventually, even the occasional battle front. Their presence on the staff also forced newspaper establishments to contend with unfamiliar issues such as maternity leave.

However, women began entering the press in more significant numbers during the mid-1970s. A number of factors may have contributed to creating this sizeable third wave. The ripple effects of the growing international women's movement were stirring the waters in India, too, during this period. This was also the time following the bitter experience of the Emergency, which served to alert both journalists and other citizens to the importance of safeguarding civil liberties and democratic rights, including freedom of expression. Newly liberated by the fall of this short-lived quasi-dictatorship, the press in

---

[1]In my opinion, nothing short of a massive exercise covering a sample of at least those newspapers and magazines in each major genre occupying the top two or three spots in the circulation sweepstakes in each language would provide the basis for anything close to a realistic estimate.

India became far more vigorous and vigilant than it had been since Independence. Investigative journalism became a catchphrase and added to the attractive, exciting new image of the press. A magazine boom followed in the early 1980s, which vastly improved and expanded the job market for journalists, which in turn enlarged the opportunity for women, who found greater acceptability in the magazine world than in daily newspapers.

The late 1970s and early 1980s represented a period of sociopolitical ferment and cross-fertilization in India, the effects of which were reflected, to a considerable extent, in the press. There is little doubt that women in the profession contributed significantly to this process. A number of women entering the field at this time were associated with, or at least sympathetic to, the women's movement, the human rights and civil liberties movements, various grassroots movements for social and economic justice in different parts of the country, and the nascent environmental movement. Many of them brought this new consciousness to their work as journalists. Under these circumstances, it was not surprising that women comprised four out of the six winners of prestigious awards for human rights reporting in the 1980s.

A study of the coverage of women's issues in the press in the 10-year period from 1978 to 1987 (Joseph & Sharma, 1994) found that the presence of women in strategic positions within the press at that time made a substantial difference to the coverage of such subjects, although the contribution of some male journalists in this area was also noted. For example, the survey revealed that *The Statesman* carried proportionately more editorials than news reports on women's issues. This anomaly could only be explained by the presence on the staff of a relatively senior woman journalist with access to the editorial page, who wrote those editorials despite the fact that those in charge of the news pages did not deem the subjects worthy of detailed coverage. The same journalist later explained that she had chanced upon gender issues when, as a newcomer to the editorial page, she was looking for areas left uncovered by her male colleagues (Joseph & Sharma, 1994).

Naturally, not all journalists and not all women in the profession during this period were necessarily involved with issues and/or movements. In fact, many media women chose to keep their distance from causes in their effort to uphold the hoary, if questionable, tradition of journalistic objectivity. Although some were personally interested in such issues, they chose to tread a discrete professional path, although quite a few others contrived to work at both levels. A number of women were also able to break into the coveted area of hard news reporting during this period. Many among them came to be widely recognized because of their reports from various areas of conflict in and around the country. Several broke exclusive stories and managed to secure rare interviews with leaders of militant organizations operating in these hot spots. Quite a few women also made names for themselves in the prestigious field of political reporting and analysis.

The fourth wave of women to enter print journalism, during the 1990s and into the new millennium, has assumed the proportions of a tidal wave, at least in those parts of the country where the first three smaller waves had prepared the ground. Even in many other places, the slow trickle that had been perceptible over the past few decades had by this time established itself as a steady stream. Only in a few places did women have to wait until the 1990s to even get through the dykes.

The new recruits entered a vastly altered playing field because there was, by then, fairly widespread acceptance in most parts of the country of women's active participation in the world of work. Even diehard opponents of women's entry into unconventional fields like the media had to accept that it was not possible to turn back the tide. If any resistance or even hostility persisted, they had to be expressed in less direct ways. A variety of female role models was already available at senior levels in the profession and in virtually all areas and genres of journalism, especially within the metropolitan English-language press. In addition to editors (including political and financial editors), chief reporters, chiefs of bureaux, special and foreign correspondents, and columnists, not to mention magazine editors and feature writers, there were even a few sports reporters and photojournalists, as well as a couple of cartoonists.

The press itself had undergone significant changes during the 1990s, a decade that also witnessed the dawn of a new era of economic liberalization and globalization, satellite television and unbridled consumerism in the country. The overarching political and economic climate of the late 1980s and the 1990s had a major impact on the press and therefore on the practice of journalism in India. The ongoing corporatism of the press yielded financial benefits to some journalists, with more attractive salaries and perks on offer than could ever have been imagined before. However, not only was this not a universal phenomenon, but the system of employment by contract (as opposed to permanent or tenured employment) that became increasingly prevalent in many press establishments, introduced an unfamiliar and uncomfortable element of job insecurity.

Under the new dispensation, journalists seemed to have less say than before in the editorial content and policies of their publications. The role and responsibilities of editors changed significantly. In addition, editors and corporate managers began to interact far more closely than in the past, often planning and executing joint strategies. For example, on April 16, 2000, the front page of the Sunday edition of *The Times of India* (*TOI*)—which describes itself as "the world's number two broadsheet general interest daily newspaper in English" (Ram, 2000, p. 253)—was given over to a spectacular advertisement announcing the launch of a new Indian Internet portal. In reality, the four-page advertisement comprised an outer cover to the newspaper proper, but the illusion was maintained by the use of the traditional, official *TOI* masthead at the top of the first page of the ad. The apparent and unprecedented "sale" of the front page of a major newspaper sparked a furious debate in media circles but the executive managing editor of the paper was clearly unfazed by the controversy, saying,

"It was just an innovative business decision. Why make such a fuss over it?" (Tripathi, 2000, p. 14).

In this new environment, commercial interests sometimes overrode professional judgments, with some media managers popularizing the view that newspapers and magazines were essentially brands to be marketed like other consumer products. For instance, a vice president of Bennett, Coleman & Co. Ltd., "the country's largest, multi-product and most powerful newspaper publishing company" (Ram, 2000, p. 253), whose flagship is *TOI*, had this to say about the raison d'être of the print media:

> For the moment, print media cannot do without advertising as it accounts for 80% of your revenue. The advertiser, thus, becomes the primary customer of the print media. . . . So, I, the print media, am not trying to get readers for my product, but I get customers, who happen to be my readers, for my advertisers. . . . I have a mental picture of the ideal *Economic Times* reader, his lifestyle, consumption habits, etc. So I can create the brand to cater to this reader. (cited in Das, 1999, p. 58)

The prevailing atmosphere ensured that there was more and more emphasis on the entertainment aspect of the media. Strong, unconventional views on a number of issues simultaneously became less and less acceptable within the mainstream media. Celebrity and lifestyle journalism became new growth areas within the press as it sought to meet the challenges posed by other, newer media. According to the media executive just quoted:

> News or information is no longer the logic for buying a newspaper. . . . The question what will make people buy and read the newspaper is getting more and more challenging. You have to entertain them, constantly. . . . I tell my journalist friends that these days each headline is looked at for entertainment. And what's wrong in it? When business and political sentiments are down why not offer feel-good journalism? In a happy mode you consume more. And that's what every advertiser wants . . . (cited in Das, 1999, p. 58)

Some of the "deeply worrying tendencies" in the Indian press at the turn of the millennium have been identified as:

> Increasing concentration of ownership in some language sectors of the Indian press; higher levels of manipulation of news, analysis, and public affairs information to suit the owners' financial and political interests; the downgrading and devaluing of editorial functions and content in some leading newspaper organizations; the growing willingness within newspapers to tailor the editorial product to serve advertising and marketing goals set by owners and senior management personnel; Murdoch-style price wars and aggressive practices in the home bases of other newspapers to overwhelm

and kill competition, raising fears about media monopoly; and rampant corruption. (Ram, 2000, pp. 256-257)

It was this brave new world that the ever higher numbers of women aspiring to be journalists entered in the 1990s. It was also in this radically altered setting that a number of the more experienced media women neared the top of the editorial ladder and a handful achieved what would have been unthinkable just a couple of decades earlier.

By the end of the decade, it was evident that the number of women in journalism in India had reached an unprecedented high, although there is still no quantitative data to corroborate this observable reality. Equally obvious was the fact that women were playing an increasingly visible and valuable role in the press, both as writers and editors. Bylines by women had become commonplace not only in magazines and feature sections but also on the news and editorial pages of dailies. Women were writing on a wide range of current events and issues, including subjects related to the high-prestige areas of politics, business and economics, international relations, and what is euphemistically known as defense.

The high visibility of women in news and current affairs programs of the newly burgeoning television medium—as correspondents, anchors, and hosts—had added to the impression among people, both within and outside the media, that the metropolitan media in India were virtually on the brink of a female take-over. It was perhaps a sign of the times that the heroines of a number of recent feature films and television serials in several Indian languages were intrepid female journalists. In the Hindi movie, *Dil Se*, for example, a female human bomb or suicide bomber masqueraded as a newspaper journalist to gain access to her target. Women as journalists had obviously entered the popular imagination.

However, as the century and the millennium drew to a close, it was not clear whether women's participation in other sections and aspects of the press was as widespread as it seemed from the evidence in English-language publications located in media centers like Delhi (the political capital) and Mumbai (the commercial capital). Nor was it clear what larger numbers meant in terms of women's professional status, mobility, and influence within the press. Furthermore, little was known about their experiences in a hitherto male-dominated field that was still widely viewed in many parts of the country as an unconventional—if not inappropriate—career for women. Also unclear was the question of how women in journalism saw themselves in the context of the profession and the society to which they belonged.

WOMEN'S EXPERIENCES AND PERSPECTIVES

In the research reported here, I interviewed a convenience sample of more than 200 Indian women working as journalists in different parts of the country (and some locations overseas), in the press in English as well as other Indian languages, at various levels in the editorial hierarchy, and in different branches of journalism. Although I attempted to cover as wide a spectrum of journalists as possible, the choice was dictated by a number of factors: professional placement, personal acquaintance, mutually convenient availability, and referrals where I depended on third parties to effect introductions. However, I did strive for a geographic and linguistic spread and I also made a deliberate effort to include women journalists of different ages and levels of experience, who represented not only different persuasions and perspectives but were also engaged in different spheres of journalistic activity. In the end, I was able to meet women journalists in four metropolitan cities, three state capitals, and three other cities. In addition, I received responses to questionnaires from women working as journalists in six more cities in the north, south, west, east, and northeast regions, as well as a few working abroad.

Women in journalism clearly cannot be herded into a single, stereotypical category. The experiences and perspectives of women in different sections of the press, at different levels, in different parts of India are, unsurprisingly, different. Apart from gender, a variety of factors influence both their experiences and their perceptions. These include their socioeconomic and cultural location as individuals, their political perspective, the sociocultural milieu in which they live and work, as well as the economics and culture of the media establishments to which they belong. However, it is clear that Indian women in journalism are bound together by a number of common experiences—whether or not they like or choose to acknowledge the fact. Most of these arise from the reality that gender continues to play a significant role in the way women are perceived and treated by others, both within the profession and in the wider society. Evidently, even if women journalists wish to "transcend gender," "de-sex" themselves and to be viewed and treated as "professionals like anyone else"—as many of them put it—it is not always possible because they are perceived first as women by many of those they have to deal with on a daily basis. In any case, the shared experiences lead, necessarily, to some common ground.

It appears from this study that the self-image of women journalists is remarkably positive and that even those who have had unpleasant experiences or who function in hostile environments seem to have resisted blaming themselves for their situation. The confidence and clarity with which women describe and analyze their position and condition within the profession is striking. Nevertheless, there is considerable convergence of opinion about the obstacles that women journalists still encounter because of their sex. The few gender-linked advantages cited by some women seem insignificant compared to the long list of gender-based disadvantages outlined by the majority.

The growing number of women in the media workforce, particularly in media centers like Mumbai and Delhi, has created the impression that the barriers that once restricted women's entry into the press have been overcome. However, in many parts of the country and certain sections of the press, resistance even to the recruitment of women persists to the present day. According to a young Hyderabad-based journalist who found it difficult to land a job after graduating from journalism school, "Although job advertisements do not specify gender, women's applications are often not considered. Telugu newspaper managers think ten times before they hire a woman because they are not convinced about women's capabilities or long-term interest in the profession."

The increasing visibility of women in the so-called mainstream, national press—as both writers and editors—may suggest that there are no more impediments in women's path to the top of the editorial pyramid. However, many female journalists still experience slow and limited progress, if not total stagnation, in their careers. In addition, the existence of invisible barricades that currently keep women from occupying the very top spots in the hierarchy (of major newspapers in particular) is widely acknowledged, even by women who have reached relatively high positions within their news organizations. The infamous glass ceiling may have developed some cracks in a small, although admittedly influential, section of the press, but it has still not been shattered. Elsewhere in the press the ceiling—glass or otherwise—is so far above them that it is not within most women's sights.

The spectacular success of a number of women in a wide range of high profile areas of journalism, hitherto assumed to be male terrain, implies that there is nothing to stop competent and determined women from fulfilling their professional dreams. However, the tendency to relegate women to particular functions and beats within the press has not disappeared: Many women state that they are not given a chance to demonstrate their capabilities, especially in what is known as hardcore, mainstream journalism. "There is still a weird idea in Marathi journalism that women don't and can't know much about politics. They prefer women to do 'harmless' things," said a Pune-based journalist who has handled several beats and developed good sources even in the supposedly rough world of labor unions.

At the same time, a number of women question some of the hoary traditions of the profession. For example, a significant proportion disagree with the separation of news and issues into 'hard' and 'soft' categories and especially the privileging of the former over the latter. Most acknowledge that it is necessary to break into the high-prestige hard news areas of political or financial writing in order to get ahead under the present system. But quite a few also believe it is time to demystify some of the age-old holy cows of journalism, such as the assumption that coverage of politics is the acme of journalism. Such internal questioning of the hard versus soft news dichotomy is significant because traditional categories and hierarchies are often seen as immutable realities by many media professionals.

In addition, a large number of women in the profession is concerned about recent shifts in the agendas of major sections of the media, and the consequent dramatic increase in the quantum and prominence of celebrity and lifestyle journalism. In the words of a Delhi-based journalist with a special interest in development, "The Indian media have become increasingly obsessed with politics, the corporate world, fashion, personalities, 'pop' culture, and the world of entertainment. Scant attention is paid to the problems of living which confront people at the turn of the century."

As in many parts of the world, there are minorities within minorities in terms of disadvantage in India. There is little doubt that class, caste, creed, and ethnicity play a significant role in determining who, even among women, gains entry into the media and has the opportunity to rise in the profession, although there is currently no data on the socioeconomic and cultural composition of the Indian press corps, male or female.

Meanwhile, the controversy over women and night work continues to rage in many parts of the country even now. Some establishments still try to evade statutory provisions for women working late hours (such as transport or dormitory facilities) by excusing women from the night shift and/or using night duty to justify not hiring female staff. A number of women seem ambivalent about the issue, mainly because of anxieties about safety, domestic responsibilities, and social disapproval. On the other hand, many women are critical of female colleagues who are reluctant to work on the later shifts, pointing out that women cannot hope for career advancement if they demand special concessions. Under the circumstances, quite a few women seem to feel that they are damned if they do work at night and damned if they do not.

To make matters worse, women's struggle to reconcile the conflicting demands of work and family endures. For journalists, this universal problem is exacerbated by the long, late, and irregular hours as well as the erratic and unpredictable work schedules that commonly characterize the profession. In India, women continue to shoulder primary responsibility for home and family, with few formal, organized, dependable support systems to lighten their domestic burden. The problem is particularly acute for women from tradition-bound, middle-class families who cannot afford to hire full-time domestic help.

In addition, a number of women confess that they continue to feel the oppressive pressure of constantly having to prove themselves in a profession dominated by men and masculine attitudes, despite the proven track record of a number of women. Many also mention difficulties with cultivating news sources, who are still overwhelmingly male and, especially in some parts of the country and certain fields, not accustomed to dealing with women on a professional footing.

Interestingly, however, these difficulties pale before the problems that many women seem to encounter in their relationships with their male colleagues. These range from condescension and belittlement at one end of the spectrum to sexual and professional harassment at the other. Curiously, most of them have more complaints about contemporaries than about seniors in the profession, including editors, suggesting that male peers are more problematic than older and/or more powerful men in the profession.

Young women entering the profession in the 2000s naturally reflect many of the attitudes and mores prevalent in middle and upper class Indian society in the 21st century. Having gained from the experiences and struggles of their predecessors (whether or not they acknowledge this), they may be well placed to push aside the remaining obstructions in the career paths of women in the media. On the other hand, they may need to carefully sidestep fresh pitfalls, such as new *avatars*[2] of the "ladies' beat," as both the media and society change with the times. For example, if in the old days women in the field were asked to cover flower shows, dog shows, baby shows, and the like, today there is a preponderance of young women on the pop culture and celebrity beat, covering fashion shows and beauty contests, Valentine's Day celebrations, and high-society parties.

Indian women have not only arrived but are clearly determined to stay in journalism, despite the trials and tribulations that many of them report. What is more, they have already made an impact in the profession, with many excelling in the conventional, prestigious and glamorous areas of journalism and many more expanding the boundaries of the field in terms of the scope, breadth, depth and approach of media coverage. At the same time, it is clear that the attitudes of colleagues and family members still place stumbling blocks in the paths of a number of media women. It is also obvious that the structures and systems of media organizations, not to mention society, have yet to be sufficiently transformed to enable women's full, free, fearless, and unfettered participation in the profession.

GENDER AND PROFESSIONALISM

The focus of this section is on the possible role and impact of gender on the perceptions and performance of women in the profession. Like professional women in many other parts of the world, journalists in India tend to shy away from identification or classification by gender. Although only a few women were vehemently opposed to the term *woman journalist*, most confessed that they were uncomfortable with what they perceived to be an unnecessary, unflattering, and, indeed, pejorative label that, for them, implied some degree of inferiority or disability. They expressed concern about the negative connotations of a gender-based category, which could accentuate difference and exacerbate disadvantage. A few journalists saw the term as entirely favorable, convinced that women tended to be better journalists because their experiences as members of a disadvantaged social group led them to question the status quo—an approach that they saw as an asset in the profession. Others maintained that recognition of

---

[2]Incarnation, manifestation

gender as a crucial component of an individual's identity did not presuppose any contradiction between being a woman and being a professional.

In addition, a number of interviewees called attention to the likely social benefits of their gender identity in creating positive role models, encouraging successive generations of women to enter the profession and expanding the spaces within the media to highlight gender-related issues. According to some, spotlighting women's growing presence in the high-profile and traditionally male world of journalism could also have a favorable impact on society at large, countering outdated ideas about gender-segregated professions and promoting "the democratization of social norms." Others suggested that it was, in the end, a matter of individual choice. As one of them put it, "Some people see gender as a significant aspect of their identity, others want to transcend the fact of being a woman and be treated as a person." But, according to several women, the question was not so much personal preference as societal perception: Women might prefer to be identified as human beings and treated as "people," but they were nevertheless compelled by external forces to remember that they belonged to the "second sex."

Despite differences of opinion on gender as a distinguishing feature, there was a surprising consensus on what qualities could be associated with female journalists. Even many of those who disapproved of classification by gender seemed to think that women in the profession shared a number of positive characteristics. Words like *conscientious, sincere, committed, earnest, responsible, dependable, hard working, efficient, thorough, meticulous,* and *fastidious,* for instance, were repeatedly used by a wide range of female journalists to describe the attributes that they think women have traditionally brought to their jobs in the press. Many women in the profession said they believed that women—in both the English and the vernacular press—tended to have a greater command of language as well as better writing skills than most men. Several interviewees suggested that women journalists as a group were less likely to be corrupt and corruptible than some of their male counterparts. A number of them also pointed out that women often demonstrated more staying power than their male colleagues, especially when it came to the consistent coverage of undramatic and unglamorous but important social processes. Some women said they saw evidence of women's steadfastness in other aspects of work, too. As one woman put it, "In a crisis situation, women generally come out better. They are more steady as human beings." Few seemed to dispute these obvious generalizations, not even those who vociferously opposed categorization by gender.

However, the question of whether women bring any special perspective to their work as journalists appeared to be quite contentious. Some journalists pointed out that gender was such an integral aspect of a person's identity that it could not help but influence professional perceptions and choices. They suggested that women brought more sensitivity, passion, and depth to media coverage of news and issues. According to them, women were more likely to put faces to events and numbers and to focus media attention on social trends. Several interviewees were of the opinion that women usually have a more comprehensive perspective than men, possibly because of the wide range of interests, activities, and responsibilities that form a routine part of their daily lives. They said they believed that women were less prone to tunnel vision, more given to looking at things "in the round" and thereby more likely to see the bigger picture.

But a number of those interviewed said they could not say for sure whether women actually introduced a different worldview or adapted to the prevailing norms of the profession. As a senior journalist pointed out, "Some women bring in different perspectives, others don't. The longer you remain in the profession the less likely you are to retain a fresh perspective." Claiming that the worldview of many media women was not significantly different from that of their male colleagues, another said, "I sometimes wonder whether the perspective they project is their own or one adopted early in life as the best way to get on in the world, especially the media world. At times I wonder whether the reason why women now seem to be getting jobs in the media with relative ease is because there is no danger that a different perspective will intrude on mainstream media content."

Many agreed that differences in perspective depended less on gender than on an individual's background, interests, and convictions. Some suggested that consciousness of gender as a social construct and awareness of what are known as "women's issues"—both of which are more common among women than men—could be a professional asset, fostering the critical, questioning approach required to discharge the media's watchdog function.

The question of whether women in journalism have a special role and responsibility on account of their gender, particularly in terms of ensuring more and better coverage of women's issues, aroused strong feelings. Some journalists rejected outright the idea that they were duty-bound to promote the cause of other women. Others not only accepted the additional charge but also bemoaned the fact that many women in the field shunned what they see as a vital responsibility. A middle position was taken by those who view gender-related issues as just one of the many areas they think they should cover as part of their professional duty. Many journalists asserted that the onus of writing about gender-related issues should not be on women alone. They pointed out that both men and women in the profession ought to be gender sensitive and to feel responsible for balanced media coverage of all newsworthy events and important issues, including those likely to have a special impact on women.

If some women in the profession prefer not to be associated with any cause, let alone women's issues, it is not always because they are disinterested. From my inquiries, it would appear that at least some of them choose to adopt such a stance, irrespective of personal inclination, in order to avoid jeopardizing their professional prospects. Apart from their understandable desire to avoid labels and ghettos, there is an additional disincentive in the form of the current devaluation of the concept of social responsibility within the profession as a whole.

Under the circumstances, it is remarkable that a number of young women in the field said they consider gender an important issue to focus on. As one of them put it, "Women's issues are part of the basket of issues I would push to write on—not because I'm a woman but because they are important and because they relate to a section of society that doesn't easily find a voice in the media." According to another young journalist, "Our generation has little idealism left. But the little that remains seems to be with the women."

There was considerable ambivalence on the question of whether the increasing presence of women in the press has had any impact on media content or media organizations. There were those who believed that it had made a significant difference. For instance, a number of interviewees credited women with having introduced more human interest in media content. They suggested that women journalists had a tendency to look at the human side of a story even while covering hard news.

Others suggested that those publications that were run or controlled by women tended to reflect the generally broad outlook of their female editors, covering a wide range of subjects, offering a good mix of serious and light stories and thus catering to a diverse audience. Some pointed out, however, that this trend could have a downside, especially for dailies, if mainstream journalism became too "featurish" and lifestyle-oriented at the cost of hard-core political coverage. Most interviewees acknowledged that women had contributed significantly to broadening the scope of press coverage, and not just in the context of women's issues. According to them, women had made a considerable difference to the coverage of social issues in general (education, health, children's rights and welfare, environmental degradation, etc.) and women's issues in particular. Many of these issues related to human development and rights, social and economic justice, culture and other vital aspects of life and society that had been neglected by a press traditionally preoccupied with politics (in the narrow sense) and government.

Some professionals, however, are not convinced that women have made a major difference to journalism as a whole, especially in the area of political reportage and analysis. As one senior woman journalist put it, "A few individual women journalists have produced some great journalism but as a category they have not made a qualitative difference. If women do produce a different brand of journalism, here it is still journalism in the making." In this context, some journalists suggested that if women had not yet had a major impact on the media it was because few occupied decision-making positions and even fewer had the confidence and courage to risk treading a different path even if they wanted to.

There was considerable divergence of opinion, especially among young women, on whether gender makes a difference to leadership style. A number of interviewees said they did not believe women at or near the top influenced work culture in any special way. Some acknowledged that this could be because women professionals had little option but to conform to the prevailing culture of the organization they were working in. A few suggested that senior, successful women journalists were often no better and occasionally worse than their male counterparts. A number of them were seen as aggressively ambitious and autocratic in their professional dealings, and not particularly supportive of other women.

The perception among some young journalists that female bosses were less sympathetic and more strict than equivalent men was attributed by others to the fact that juniors with a tendency to cite gender-related reasons for professional lapses would find it more difficult to get past senior women with lame excuses. As one respondent put it, "A fellow woman can't be fooled as easily as a man who may hesitate to call a female junior's bluff"—for fear of being misunderstood, if nothing else. Another pointed out that concurrence with patriarchal notions about female roles and responsibilities could also make paternalistic male bosses indulge demands by some women for special concessions and privileges.

Still, a number of interviewees claimed that female editors tended to be more empathetic, less egotistic, more willing mentors and better bosses than men, especially for other women in the profession. Several women editors suggested that their awareness and understanding of the numerous roles women play and the multiple pressures they function under usually encouraged them to accommodate female colleagues' special needs, particularly at certain points in their lives. Others who headed editorial departments said they had been able to build cohesive and effective teams and bring out the best in their staff because of their approach to managing people, which included getting to know colleagues at an informal, personal level and establishing a rapport with them both emotionally and professionally.

There seemed to be some agreement among the women journalists interviewed on the proposition that gender may be a less critical factor in determining editorial-management style than individual personality. Yet most journalists admitted that women working together usually created a warmer, friendlier working environment, significantly different from the atmosphere in male-dominated media workplaces, especially when a woman was also in charge. Many suggested that offices with a preponderance of women were often marked by camaraderie and intimacy. Some pointed out that newsrooms including women were less likely to be hotbeds of bad language and sexist or risqué humor.

Highlighting the advantages of a female-dominated workplace, the editor of an Indian women's magazine said,

> Women have a different working style. Men tend to push work into the evenings. They don't have an internal alarm—so they hang around, loiter, and shoot the breeze. Women tend to be more focussed workers: working hard through the day and getting out of the office at a decent hour. Also, since women are used to managing chaos they are able to manage work as

well. When women work together there is less tension and conflict about how work is to be organized. At one time, one thought one had to desexualize oneself and be more like a man. But now, surrounded by women, one doesn't have to play the male any more. One doesn't have to deny the fact that one has a home and children and a life outside the office. (Joseph, 2000, p. 215)

CONCLUSION

It is clear that women in print media in India have divergent views on the role and impact of gender on their professional selves and working lives. There is a conspicuous dichotomy in their perceptions of themselves as individuals and journalists, and as women. Despite the fact that many women have been publicly recognized for their excellent work, to a large number of them "female" continues to connote inferiority. On the other hand, many women in the profession—including some who oppose classification by gender—voluntarily propose that women possess certain inherent qualities that enhance their contribution to the press in a number of ways. A majority also admits that women face special, gender-linked problems within the profession.

The apparent contradiction in these positions is not as curious and puzzling as it may seem. Women are deeply influenced by gender ideology, especially if they have not been exposed to feminist critiques of the patriarchal worldview and empowered to question the assumptions that underlie it. A number of other identities (class, caste, creed, race, and ethnicity, among others) influence women's access to and experiences in the profession, their interactions with its structures and other individuals within it. These, in turn, are bound to determine their perceptions to a significant extent.

The discussion in India on gender identity and professional identity raises questions about the relative influence of gender and other factors on women's practice of and performance in journalism. I am inclined to think that some characteristics and contributions attributed to women in the profession may be influenced by factors other than or, at least, in addition to gender. For example, the generalized assumption that women journalists are exceptionally conscientious and hard working could be due to the fact that they are, as a group, still under pressure to prove themselves.

Similarly, the expansion in the scope of press coverage since the mid-1970s was clearly influenced by events and processes within and outside the country, such as the State of Emergency (1975-1977) and the growth of popular movements for women's empowerment, human rights, environmental protection, and so on. These developments obviously stimulated public concern about and media interest in these issues. When, in the mid-1970s, women began to enter print journalism in significant numbers, they brought these concerns into their work, as did several men. Although gender may well have played a part in making media coverage more broad-based (and I believe it has), other factors are also likely to have contributed to this development.

The controversy over perspectives may also arise from the fact that gender is not the sole determining feature of an individual's life. Although most women are likely to have similar reactions to certain issues—such as violence against women—their analysis and their views on other, less emotive gender-related issues may very well depend more on their exposure to information and ideas and the overall ideology to which they subscribe than on the mere fact that they are female.

In the final analysis, there is little doubt that women have made a perceptible mark on major sections of the Indian media and altered the atmosphere in those newsrooms where they have a significant presence. At the same time it is also quite clear that the increasing presence of women in the profession has neither democratized nor feminized the Indian press. Indeed their large-scale entry into the profession during the 1990s and their unprecedented professional achievements during this period also, paradoxically, coincided with the dilution of core journalistic values and a reduction in journalistic independence from proprietorial control. It is also clear that the structures and systems of media organizations, not to mention society, have yet to be sufficiently transformed to enable women's full and unfettered participation in the profession. Against this background, it remains to be seen whether women's rise in the media—in terms of numbers as well as seniority and decision-making powers—will translate into a transformation of media content, structures, and systems.

REFERENCES

Census of India, (2001). Delhi: Government of India. URL (consulted October 2001: http://www.censusindia.net/results/resultsmain.html)

Das, B. (1999, June). The paper chase. *Gentleman*, pp. 57-61.

Indian Readership Survey, (2001). Delhi: Business Standard/The Hoot URL (consulted October 2001): www.thehoot.org)

Joseph, A. (2000). *Women in journalism: Making news*. New Delhi: The Media Foundation/Konark.

Joseph, A., & Sharma, K. (1994). *Whose news? The media and women's issues*. New Delhi: Sage.

Manorama Yearbook 2001 (2001). Kottayam: Malayala Manorama.

Ram, N. (2000). The great Indian media bazaar: Emerging trends and issues for the future. In R. Thapar (Ed.), *India: Another millennium?* (pp. 241-292). New Delhi: Viking/Penguin India.

Tripathi, P.S. (2000, April 20). Day the news went missing. *The Asian Age*, p. 14.

10

Gender in the Newsroom: Canadian Experiences

Gertrude J. Robinson

CANADIAN PRINT
AND BROADCAST PERSONNEL

Women's entry into the Canadian media professions was not chronicled until the early 1970s when I began to survey their position in the daily press. This research demonstrated that women's status in this "prestige"—read "male"— profession was that of a minority, even though North America's post-World War II economies had opened up the public world of work for women. In Canada more than 3 million women entered the labor force between 1970 and 1994, and their workforce participation increased from 34% to 45% (Statistics Canada, 1995). Both the press and broadcasting benefited from this labor market shift (Robinson, 1975, 1977). In the 20 years between 1974 and 1994, women increased their presence on daily newspaper staffs from one in five to almost one in three (21% to 28%), whereas in broadcasting their presence quadrupled from a low of 10% to a high of 38%.

To gain an up-to-date snapshot of women's professional progress in the Canadian print and television studios I surveyed the role and position of Canadian female and male journalists in both 1974 and 1994. Survey I covered all of Canada's 114 dailies and 118 television outlets. It involved a telephone interview to determine the number, distribution, and organizational position of female and male editorial newspaper and television staff in Canada's five regions. Survey II (the attitude survey) was conducted in 1995. It constructed a

regionally weighted proportionate representative sample of 134 female and
male journalists, matched by age, position, and geographic location, to probe
gender differences in the workplace. It was designed to assess diverse workplace experiences, management attitudes including affirmative action policies,
journalistic self-perceptions, journalistic goals and values, as well as the news
production values of female and male practitioners. The response rate to this in-
depth quantitative and qualitative questionnaire was 92%, based on the return of
123 questionnaires.

These surveys indicate that half the new media recruits in Canada were
women and, as in the United States, the median age of female personnel continued to be lower than that for males in the profession. In Canada it stood at 34
and 40 years, respectively, for females and males, and in the United States at 30
and 33 years (Weaver & Wilhoit, 1991). In Canada, the reduction in median
ages is primarily found in television, where station growth opened up new
opportunities for the recruitment of younger professionals. Canadian newspapers, in contrast to the United States, have stagnated and therefore employ proportionally more older personnel. Age reductions for women according to
Scandinavian research exemplify the effectiveness of affirmative action programs in recruiting females and minorities into the media professions in those
countries and elsewhere (Lofgren-Nilsson, 1993).

Gendered Work and Family Expectations

Despite the fact that gender and communication studies have begun to demonstrate that newsroom work is different for female and male personnel, communication scholarship continues to perpetuate the orthodoxy that women's different experiences are a result of their lesser numbers in the newsroom. In studies
of this kind, gender is considered a biological attribute that exists in isolation
from social characteristics like ethnicity, status, and education (see Pritchard &
Sauvageau, 1999). Although this might have been a persuasive argument in the
1970s, gender studies have indicated that such a view is not only oversimplified, but factually wrong today: Newsroom work for women is different
because of systemic biases in the social reproduction of the profession (see
Creedon, 1993) These systemic biases are recreated through classificatory
and evaluative procedures, which use gender dualisms to define women
and ethnic minorities as "different" and then fall back on these classificatory
differences as reasons for the unequal evaluations of women's newsroom
activities.

In Canadian society, as in North America and Europe, the systemic biases
that affect how female and male journalists perform their jobs are grounded in
gender-based assumptions about how work and family obligations should be
combined. Traditional role norms prescribe work and family responsibilities by

gender, but by the end of the 20th century, a new option for integrating these two roles had emerged. Married women's increased employment introduced a reduction of women's family roles, but, virtually no increase in the husband's family involvement (Armstrong & Armstrong, 1990). As a consequence, Pleck (1984) noted, employed wives face strain and exhaustion in combining their work with their family roles. The husband's family role is unresponsive to changes in the wife's working role (men do not take on more household tasks when their wives work) and women are expected to place family obligations above their work roles.

These gendered work and family role expectations have effects on how women journalists organize their working lives and may explain why there are still fewer women than men in the profession. Our findings show several gender-based difficulties women encounter in trying to combine their family obligations with their professional ambitions in the Canadian media. They are differential rates of marriage, differential numbers of children for female and male professionals, the strains of "meshing" work with family responsibilities, and the effects of what may be called "masculinist" career notions.

Marriage Rates

Our proportional gender sample ($n = 62$ women; $n = 61$ men) indicates that in the mid-1990s, only 65% of the female journalists were married or lived with a partner, whereas 81% of the 61 males were married.

Number of Children

Even more striking, nearly two thirds of female journalists had no children, whereas only one third of males were childless. Female journalists with children, furthermore, had fewer children than their male counterparts. Of the 26 female journalists with children, the greatest number (17) had only one, with the remaining 5 females having two children, and only 4 women in the sample had three or more children. In contrast, of the 42 males with children, the numbers of children were substantially higher. Eleven men had one child, 18 men had two, and a 13 men had three or more children.

Work and Family Responsibilities

The small group of female journalists with children had greater difficulty reconciling work and family responsibilities than did their male colleagues. As expected, a greater proportion of working mothers (42%) than fathers mentioned child-care arrangements and other obligations that interfered with their work schedule from time to time. For working fathers, only 31% voiced the same complaints. Interestingly, the 68% of men who saw no problem combining work with family responsibilities were of this opinion, irrespective of whether they had children or not, indicating that their wives assumed (or were expected to assume) all family-related responsibilities. Pleck (1984) pointed to this as a manifestation of the fact that work–family roles for women and men continue to be segregated by a dual market and also by what he called *asymmetrically* permeable boundaries. Working women are expected to do most of the housework and their family roles are expected to intrude on their work roles. For instance, when there is a crisis at school, it is the working mother, rather than the working father who is usually called to take responsibility. For the husband on the other hand, the work–family permeability is in the opposite direction. The working father is expected to manage his family responsibilities so that they do not interfere with his work efficiency. Consequently, as is seen here, male journalists are much more able than their female colleagues to participate in the after-hour "pub culture" and to benefit from the informal, mostly male networks created through these encounters.

"Masculinist" Career Notions

This career model penalizes females but not males for work interruptions. Our attitude survey showed that overall, 27% of all female journalists, but only 19% of men, at all levels of the newsroom hierarchy had interrupted their careers at least once. For women, these interruptions were overwhelmingly caused by the birth of a child. Men listed study, travel, or relocation as their main reasons for the interruptions of their journalism careers. Interviews established that the evaluation of career interruptions was different for male and female media workers. For males, these interruptions are interpreted as career-building strategies, whereas for females, because they have to do with childbearing, they were seen as career inhibitors. These differential outcomes seem to be closely connected to a traditional view of motherhood. (Such a view is also reflected in the miserly maternity leave policies in North America, which in contrast to Europe, offer only between 2 weeks and 3 months of paid family leave after child birth.)

All of this evidence adds up to the understanding that journalism has a work culture that is nonhomogeneous (Melin-Higgins & Djerf-Pierre, 1998), in which women and minorities are not equal participants, but must conceive of themselves as "different," and inferior. Within this nonhomogeneous culture, the male understandings of professional practice are systematically advantaged. Females within the working community, by reason of their unique work–family relationships, will not only have to develop different strategies for building their professional careers, but also create different understandings of how to perform their work roles in the heterosexual newsroom. All of these social practicessystematically discourage Canadian women from entering the journalism professions.

PROFESSIONAL "CLIMATE" IN THE NEWSROOM

Professional climate in the newsroom and the ways in which females are supposed to "enact" their working roles, are also culturally constructed and therefore gendered. The attitude survey illuminated different aspects of the journalistic culture and its effects on female practitioners. Although it was initially assumed that the newsroom's working "climate" was a relatively simple variable, which was conceived as a neutral "professional ethos" (Löfgren-Nilsson, 1993), comparative research has shown that it too is organized around a man-as-norm and woman-as-interloper structure (Ross, 2000). This suggests that the informal workplace activities reinforcing the systemic marginalization of female colleagues, need further scrutiny. Several researchers in Sweden, the United Kingdom, and Germany (Djerf-Pierre, 1996; Klaus, 1998; Melin-Higgins, 1998; Ross, 2000) discovered that newsroom climate is sexist in both tone and practice. This means that irrespective of competence, the male incumbents try to reinforce their power superiority in the workplace through a variety of symbolic practices.

Several of these practices have, by now, been widely documented. The first is the "communicative style" between colleagues that permeates the newsroom. Melin-Higgins & Djerf-Pierre (1998) called it "locker room humor," whereas other researchers refer to it as "banter." In Britain, this humorous banter focuses on team sports such as soccer, cricket, and rugby and also contains sexist and racist jokes (Melin-Higgins & Djerf-Pierre, 1998). In Canada, my interviewees mentioned that it utilizes football and ice hockey as its vehicle, team sports where women are not yet widely legitimated. Because females are generally not as interested in contact sports, this informal communication practice turns out to be a not too subtle mechanism for excluding women reporters from workplace interactions and making them feel like outsiders.

The "competitive culture" of the newsroom is another aspect of symbolic newsroom practices that female respondents have identified. It draws attention to the fact that story assignment is not cooperatively worked out, but struggled over. In this contest, not only story areas (beats), but also interview assignments are gender stereotyped. High-profile interviews with federal politicians will be assigned to males, whereas low-priority school and health stories go to female reporters. Bourdieu explained this contest as an asymmetrical prestige exchange process, in which male incumbents are able to convert their "political capital" based on power, into "cultural capital," namely desirable story assignments (Bourdieu, 1991). In the heterosexual newsroom, this exchange process is tilted against female reporters because their cultural capital will not be accepted as equal to that of the males in the newsroom hierarchy. Clearly, such gender-role positioning places female practitioners into an attitudinal double-bind, pitting their status against their competence (Klaus, 1998). One of our interviewees, a Canadian press reporter touches on the struggle to compete for stories by remarking:

We have helped bring issues traditionally deemed "women's issues" such
as health, parenting, and family or relationship concerns to the forefront.
Not only do we ensure these issues get covered, we are getting them off the
lifestyle pages and on to the front pages of newspapers. . . . Although we
still have a way to go.

A third and final aspect of newsroom culture, which has already been allud-
ed to, also disadvantages women and thus helps to marginalize female reporters.
It is the after-hour pub tradition, which extends the already long working day
into the wee hours of the night. Only female reporters without family obligations or children are able to participate in the drinking bouts, where the "old
boys network" is created and sustained. This network informally influences
work assignments, affects promotions, and also creates gendered work-role
expectations that are sterotyped in film and elsewhere by the hard drinking,
trench-coated reporter. Humphrey Bogart plays this character to perfection in
the movie *Casablanca*.

To test whether these gendered workplace expectations translate into differences in how females and males enact their newsroom roles, the Canadian
sample was asked whether women had to perform more of the "private sphere"
activities, those in which feminist researchers have suspected differential
performance criteria, such as: pick up after others, answer phones, look for
documents, comfort colleagues, be a lightning rod, or make or get coffee.

Women and men showed a marked difference in specifying the tasks that
women perform more frequently than men in the newsroom. The performance
of three tasks stood out: comforting colleagues (54% of the females compared
with 19% of males); being a lighting rod (41% females compared with 13%
males); and answering the telephone (39% females compared with 8% males).
In addition, women were seven times as likely as men to say that they "pick up
after others" (22% of women compared to 3% of men) and four times as likely
to say they "look for documents" (22% of women compared to 6% of men). The
perceived gendered distribution of these tasks demonstrates that the heterosexual newsroom continues to assign the labor-intensive relationship-building
"mothering" and "housekeeping" roles to female professionals, even though
women and men should arguably be equally responsible for the smooth functioning of newsroom relations and tasks. Only one traditional activity, that of
"coffee making" has, over the years, become de-gendered, indicating that even
in the newsroom, stereotypical task assignments *can* be shifted.

Despite increased recruitment of women into the field, the Canadian findings demonstrate that workplace expectations continue to be unequal and
gender-based. These gendered expectations force female professionals to enact
their newsroom roles either in conformity with these expectations or in opposition to them. Even when they conform, the evidence shows, females are either
systematically excluded through such negative symbolic practices as banter and
competitive attitudes, or they have to do more of those types of tasks which are

relationship- and efficiency-building for everyone on the job. All of these strategies are designed to perpetuate the male power structure of the profession.

Gender researchers in North America and Europe agree that increased numbers of women in the profession will not automatically lead to changes in newsroom practices. They also concur that equity policies, which strive for merit-based equality of opportunity for all, are essential for creating change in the 21st century. I support this prediction on the grounds that the median age of Canadian professionals has decreased from 40 years to 37 years in the past two decades. This means that the older generation of journalists (those over 55 years of age with a lower level of education), will be retiring over the next 10 years and a younger generation of Canadian practitioners will become more dominant—a generation that has been used to the presence of female colleagues and has become sensitized to equity issues in the workplace.

Gendered Workplace Pressures?

Despite the inequalities women journalists face in the newsroom setting, research shows that female professionals rarely feel discriminated against on the job (Weaver & Wilhoit, 1991). Their job satisfaction rates are consequently as high as those of their male colleagues. How can these findings be reconciled with the evidence that women are expected to perform their roles differently from men? Is there any evidence that female colleagues develop different strategies for dealing with workplace pressures? How do these pressures affect the female understanding of their reportorial role? There are clearly no simple answers to these complex queries. Gender differences alone cannot explain the variegated workplace strategies that female journalists employ. Other relevant considerations, as we have seen, are such social characteristics as marital status, numbers of children, position in the newsroom, as well as individual responses to the power structure. At present, there are no studies that systematically interrelate the afore mentioned and other social factors with gender. However, some researchers have begun to explore female responses to the power structure at work through in-depth interviews.

For example, Melin-Higgins and Djerf-Pierre (1998) documented three types of coping strategies that female professionals develop, depending on the type of organization in which they are employed. Some women adapt by becoming "one of the boys" and embracing the male values and employing their "objectivist" reporting style. Others oppose the prevalent culture and choose what Melin-Higgins and Djerf-Pierre called a "mission" approach. These female reporters follow an ethic of "making a difference to people and society." One might call this group of professionals, journalists with a "feminist" outlook even though they need not belong to an organized women's movement. What they do have in common is that they conceive of their reporting role in light of equity criteria and are concerned with understanding and explaining women's social existence. Consequently, their political stories explore and enhance the opportunities for female politicians, or they focus on rape and child abuse as important health issues for which women should seek professional help. Because this group of professionals was perceived as having developed a female "counterculture" in the newsroom, their capabilities were frequently undervalued and they faced substantial promotion difficulties. A final strategy for female journalists is to "opt out" of the gendered newsroom situation and its long hours of work, by becoming freelancers. This group of females and males tends to want to combine work with children. They additionally wish to do more critical and in-depth analysis than is possible on the tight newsroom schedules (Melin-Higgins & Djerf-Pierre, 1998). Exactly when and under what circumstances female professionals opt for one of the three coping strategies requires further research.

The extent to which Canadian journalists chose to opt out and become free-lancers is extremely difficult to evaluate for two reasons: The national census does not cover this professional option and second, it appears that freelancers rarely join the professional associations. Our survey discovered that there were six times as many freelancers in the Canadian press (298) as in television (54) in 1994, constituting about 9% of the newspaper labor force of 3,451 but only 4% of that in television (1,305). The gender ratio among newspaper freelancers is about equal: 53% women and 47% men, but in television women are in the overwhelming majority and constitute 74% of this group. These statistics suggest that the option of freelancing is chosen by slightly more women than men, but overall, is not that popular. Clearly, more work needs to be done on this question in order to illuminate whether there are differences in social and work characteristics between the two groups and to determine the circumstances under which females and males choose to become freelancers.

What this admittedly limited evidence indicates is that the majority of female professionals do not choose to follow the two extreme alternatives previously mentioned: becoming "one of the boys" or opting out. Most carry on as though they were equal in the heterosexual newsroom and use their gender strategically under certain circumstances. This indicates that one cannot speak of simple, bifurcated "female" or "male" role conceptions, but has to acknowledge that human beings are active agents in the construction of their professional persona. Consequently, both females and males fall back on their gendered socialization experiences to explain their professional behavior to themselves and to others. Yet, because they are symbolically marked as "different," it is easier for women to become aware of their status discrepancies in the male newsroom. Interviews in both Germany and Canada reveal that there are situations in which female journalists put their subordinate and conflictual status as "woman" to strategic use, to gain otherwise inaccessible information. Klaus (1998) gave examples where a legal reporter compensated for her exclusion from the male only pub crawls by taking her colleagues aside individually and appealing to their legal expertise to "explain" a court situation to her. This yielded hitherto unrevealed reportorial material, and provided her with a new angle for her story. Another "scooped" her colleagues through superior social connections, and an invitation to an exclusive wedding, from which the press was otherwise barred.

In our own research with Canadian journalists, we were told that the roles of "buddy" or "motherly confidant" were sometimes used by female professionals to acquire information not otherwise obtainable. One female reporter furthermore noted that she combined her professional with her social instincts and often queried male politicians on their personal feelings about issues, something that was never done by her colleagues. These examples indicate that the bifurcated notion of a gender-specific journalistic role conception is an oversimplified notion that can no longer be entertained. Professional role identities, just like gender identities, are not fixed but malleable. They are not something we "have" but something we "create" and change, depending on the social—and work environment in which we find ourselves.

GENDERED PROFESSIONAL OUTLOOKS?

Defining journalists' social role and the media's mission in contemporary democracy have been matters of public debate in Canada since the time that both the media and the profession endorsed the social responsibility mandate in the late 1950s (Saint-Jean, 1993). Before entering the debate, a definition is in order to ground the following discussion. When I talk about a journalist's social role conceptions, I am referring to the mind-set and behavior of an incumbent in an organizational position that covers how a person thinks about and does his or her job. Because it is difficult to define the journalistic mediator position, which is located between politicians and their public in a democratic state, U.S. researchers initiated studies early in the 1970s to investigate how working reporters define their social role. For Johnstone, Slawski, and Bowman (1976), the key interest was the extent to which journalists in the 1970s viewed themselves as neutral "messengers" or as active "agents" in the social communication process. Today, this dichotomous thinking has been superceded by a more complex tripartite notion of the role. Factor analysis has discovered that the professional understanding of U.S. journalists include three attitude clusters: the adversarial, interpretive, and the disseminator roles (Weaver & Wilhoit, 1991). How do these findings stack up with Canadian stances and are there gender differences in journalistic role conceptions?

To answer these questions, the Canadian attitudinal survey adopted Weaver and Wilhoit's (1991) methodology and added gender as an important variable. Using a list of "things that the media do or try to do today," respondents were asked to rate the importance of eight media roles on a five-point scale, ranging from *very important* to *not important*. The findings showed marked gender differences in percentages of the top two responses. Although female and male reporters chose the same four social roles as most important, their order of importance differed. All Canadian professionals interpreted their four most important social roles as agents of change, neutral witnesses, uninvolved conveyors of information, and craftspersons. Female professionals, however, considered the role of agents of change (55%) most important, followed by neutral witness, which received 47% of the group's approval. For males, two roles were considered of equal importance: neutral witness (51%) and the craftsperson role at 50%. Surprisingly, male professionals did not see themselves as agents of change, which only 39% of the group supported. Although these differences need to be further explored, they do suggest that female professionals seem to be more socially conscious in their outlook and bring this attitude into their newsroom work. The male choices, in contrast, with their emphasis on the craft components of the profession, seem to foster neutrality and distance. Together, these attitudinal differences lead to variations in topic selection, attitudes toward the public and narrative styles.

To explore whether the differences in social role conceptions had consequences for journalistic practice, respondents were asked to evaluate the various tasks involved in reporting; "In your opinion, what tasks should journalists perform?" Once again, both women and men assigned top priority to the same mix of four tasks, all of which received more than 90% approval: report events, investigate, explain events, as well as explain in simple terms. However, there are three secondary tasks with 70% to 80% approval ratings that are ranked in a different order by each group. The female group supported, in declining order of importance, giving background information (83%), educational tasks (79%), and the watchdog role (71%). The male group gave higher ratings to playing the watchdog role (77%) and to "condemning governmental wrongdoings." Although the evaluative differences between women and men are not large, it is interesting to speculate that "educating the public" is one of the ways in which women translate their social commitment into journalistic practice. Men's greater interest in the watchdog and condemnatory tasks seems to grow out of the competitive and adversarial stances prevalent in the newsroom.

Another way in which social role conceptions may affect journalistic practices is through an analysis of the methods that reporters are willing to use in acquiring story material. Once again, both females and males support the same three methods, but gender makes a difference to the level of support. Feminist research on women's psychology and workplace behavior suggests that gender differences manifest themselves in a tendency for women to comply with authority more than their male counterparts (Löfgren-Nilsson, 1993). Their socialization patterns, which stress cooperation, tend to make them feel uncomfortable with legally and morally questionable actions. When asked, "Given an important story, which of the following methods do you think may be justified and which would you not approve of under any circumstances?" Agreeing to protect confidentiality and not doing so, and claiming to be somebody else were among the least approved methods for both women and men, generating an approval rate of only 3% and 7%, respectively. Substantial gender differences are evident, however, in the responses to the practice of badgering unwilling informants to get a story. Here, only 23% of females compared to 37% of males approved of this strategy, suggesting differences in socialization patterns concerning coercion between females and males. A similar pattern is visible in response to "making use of personal documents without permission," where the responses of female professionals were six points below those of males (14% compared to 20%).

GENDER AND NARRATIVE FORM

Another set of questions closely aligned with the issue of gender-specific role conceptions has to do with the circumstances in which gender affects reportorial approaches and narrative forms. Here, too, so called "standardized survey instruments" have yielded no empirical evidence, even though women journalists can all give examples of differences in reportorial approaches between females and males. It has been claimed that women have introduced a set of new topics, that they select different perspectives to cover, and that they choose different emphases for their stories. In order to try to verify these claims, our Canadian sample was asked to record on a five-point scale: "Where did the presence of female journalists bring about the most changes?"

The responses showed that usually female and male respondents made the same grand choices concerning the four top response items. Changes attributed to females in the profession were wider range of topics covered (86% females: 60% males); different angles of coverage (82% females: 57% males); increased range of experience (63% females: 43% males), and greater sensitivity toward sexism (64% females: 70% males). Overall, except on the issue of sexism, female professionals gave higher rankings to changes attributed to females than their male colleagues. This could mean that female journalists are more conscious than males of the changes they have brought about in the profession. This is an expected reaction from a minority that is still fighting for equity in the workplace. Both women and men agree that females do bring a different perspective to their work. A male journalist exemplified this view when he noted that: "obviously women bring different life experiences, sensitivity and *Weltanschaung* to the job." The findings seem to confirm that gender is an intervening variable that colors all communicational activities. Yet, as an intervening variable, gender also has highly differential effects, when combined with different attitude clusters.

A little over two fifths (44%) of females and 40% of males believe that the newsroom climate has improved over time. This is a puzzling unanimity, considering that "climate" referrs to those practices that are designed to exclude females. However, in the in-depth interviews it became clear that female reporters were comparing their current experiences with those of the previous decades, when sexist practices were even more rampant than they are today. The very low percentages of journalists (15% of the women and 25% of the men) who believe that there has been a reduction of competitive practices in the newsroom, and that management has supported more cooperation (33% of women and 20% of men) in response to women entering the media, indicates that both groups are becoming aware of the negative outcomes of these attitude clusters. Thus, both females, as well as males, seem to be looking forward to a more egalitarian future.

CONCLUSION

What do these findings mean with respect to the impact of gender on reportorial practices? On the question of differences in topic choices one respondent opines: "I believe the industry still covers 'male issues' and that a female presence is necessary to give viewers a female perspective of events, as well as to ensure 'female' issues are addressed." This is a call to utilize gender as a strategy for exploring all topics and to draw female viewers, listeners, and readers—who are frequently overlooked—into the public sphere. A male respondent indicated that there is no competition involved in such a strategy but that it is more a matter of equity. "Women can show leadership in approaching issues important to women exclusively or generally, just as men can show leadership in approaching issues important to men exclusively or generally."

Elsewhere, researchers have documented instances of gender differences in topic choices, although this doesn't mean that topic selection can be explained in terms of gender alone. Historical issues may also be involved (Klaus, 1998). Over time, topics that remained uncovered because they belonged to the private sphere of personal responsibility, have moved into the "public realm" of reporting and Zelizer (1993) documented that such shifts occur at different times in different countries, depending on the salience of the issues addressed. In Germany, for example, the issue of abortion and women's reproductive rights became a trigger for moving abortion from the private to the public discussion agenda in the early 1990s. At that time, reunification required the German parliament to discuss the in- or exclusion of abortion under health insurance (Klaus, 1998). In Canada, a similar debate occurred 10 years earlier. More generally, topic shifts have been accompanied by the development of more experience based reporting styles in both North America and in Europe, a narrative form often deprecatingly called "entertainment journalism" (Frankel, 1999).

But the question of whether a gendered news discourse exists or not, may simply be wrongly formulated. It posits differences where none may exist, namely in professional performance, where the above evidence presented here demonstrates that commonalties outweigh differences. Most professional performance occurs both in a particular reporting situation and in a work hierarchy where male power dominates. Yet, it is this power differential, in turn, that encourages some female professionals to question the gendered assumptions on which newsroom work is based. It is this same power differential that encourages them to try to insert their own life experiences into their work environment. These experiences, however, are only sometimes relevant for their reportorial work and for the selection and interpretation of news stories. It is the job of future research to further clarify and pinpoint those situations and themes where gender becomes relevant for interpretation, rather than to make the global assertion that female and male reporters do their work differently.

Some researchers (see Ross, 2000) have argued persuasively that increasing the numbers of women has had an impact on the process and structure of the profession, and that their presence can widen the scope of what issues, events, and stories are now regarded as newsworthy. Not only a more diverse range of issues is now covered, but many of these new story types are of particular interest to women. Others have focused on concerns about what they call the "feminization" of the media and the sector's consequent loss of prestige (Creedon, 1993; Fröhlich & Holtz-Bacha, 1995). But such an assessment implies a dual use of the term *feminization*, which can be misleading. On the one hand, it could refer to the "widening of the news agenda" and thus a rethinking of the male defined values and norms of the profession. On the other hand, it suggests a reduction of the overall salary level within the profession. The shift toward a more informal style of news reporting with more personal and human interest content—the "soft journalism" practiced today in both print and television—is an example of the first meaning of the term. Yet, this outcome was not achieved solely through the agitation of female professionals, but also (and perhaps mostly) by commercial concerns about the loss of audience share. Throughout the 1990s, both North American print and broadcasting found that they were losing their female readers and viewers and were likely to continue to do so unless they adjusted their content.

As to the concern that increasing numbers of women in the media diminishes the status and pay scales of the profession, the so-called velvet ghetto, this is still hard to verify, at least in Germany and Canada. Even though a proportionally greater number of women are employed in the less well-paid freelance domain of media work in both countries, there is no evidence that this "ghettoization" has affected the salaries of full-time professionals. In both countries, this argument was used in the 1960s to justify recruiting practices that were clearly discriminatory and that have ceased in response to equity legislation. Salary comparisons by Lünenborg (1997) in Germany, who compared salary scales of west and east German professionals and my own comparisons showed no systematic reduction in salaries since the 1970s, but rather a significant increase. In Canada, median salaries in the so-called knowledge economy services have increased faster than in manufacturing. Furthermore, between media fields, women did better in broadcasting, where a larger recruitment took place in the 1980s, than in print. Also in larger metropolitan media outlets they receive better salaries than in smaller markets (Robinson & Saint-Jean, 1997). Finally, better salaries in the broadcast sector are a result of collective agreements that contain salary equity planks and thus counteract the supposed salary erosion. What these comparisons show is that the "feminization" (reduction) of salaries as a result of women's entry into the journalism profession is yet to be verified. Moreover, it needs to be challenged because it once again oversimplifies the complex societal interrelationships between the meaning of gender and its practical implications.

REFERENCES

Armstrong, P., & Armstrong, H. (1990). *Theorizing women's work*. Toronto, Canada: Garamond.

Bourdieu, P. (1991). *Language and symbolic power*. Cambridge: Polity Press.

Creedon, P. (Ed.). (1993). *Women in mass communication* (2nd ed.). Newbury Park: Sage.

Djerf-Pierre, M. (1996). *Gröna Nyheter. Miljöjournalistiken I televisionenes nyhetssändingar 1961-1994* [Women journalists in television]. Göteborg: Department of Journalism, Media and Communication, University of Göteborg.

Frankel, F. (1999). *Media madness: The revolution so far* (Communication and Society Report). Aspen: The Aspen Institute.

Fröhlich, M., & Holtz-Bacha, C. (1995). *Frauen und Medien: Eine Synopse der deutschen Forschung*. [Women and media: A synopsis of German research]. Opladen: Westdeutscher Verlag.

Johnstone, J., Slawski, W., & Bowman, W. (1976). *The news people: A sociological portrait of American journalists and their work*. Urbana: University of Illinois Press.

Klaus, E. (1998). *Kommunikationswissenschaftliche Geschlechterforschung* [Gendered communication research]. Opladen: Westdeutscher Verlag.

Löfgren-Nilsson, M. (1993). *Climate and gender: Journalists' perceptions of the newsroom "climate"* (Working Report 30). Göteborg: Department of Journalism, Media and Communication, University of Göteborg.

Lünenborg, M. (1997). *Journalistinnen in Europa* [Women journalists in Europe]. Opladen: Westdeutscher Verlag.

Melin-Higgins, M., & Djerf-Pierre, M. (1998, July). *Networking in newsrooms: Journalist and gender cultures*. Paper presented at the conference of the International Association for Media and Communication Research (IAMCR), Glasgow.

Pleck, J. (1984). The work–family role system. In P. Voydanoff (Ed.), *Work and family: Changing roles of men and women* (pp. 9-19). Palo Alto: Mayfield.

Pritchard, D., & Sauvageau, F. (1999). *Les journalists canadiens* [Canadian journalists: A millennial portrait]. Quebec, Canada: Laval University Press.

Robinson, G. J. (1975). *Women journalists in Canadian dailies: A social and professional minority profile*. Montreal: McGill University Working Papers in Communication.

Robinson, G. J. (1977). The future of women in the media. *McGill Journal of Education, XXII*(1), 123-133.

Robinson, G. J. (1995). Women politicians in Canadian news reporting: Different gender discourses? In *RIWE Yearbook on work, education, culture* (Vol. 13, pp. 181-198). Recklingshausen: RIWE

Robinson, G. J. (forthcoming). Theorizing the impact of gender in Canadian journalism. In R. Fröhlich & S. Lafky (Eds.), *Women journalists in the western world: Equal opportunities and what surveys tell us.* Cresskill, NJ: Hampton Press.

Robinson, G. J., & Saint-Jean, A. (1997). *Women's participation in the Canadian news media: Progress since the 1970s* (SSHRC Summary of findings). Montreal: Graduate Program in Communications, McGill University.

Robinson, G. J., & Saint-Jean, A. (1998). Canadian women journalists: The "other half" of the equation. In D. Weaver (Ed.), *The global journalist, news people around the world* (pp. 351-372). Cresskill, NJ: Hampton Press.

Ross, K. (2000, July). *Sexing the news: Gender politics and newsroom culture.* Paper presented at International Association for Media and Communication Research (IAMCR), Singapore.

Saint-Jean, A. (1993). *L'Évolution de l'éthique journalistique au Québec de 1960 à 1990* [The evolution of journalistic ethics in Quebec from 1960-1990]. Unpublished doctoral thesis, Montreal Graduate Program in Communications, McGill University.

Statistics Canada (1995). *Women in Canada: A statistical report* (3rd ed.). Ottawa, Canada: Ministry of Industry.

Weaver, D., & Wilhoit, C. G. (1991). *The American journalist: A portrait of U.S. news people and their work.* (2nd ed.). Bloomington: Indiana University Press.

Weaver, D., & Wilhoit, C. G. (1998). Journalists in the United States. In D. Weaver (Ed.), *The global journalist: News people around the world* (pp. 395-414). Cresskill N.J: Hampton Press.

Zelizer, B. (1993). Journalists as interpretive communities. *Critical Studies in Mass Communication, 10*(2), 219-237.

11

Coping With Journalism: Gendered Newsroom Culture

Margareta Melin-Higgins

In this chapter, I seek to understand Scottish and English journalism. That is a strong statement, and needs substantial theoretical and empirical support. The first part of this chapter is a discussion of what I consider to be a useful theoretical approach to the study of journalism, a culturalist perspective, where culture is seen as the production and reproduction of meaning. My intention is to use the theories and methodologies of cultural studies in the study of journalism. I argue for the usefulness of three concepts. The principal concept is *journalist culture,* which encapsulates the production and reproduction of meaning of a professional group (journalists) and the power play that takes place within that reproduction. This is closely connected to two other concepts that I use in a journalistic context, Bourdieu's idea of a *social field* and de Certeau's concept pair *strategy and tactic.* My main argument is that these concepts are particularly useful when studying journalism from a feminist perspective, because the latter approach draws away from an essentialist notion of the importance of the sex of journalists and focuses instead on gender, that is, the social and cultural reproduction of meaning and ideology that is inherent in gender and definitely in journalism. In the second part of the chapter, I use these concepts and discuss journalist culture as I have found it in England and Scotland in the 1990s, looking particularly at the gendered nature of this culture.

STUDYING THE GENDERED CULTURE OF JOURNALISM

Journalist Culture

Traditional approaches to the study of journalism have provoked some criticism and a call has been made for a new way to study journalism using a culturalist perspective.[1] By taking a cultural perspective on news, Schudson (1991) argued, the researcher will be better able to study the content and form of the cultural milieu of journalism, which in turn will reveal the social structures and ideology of journalism, and also the importance of sources and audience for the social construction of journalism. I argue, like Schudson (1991) and McNair (1994), for the importance of studying journalism from a cultural perspective. I have been greatly inspired by Raymond Williams and have used his definition of culture as a fundamental base in my line of thinking. He sees culture as a way of life for a particular group of people at a particular point in time (Williams, 1976, 1981).

From these lines of thoughts, I tried to draw links with the study of journalism and soon came up with the concept of *journalist culture*, which I then defined as the production and reproduction of culture, meaning, and ideology for a particular professional group (journalists; Melin, 1991). This definition is, however, far too wide and thus difficult to use empirically. Zilliacus-Tikkanen (1997) also used the concept of journalist culture. She sees it as a synonym to *discourse*, that is, "a model in the journalists' head, which is realised in the work process" (p. 41). She gives, however, no acceptable explanation to how the model ended up in journalists' head in the first place, and how it stays there.

Drawing from Raymond William's work on culture, I define *journalist culture* as what a particular body of journalists, at a point in history, feels, thinks, acts, and is. Journalist culture is creation and re-creation of meaning and reality, constantly negotiated and determined by power. Journalist culture is thus, a shared worldview—reality—for a group of journalists, which of course comprises a set of ideals, values, and rules of how to handle things (like news) and how to enact that perspective. As culture, journalist culture is not homogenous. In the process of hegemony, a dominant culture is created that is seen as "normal." Against this, opposing meanings are created, which are seen as deviant. There is a constant fight between the dominant culture and different oppositional cultures, a fight for the symbolic power of creating the meaning of journalism (Melin-Higgins, 2004; Melin-Higgins & Djerf-Pierre, 1998).

---

[1]Schudson (1991) argued for a culturalogic perspective, which is basically the same as McNair's (1994) culturalist perspective.

The differences within the culture are, in fact highly interesting and vital in order to understand the culture as a whole. What I mean is that there are obviously groups of journalists that disagree with the common understanding of what journalism is. This causes conflict. To understand the nature of these differences and conflicts, and indeed to thus understand the inherently gendered nature of journalism I shall explore Pierre Bourdieu's concept *social field* and apply it to the field of journalism.

Journalism as a Social Field

The notion of a professional culture (in this case, journalism) can easily be related to what Pierre Bourdieu called a *social field* (see Bourdieu, 1984, 1990, 1991). Journalism, as a social field in Bourdieu's terms, means that every part of this field embodies meaning, ordered within a hierarchy. Hard news is more important than soft news, broadsheet newspapers have more status than tabloids, and so on. There is, however, nothing objective about this hierarchy. It is a social construction, the outcome of a struggle for symbolic power. This struggle is really a fight for the power of definition. The winners define what— in this case journalism—is. This is the group's *doxa*, to use another of Bourdieu's concepts, that is, the official definition of what is reality, what *is* journalism. And the doxa represses and excludes all other definitions so that the definition of journalism by the dominant group is seen as the objective truth by dominator and dominated alike. Previously, I argued that in a journalist culture, there is a dominant group and then oppositional groups which oppose the doxa. I would, however, argue that oppositional groups are aware that the doxa is a mere set of values, created meanings and they oppose these as they enter into the battle for symbolic power. Obviously, therefore, oppositional groups are seen as a threat by the dominant group.

The point of connecting the concept of journalist culture with that of Bourdieu's social field and symbolic power is that together, they become a powerful tool in explaining the gendered structures and conflicts within journalism and thus facilitate a deeper understanding of female journalists' terms and conditions. In a discussion of the feminist thinking of Bourdieu, Järvinen (1999) pointed to how *habitus, symbolic power,* and *doxa* are inherently gendered. The classifications that are made in the social field are based on the distinctions between different habitus and ultimately the distinction between men and women (see also, Bourdieu, 1984, 1999). The struggle for symbolic power can thus also be seen as a struggle between the sexes.

To say that journalism is a male bastion is hardly an overstatement. Almost all research on journalism, from a variety of countries and that uses a feminist perspective, argues that journalism is a male construction (e.g., de Bruin, 1998; Melin-Higgins, 1996a; van Zoonen, 1988a; 1998b; Zilliacus-Tikkanen, 1997). In other words (or translated into the concepts I previously outlined), the dominant journalist culture is masculine and the dominant journalist culture consists of mainly male journalists who have defined the doxa of journalism. It is thus the preferred meaning of male journalists that is seen as the norm, the objective truth. Against this, there are a number of oppositional cultures, some of which consist mainly of female journalists who struggle to define what an alternative journalism is—or could be (Melin-Higgins, 2004, Melin-Higgins & Djerf-Pierre, 1998).

Strategies or Tactics

Another way of looking at the relationship between dominant and dominated is to see it as warfare. And de Certeau (1984) uses the very metaphor of warfare to explain actions in relationships. He argued that strategy is

> the calculation (or manipulation) of relationships that becomes possible as soon as a subject with will and power (a business, an army, a city, a scientific institution) can be isolated. It postulates a place that can be delimited as its own and serve as the base from which relations with an exteriority composed of targets or threats (customers or competitors, enemies, the country surrounding the city, objectives and objects surrounding the research) can be managed. (p. 39)

Strategy is for the strong and the powerful. They pin their hopes on the resistance that the establishment of place puts up against the erosion of time. Tactics, on the other hand, are used by the weak. They have no place on which to rely so they need to rest on "a clever utilization of time, of the opportunities it presents and also of the play that it introduces into the foundations of power" (p. 39). Just as a strategy is organized by the holders of power, a tactic is determined by the absence of power and limited by the possibilities of the moment. Open warfare against the powerful would only lead to defeat, so the weak seek out the weaknesses of the powerful and use deception, and guerrilla warfare as tactics.

Again, looking at the social field of journalism, *strategies* and *tactics* are two useful concepts to help in understanding the gendered power play of the newsroom. In fact, when the Swedish journalist Ami Lönnroth spoke about her experiences of working as a journalist at a conference on *Women and the Media*, she argued that the newsroom is a place of gender-based power, conflict, and culture clashes and that female journalists had to use guerrilla warfare to assert their ways of writing and being a journalist (Lönnroth & Boëtius 1991).

Strategies or Tactics of Female Journalists

In journalism then, the members of the dominant culture, which is a masculine construction and where most members are male, use various strategies to main-

tain their place and power to define the doxa of journalism. Different oppositional cultures lack the power of place and are therefore bound to use various
tactics. And indeed there are a number of studies, which show that when women
enter journalism, they need to employ strategies to survive in the masculine
domain that is journalism. Some of these are oppositional and thus cause culture
clashes and others accept the hegemonic doxa and work within it. I would, however, argue that it is wrong to talk of strategies when discussing the different
paths female journalists take to survive in the male culture of journalism,
because they have no place or power to employ strategies: therefore, women
can only use tactics.

There seem to be two tactics that do not challenge the existing doxa.
Schlesinger (1978) talks of a *female ghetto* in journalism and van Zoonen
(1998a) used the term *marionette* to describe women journalists (or the tactics
used by them) who do not challenge the "order" but instead take on the role of
"woman journalist" as defined by the dominant culture. These women are,
therefore, not seen as threatening and are often left to get on with their business,
which is, anyway, not perceived as being important or having status. Soft news,
women's magazines, women's pages, and so on are places or ghettos where
these women "are kept."

The second of the tactics, which does not challenge the doxa itself, is seen
as more threatening by the dominant culture. Women who employ this tactic
challenge the gendered hierarchy of journalism by wanting to be one of the
boys. They challenge the male prerogative of being able to make choices and
try to infiltrate the male, status-filled world of journalism by stepping into masculine territory, for example by wanting to cover hard news, of becoming a foreign correspondent, or working, on the news desk of big national newspaper.
Although not challenging the fundamental values of the dominant culture, these
women are seen as a threat as they challenge the male supremacy and "natural"
right to the most status-filled positions in journalism. The dominant culture thus
employs various strategies to cope with these women. Name-calling is one strategy, and terms like *aggressive* and *unfeminine* are words often attributed to
them (Egsmose, 1998; Eide, 1995; Melin-Higgins 1996a; van Zoonen, 1998b).

A third strategy is that of being one of the girls (Melin-Higgins, 1996a; van
Zoonen, 1998b). Contrary to the other two tactics, this is an oppositional tactic
in that it challenges the very doxa of journalism and attempts to make it more
feminine, for example, by raising the status of feminine subjects. It is seen as
threatening by the dominant culture, which tries to repress the opposition by, for
example, belittling women and the work they do (Egsmose 1998; Eide 1995;
Melin-Higgins 1996b; van Zoonen, 1998b; Zilliacus-Tikkanen, 1997). Being hit
by aggressive or defensive strategies by members of the dominant culture is
routine for most female journalists. Eide (1995) called this a "Catch 22 situation"; you are damned if you want to cover hard news (being seen as aggressive
and hard-nosed) and damned if you want to cover soft news (being seen an
incompetent little girl). There seems to be no escape.

The most extensive attempt to describe female journalism and tactics (strategies in her words) is made by Zilliacus-Tikkanen (1997; see also, van Zoonen, 1998b). Based on secondary sources (journalist studies) from a number of Nordic countries and interviews with Finnish radio journalists, she has listed seven areas in which female journalism (seen as an oppositional culture) is in conflict with the dominant journalist culture:

1. *Hard versus soft news.* Traditionally, hard news has higher status, but female journalism prioritizes soft news.

2. *Isolating facts versus wholeness.* Traditionally, news is rarely put into context, whereas female journalism argues for discussing processes and putting news in context.

3. *Competition versus consistency.* The dominant journalist culture is mainly interested in the fight (!) between competitors in the game (!) for power, whereas female journalism is more interested in the reasons behind events and their consequences.

4. *Distance versus involvement.* The dominant culture argues that a good journalist is neutral and distant, whereas female journalism prefers journalists to be subjective and involved.

5. *Individualism versus collectivism.* The tough, free, lonely journalist who investigates and writes stories independently is an ideal in traditional journalism. Women's journalism, on the other hand, emphasizes collaborative projects and work processes and women also tend to prefer to work in nonhierarchical news organizations.

6. *Work versus private life.* The latter should be subordinate to the former or rather, private life is a continuation of work life for (male) members of the dominant journalist culture. This means, for example, that it is seen as important to continue news room discussions in the pub after work (see Egsmose, 1998; Melin-Higgins, 1996b). For female journalism, it is the other way around: private life, with its lifestyle and values, will influence work life.

7. Formal versus experimental. The dominant culture adheres to traditional forms and ways of working. News journalism particularly is characterised by stock clichés and "molds" for news. Female journalism, on the other hand, is much more interested in experimenting with form and content and willing to cross the boundaries between genres.

One way of interpreting these points is to say that female oppositional culture actually challenges the common news values of journalism (see Galtung &

Ruge, 1973; Gans, 1979). Zilliacus-Tikkanen suggested that this is a definition of *female journalism* and is the goal for which most women journalist strive although they employ different strategies (i.e., tactics, in de Certeau's terms) to get there.

METHOD

In 1992, I undertook thematic interviews with 33 British journalists (16 women and 17 men). I chose to interview journalists working in national media in England (London) and Scotland (Glasgow and Edinburgh). Specifically, I interviewed 17 Scots, 14 English, 1 Irish (working in Scotland), and 1 American working in England. The media they worked for included national television (news and current affairs), radio (news and discussion programs), national broadsheets, and tabloids: Some worked as freelancers for national media on a variety of beats. The sample was chosen using two principal methods. One was through deliberative sample in an effort to find men and women working in different media and covering different beats. The other method was the *snowball method* (see Köcher 1985, 1986) in which one journalist would give me the name of others who might be interested in participating. In 1998–1999, I followed up on the journalists I originally interviewed.[2] I conducted interviews with nine of the original journalists—three men and six women: Three interviews were held in England, six in Scotland. I chose the follow-up journalists strategically. Either they represented different cultures or tactics, or their lives or careers had taken an interesting turn in the intervening years between interviews.[3]

All the interviews were informal and discussions ranged across a number of themes including why they became journalists, what they wanted to achieve in their jobs, their definition of good journalism, examples of a good job they had done, objectivity, and their personal background so during the second set of interviews, I also discussed what had happened to them in the past 6 years and issues relating to child care. The theme of this chapter, "how to cope with journalism," was not planned, but was an issue brought up by the journalists interviewed. The interviews lasted anywhere from 90 minutes to a whole working day and were held in newsrooms, offices, restaurants, or pubs depending on the preference of the journalist interviewed.

---

[2]Two of the journalists had died and five had moved without anyone knowing their present job or whereabouts.

[3]I tried to interview more journalists than I managed in the end. The failures were due to deaths, illnesses, foreign jobs.

Seeking to understand British (Scottish and English) journalism, as is my aim, implies not only a firm theoretical framework, but also a solid empirical ground. Can 33 journalists provide deep and valid enough knowledge to achieve my aim? Most studies on the profession of journalism have used questionnaires (see Weaver, 1998; Weibull, Asp, Börjesson, Lötgren, Melin, 1991) and large-scale questionnaire-based studies will render the study's findings a certain level of generalizability. But from my own experience of working with these kinds of studies, I believe that there are at least two serious problems regarding validity. One is that a rigorous (and randomized) sample frame is vital for statistical reliability. In some countries, this is possible through the availability of lists of trade union members (see Weibull, Asp, Börjesson, Lötgren, Melin, 1991; Melin-Higgins, 1996a). In Britain, however, such lists are not easily accessible. Köcher (1985, 1986) used the snowball method and Henningham and Delano (1998) used staff (full time) lists from national media. The other problem is that attitude scales and question batteries (which are then often factor analyzed) are easily misinterpreted and the views of individual journalists are lost. So, although interviewing hundreds of journalists is seen as producing data that are supposedly generalizable, they provide shallow (if not erroneous) knowledge and little understanding of the process of journalism that they set out to study.

So, due to my own frustrating experiences working with large quantitative journalist studies, and also from reading many journalism studies of poor statistic quality, I have tried to find other methods and approaches. Greatly inspired by theories of knowledge in feminist epistemological discussions, I have constructed a method, which I believe gives me understanding of both the individuals I meet in interview situations and the culture of which they are part and reflect.

There are three feminist epistemological issues, which I think are important for any study. The first is that of reciprocity, that is, breaking down the distinction between subject and object. Good research should rely on a nonhierarchical research setting based on a dialogue where the experience, knowledge, and wisdom of the researched is acknowledged (see Armstead, 1995; Fonow & Cooke, 1991; Ramazanoglu, 1992; Spender, 1985; Stanley, 1995). The other is that of reflexivity, that is, breaking down the distinction between subjectivity and objectivity. This entails taking a subjective stance, recognising oneself as a human being (with feelings and thoughts and values and experience) and as a necessary instrument through which research occurs. It is not a rejection of being critical, rigorous and accurate, but quite the contrary, it makes interpretative schemes explicit and enables self-criticism (Harding, 1987; MacKinnon, 1989).

The third issue is the recognition that knowledge is always political and research is always done *for* someone. The consequence is, again, to make this explicit. Research should be political and oriented towards action and change (Jónásdottír, 1991; Ramazanoglu, 1992).

Obviously, such points are often found as indicators of interpretative (qualitative) research more generally. For example, the Norwegian psychologist Steinar Kvale (1997) likened the interviewer with a traveller who seeks and constructs knowledge through interaction and understanding. He also pointed out that both the produced knowledge and the interaction itself can be used to change the interviewer's situation by, say, creating awareness. Thus, understanding is the fundamental goal of the researcher, and the story told in the interaction between interviewer and interviewed can be the basis for the understanding of, in this case, journalist culture: Looking at a culture over time will capture the inevitable change at both the personal and the cultural level.

So I believe that my study of interviews with 33 journalists, some of them conducted over time, can indeed provide valid knowledge of the journalist culture I seek to understand. And it can, arguably, also provide findings, which are possible to theoretically (or analytically) generalize (Kvale, 1997; Larsson, 2000). The heterogeneity and contextuality of the knowledge and the logic of statements and analysis can suggest some aspects of typicality and commonality, give insights into what might be (in another situation), and finally what could be (the ideal) (Kvale, 1997).

THE DOMINANT JOURNALIST CULTURE AND ITS DOXA

The Social Field

British journalism reflects, to a high degree, the values of contemporary British (English and Scottish) society. This is hardly surprising. Köcher (1985, 1986) argued that journalism is always determined by the social context in which it exists, that is, by the history, legal and political system of the particular country in which it operates. So British journalism (what I call *journalist culture*) is characterized by a strict organizational and structural hierarchy, a strong and important old boys' network, a very traditional view of women, and very little support for working mothers (see Christmas, 1997; Egsmose, 1998; Galloway & Robertson, 1991), all unsurprising given the structure and culture of Britain. In Britain, class distinctions are firm and the dominant British culture has a lot of power (Egsmose, 1998; Köcher, 1985, 1986). It is the same in journalism. The dominant journalist culture is indeed very dominant, which means that the doxa is taken for granted as the objective truth, and goes unquestioned by the majority of journalists or the British population. On the other hand, there are also strong oppositional groups that need to speak loudly to make their voices heard.[4] The characteristics of journalists are, however, not a reflection of Britons in general. Henningham and Delano (1998) showed that journalism is truly "the domain of White Anglo-Saxon Protestants" the typical journalist identifying him or herself as European (90% of British journalists), Protestant (56%), middle class (63%), and male (75%).[5]

Looking at English and Scottish journalism as a social field, there were three issues that struck me during the interviews. One was the hierarchy among journalists, a hierarchy that every one of the journalists I interviewed was aware and related to. For example, the very clear distinction between the important hard news (for example, foreign, political and economic news), and the unimportant 'soft' news (e.g., culture, education, human interest stories) was real and vital for all the journalists I interviewed. For them, the fight for stories and beat is really a fight for status and recognition in the organization (see Egsmose, 1998; Schlesinger, 1978; Tunstall, 1970; van Zoonen, 1998b; Zilliacus-Tikkanen, 1997).

It has been argued by many scholars that journalism is a man's world and a masculine space, which is also true of British journalism (see Baehr, 1980; Beasley, 1989; Christmas, 1997; Eide, 1995; Gallagher, 1995; Robinson & Saint-Jean, 1998; Steiner, 1998; van Zoonen, 1998a, 1988b). The overall result of my study does indeed corroborate these arguments, and from that I argue that the dominant journalist culture in England and Scotland is very masculine and sexist. As one female editor exemplified:

> I wouldn't like to work on the news desk. I'm not tempramented for it. Favourites are picked there more than in other places. It's the old style

---

[4]In my own experiences (from living for than a decade in Britain), oppositional groups like the gay movement and the feminist movement are more vocal than equivilant movements in Sweden, my present home country. Lindvert (2002) and the political columnist, Heidi Avellan (2002) both argued that in Sweden feminism has become a State feminism, present in almost all party programs, but of a luke warm temperature. In other countries, feminism is part of the opposition, and therefore needs to be hotter, more radical to be heard.

[5]Reliable statistics of British journalists is hard to find — due to the problems with sample frame as discussed previously (see van Zoonen, 1994). In Henningham and Delano's (1998) study one must remember that the sample frame is full-time permanent staff-lists. Another important point is the difficulty of statistically measuring factors like ethnicity and class, that can both be an objective description or an identity creating factor (i.e., perception of class membership). In this case, class seems to be measured in the former way by the occupation of the journalist's father or mother (breadwiner). Gender, although seemingly simple to measure, is also difficult (see van Zoonen, 1994). For example, the number of British female journalists is shown to vary between 16% and 25% (Bertagna, 1991; Henningham & Delano, 1998; Van Zoonen & Donsbach, 1988) whereas Gallagher (1995) talks of 38% female media workers.

'guys-go-down-to-pub'. The guys hang out together and the camaraderie doesn't accept women—apart from flirtation. . . . It's a deeply sexist country compared to America (Clara, women's news, department editor, broadsheet, England).

The distinction between soft and hard news often seems like another aspect of the classical enlightenment dichotomy man–woman, strong–weak, public–private, hard important news–soft unimportant news (see Hirdman, 1990; Jónasdóttir, 1991). It is the former that hits the front page and that has the highest status among journalists.[6] *Every* woman I interviewed related to this dichotomy in one way or another, often with a great deal of frustration. Given this, I am not surprised that twice as many women as men believe it is more difficult for capable women journalists to get ahead in their career. As only 7% of editors of the press are women (Henningham & Delano, 1998) this is quite likely reality, not only perceptions (see Robinson & Saint-Jean, 1998).

The third striking aspect of the result I found was the resilience and valorization of the archetypal journalist as a tough, ruthless male reporter with a pen and notebook in this hand, a cigarette in his mouth, and a whisky bottle in his pocket, digging up the truth that some politician has tried to hide and saving the country from corruption—the working-class hero has become a journalist. Almost all the men I interviewed made passing remarks on their own or colleagues' class background, and they clearly want to live up to this working-class ideal, and furthermore, quite a few succeed. Dave,[7] for example, had become editor of an English tabloid between my two interviews with him, and he said his working-class background had been partly responsible for the position he now had.

Given the general gentrification of journalism (Melin-Higgins, 1996a, 1996b; Weaver, 1998) and Henningham and Delano's (1998) result about British journalism in particular, this attitude is quite astonishing. Perhaps this should be seen as a strategic institutionalized identity creating process (de Bruin, 1998; van Zoonen, 1998a), where working class and masculinity is coupled together, along with pub-going, banter among the boys, but also with objectivity and professionalism.

---

[6]This assumption can indeed be problematised, as van Zoonen (1998a) does in an article about the feminisation of news.

[7]All the names of journalists are fictitious. When a year is written, it indicates that I did two interviews with that journalist, and the quotation is from 1992 or 1998, respectively. When no year is mentioned the interview was held once, in 1992.

THE DOXA

The apparent homogeneity among British journalists (see Bertagna, 1991; Henningham & Delano, 1998; Köcher, 1985, 1986) makes the doxa even stronger. McQuail (1994) argued that neutrality is the most common value among journalists and interestingly, British journalists tend to have a much stronger belief in objectivity and neutrality than their colleagues in other European countries (Donsbach & Klett, 1993; Köcher, 1985, 1986; Melin-Higgins, 1996a, 1996b). In the book, *The Global Journalist* (Weaver, 1998) one can see that British journalists are among the strongest believers in their information-transmission role in the world and my own study supports these findings. There is a very strong belief in neutrality, and of remaining distant at all costs. One has to be impartial, which does not mean uncritical—one can do both.

> You report what people think—not reflect it, or support it—from their point of view. Your duty is to inform as much as you can, as impartially as you can. (Diana, home affairs correspondent, broadsheet, England).

> The whole point is to be a neutral reporter of events, as I see it. A reporter should report what he sees. (Billy, crime reporter, tabloid, Scotland)

> Journalists are there to question authority. Report, question and discuss what goes on in society. You can do a professional job. You can be neutral. (Heather, home affairs correspondent, broadsheet, Scotland)

> Yes, we can be objective . . . in terms of treatment of news stories, even if we don't agree. . . . We can all have our own subjective views, but we can stand aside from it as professional journalists. That's the difference between BBC and the tabloids. (Brian, deputy editor, BBC, England)

Putting these findings another way, the doxa of English and Scottish journalism is very clearly objectivist. Another intrinsic value of the doxa is that the news-gathering process is also seen as fundamental—it is the *hunt* for news that is the most important. Previous studies on the roles of British journalists have all pointed to the strong bloodhound or investigative role (Donsbach & Klett, 1993; Köcher, 1985, 1986). Most of the journalists I interviewed talked of the information-gathering process as being what constitutes good journalism, either in terms of finding "The Truth" and/or being critical of the powerful (i.e., politicians) and also conducting good (i.e., tough) interviews.

> It's important to have distance to yourself. If you can't have distance, you can't be subversive. It is necessary not to be part of the establishment that

you should police. You have to be an outsider as a journalist. One has to know the system and be sceptical, then you fight back. (Bob, general reporter, broadsheet, Scotland)

[the journalists' role] is being pushy. To be in the right place at the right time, to shoot things that people don't want you to do. (Edward, Scotland reporter, TV, England/Scotland)

Furthermore, in hunting for "The Truth," most means were allowed. Several of the journalists (all male) took pride in regularly breaking ethical codes to get their story. They told me about tricks they used particularly when interviewing people not used to journalists, for example, relatives of murder victims.

To get the story before someone else is ultimate. And to do it you have to use your contacts and knock on the doors as hard as you can. . . . You have to do the job, to talk to people, even if it causes grief. You have to cry with them if necessary—to get the photo and the information. I'm stone dead, cold blooded. I can do it if it's a question of getting the story first. It's something you get used to. (Billy, crime reporter, tabloid, Scotland)

The approach to news and the news-gathering process is obviously funda-mental and obviously influences the stories, which get to make the news (e.g., which stories, what angles). Part of the doxa is also the glorification of what could be considered as the tough part of journalism—the working hours and the stress. Schlesinger (1978) spoke of this as being part of the glamorous side of journalism, which has become fetishised in the mythology of journalism. The same can be said about the semi-alcoholic, overworked, working-class guy I discussed previously. "Och, he won't stop until he drops down dead" one jour-nalist said with considerable admiration, about a colleague I tried to reach for an interview. The pub is central to this mythology. Although the differences between Scottish and English journalism are few, the importance of alcohol and the pub is one of them. For example, all the journalists I interviewed in Scotland (on both occasions) chose to meet me in a pub or a restaurant, whereas all the journalists (with one [Scottish] exception) in England chose to see me at their workplace.

Pubs are different here; you go to a pub before going somewhere else. People *do* go out, but only for a couple of drinks. Most people in the news-room don't drink at lunchtime. "Drunken journalists" don't apply anymore. (Brian, deputy editor, BBC, England)

THE STRATEGIES TO RETAIN POWER

The Gatekeepers

The dominant culture uses a number of strategies to retain power. The first is to guard the *entrance into journalism*. A strong old boy network is the main strategy, which means that being the right sex (male), well connected, coming from the right schools, or at least places, will make one recognized by the gatekeepers. Another is the extremely tough and sexist attitudes on journalism training courses, which was mentioned by four of the women I interviewed.

> Both my parents were journalists and my mother wrote a woman's column. I only became a journalist because she walked up to the editor of xxx [the regional broadsheet] and kept asking him to take me on. Eventually she persuaded him. It's a deep-rooted idea that women's place is not in a newspaper. (Anne, retired editor of woman's page, broadsheet, England)

> There were mostly women on the course in Cardiff, and on the BBC training course it was 50–50. They said they would prepare us for the newsroom. And they did. It was awful. Sexual jokes and innuendoes all the time. . . . there was just one type of journalism taught: short-hand, law, and being a tough guy. (Frances, presenter/reporter, radio, Scotland, 1992)

The Routines

Another strategy is the very structure of the media organization itself, which is formalized *in everyday routines*. The newsroom is generally very hierarchical and jobs are given out at morning meetings to individual journalists, who are often specialists in a particular subject area. These meetings tend to be tense if there are journalists (for which read "women") who challenge the "natural" order of the distribution of jobs, like the gendered dichotomy, hard-soft news previously discussed. So, rituals like the morning meeting also serve to keep up the distinction between the different groups in the social field of journalism (see Burns, 1977; Egsmose, 1998; Schlesinger, 1978).

> As a woman you're certainly in a minority. Men are quite patronising. But I don't find it a problem. I get my stories in. But in meetings you're thought of as . . . well you're not taken seriously. (Ailsa, fashion editor, tabloid, Scotland)

> They [men and women] are not really different. It's tough, more difficult for women to be on TV because they have to dress differently every day otherwise people complain. Also, they want to be prima donnas and stars much more than men. . . . Men don't treat women inferior and they don't

feel like that. It's like "horses for courses": women are used in certain stories because they are good at it, that is, soft stories. (Steve, general reporter, TV, Scotland)

At meetings, well I always do, I let every journalist come up with ideas and say what they want to do. Also women. There are, though, some things women are better at. (Dave, editor, tabloid, England, 1998)

The Newsroom Culture

Not only is the structure of the newsroom sexist, so is its *culture and attitude.* Football/cricket/rugby stories and sexist and racist jokes are part of the everyday newsroom culture. Belittling women with attributes like *girl, hen, darling* is also part of this strategy. This is seen as offensive by many women who try to avoid places where these are heard. Power is thus restored—one more battle is won. When belittling successful female journalists, other adjectives are used. *Hard-bitten old hag, tough as old boots, she slept her way to the job* were comments about famous women journalists, that came up frequently[8] during the interviews. And this to a female researcher.

The Pub

The sexism goes on after hours *in the pub,* which is really a continuation of the newsroom. In the pub, there is not only football talk. The pub is also where the next day's jobs are often given out, where promotions are discussed, and where stories are made (see also, Egsmose, 1993). The local pub is often where many sources go, (e.g., local politicians), and this is particularly the case in Scotland. Most of the male journalists I interviewed said they left home at 8 or 9 in the morning and usually did not get home until 10 or 11 at night. With these hours, one would think that a private or social life is impossible, but journalism *is* the private *and* social life. It is a *way* of life. Obviously, one needs a very supportive and understanding partner with this lifestyle, and some of the male journalists spoke very highly of their wives in this respect.

My wife doesn't mind me being away so much, and it doesn't impose on our marriage, because she is used to it—over the years. (Barry, Scotland correspondent, broadsheet, England)

---

[8]With three exceptions, all the men I interviewed made some derogatory comment on female colleagues.

Pubs are very big. It's a meeting place, where you can take people for a drink, and where you try to draw stories out of sources; a few drinks can open up people. Most guys in the paper go for a drink after work. So do I sometimes. And sometimes I go out with detectives and gangsters. (Billy, crime reporter, tabloid, Scotland)

I could never have become editor for xxx [taboid] if it wasn't for my wife. . . . No, she doesn't work. She looks after our children. She used to be a journalist. (Dave, editor, tabloid, England, 1998)

When asked, most of the men in the study did not find sexist attitudes a problem and in fact did not see it as sexist and talked of the equality programs in their organizations. They did not think that female journalists—today at least—had any problems as a result of their gender. On the other hand, *all* the women I interviewed *did* find this a problem, although in different ways. Unprompted, they all commented on sexism in the newsroom, how they suffered from it, that they are treated like "wee lassies," and as a consequence were unable to do the kinds of stories they wanted to.

I didn't like the politics of the newsroom, that's why I left. Its a male dominated area: it's a middle-middle class, bright grammar school, boys' culture, and if you're not into sexist and racist jokes, and don't like cricket, you've had it. Then you're isolated. . . . It's a men's game: there are women that play it and women that don't. Those that don't, go into a different kind of journalism. (Ruth, producer, radio, England, 1992)

In their work, Henningham and Delano (1998) found that 60% of their women respondents said they had personal experience or knowledge of women who had been victims of prejudice in the newsroom, compared with only 31% of men. From my own experience, I am surprised the figure for women is not higher. Also, in Henningham and Delano's study, 53% of British female journalists were single compared with only 31% of male journalists.[9] *All* the women I interviewed talked of the problems that having a family or a partner caused. Some talked of the choices they had made to become, or remain a journalist: no children, no husband.

---

[9]The 31% single male journalist figure should be compared to 29% of the British population in general, and similarly 53% female journalists compared to 21% female Britons aged between 20 and 65 (Henningham & Delano, 1998).

COPING WITH JOURNALISM—
THE TACTICS OF FEMALE JOURNALISTS

With frustration running very high, it is perhaps not surprising that the women I interviewed had very clear and outspoken tactics for coping. I found four principal tactics, that are used, which are not dissimilar to those found in other studies (Egsmose, 1998; Eide, 1995; Melin-Higgins, 1996b; Schlesinger, 1978; van Zoonen, 1988a, 1998b; Zilliacus-Tikkanen, 1997).

Dominated Marionettes or
Women With Place and Power?

The first two tactics share the fact that they accept the doxa and play by the rules of the dominant culture. In fact, they enter and become part of the dominant culture.

> There are two ways of getting on as a woman: 1) become one of the boys, 2) have the figure and face, the vital statistics. (Iona, freelance court journalist, Scotland)

The second of these tactics is used by those who are either young and new to journalism, or who have no wish to fight for a place among the boys. They have in common that they (albeit to various degrees) adapt to the traditional view of women, that is, to accept that they will be seen as a woman first and a journalist second, to accept that they will cover the soft stories even if they once thought they could become a political correspondent. Some of the women who use this tactic commented on newsroom gender relations, which they saw as friendly banter rather than sexism and were more upset by the lack of promotion.

> I always wanted to be a news-reporter and the last job I wanted was as women's reporter. I was, though, pitched in by the editor, since they needed somebody for the job. . . . I hope to be able to write an important story as well as a man. . . . Women and men are not treated differently on [name of newspaper]. The joshing and joking is between individuals. Chauvinism has more to do with society than [our newspaper]. The tabloid papers, though, are difficult for women. They are either very tough and see themselves as "one-of-the-boys," or they do the "bimbo jobs" (following starlets that will marry a football-star). But it is up to individual women what kind of job they want. (Mary, editor of a woman's page, broadsheet, Scotland)

> When I was 19 I was given the woman's page to write. I cried and thought
> it was the end of my career . . . I left because there was no possibility for
> promotion. I saw all the young men jumping over me. It was also then that I
> had my daughter. (Anne, retired editor of women's page, broadsheet,
> England)

At one level, it seems that the women employing this tactic are the biggest
losers in the war between cultures. It struck me, however, that they had created
a place for themselves, a place in which they had power. Fashion pages,
women's pages, woman's hour radio programs, and so on do not have particularly high status among male colleagues, but this did not seem to bother these
women. Instead they sought appreciation from their audience.

One of the Boys, or Women With Attitude?

To get on in a man's world, perhaps the best option is to adapt to the dominant
culture, to be "one of the boys" (see Egsmose, 1998; van Zoonen, 1998b). This
entails adopting the values and ways of the dominant culture, that is, to adopt a
neutral and distant approach to news, and it means trying to cover (and hunt for)
the hardest of the hard news. As Charles said in 1992:

> Women are shunted off into softer, women's interest-type stories. Women
> that are in news journalism have to deny their femininity: be a man—come
> and drink with us. Unfortunately, some women have made themselves part
> of the pub-culture because they think that's the way it should be. (Charles,
> arts columnist, broadsheet, Scotland, 1992)

The women who adopt this strategy tended to accept journalism as a
lifestyle, that is, they usually went to the pub with the boys, although they commented that it was unusual for women. They had often made the choice of not
having any children as it would hinder to their career.

> I'm deep into the pub culture, which is quite rare for women journalists:
> women go home, men go to the pub. The pub culture which is prevalent
> among Scottish journalists is for men, and it extends to the workplace: they
> talk at work the way they would in the pub, hence women are seen as being
> boring, gullible and not witty, since they're not in the talk. (Frances, pre-
> senter/reporter, radio, Scotland)

> I used to hang around with the guys in the pub all the time. But my mar-
> riage nearly hit the rocks because of it. It's not really a man–female thing,
> more family–or not. When I got pregnant my [journalist] friends pitied me
> for having to stay home. But now I just want to get home to my daughter.
> (Ruth, producer, radio, England, 1992)

The reason these women choose this tactic is that they want to avoid the sexism and low status of covering soft stories, and the disrespect that follows from that. Trying to be one of the boys is, however, frustratingly hard work, as Frances, a Scottish radio journalist said in 1992: "So, what do you do when you want to cover political news and there is a middle-aged man already doing it?" Her answer to herself was that, "The only way is by being better and more of a man than the man himself." It seems to be a successful tactic, in that during the years that passed between the two sets of interviews, all the women who seemed to use this tactic had climbed the career ladder.

One of the Girls, or Compassionate Journalism With a Mission?

A quite different way of coping with the dominant newsroom culture is to create one's own culture. The women who adopted this tactic clearly rejected the dominant culture and its values. They rejected the objectivist approach and spoke for a subjective journalism, where the journalist's feelings and opinions are important. Most of the women I interviewed had a very clear mission with their job—it was more than just a job to them. They really believed they could make a difference to people and to society, and they therefore chose the subject area they found interesting and important. One covered politics in order to be able to enhance the possibilities for female politicians and feminist politics. One covered health issues to better (than male reporters) cover rape cases and child abuse, and one covered "women's issues" and emphasized the importance to women of cooking and fashion.

> I understood that I had to create a niche for myself otherwise I'd end up doing crap jobs, since the hard stories are exclusively for men. I chose health, because I thought it was important. (Diana, social affairs correspondent, broadsheet, Scotland)

> We have a kind of mission. . . . My role is to tell women. . . . it's not a feminist program, but it should reflect that women succeed in society. There are not enough of them though. I look for women speakers and sources. (Flora, editor of woman's program, radio, England)

> . . . fashion is to educate people, to make them use their own creativity. Try to give people some information, that women in particular are interested in. (Ailsa, fashion editor, tabloid, Scotland)

A more radical way to oppose the dominant culture is to create one's own environment, be it the women's page, *Women's Hour* on radio, or a women's magazine such as *Harpies and Quinnes*. All the women who worked in these female contexts talked of the positive working environment they experienced compared to a mainstream newsroom.

> *Harpies and Quinnes* is spare time and not paid. My tasks there are also more managerial. I love it. . . . working with other women. We get things done. There's not so much politics and playing with egos going on. Its more cooperative. (Lilidh, general news-reporter, tabloid, Scotland)

> It's important that it's the women's page I work for. That is more the feminist side of me, than a burning desire to be a journalist. (Mary-Ann, deputy editor of women's page, broadsheet, England)

When I interviewed Ruth in 1998—she then worked at BBC TV—I spent the whole day with her. One of her fellow (part-time) producers, Liza, a woman in her 30s, with two small children, produced the show of the day. Liza was the object of many comments from her colleagues, particularly when she said she didn't have time to answer my questions. Women made comments like: "You know, she is really stressed and tries to do it all in half a day. God, I don't know how she can do it." Her three male colleagues, on the other hand, made more derogatory comments such as: "She used to be out and about much more before she had kids. She was much more fun then" and "Watch it, she'll bite your head off. Motherhood makes strange things to a person."

The problems many women experienced were that they were treated as "wee lassies" with little respect, as what they were doing was not considered important. Perhaps the biggest problem was a personal one: They all tried to be and do everything—successful journalists, active feminists, and good mothers.

Retreating From the Newsroom— or Getting a Place?

Creating a niche, a space, or even a new medium is a luxury few female journalists can manage. Another strategy to avoid the pressure and sexism of the newsroom is to leave it altogether. A lot of freelancers (particularly women) give up their salaried positions in media organizations for that very reason. One woman courtroom freelancer said that she left her job because as a freelancer she could be more critical and do better analysis (and therefore do a better job), which was almost impossible with the tight deadlines of a mainstream newsroom. One often quoted reason for becoming a freelancer was that it enabled women to be journalists, despite having partners and children. Indeed, some of the interviewees saw becoming a freelancer the only option if they were going to have children and a career.

A more tragic strategy (tragic mainly for journalism) is that some women cannot cope with the pressures and leave journalism altogether. The 6 years that elapsed between the two sets of interviews saw several women leaving the newsroom. One quit to work in public relations and has now become a lecturer in journalism. Three women have taken time off to have children. They now want to get back into journalism, as freelancers, producers in television or working with Web journalism. One is away from work with a long term stress related illness.

CONCLUSIONS

To briefly summarize, in this study I have, by combining classical theories of sociology of journalism with feminist theories and cultural studies, found fruitful analytical tools to achieve an understanding of the British (here English and Scottish) journalist culture in the 1990s. This *journalist culture,* as a *social field,* is characterized as being highly hierarchical, trusting on the old boy network, and having a very traditional view of women. This can be seen as a reflection of the British society at large (see Christmas, 1997; Egsmose, 1998; Galloway & Robertson, 1991; Köcher, 1985; 1986). The hierarchy is exemplified with the classical distinction made between soft and hard news[10] that can be seen as an outgrowth of the equally classical Patriarchal Enlightenment dichotomy (male = rational, strong, tough, active, etc., female = irrational, weak, nurturing, passive, etc.) (Hirdman, 1990; Jónasdóttir, 1991; MacKinnon, 1989). The *doxa* of the dominant culture entails a very strong objectivist approach (i.e., a firm belief in neutrality, impartiality, and remaining distant at all cost) and an emphasis on the hunt for news, The Truth, and in this hunt the end justifies the means (i.e., ethical codes seem to be taken lightly). There is furthermore a glorification of the tough part of the job (i.e., presenteeism, long hours, stress, and alcohol).

I have argued that British journalist culture and its doxa are masculine and sexist, which is not particularly surprising, given that most feminist journalist scholars come to the same conclusion, albeit in various countries.[11] Also the strategies used by the dominant culture to defend the culture and doxa seem to

---

[10]This distinction exists in most other countries as well, which has been documented by most feminist journalist scholars (e.g., de Bruin, 1998; Eide, 1995; Egsmose, 1998; Melin-Higgins, 1996a; 1996b; Robinson & Saint-Jean, 1998; Zilliakus-Tikkanen, 1997; van Zoonen, 1998a; 1998b).

[11]The list of references to the argument of masculine news organizations could be very long. Some examples are Baehr (1980), Beasley (1989), Bertagna (1991), de Bruin (1998), Christmas (1997), Egsmose (1998), Eide (1995), Melin-Higgins (1996a, 1996b) van Zoonen (1998a; 1998b), Zilliacus-Tikkanen (1997).

be masculine in nature. These include a strong gatekeeping function to guard the entrance to the profession, macho organizational structure and routines, the pub culture, and overt sexist attitudes (see also, Egsmose, 1998; Zilliacus-Tikkanen 1997). And these strategies appear to be successful. I found for example that the doxa and dominant culture had changed little over time.

The relatively few women12 who actually enter journalism (despite the old boy network) have a hard time coping and employ outspoken tactics to do so. One way to cope and to get a career is to adapt on every level and to become one of the boys, fighting with the men for the status-filled jobs and high salaries. Another is to be like a marionette, accepting the inferior status given (as a woman journalist). Yet another way is to create an oppositional culture, for the girls, with a completely different approach: This could be creating a niche, a space in the newspaper/program, or a new medium, with the aim of creating a more interesting journalism. A fourth way is to leave the newsroom altogether and become a freelancer, as a way to do better journalism, or just to be able to be a journalist at all.

What characterized *all* the women in the study was that journalism was not just a job to them, it was a mission. They had a clear purpose and wanted to change society and change journalism. I found similar results in a study among Swedish journalists (Melin-Higgins, 1996a, 1996b). Similarly, I found in both studies that the women's approach to news stories varied from that of male journalists. All the women tended to question the idea of neutrality and objectivity. Several (particularly those who can be said to be members of an oppositional culture) tended to talk of subjectivity and a personal involvement as the only *good* approach journalism. This does, indeed, come close to what Zilliacus-Tikkanen (1997) described as female journalism in conflict with traditional journalist culture (see also, van Zoonen, 1998b).

The female journalists, on the one hand, seem to have more fragmented identities as journalists, or rather as *female* journalists, at the same time they were much more convinced in their identities as journalists, or in their approach to journalism than their male colleagues. Perhaps one reason for this can be found if one acknowledges the patriarchal structures of journalism, that is, men's professional identities as journalists and that fact that men's ideas are much less fragmented and less problematic than those of women in journalism, as journalism (as it is defined in contemporary British society) and masculinity (as it is defined in contemporary British society) are in tune with each other (see de Bruin, 1998; van Zoonen, 1998a, 1998b). To cope with journalism, women have to find tactics that deal with their identities as women (e.g., by suppressing this fact) and as journalists. From that, follows the need for women to have a stronger conviction of why they want to be, or remain journalists. It is a mission.

It is important to point out that there are men who also find the dominant culture problematic and try to change their work in ways not that different to the women. One conclusion that can be drawn, then, is that if a journalist openly opposes the dominant culture and its doxa, that journalist needs a lot of personal strength and conviction: Seeing the job as a mission and having a personal involvement, I argue, is crucial.

Following people, their lives, attitudes, and careers over time has been fascinating. British journalism culture has shown both stability and change, both on a personal and cultural level. However, the journalist culture with its doxa has remained the same through out the 1990s and so has the frustrations of female journalists. However, there have been positive changes both on a personal and cultural level for some people. Since 1992, several of the women I interviewed have been promoted to senior editorial positions. A couple of the women have gotten married and have had the children they wanted *and* have become freelancers. The male journalist who was the most critical toward the dominant culture has managed to create a niche for himself where he produces interesting and different journalism.

At an organizational level, a change of editor can mean a big change in the journalist culture. For one broadsheet newspaper, a new editor has meant a drastic increase in the number of women on the news desk, and an alcohol ban during working hours. The new editor on a tabloid newspaper enabled women who had children to work part of their hours from home. New technology has made it possible to find solutions for journalists who want to spend less time in the newsroom. The tendency for women to leave the newsroom and work freelance or as Web journalists, is, however, not always easy. Both job types tend to have less status and less pay and most workers are women. This, I argue, is an interesting area for further research.

A lot of the changes that have taken place are due to the hard work, support, and networking of individual journalists, particularly women.[13] For further changes to take place in British journalism, to improve the terms and conditions of both female and male journalists, they have to be preceded by structural changes in media organizations and by political and structural changes in Britain, more generally. The professional, public, and the private are inseparable, and one particular issue that must be dealt with is support for working mothers.

Structures have not changed or changed enough, because a lot of things become difficult once you have a child—and especially if you have more than one. Many of us felt it was time to fight—but it was also time to make dinner and take the children to ballet. Often the women who had the choice pulled back and there weren't enough of the others to force change to happen. I also think there has to be pressure from above, from NGOs [nongovernmental organisations] as well as from the government. People think that there isn't a problem, because so many careers are open to women now, which weren't open 20 years ago, but there will be terrible consequences if we don't change soon (Maureen Freely, writer, cited in Perkins, 2001, p. 9).

---

[13]The networking organization *Women in Journalism* has started and is doing very interesting work. It can be contacted at wijuk@aol.com.

REFERENCES

Armstead, C. (1995). Writing contradictions. Feminist research and feminist writing. *Women's Studies International Forum, 18* (5/6), 627–636.

Avellan, H. (2002). Utan röda strumpor [Without red stockings]. *Sydsvenskan Dagbladet, 10*, 2.

Baehr, H. (1980). *Women and media.* Oxford: Pergamon Press.

Beasley, M. (1989). Newspapers: Is there a new majority defining the news? In P. Creedon (Ed.), *Women in mass communication. Challenging gender values* (pp. 180–194). Newbury Park, CA, London: Sage.

Bertagna, J. (1991). Women in the Scottish arts and media. In The Woman's Claim of Right Group (Eds.), *A Woman's claim of right in Scotland. Women, representation and politics* (pp. 95–101). Edinburgh: Polygon.

Bourdieu, P. (1984). *Distinction. A social critique of the judgement of taste.* London: Routledge & Kegan Paul.

Bourdieu, P. (1990). *In other words. Essays towards a reflexive sociology.* Stanford, CA: Stanford University Press.

Bourdieu, P. (1991). *Language and symbolic power.* Cambridge: Polity Press.

Bourdieu, P. (1999). *Den manliga dominansen (La domination masculine).* Göteborg: Daidalos.

Burns, T. (1977). *The BBC. Public institution and private world.* London & Basingstoke: MacMillan Press.

Christmas, L. (1997). *Chaps of both sexes? Women decision-makers in newspapers: Do they make a difference?* Devises, Wiltshire: The BT Forum.

de Bruin, M. (1998, July). *Gender in Caribbean media: Beyond the body count.* Paper presented at the IAMCR conference, Glasgow.

de Certeau, M. (1984). *The practice of everyday life.* Berkeley: University of California Press.

Donsbach, W., & Klett, B. (1993). *Subjective objectivity. How journalists in four countries define a key term of their profession.* The Netherlands: Kluwer Academic Publishers.

Egsmose, L. (1993). Medvind og modvind i TV. Karrieremuligheder for kvindelige medieprofessionelle i Danmark og England [With and against the wind in TV. Career possibilities for female media professionals in Denmark and England]. In U. Carlsson (Ed.), *Nordisk forskning om kvinnor och medier* (pp. 201–226). Göteborg: Nordicom.

Egsmose, L. R. (1998). Et kønsperspektiv på medieprofisionelle i TV. Kvinders karrieremuligheder i BBC og Danmarks Radio [A gender perspective on media professionals in TV. Women's career possibilities in the BBC and Denmark's radio]. *Sosiologisk Tidskrift, 3*, 231–244.

Eide, E. (1995, August). *Journalist-feminismens Catch 22.* Paper presented at the Nordic conference on mass communication, Helsinki.

Fonow, M., & Cook, J. (1991). *Beyond methodology. Feminist scholarship as lived research.* Bloomington: Indiana University Press.

Gallagher, M., with von Euler, M. (1995). *An unfinished story: Gender patterns in media employment.* Paris: UNESCO.

Galloway, K., & Robertson, J. (1991). Introduction: A woman's claim of right for Scotland. In The Woman's Claim of Right Group (Eds.), *A woman's claim of right in Scotland. Women, representation and politics* (pp. 1–6). Edinburgh: Polygon.

Galtung, J., & Ruge, M. (1973). Structuring and selecting news. In S. Cohen & J. Young (Eds.), *The manufacture of news* (pp. 62–72). London: Constable.

Gans, H. (1979). *Deciding what's news. A study of CBS Evening News, NBC Nightly News, Newsweek and Time.* London: Constable.

Hall, S. (1980). Cultural studies: Two paradigms. In *Media, Culture and Society, 2,* 57–72.

Harding, S. (1987). *Feminism and methodology. Social science issues.* Bloomington: Indiana University Press.

Henningham, J., & Delano, A. (1998). British journalists. In D. Weaver (Ed.), *The global journalist. News people around the world.* Cresskill, NJ: Hampton Press.

Hirdman, Y. (1990). Genussystemet [The gender system]. In *Demokrati och makt i Sverige. Maktutredningens huvudrapport* (pp. 73–117). SOU.

Jónásdottir, A. (1991). Könsbegreppet i samhällsvetenskapen. Tre kontroverser [The gender concept in social science. Three controversies]. In *Könsrelationernas betydelse som vetenskaplig kategori* (Report nr 21). Stockholm: JÄMFO.

Järvinen, M. (1999). Immovable magic—Pierre Bourdieu on gender and power. *NORA, 1,* 6–19.

Kvale, S. (1997). *Den kvalitativa forskningsintervjun* [The qualitative research interview]. Lund: Studentlitteratur.

Köcher, R. (1985). *Spürhund und Missionar. Eine vergleichende Untersuchung über Berufsethik und Aufgabenverständnis britischer und deutscher Journalisten* [Bloodhounds and missionaries. A comparative study of professional ethics and job perception between British and German Journalists]. Allensbach: Der Ludwig-Maximilians-Universität München.

Köcher, R. (1986). Bloodhounds or missionaries. Role definitions of German and British journalists. *European Journal of Communication, 1*(1), 43–64.

Larsson, LÅ. (2000). Personliga intervjuer [Personal interviews]. In M. Ekström& LÅ Larsson (Eds.), *Metodier i Kommunikationsvetenskap.* Lund: Studentlitteratur.

Lindvert, J. (2002). *Feminism som politik* [Feminism as politics]. Lund: Borea.

Lönnroth, A., & Boëtius, M-P. (1991). Fler kvinnliga journalister—märks det i mediautbudet? [More female journalists—is it noticable in media content?]. In *Kvinnoperspektiv på masskommunikationsforskningen* [Women's perspective on mass communication research] (Report nr 22). Stockholm: JÄMFO.

MacKinnon, C. (1989). *Toward a feminist theory of the state.* Cambridge, MA: Harvard University Press.

McNair, B. (1994). *News and journalism in the UK.* London: Routledge.

McQuail, D. (1994). *Mass communication theory. An introduction.* London: Sage.

Melin, M. (1991). *Från kultur till journalistkultur. En litteraturöversikt över diskussionerna kring kulturbegreppet* [From culture to journalism culture. A literature review of the discussions around the concept of culture]. Göteborg: Department of Journalism and Mass Communication, University of Göteborg.

Melin-Higgins, M. (1996a). Bloodhounds or bloodbitches. Female ideals and Catch 22. In *Kjønn i Media* [Gender in the media]. (Report nr 2/96, pp. 100-120). Oslo: Sekretariatet for kvinneforskning (Secretariat of womens studies).

Melin-Higgins, M. (1996b). *Pedagoger och Spårhundar. En studie av svenska journalisters yrkesideal* [Educators and bloodhounds. A study of Swedish journalists professional ideal]. Göteborg: Department of Journalism and Mass Communication, University of Göteborg.

Melin-Higgins, M. (2004). *Dominant culture and gender opposition in British journalism.* Göteborg: University of Göteborg.

Melin-Higgins, M., & Djerf-Pierre, M. (1998, July). *Networking in newsrooms— Journalist and gender cultures.* Paper presented at IAMCR, Glasgow.

Perkins, A. (2001, May 31). Hands up who fell off the career ladder as they hit motherhood. *The Guardian*, p. 9.

Ramazanoglu, C. (1992). On feminist methodology: Male reason versus female empowerment. *Sociology, 26*(2), 207–212.

Robinson, G., & Saint-Jean, A. (1998). Canadian women journalists: The "other half" of the equation. In D. Weaver (Ed.), *The global journalist. News people around the world* (pp. 351–372). Cresskill, NJ: Hampton Press.

Schlesinger, P. (1978). *Putting "reality" together. BBC news.* London: Constable.

Schudson, M. (1991). The sociology of news production revisited. In J. Curran & M. Gurevitch (Eds.), *Mass media and society,* (pp. 141-160). London: Edward Arnold.

Spender, D. (1985). *For the record. The making and meaning of feminist knowledge.* London: The Women's Press.

Stanley, L. (1995). My mother's voice? On being "a native" in academia. In L. Morley & V. Walsh (Eds.), *Feminist academics. Creative agents for change* (pp. 183-194). Taylor and Francis.

Steiner, L. (1998). Newsroom account of power at work. In C. Carter, G. Branston, & S. Allan (Eds.), *News, gender and power* (pp. 145-159). London: Routledge.

Tunstall, J. (1970). *The Westminster Lobby correspondents. A sociological study of national political journalism.* London: Routledge & Kegan Paul.

Weaver, D. (Ed.), (1998). *The global journalist. News people around the world.* Cresskill, NJ: Hampton Press.

Weibull, L., Asp, K., Börjesson, B., Lötgren, M., & Melin, M. (1991). *Svenska journalister—ett grupporträtt* [Swedish journalists—a group portrait]. Stockholm: Tidens förlag.

Williams, R. (1976). *Keywords. A vocabulary of culture and society.* Milton Keynes: Open University Press.

Williams, R. (1981). *Culture.* Milton Keynes: Open University Press.

van Zoonen, L. (1994). *Feminist media studies.* London: Routledge.

van Zoonen, L. (1998a). A heroic, unreliable, professional marionette (M/F): Structure, agency and subjectivity in contemporary journalisms. *European Journal of Cultural Studies, 1*(1), 123-143.

van Zoonen, L. (1998b). One of the girls?: The changing gender of journalism. In C. Carter, G. Branston, & S. Allan (Eds.), *News, gender and power* (pp. 33-46). London: Routledge.

van Zoonen, L., & Donsbach, W. (1988, June). *Professional values and gender in British and German journalism.* Paper presented at ICA, New Orleans.

Zilliacus-Tikkanen, H. (1997). *Journalistikens essens i ett könsperspektiv* [The essence of journalism from a gender perspective]. Helsinki: Rundradions jämställdhetskommitté [Finnish broadcast company's equality commitee].

12

Shifting Sites:
Feminist, Gay, and Lesbian
News Activism in the U.S. Context

Carolyn M. Byerly

Events have a way of changing history, sometimes beyond the goals of those who lead them. If second-wave feminism had set only the goal of changing news coverage about women, that would have been monumental, given two centuries of male control in U.S. newsrooms. Modern feminists, through intentional activism over the last three decades, have left their mark on news organizations and on news itself in numerous important ways. But feminist inroads into journalism also have had unanticipated outcomes. By creating the political and cultural space to question gender as a social construction and women's relations of power to men, feminists were also opening the spaces for broader issues of gender roles and sexuality to emerge, in relation to news and its production.

By the 1980s and 1990s, feminism had helped to create a context both for a feminist presence, as well as a stronger presence of gay and lesbian journalists in United States newsrooms and in news stories. Indeed, women in some news media, particularly at weekly newspapers and magazines, were found to be close to parity with men, in both journalistic and managerial ranks by the mid-1990s, according to one study. The same research, however, shows that although women may have relatively more control over selecting topics for their stories, they have less influence in organizational decisions like hiring, especially in broadcast news (Weaver & Wilhoit, 1996, cited in de Bruin, 1998). Aarons and Murphy (2000) found that most of the gay and lesbian journalists they surveyed in today's United States newsrooms were "out" and felt that this did not affect their employment or assignments. But other research questions whether progress has been uniform, pointing out that the news still underrepresents both

221

women and sexual minorities in its coverage (Aarons & Murphy, 2000; Bridge, 1994).

In addition, scholars, working journalists, and critics of journalism all say that the news media need to more fairly represent the lives of women and sexual minorities. For example, Pozner's (2001) critique of United States news coverage of female politicians comes down hard on stories that persist in emphasizing their dress size, hairstyles, and mannerisms instead of their ideas and performance.

> A search of the Nexis database turns up no essential details about [Vice President] Dick Cheney's inseam or the length of [Senator] Trent Lott's trousers—but it does reveal that before she became [New York state] senator, Hillary Rodham Clinton "whittled her figure down to a size 8" by touching little more than a lettuce leaf during fund raisers. (Pozner, 2001, p. 9)

Lesbian and gay journalists believe that the quality of news about sexual minorities' experiences, contributions, and problems (e.g., victimization and discrimination) has improved, especially the hot button issues, like AIDS and gay marriage, at the national level. But at the local level, they agree overwhelmingly that much needs to improve in terms of quantity and quality of the gay experience (Aarons & Murphy, 2000).

Together with the civil rights movement for racial equality, these movements for social justice have challenged the dominant Eurocentric, male, heterosexist paradigm in U.S. society. They have also called into question the way that news organizations mirror and reinforce this paradigm, both in the relations of power present in newsrooms and in the content of news. This chapter is specifically concerned with the gains and the hindrances that women and sexual minorities have encountered in their efforts to establish a more powerful relationship to news over the years and, in the process, to advance their presence and power politically and culturally.

TERMINOLOGY

I use the term *feminist* generally to describe the advocates (and corresponding movement) engaged in women's liberation, which includes efforts to secure civil and economic rights, social advancement, and a reappraisal of women's experience from both liberal and radical perspectives. From time to time, I find it necessary to distinguish between these, defining *liberal feminist* as that which is concerned with the fullest development of the individual (and women's need to reform society to allow such for women), and *radical feminist* as that which views women's oppression as an outgrowth of their sexual class (and women's need to re-imagine and restructure society to encompass female experience).

Gay rights refers to the corresponding political movement by gay, lesbian, bisexual, and transgendered individuals, since the late 1960s. Collectively, these individuals represent *sexual minorities*.

I use the term *intervention* to refer to any organized, intentional act aimed at interrupting sexist or anti-gay and lesbian practices with the goal of making those practices fairer and more egalitarian. Much of my own work in feminist journalism research over the years has been concerned with both liberal (reformist) and radical (revisionist) interventionist campaigns and programs aimed at giving women both a greater presence and voice in mainstream and alternative news, and I extend that work in this chapter in various ways. One way is to factor in gay and lesbian news activism, which occurs within the political space provided by grassroots feminism and the analytical space afforded by feminist theory. Incorporating and theorizing gay and lesbian activism broadens and deepens our understanding of gender relations within newsmaking.

Capitalism refers to the political-economic system characterized by private ownership in investment that results in a class structure that requires a low-paid labor pool both on local and global scales. *Globalization*—the internationalization of the capitalist political-economy—enters into the discussion in terms of media ownership and the relations of power between White wealthy male owners and women, sexual minorities, and racially diverse populations who are marginalized by global capitalism in general and by corporate news industries and content in particular.

At this point, I acknowledge the difficulty of making clean distinctions between feminist and gay/lesbian news activists, which I resort to using as a kind of shorthand. There is, of course, considerable overlap in membership between these groups. In addition, many heterosexual male journalists have actively supported both feminist and gay rights movements and the improvement of news around the issues. In my efforts to shorten terminology to keep discussion from appearing to be long-winded, I do not mean to be exclusionary or disrespectful.

NEWS AND THE PUBLIC SPHERE

To speak publicly today in a complex society that is spread out geographically requires that citizens have some kind of access to print and electronic news media. Such public speech has long been understood to be associated with the social power necessary to influence democratic processes. Citizens have viewed both mainstream and alternative media as the means to speak publicly and thereby gain access to the public sphere. The public sphere, as defined by Habermas, is an imagined space free of commercial and government influence, where ideas can be articulated and debated, and where citizens can enter into deliberations that lead to social outcomes (Fraser, 1993; Garnham, 1993).

Drawing on Habermas, Garnham argued that institutions and processes of public communication—like that afforded the news media—are integral to democratic political structures and what they do. Such notions have long resonated with women seeking fuller social participation. Like their 19th-century foremothers, feminists since the 1960s have sought to increase their visibility and public voice through the media in order to challenge sexist stereotypes, to circulate new ideas about women's advancement, to mobilize political followers, and to publicize their achievements. Since the early 1970s, gay and lesbian citizens have similarly sought mainstream news attention toward securing their own civil rights and legitimizing their gains.

GENDER AND THE POLITICAL ECONOMY OF NEWS

Canadian political-economist Isabel Bakker (1994) observed that most political-economic theory is male-oriented, even though it may appear to be gender-neutral. Social cohesion between men is enhanced, she argued, by the exclusion of women. Following this thinking, political-economic theory may be said also to be heterosexist in that it usually does not recognize the social exclusion of sexual minorities, whose orientations and behavior contradict traditional norms for men and women and historically have caused them to be marginalized. The result is cohesion and privileging of heterosexual male economic and political power. Both feminist and queer theorists have done much these last years to study the overlapping elements of oppression experienced by women and non-heterosexual citizens, as well as ways that their respective movements have legitimized their presence and helped to secure their civil rights in society. In this discussion, there is value in showing the ways in which economic and other structures of power work together to perpetuate a dominant culture, in part through the news media. Large, corporate media tend to be centrist-to-conservative politically, and in the United States, this has meant the news (particularly broadcast news) has tended to privilege the events, issues, and contributions of White male elites. In this discussion, I explore the ways that feminist and gay rights journalists and activists have applied interventionist strategies for changes within newsrooms and news content, and their allies have intervened similarly from the outside.

Feminist journalism historians Beasley and Gibbons (1993) remind us that women have played active roles as publishers and journalists since the colonial American era in what might be called the general purpose publications of their day. And, although this was true—and important to consider in recognizing women's long professional involvement—there is no evidence that women then or since have ever represented a critical mass in either ownership or control over news enterprises. Au contraire, female ownership and control have been and remain the exceptions to the rule. One review of boards of directors of some of the largest global media corporations in 2001 revealed that women are not moving into leadership positions in numbers that reflect society at large, either in the United States or other nations (IWMF, 2001). Although women are still more than half the world's population, men routinely decide what news the society should hear and read. In the United States, the Radio-Television News Directors Association, reports that women make up only 24% of the news directors in television and 20% in radio. The American Society of Newspaper Editors (ASNE) reports that women hold only 34% of newsroom supervisor positions in the United States (cited in IWMF, 2001). Even powerful women who make it to the top of news corporations recognize the limitations of their gender in the field. The late Katharine Graham, chairman of the board of the agenda-setting *Washington Post*, once observed that "there is a difference between having the authority to make decisions and the power to make policy" (cited in Weaver, 1997, p. 39).

Down in the trenches of newsrooms, the scenario is somewhat better. Research shows that as individuals, female journalists exercise relatively more control over their own work than their male counterparts are able to do. By the early 1990s, female journalists, particularly in broadcast, were reporting that they had control over which of their stories aired 42% of the time, whereas their male colleagues said they did only 25% of the time (Weaver, 1997). Even so, there are still fewer women in newsrooms than men, and they make less money than men during the first 15 years of work.[1] Neither are female journalists often able to bring a feminist frame to their stories.[2]

These data become particularly troubling when one considers the fact that women have outnumbered men in United States schools of journalism since the early 1970s—60% women to 40% men in most schools. And yet, by the time these women enter the profession, the trend rapidly changes, with male journalists continuing in mobility, and women either dropping out or remaining fairly static in position (Lafky, 1993; Marlane, 2000). Economics also enter the picture in a major way, because in all areas of journalism, women's pay is likely to be lower than men's, in part because women are less likely to be considered for supervisory positions (Lafky, 1993). Although some individual enterprises have made progress in promoting both women and ethnic minorities, the fact remains

---

[1]Weaver's (1997) data show that female journalists today begin to reach parity with their male colleagues in salary between 15 and 20 years of service. His data also reveal, however, that at this level of experience, men outnumber women three to one.

[2]Huddy's (1997) empirical work shows that all journalists, including females, are pressured to limit their feminist-identified news sources and to greatly simplify feminist definitions and perspectives in their stories—despite a continuing feminist movement these last few decades. Such industry self-censorship continues to marginalize women as social actors and renders their activities less important than men's. The practice is misogynistic.

that after nearly three decades of affirmative action and activism, there is little evidence that either ethnic minority males or females overall in newsrooms are moving in and up. In a Ford Foundation-sponsored study, 61% of the 448 female ethnic minority respondents said that racial discrimination was a persistent barrier to their advancement in journalism; nearly 50% said that they believed they had no access to jobs with high visibility or authority (IWMF, 1999).

We have no comparable longitudinal data to show the political and economic relations of power between gay/lesbian journalists and their heterosexual counterparts. However, anecdotal evidence tells us that gay men and lesbians, in small numbers, have both owned and controlled news and other media. For example, the posthumous disclosure of *Forbes* magazine billionaire Malcolm Forbes' homosexuality by gay magazine *Outweek* publisher Michael Signorile in 1990 made at least one such owner known, albeit in an ethically questionable manner (Alwood, 1996; Gross, 1993). *Oakland Tribune* Vice president Leroy Aarens disclosed his own gay identity in April 1990, as he prepared to help the ASNE conduct the first survey research among gay and lesbian journalists. And, that at least one lesbian made her way into media management became known when Linda Villarosa, executive editor at *Essence*, announced her lesbianism in a 1991 article.

A bit more is known about gay and lesbian journalists working in United States reporting. Recent research suggests that sexual minority news professionals in general have been systematically marginalized just as females have been in their work. The 1990 ASNE study revealed deep anti-gay bias in many newsrooms, including the perception that gay and lesbian employees delivered poor to mediocre reporting (Aarons & Murphy, 2000). These attitudes engendered fear and silence, contributing to the invisibility of sexual minorities by keeping them in the closet. Even 10 years later, when ASNE repeated the survey, researchers Aarons and Murphy noted they found their 363 subjects through solicitation because a random sample was still not feasible "since many [still] remain closeted and invisible" (p. 8). A closer look at the journalistic closet can be found in the stories of gay men and lesbian reporters told to Edward Alwood (1996) in *Straight News*. Alwood, a former CNN reporter, recognized that although gay male and lesbian reporters have both suffered discrimination, the experiences have been more severe for lesbians. Already fewer in number and lower paid than males, lesbians have routinely faced harassment and possible firing. In his 5 years of interviews and research for the book in the early 1990s, Alwood found few lesbian print journalists and no lesbian broadcast journalists willing to share their histories with him.

Since the mid-19th century, the United States news media have been almost exclusively private commercial, profit-making operations run for the aggrandizement of their owners, stockholders, and chief executives. More recently, even what has been known as the Public Broadcasting System (PBS) has gradually taken on a corporate commercial demeanor, launching a for-profit record label (in collaboration with a Hollywood company), placing ever lengthier commercials for its corporate sponsors on its television network, entering into joint ventures with Viacom's Nickelodeon and other cable competitors, and otherwise emulating the enterprises it was meant to serve as an alternative to (McChesney, 1999).

That any mainstream print or broadcast medium today serves the public's interest or fosters a marketplace where diverse ideas compete is open to serious question. As the carriers of corporate financial data, as well government news, entertainment, and advertising, the news (and I should add entertainment) media have been central to creating and normalizing the global economy. Media corporations serve to consolidate the wealth and power of White, mostly United States-based, wealthy male owners. By the mid-1990s, the United Nations put the telecommunications industries at the top of the revenue hierarchy, with most of those companies being U.S.-based. Because the largest of these companies are mixed conglomerates, stockholders and executives can minimize losses. In other words, when one company drops in profitability, another simply shores up the conglomerate's revenues. But most of the media operations don't lose money—they rake it in. When media scholar Robert W. McChesney (1999) wrote his instant classic *Rich Media, Poor Democracy*, there existed half a dozen major companies owning most of the world's media. Compare this to the 53 media companies two decades before. In Fall 2000, the Federal Communications Commission (FCC), the agency charged with regulating U.S.-based broadcast and monitoring anticompetition among all media, gave tentative approval to the merger of America On-Line (AOL) and Time-Warner in 2001, thus allowing the largest media conglomerate in history to form. A few months later, in March 2001, the FCC approved 32 radio mergers—26 of them in a single market—in one decision, with FCC Chairman Michael Powell saying that "public interest is served by inaction" (cited in Srinivasan, 2001, p. 7A). The 32 radio mergers are permitted by the Telecommunications Act of 1996, which removed restrictions on how many radio stations a single company could own nationwide, as well as eased caps on how many stations a company could own in one market. Thus, media conglomeration, under the control of a wealthy male elite, rushes on with the approval of both Democratic and Republican presidents and congressional leaders.

For women, sexual minorities, and others historically marginalized, this concentration of wealth and power has intensified the challenge to open up access to their voices, concerns, and analyses. The news media will remain an important site of struggle for truly free speech.

CONSCIOUSNESS AND ACTIVISM

Organized intervention campaigns targeted at the news media are the manifestations of political consciousness by a group that recognizes that it has been

maligned or neglected by the media, and that it needs mainstream news channels for greater visibility and voice. Seeking the right and means to speak has
been part of every movement for self-determination (Kielbowicz & Scherer,
1986). Leadership toward this goal is key to inspiring others to act. Little known
is the fact that race, sex, and sexual identity have often been overlapping motivators to leaders who inspired a following. For instance, the mainstream media
of the mid-19th century ridiculed all early feminists, but they rendered African-
American feminists particularly irrelevant. Maria Stewart became the first
African-American female journalist to challenge the marginalization caused by
these attitudes by writing in opposition to women's slavery in William Lloyd
Garrison's abolitionist newspaper, *The Liberator*, between 1831 and 1833. Men
threw stones at her for her defiance (Streitmatter, 1994), but Stewart had opened
the door for others, like Gertrude Bustill Mossell, to follow her. An influential
post-Civil War writer for both Black-owned and mainstream White-owned
newspapers and magazines—including *the Ladies Home Journal*—well-educated Mossell was both a feminist and an advocate of Black progress. Mossell covered stories about White exploitation of Black workers and encouraged women
to get their education and go into journalism—a valuable route, she believed, to
fighting lynching and other forms of racism and inequality (Streitmatter, 1994).
Ida Wells Barnett, Josephine St. Pierre Ruffin, Marvel Cooke, and, more recently, Dorothy Gilliam, Charlayne Hunter-Gault, and others represent a long line
of African-American female journalists who have used their profession to
advance women's rights and anti-racism.

One of the first White feminists to recognize that something had to be done
was suffragist Susan B. Anthony (1820–1906). Anthony believed that as long as
newspapers and magazines are controlled by men, women's ideas and deepest
convictions will be prevented from reaching the public (cited in Gallagher,
1987). At first, Anthony and other pre-Civil War suffragists sought alternative
venues, publishing their stories and commentaries in abolitionist newspapers
like Frederick Douglass' *North Star*. After the war, some began their own publications. Anthony and her friend and lifelong collaborator Elizabeth Cady
Stanton founded the newspaper *Revolution* in 1868, and it lasted for 2 years,
putting Anthony deeply in debt. Suffrage leader Lucy *Stone's Women's
Journal*, which enjoyed a long life under several editors, and more than a dozen
other suffrage papers in different parts of the country, sprang up between the
late 19th and early 20th centuries. These papers contributed to the making of an
early feminist community and cohesive suffrage movement with well-articulated political analyses and goals necessary to mobilize women and male supporters to secure women the vote—something finally accomplished with passage of
the Nineteenth Amendment to the United States Constitution in 1920 (Beasley,
1993; Steiner, 1983).

Today's high profile liberal feminist writers like the *Boston Globe*'s award-
winning Ellen Goodman, former *Wall Street Journal* writer (and Pulitzer recipient) Susan Faludi; the *Atlanta Constitution*'s Cynthia Tucker, and Molly Ivins

of both print and broadcast notoriety are regularly seen in mainstream media. Even socialist feminist Barbara Ehrenreich, who became a *Time* magazine columnist in the 1990s, gets to speak publicly in the mainstream. Neither should we forget the other manifestations of feminist consciousness—from *Ms.* magazine and, *off our backs*, both since the 1970s; the short-lived but important magazine *On the Issues*, in the 1990s; Pacifica radio network and Women's International Newsgathering Service (WINGS) syndicated radio, since the 1950s and 1970s, respectively; and today's ever-increasing online women's news sources, including Women's International Net Magazine, Aviva, and Women's eNews. Together, these are almost enough to make us forget the overall dearth of coverage of women's lives and political behavior in the mainstream news outlets. But not quite.

Gay political consciousness and its accompanying visibility arose cautiously through underground newsletters, beginning in the 1940s and gaining steam through the counterculture and women's movement in the 1960s (Streitmatter, 1995). The gay press clearly contributed to the construction of both a political identity and cohesive cultural community strong enough for gays and lesbians to begin to challenge homophobia through the McCarthy era of the 1950s and finally to openly confront official authority publicly. In 1969, gay men, some of them in drag, clashed with police in what would be several days of violence after police raided the Stonewall Inn in New York City's Greenwich Village. The event, which has become known as "Stonewall," galvanized gay resistance to harassment and oppression and marked the beginning of a gay liberation movement, both in the United States and internationally. Feminism, by this time, had helped strengthen lesbians' own political identity, leading to a separatist lesbian-feminist movement. Recognizing that the gay press was dominated both by male control and content, lesbian feminists began their own publications. The periodical *off our backs*, particularly, has contributed to the social construction of a radical lesbian feminist identity and dialogue on violence against women, sexuality, pornography, and other issues since the 1970s. Streitmatter (1995), who has done the definitive work on the gay press and its relationship to mainstream news media, noted that the schism between gay male and lesbian media did not end until the AIDS crisis of the 1980s, which brought lesbian and gay male leaders and working relationships closer.

The need to speak publicly about AIDS, hate crimes, gay civil unions, antidiscrimination laws and other commonly shared problems and goals has indeed brought gay male and lesbian writers and voices more forcefully into both mainstream and gay-oriented media. Lesbian journalist Deb Price's syndicated column on gay experience became a regular in the mainstream Gannett chain in the 1980s, and the *Miami Herald* recently launched its own gay columns and articles to reach its large southern Florida gay and lesbian audience. Gay media also enjoy greater visibility and circulation, especially in larger cities. The slick, high-profile weekly magazine *The Advocate*, and city weeklies like the *Washington Blade* are both agenda-setters in articulating events, conflicts, and political issues for gay and lesbian communities. Internet sites like PlanetOut and Gay.com have moved gay presence into cyberspace. In fact, the recent mega-merger of these two companies into PlanetOut Partners has sparked a debate within gay journalism circles about gay media capitalism and whether its foray into the global economy is hurting serious gay journalism (Ocamb, 2001).

FORMS OF NEWS ACTIVISM

None of these advancements in the news came easily—they are rather the fruits of long-term effort. In more than a century and a half of agitation, feminists have employed two main forms of news activism to create a stronger presence for women's ideas and experiences in mainstream print and broadcast media. Gay and lesbian activists have also employed similar strategies. The first of these may be defined as external campaigns waged by activists against mainstream news corporations, usually with the goal of eliminating stereotypic or negative coverage, as well as gaining more or better coverage of feminist, gay, and lesbian activities and issues. External campaigns are sponsored and led by advocacy organizations working on the front lines of social change. They legitimize and give impetus to progressive changes within the industries.

The second form of activism takes many of its cues from external campaigns just described and may be defined as internal campaigns that are organized and led by journalism professionals. Internal agitation within mainstream news organizations has usually been for the purpose of improving policies, pay and working conditions, and eliminating overt discrimination. Improving news assignments for female reporters has also been on the agenda of internal campaigns (Byerly & Warren, 1996). Both feminist and gay and lesbian activists have also used their own movement media to circulate information to members and followers. I refer to the importance of alternative media throughout this discussion.

EXTERNAL CAMPAIGNS

The importance of external intervention by advocacy organizations should not be minimized because through them emerge the articulation of problems with and the desired standards for new behavior, with regard to the news industry and its professionals. There have been dozens of examples of such groups successfully pressuring the news media for changes through the years, using mechanisms that include public criticism (often over time), demands for specific changes, and even the carrot approach—awards. Here we consider a few to illustrate the point.

Feminist groups like National Organization for Women (NOW) began to monitor and complain about the coverage of contemporary women's lives and issues by the early 1970s. NOW founder Betty Friedan, once a reporter herself, published *Feminine Mystique* in 1963, criticizing the media for either ignoring women's lives altogether or misrepresenting them in shoddy stereotypes. In 1972, NOW took action to intervene by filing a petition against the license renewal of WABC-TV in New York. The petition charged the station with deficiencies in (a) ascertaining women's opinions on community issues, (b) news and programming on women's concerns, and (c) employment of women. The petition also criticized negative coverage of women, such as one editorial by Howard K. Smith, who had said that sex discrimination was too inconsequential for federal action (Beasley, 1993). Nervous that such challenges would lead to FCC intervention in relicensing, stations all across the country began to negotiate with feminist groups. In 1974, the Los Angeles Women's Coalition signed agreements with two network-run stations, which led to the establishment of women's advisory councils and other fair treatment action (Beasley, 1993).

NOW has continued to push for news attention to issues affecting women. In the mid-1970s, NOW hired a public information officer and incorporated a sophisticated media campaign into its state-by-state legislative reform program, which focused on updating rape and sodomy laws, and addressing barriers to women's credit, among other things. The campaign utilized press releases, media kits for journalists, and press conferences, at both national and state levels. This strategy served to increase the news coverage dramatically, as evidenced by the *New York Times'* index showing the number of stories on NOW-targeted issues more than tripling between 1974 and 1977 (Byerly, 1999).

In September 2000, NOW led a massive telephone, letter-writing, and e-mail protest against NBC's airing of the Olympics and other programs, a Nike ad depicting a woman in a jog bra and shorts and wearing Nike shoes outrunning a would-be assailant wielding a chainsaw. The ad was pulled after public pressure forced it off. In addition, the group continues to issue press releases on a wide range of matters relevant to women's status and uses its Web site to analyze media ownership, news coverage, and social concerns. Through its Watch Out, Listen Up! project, an ongoing assessment of prime-time TV's representation of women, the group continues to advance a critical assessment of women's representation in entertainment and a dialogue about how women wish to be treated. The group issues an annual *Feminist Primetime Report* summarizing its findings.[3]

Since 1985, the Gay and Lesbian Alliance Against Defamation (GLAAD) has been the principal leader in media reform on behalf of the gay community,

---

[3]NOW's media Web site can be found at www.nowfoundation.org/communications.

utilizing a system of punishments and rewards. The organization, which includes academics, celebrities, political figures, and others on its board and in its leadership, regularly issues press releases making reasoned criticism of media-related issues and events. Then it invokes followers to speak out through demonstrations and letter-writing campaigns. When comedian Bob Hope used the word "fag" on NBC's *Tonight Show* in 1988, GLAAD generated such a public outcry that Hope produced a public service announcement condemning anti-gay violence to represent his apology. Two years later, when CBS *60 Minutes* commentator Andy Rooney made homophobic comments, GLAAD-generated protests led to Rooney's reprimand and temporary suspension from the program. In 1998, when gay University of Wyoming student Mathew Shephard was brutally murdered near Laramie, GLAAD staff helped manage media coverage by organizing student and community press conferences, issuing numerous press releases, and having GLAAD spokespeople speak to reporters about the link between hate crimes and religious political extremism toward hatred and intolerance (GLAAD Web site).

More recently, GLAAD surfaced as the leading voice in protest of White hip-hop musician Eminem's violent, anti-gay and anti-woman song lyrics and the musician's nomination for several awards for his 2000 release, the *Marshall Mathers LP* album. GLAAD also distributed an open letter to Elton John just before the Grammy ceremony in late February 2001, asking John not to perform at the event with Eminem—a request that proved futile.

GLAAD's annual Media Awards Ceremony serves as a reward system for news and entertainment media that do exemplary jobs representing gay and lesbian experience or characters. The organization also offers itself as a resource, meeting with media personnel to give advice on news coverage and entertainment programming. Overall, these GLAAD campaigns have pushed gay and lesbian analysis of popular culture and social issues into the news media on a regular basis for a decade and a half, and served to shape new standards for news coverage of gay and lesbian lives, problems, and social contributions.

INTERNAL CAMPAIGNS

For more than 100 years, female journalists have led internal campaigns in their newsrooms, using both *ad hoc* and more permanent organizations to advance themselves in the profession or to change something they objected to. By the Civil War era of the mid-1800s, women had established themselves as serious writers on political and social events for mainstream newspapers circulating in both the north and south. By 1879, slightly more than a decade after the war's end, there were 166 women listed as Washington correspondents. But discrimination against females in the field had already become entrenched by then. Only 20 of 166 had gallery privileges in Congress, and Beasley and Gibbons (1993) noted that female reporters more and more were being relegated to writing society news and gossip.

Washington women journalists formed the Ladies Press Club in 1881, with the goals of "mutual help and encouragement" (Burt, 2000, pp. xi-xvii). By the end of the 19th century, some two dozen women's press clubs existed in California, Colorado, Michigan, Missouri, Illinois, Ohio, Washington, DC, Massachusetts, New York, and Mississippi. Within another 50 years, press women had established similar organizations in nearly all of the states. Burt (2000) noted that these organizations served as networks of support, as well as mechanisms to promote the legitimacy of women journalists. They accomplished the latter, in part, by trying to cover women's activities in communities where they worked, in addition to their regular news assignments.

Women's organizations in journalism became more overtly political by the early 1970s, after modern feminism sparked the founding of feminist lobbies like NOW and Women's Political Caucus and generally electrified women's political activism across the country. The time was right for greater militancy. Passage of the federal Title VII in 1972 created the legal framework for women to challenge sex discrimination in employment, something that would usher in an era of lawsuits by women journalists. That year, women at *Newsweek* and *Time* magazines filed separate complaints of sex discrimination with the federal Equal Employment Opportunities Commission (EEOC). Both suits would eventually be settled when employers agreed to establish affirmative action policies to make hiring, training, promotion and higher pay more available to women (Beasley & Gibbons, 1993). Also in 1972, women reporters and staff at *The New York Times* established their Women's Caucus to address underemployment and low pay. At first caucus members pressured management to agree to raise wages and advance women into senior positions. But the glass ceiling remained intact, and by Fall 1974, six members of the caucus sued *The Times* for sex discrimination. The suit was settled in 1978 (Steiner, 2000). In the following years, women at *The Washington Post*, Associated Press, *Newsday*, *Detroit News*, *Baltimore Evening Sun*, *Readers Digest*, NBC and other broadcast media, and scores of other news organizations filed—and won—discrimination suits against their employers.

In many newsrooms, the internal organizations that had helped women campaign for both legal challenges and incremental policy changes remained intact even through the conservative 1980s and 1990s (Byerly & Warren, 1996). In survey research in the mid-1990s among journalists at major U.S. newspapers, Warren and I found that activism among females and racial minorities had been both continuous and episodic in the previous 20 years. Some established groups (often called women's caucuses or minority caucuses) had drifted into social support groups, meeting only periodically. Others had become dormant altogether. The study also revealed that journalists are far from immune from the political and social currents around them that become the stuff of news. In fact, many identify with and may be members of activist organizations that address racism, sexism or homophobia. Seventy-nine percent, including both male and female respondents, considered themselves feminists, and 84% said they were concerned about the lack of minority reporters. Respondents also said they were motivated to act out of self-interest and social conscience within their professional spheres, particularly when they perceive a common threat or interest (Byerly & Warren, 1996). Such was the case in Summer and Fall 1991 when the need arose to protest many newsrooms' handling of two high-profile events. The first was Senate confirmation hearings of nominee Clarence Thomas, which brought forth law professor Anita Hills' allegations that Thomas had sexually harassed her a few years earlier. The second was the William Kennedy Smith rape case in Florida, which had prompted many newsrooms to publish or broadcast the name of the victim, Patricia Bowman. In both instances, female journalists—of all ethnicities—said they identified with the victims and resented the way these women were vilified by their news organizations. Male colleagues joined with females in petitioning their editors to issue apologies or run fairer stories about both Anita Hill and Patricia Bowman (Byerly & Warren, 1996).

Internal campaigns within U.S. newsrooms have also been waged by both feminist and gay and lesbian reporters who doggedly demanded to cover events and issues raised by their movements. In the 1980s, many of the female journalists, who insisted on covering feminism began to write first-person books chronicling these efforts. Broadcast journalists Marlene Sanders and Marcia Rock's (1988) *Waiting for Prime Time*, former *New York Times* reporter Nan Robertson's (1992) *The Girls in the Balcony*, and former *Los Angeles Times* reporter Kay Mills' (1988) *A Place in the News* are among them. First-person gay journalists had also begun to write about covering gay experience by then. The late Randy Shilts' (1987) of the *San Francisco Chronicle*, for example, wrote *And the Band Played On*, recounting the emergence and coverage of the AIDS epidemic through his personal lens as this newspaper's leading reporter. The AIDS epidemic helped to catapult gay male reporters into new visibility and demand, while marginalizing other news about gay experience through the 1980s.

In response, a year later, *Oakland Tribune* executive editor Leroy Aarons, organized the National Lesbian and Gay Journalists Association (NLGJA). The organization today has more than 1,200 members, holds an annual convention that draws high-profile reporters from throughout the industry, and offers a range of other services to its members. Working through statewide chapters, NLGJA provides a professional network and also lobbies for news attention to gay and lesbian stories. In February 2001, the NLGJA conducted a poll of members to help in long-term planning, with many questions taking a decidedly political direction, asking whether members wanted the national office to lobby harder for gay content and better newsroom conditions for its members. Through its listserv to members, NLGJA affirms the effectiveness of gay and lesbian newsroom activism. In March 2001, for instance, the group issued a news item to members via the listserv, announcing that the Tribune Company had just adopted domestic partner benefits, as well as added sexual orientation to its nondiscrimination policy. *Newsday* assistant news editor Karen Bailis, who had authored the news item, ended with "Thanks to all who lobbied for these benefits!" (Bailis, 2001).

SCANNING THE HORIZON

Internal news activism has taken a new, and I believe important, direction over the last decade or so in the form of what might be called *multicultural advocacy groups*. These groups are comprised of national and international journalists whose demographics and interests cross race, ethnic, national, and sexual orientation lines. Their politics are decidedly mainstream and liberal, aiming to educate and to mobilize members broadly toward equality and greater representation within the profession. However, liberal concerns are also valid concerns and when addressed, these offer the possibility for greater egalitarianism within and by the news industries. In addition, radical ideas do surface within liberal forums and these have the potential for being incorporated and hence influencing the direction of organizations.

One such group is Unity, a coalition comprised of four organizations, each representing journalists of Asian, Black, Hispanic, and Native American ethnicity. Since 1994, Unity has also had a working partnership with National Lesbian and Gay Journalists Association. Unity holds conventions where panels and keynotes explore the problems and views of working journalists. The Unity '99 convention, for instance, which was co-sponsored by the NLGJA, included examinations of common ground issues related to gay and ethnic issues in news. At that meeting, keynoter Oscar Gandy, a Marxist academic who teaches communication at University of Pennsylvania, criticized the framing of news stories in ways that encourage White audiences to believe that inequities in social status are African Americans' own fault (Hamilton, 1999). Gandy studies race and representation in the media, considering how capitalism leads to the commodification of certain stereotypes and messages by profit-driven enterprises. Gandy's presence conveys a concern by Unity members for the ways that their professional work is shaped by structural elements of the capitalist political economy. Awareness and dialogue are necessary antecedents for strategies and change.

Unity's publication, *Newswatch*, published by the Center for Integration and Improvement of Journalism at San Francisco State University, circulates reports of conventions, new developments in the field, and critical commentaries about reporting and newsroom politics, including problems of discrimination.

A newer multicultural, international advocacy group is the International Women's Media Foundation (IWMF), headquartered in Washington, DC. Founded in 1990, and with members in more than 100 countries, the IWMF promotes female advancement in the profession and champions news with women as part of the story. Funded by grants from Freedom Forum and other groups, the organization's philosophy is that "no press can be truly free unless women have an equal voice." The group develops regional networks of women journalists, sponsors seminars and fora, and makes awards to women who have accomplished something heroic in the line of work. IWMF's research arm produces several reports, as well as a regular newsletter to members, during the year. The 2001 co-chairs were two high-profile U.S. journalists of color—Carole Simpson of ABC-TV and Cynthia Tucker of the *Atlanta Constitution*. In its report, *Will Women Change the News Media* (IWMF, 2001), the IWMF strongly argued for advancing women into media decision and policymaking. One voice was that of Gail Evans, executive vice president of CNN in the United States, who said: "If there are six seats at the [management] table, and five of them are held by men, and one is held by a woman, every other women in the organization thinks there is one seat open. . . . There isn't. There are six seats open. . . . We pit ourselves against each other because we only see that one seat."

IWMF research among female journalists, both in the United States and other nations, indicates that its members believe the news would be different if more women held leadership positions in media companies The critical mass hypothesis is an enduring one, advanced by other feminist scholars, like Gallagher (1981) and Eisenstein (1981/1993), who suggested that male-dominated organizations are more likely to become responsive to women's needs and concerns when there are sufficient numbers of females within them asking for change. Feminist empirical research shows that such change is most likely to come about when women are organized and with a strong external feminist movement in place (Byerly & Warren, 1996). Similarly, news content has been more likely to incorporate feminist themes and sources when feminist movements have been strongest. So, although groups like IWMF—heavily sponsored by corporate funding and focused on mainstream journalism and its female practitioners—is liberal in its goals, it could well help to create a more radical effect over time, particularly if it succeeds in putting women into management and also into more key economic and political reporting assignments. A high-profile international organization with experienced female journalists places a longer vision into circulation and serves as a forum for strategy to be articulated and progress to be monitored and made public. Whether this particular organization will follow the path of Unity and become a forum for critical questions about whether capitalism serves women's interests, including those of female journalists, remains to be seen.

EPILOGUE

This chapter was written in the midst of a significant political shift in the United States. George W. Bush was elected president in what many believe was a stolen election. As court suits challenging the election of November 2000 were filed and pundits tried to make sense of the nonsensical, a phalanx of extreme-right politicians deeply invested in corporate power took over the nation's government. Although some of Bush's new cabinet appointments were women and ethnic minorities, none had ties to feminist or progressive politics and few if any were openly gay. The American political landscape, therefore, looked bleakly white, male, corporate elite, and heterosexual more than at any other time in history.

At such moments, it is useful to remember that there is a dialectical process at work within U.S. society that also encompasses the activism taking place within the news and information media. The situation just described was not static by any means. I tried to show the structure and history of dissent, both within the mainstream and on the margins of journalism. American journalism was born in dissent 300 years ago when growing numbers of colonists came to resent the oppression by a monarchy thousands of miles away and they used the press of the day to transmit a radical critique and agenda for rebellion. The oppressive force today is not distant but omniscient in the form of giant, powerful media companies that dominate newsmaking in the United States and thereby control the nature and flow of ideas. Whether feminist, gay, and lesbian journalists, and the external organizations that support their mission, will be able to continue effecting significant change in relations of power within those industries in these next years is an empirical question.

In drawing attention to the urgent need for journalists of conscience to act, Laura Flanders (1997), of Fairness and Accuracy in Reporting, noted that the sidelines are no place to sit and wait:

> The media-moguls at the huge corporations like Disney/ABC or Time Warner/Turner are not the ones we should expect to make the change. Horizontally, as well as vertically, the centuries-old movement for freedom of expression needs to be updated into a movement for the right to communicate. The ones who own the means right now aren't about to give them up. Why would they? As we say on radio: Over to you. (p. 9)

Flanders' call to action should motivate everyone inside or outside the news industry to take stock of the need for strategic intervention in ownership patterns, monopoly formation, and the equal access to citizens of diverse interests and backgrounds. The newsroom will remain a site of struggle, of course, but activists of all kinds must also now look to government—executive, legislative, and judicial branches—to shape new policies that will democratize the news media.

REFERENCES

Aarons, L., & Murphy, S. (2000). *Lesbians and gays in the newsroom, 10 years later* (report). Los Angeles, CA: Annenberg School for Communication (University of Southern California) and National Lesbian and Gay Journalists Association.

Alwood, E. (1996). *Straight news: Gays, lesbians and the news media.* New York: Columbia University Press.

Bailis, K. (2001, March 6). Chapter memo. National Lesbian and Gay Journalists Association, New York Chapter. <www.nlgjany.org>

Bakker, I. (1994). *The strategic silence: Gender and economic policy.* London: Zed Books, in cooperation with the North-South Institute.

Beasley, M. (1993). Newspapers: Is there a new majority defining the news? In P. J. Creedon (Ed.), *Women in mass communication* (2nd ed., pp. 118-133). Newbury Park, CA: Sage.

Beasley, M., & Gibbons, S. (1993). *Taking their place* Washington, DC: American University Press, in cooperation with Women's Institute for Freedom of the Press.

Bridge, J. (1994, January/February). The media mirror: Reading between the (news) lines. *Quill, 82*(1), 18-19.

Burt, E. V. (2000). *Women's press organizations, 1881-1999.* Westport, CT: Greenwood Press.

Byerly, C. M. (1999). News, feminism and the dialectics of gender relations. In M. Meyer (Ed.), *Mediated women: Representations in popular culture* (pp. 383-403). Cresskill, NJ: Hampton Press.

Byerly, C.M., & Warren, C.A. (1996). At the margins of center: Organized protest in the newsroom. *Critical Studies in Mass Communication, 13*(1), 1-23.

de Bruin, M. (1998, July). *Gender in Caribbean media: Beyond the body count.* Paper presented at the 21st general assembly & scientific conference of the International Association for Media & Communication Research, Glasgow.

Eisenstein, Z. (1993). *The radical future of liberal feminism.* Boston, MA: Northeastern University Press. (Original work published 1981)

Flanders, L. (1997). *Real majority, media minority: The cost of sidelining women in reporting.* Monroe, ME: Common Courage Press.

Fraser, N. (1993). Rethinking the public sphere: A contribution to the critique of actually existing democracy. In C. Calhoun (Ed.), *Habermas and the public sphere* (pp. 109-142). Cambridge, MA: MIT Press.

Friedan, B. (1963). *The feminine mystique.* New York: Dell.

Gallagher, M. (1981). *Unequal opportutunities: The case of women and the media.* Paris: UNESCO.

Gallagher, M. (1987). W*omen and media decision-making.* Paris: UNESCO.

Garnham, N. (1993). The media and the public sphere. In C. Calhoun (Ed.), *Habermas and the public sphere* (pp. 359-376). Cambridge, MA: MIT Press.

GLAAD website, http://www.glaad.org. (See link to GLAAD accomplishments.)

Gross, L. (1993). *Contested closets: The politics and ethics of outing.* Minneapolis: University of Minnesota Press.

Hamilton, S. R. (1999, Fall). Now's the time, here's the place. *Newswatch,* Center for Integration and Improvement of Journalism, San Francisco State University), inside cover.

Huddy, L. (1997). Feminists and feminism in the news. In P. Norris (Ed.), *Women, media and politics* (pp. 183-204). New York & Oxford: Oxford University Press.

International Women's Media Foundation (1999). Survey reveals barriers remain for minority women in U.S. newsrooms. *IWMF Wire* (Newsletter of International Women's Media Foundation), *9*(3), 1-2.

International Women's Media Foundation (2001). *Will women change the news media?* Washington DC: Author.

Kielbowicz, R., & Scherer, C. (1986). The role of the press in the dynamics of social movements. *Research in Social Movements, Conflict and Change, 9*, 71-96.

Lafky, S. (1993). The progress of women and people of color in the U.S. journalistic workforce: A long, slow journey. In P. J. Creedon (Ed.), *Women in mass communication* (2nd ed., pp. 87-103). Newbury Park, CA: Sage.

Marlane, J. (2000, April). Barriers to women in TV lowered—Not dismantled. *IWMF Wire* (Newsletter of International Women's Media Foundation), *10*(1), 9, 11.

McChesney, R.W. (1999). *Rich media, poor democracy.* Urbana and Chicago: University of Illinois Press.

Mills, K. (1988). *A place in the news.* New York: Dodd, Mead.

National Organization for Women (NOW) website, < www.now.org>.

Ocamb, K. (2001, Winter). Gay media mergers raise questions, fears. *NLGJA News: Alternatives, 10*(1), 1, 10.

Pozner, J. L. (2001). March/April). Cosmetic coverage: Media obsessed with cutting political women down to size. *Extra, 14*(2), 8-10.

Robertson, N. (1992). *The girls in the balcony: Women, men and the New York Times.* New York: Random House.

Sanders, M., & Rock, M. (1988). *Waiting for prime time: The women of television news.* New York: Harper & Row.

Shilts, R. (1987). *And the band played on.* New York: St. Martin's Press.

Srinivasan, K. (2001, March 13). FCC sends a signal on 32 radio mergers. *Ithaca Journal, 187,* p. 62.

Steiner, L. (1983, Summer). Finding community in nineteenth century suffrage periodicals. *American Journalism, 1*, 1-15.

Steiner, L. (2000). The *New York Times* women's caucus, 1972-present. In E. V. Burt (Ed.), *Women's press organizations, 1881-1999* (pp. 164-170). Westport, CT: Greenwood Press.

Streitmatter, R. (1994). *Raising her voice: African-American women journalists who changed history.* Lexington: University of Kentucky Press.

Streitmatter, R. (1995). *Unspeakable: Rise of the gay and lesbian press.* Winchester, MA: Faber & Faber.

Weaver, D. (1997). Women as journalists. In P. Norris (Ed.), *Media, women and politics* (pp. 19-40). New York: Oxford University Press.

Weaver, D., & Wilhoit, G. (1996). *The American journalist in the 1990s. U.S. news people at the end of an era.* Mahwah, NJ: Erlbaum.

13

Does Gender Matter in the Newsroom? Some Remarks on Gendered Discourse and Estonian Journalist Culture

Barbi Pilvre

ABOUT ESTONIA

The core of Estonian identity is partly related to the country being one of the European Union accession countries, joining EU in May 1994. A former Soviet Republic (1940-1991), Estonia regained its independence in 1991 during Gorbachov's reforms, and has been developing rapidly since then. Estonia, with its population of 1.4 million people, has chosen quite a liberal capitalist way of development, so that the contrasts in the society are striking, which is typical of east-European post-Soviet countries. The atmosphere could be like any Western city in some of Tallinn's offices, department stores, or nightclubs, but in the countryside or in small towns, it can feel as if time had stopped somewhere in the 1950s. Striking contrasts can also be found in Estonian society. The country is outstanding when considering the pace of the information and communication technologies revolution or the purchase of cars or mobile phones, but there are also very traditional ways of living outside the capital area and very traditional ways of understanding gender roles, for example. Some politicians have ambitions to present Estonia to the world as a Nordic country, but at the same time there are also critical voices stressing the essential differences in social policy, level of infrastructure, security, or general quality of life in Estonia compared with Nordic countries.[1]

---

[1]For detailed information on Estonian country, society, and culture see the homepage of Estonian Institute (www.estonica.org).

The Estonian media scene is varied with three main TV channels (one state and two commercial), several state-owned and private radio channels, two main privately-owned quality papers, a privately owned business paper, an evening paper, some weeklies, and several different journals. The scene has changed since 1990 when most of the media companies became privatized or reorganized.[2] The volume of foreign investment in Estonian media organizations, both TV and press, is substantial. Estonia's two major dailies are owned by Norwegian Schibsted (*Postimees*) and Swedish Marienberg (*Eesti Päevaleht*, partly) companies and foreign ownership is remarkable, including commercial TV channels. One could argue that if there has been any impact of Nordic journalistic culture on Estonian press and TV organizations, it is as a result of changes in ownership. It is obvious that foreign ownership has not automatically brought with it equality policies in the Nordic sense (no special quotas for women or women´s career promotion, no demands for equal salaries for men and women doing similar jobs, etc.), because Nordic owners do not directly interfere in the daily work or content of the press or TV.

MISSING RESEARCH ON GENDER AND MEDIA

Discussions on gender in the workplace have not been a popular topic in Estonia generally, nor specifically within media organizations. When it is discussed, it is usually in the context of foreign research projects (as is the case now) or an international project or seminar financed by a foreign country or international fund. I have, for example, recently produced an essay on men, women, and gender as a project for a United Nations Development Programme (UNDP) development report although it had never been raised as a hot topic in the country more generally (see Pilvre, 2000b). When some activists, including myself, were preparing a national report on women for the Bejing Women´s Conference in 1995 (Joonsaar, Jõeorg, & Karro, 1995), I tried to find out whether there was any information available on gender divisions in Estonian media organizations, numbers of men and women working in the media, or any information on salaries, and the answer was "no." So I had to contribute a section on media and women here without having any research data to which I could refer.

Research on media organizations has not given any special attention to gender until now because there is a common understanding that there are several more important issues on which to research, especially when resources, both human and financial, are limited. When I asked my colleagues about men and

---

[2]Details on Estonian media scene in the 1990s can be found in the media survey organization Baltic Media Facts homepage (www.mediafacts.com).

women in the media in 2000, I found that Professor Epp Lauk from Tartu University had collected data on the situation in the 1990s during her doctoral thesis on the professionalization of Estonian journalism (see Lauk, 1995, 1997). My own personal research interests have also been been on media respresentation and my doctoral project is on cultural change and the construction of gender in Estonian media. As part of this work (Pilvre, 2000a), I analyzed whether the gender of the journalist has any influence on the way men and women are represented in news reports. I did not, however, go very deep into this issue as it was not my main focus.

Taking into account the lack of relevant research, this chapter mostly comprises personal views on the problem and various perspectives of my journalist colleagues. As one of the founders of the Women´s Studies Centre at the Tallinn Pedagogical University and a well-known feminist, journalist, and media researcher, I have often been asked to talk on the issue of women journalists, although I never have conducted any research on it. For this chapter, I undertook a small study among my colleagues at the weekly newspaper where I work and at one daily newspaper, to identify whether my speculations on the theme have some relevance for other women and men: The findings from this small study are discussed in the "Other Case Studies" section.

ON JOURNALIST IDENTITY

Journalists probably do not identify themselves very often by gender in Estonia. They tend to regard themselves as journalists writing on politics, economy, or culture or journalists working on TV, radio, dailies, or women´s magazines. Women journalists do not have any special network, which suggests that they do not identify themselves as women in journalism. There is no women's section in the union of journalists in Estonia. If gender questions are discussed, this is done in individual conversations (if ever). Most of the interest around the issue of organizing women journalists has come from foreign colleagues, similarly to research questions. For instance, the Finnish Women Journalists' Organization has been very interested in initiating the founding of a similar organization in Estonia and I, among others, have repeatedly been approached with this idea. I have agreed that it is a good idea, but there has to be some interest from the side of Estonian women journalists to organize themselves if it is going to work. I don't feel this interest and what concerns me personally is that I haven't identified myself in the first place as a woman journalist. It is obvious that woman journalists have to identify themselves as a group that has shared special interests and common problems in order to organize, and they hardly do in Estonia yet. Maybe it is just a question of time.

But one has to keep in mind the general unwillingness of the journalists to organize themselves. This is probably due to the journalists' labor market, where the status of our union is not very high because of the ambiguous role of journalists and media organization in the Soviet era, now regarded as part of Soviet nomenklatura.[3] Also, many good journalists, women among them, prefer not to belong to any trade union because they are not in favor among the employers and journalists do not feel empowered when they belong to the union. Probably it has also been more financially rewarding for good journalists not to organize themselves. Professional solidarity in Estonia is not very common among journalists, nor elsewhere in society.

In 1988, the journalist community in Estonia comprised 44% of women and 56% of men and by 1995, the proportion of women had grown to 49% (Lauk, 1995). Estonian women have, during the whole Soviet period (as a result of the official equality policy) been active in the labor market and so we cannot map women's progression exactly against the gains made by women in the West. Even before the Soviet period, since at least the 1920s, there have always been women journalists as there have been women working in other fields of public life in the country, nor has journalism been a predominantly male profession after World War II as it mostly was in the West. In fact, the history of women journalists goes back as far as the end of the 19th century. There is no exact data on which organizations employ women journalists in Estonia but it is clear that there are more women in the state-owned TV station ETV and state-owned radio that have partly maintained their old, soviet organizational structures, than in the commercial sector. Nor does there exist data on men and women in private media companies but there are demonstrably fewer women than men working in the private press, commercial radio stations, and private TV companies. Probably we can say that in Estonia, men go where the money is, and the private companies have far more resources than the state-run organizations.

Women are in the majority as journalists in women's and society magazines. Such magazines comprise those unusual kinds of media organizations that have women as editors-in-chief in Estonia as well as of some of the managers in the publishing houses of the magazines. This is perhaps not surprising as women are universally regarded as experts on human relations and beauty world. All the powerful media organizations are still in men's hands however. The big dailies and evening papers have men as their editors-in-chief, TV stations have male heads, and so on, although there are some women as CEOs of local papers. The weekly *Eesti Ekspress* where I work has again had a woman editor-in-chief since 2002. (The weekly had a female editor-in-chief some years ago, but the journalists did not regard her as a good editor, which was probably quite a fair evaluation and one made not because of her gender.)

Women do not appear to seek senior positions in the dailies or other big media organizations. This perhaps reflects a general tendency in top manage-

---

[3]Officials being closely connected with the communist party, enjoying the privileges of the communist system.

ment in Estonia—you rarely find women as heads of large companies or corporations. There appears a "commonsense" view that women are afraid of taking major responsibilities, risks, or challenges and many women seem to have accepted this perspective without question. Most women do not find acceptable the widespread so-called masculine culture of the business organizations, complete with working late nights and weekends. Lots of women seem to have other priorities and this cannot be regarded only as cultural pressure but also as women's free choice. Women can make remarkable careers in Estonian media organizations as top reporters or editors but seldom, if ever, as senior managers. There appears to be no existing research on what women journalists really want: Are they ambitious at all? Do they strive for high positions? Why they do not reach them? I assume that there are several types of women in the journalism field—more and less ambitious—but many women hardly show any ambition to achieve the top jobs.

WOMEN AND CHANGE IN THE ESTONIAN MEDIA SCENE

When the big changes—privatization and introducing the capitalist economy—in Estonia began following the end of occcupation by the Soviet Union and the restoration of independence in 1991, young men were active in seeking new opportunities. Journalism became big business and the new business generation included hardly any women in key positions, although all jobs were in principle open to women as well as men: It was not forbidden to go into business for women. Probably due to unwritten cultural restrictions and common understanding about the division of labor between sexes, however, few women chose to enter the business world at that time, including media businesses. There was also a general negative reaction to the image of the Soviet woman—a cartoon image of a masculine woman tractor driver. Women wanted change and there seemed to exist a general fatigue about the position of the Soviet working woman burdened with social and state duties and who did not have any time or energy to enjoy a private life, family, and children.

There was also nostalgia in the air at the beginning of 1990s toward the 1930s, when Estonia had its legendary golden age as an independent Estonian Republic. Accordingly, the gender divison of those times was romantized for a while and capitalism and consumer culture in the 1990s brought new possibilities for gender identification. A career seemed to be old-fashioned and somehow Soviet-labeled in this new context because it was an everyday routine since the 1950s that women worked and had careers. Therefore, not to work, to stay home and care for the family was regarded as more Western (and therefore modern), as images of the West were uncritically interpreted from TV soaps and fashion magazines. (For more on gender discourse in the transition period in Estonia see Narusk, 1996; Pilvre, 2000c).

Thus, it was men and not women who were privatizing the big state-owned papers and founding new papers and TV stations in the 1990s. Looking back, there seem to be no women among the leading figures of the new media organizations founded in the 1990s although there have been many in the teams organizing new newspapers like *Eesti Ekspress* (1989), *Hommikuleht* (1993-1995), or new TV channels (TV1, Kanal 2). But as usual, in the written history of those new organizations, it is mostly men's names that remain in the spotlight because they have been in leading roles (as the the popular history of the first private weekly *Eesti Ekspress* by Tiina Jõgeda clearly shows; see Jõgeda, 1999).

The general view about the gender "problem" in news organizations, from the point of view of colleagues with whom I have spoken, is differential salaries. Women journalists are generally better educated than men (Lauk, 1995) and generally have higher qualifications. There is no data about how this influences the level of wages or career possibilities, but we can ask whether education influences a person's salary and career or do other characteristics have more influence? I dare to speculate that education in itself does not influence one's career nor salary, at least not in news organizations. So it is not surprising that women with better formal education can earn less or be in lower positions in the organization than men.

It seemes to be a silent "common knowledge" that women journalists earn less then men, although there are no data to prove this assumption. However, more men are discontented with their salaries than women—38% of women and 46 % of men (Lauk, 1995). But differences in wages are not publicly discussed, so few people will know other's salaries. Media organizations are mostly private companies in Estonia and the wage question is highly confidential. Very few people have any idea of the exact salaries of journalists, and those who do are senior managers who generally do not share the information they know. The Journalists' Union does not know the exact level of wages either and has no power to influence negotiations on wages. Even in the state-owned TV and radio companies, wage negotiations are highly confidential and the income of different journalists can differ greatly and not only because of gender.

At least one senior female manager of a big daily who was asked about her experiences with gender-related differences at the workplace confirmed that there is a noticeable difference in salaries in the newsroom. Management tends to share a common understanding that women are the cheaper labor force. She said the salaries that are offered to women journalists at negotiation are generally lower. And what is generally known is that women ask less and get less in salary discussions. Perhaps they do not value themselves as professionals as highly as men who generally have more developed self-esteem. Despite the fact that in many families, women's income makes a noticeable part of the family income (Narusk, 1994), there is a commonsense notion that men are the mainbreadwinners. Managers in media organizations often tend to think that women's work is like a hobby, that they work if they like to and the salary is not important because their husbands provide money for the family. Maybe in such micro-societies—senior managers of successful private companies—this model of the family is common. However, this is a very strange perception when one looks at Estonian society more generally. Most Estonian women work and earn money to provide for their families, together with their husbands. Many women journalists working in the private sector earn more than their husbands working in state organizations, even in senior positions.

A PERSONAL STORY

Before I describe my colleagues' attitudes to the gender question, I give some insights on my personal experience gained while working in different places in journalism since the mid-1980s: in a literature journal, a daily, and a weekly. As a journalist who was not professionally trained—I was first a philologist and psychologist—I have never been a reporter for a daily but always worked as an arts editor. In general, I have not experienced any gender discrimination except in wages policy: For sure in some cases I have been a cheaper worker than my male colleagues. However, in terms of ideas or quality of work, my male colleagues have always regarded me as an equal as far as I know. It seems to me somehow impossible to think that I would not be taken seriously as a journalist, cultural critic, or columnist by my male colleagues. I have been invited to work in journalism (after spending some time teaching) by senior male colleagues probably because of my reputation of a busy career-oriented person and not because of any specific "feminine" qualities. As far as my feminist orientation is concerned, I know it has sometimes irritated both my male and female colleagues and I have been criticized by women as well as men on that issue as being too preoccupied in trying to find gender issues in Estonia. However, as for my feminist image, I consider it helpful in creating a distinct trademark in the journalist market. As I have not had any serious ambitions to make a career in media management I cannot say whether my female gender or feminist reputation has influenced possible promotion. Still, since 2003, I am working as a head of the arts section of the weekly. I was promoted by a woman editor-in-chief.

OTHER CASE STUDIES:
WOMEN AND MEN TALKING

As already mentioned, I undertook a small-scale study of other journalists for this chapter, and asked some of my colleagues to comment on the question of whether they have noticed any differentiation or discrimination in terms of gender in their workplace. The questioning was carried out using e-mail and I chose the interviewees among my colleagues who are prominent mid-career journalists who have worked on mainstream newspapers and for state TV. It is important to stress that I have made my selection based on those people whom I thought would take this question seriously. Therefore, what follows is not a rigorous and random study but it does provide insights to the theme.

Tiina J.

Tiina J. (39 years old) is a prominent investigative journalist who was one of the key figures in the foundation of the weekly *Eesti Ekspress*, the first private weekly in Estonia and who has written mostly on economic issues including corruption. She says that in general, her gender has not been an issue for her. She has met lots of men during her 10-year career in journalism who have expressed their surprise about the fact that she—a female journalist—is interested in the "hard" themes like business on waste metal, mafia, criminal issues. She remembers such attitudues mostly from the beginning of the 1990s but now she faces this kind of stereotypical perspective rarely. Most of the people she has interviewed do not seem to worry about the gender of the journalist doing the interview, and in fact many people have praised her, as a woman who understands such difficult things (Tiina J. says this with irony). Tiina J. took up—without asking—the question of whether women journalists use sex in order to promote their careers She says nobody has ever made any attempt to force her to have sex in order to get some hot information. Here we clearly see that in Estonia, there is (or at least there has been) a stereotypical understanding about appropriate issues for women journalists to write about which do not include sensitive issues connected with big money and power. A woman as a top reporter on hard issues is admired or regarded strange.

Tiina K.

Tiina K. (37 years old) is another prominent journalist, an editorial manager, who says that from her experience in radio and in different newspapers, she believes that it is easier to be a woman journalist than a male. She says that attitudes toward women reporters are less prejudical, easier, nicer, and less official. As the interviewees are usually male, women have easier access to people and to the desired information. Tiina K. suggests that gender is most problematic in terms of negotations on work and salaries. Mostly, the employers presume that women have more modest expectations during salary negotiations. Tiina K. rationalizes this by articulating the common-sense view that a woman (journalist) works for fun, that she would otherwise feel dull at home, that her husband is the breadwinner anyway, and that a female journalist´s motivation is not money. She argues that therefore the price for a woman journalist is 20% cheaper than her male colleague with the same qualifications.This is quite a shocking statement, but I am sure that we can believe her because Tiina K. has access to inside confidential information, although obviously this is a subjective opinion and does not have any basis in research.

Gerda K.

Gerda K. (41 years old) is a senior female TV producer and a theater editor. She says that gender in the newsroom is a difficult problem. It is questionable whether gender is always to blame for different attitudes toward women and men in the newsroom. Nobody ever says to a woman openly that she would not get the best beat because she is a woman or that women are paid less than men. However, Gerda still feels that it is easier for male colleagues to be allocated jobs that include foreign travel. She is sure that in getting some jobs, men are in preferred positions. Women can have excellent experience but men are hired anyway. Mediocre male journalists can more easily get certain jobs than talented women. Salary negotiations are confidential but she believes that the price which is the basis for discussions is lower for women than men. She cannot say that anybody has discriminated against her personally as a woman in journalism but she says that she knows there is discrimination. In Gerda's case, we find one interesting attitude of woman journalists—they seem to know about discrimination but they do not see themselves as objects of it, nor do not confess or say openly that they have been discriminated against.

Ilona K.

Ilona K. (31 years old) is a young culture journalist and she says that she believes that Estonian society is male-centered but that journalism is a field where women are treated equally with men. She is sure that the distribution of stories is based on expertise in the field and not by gender. She does not see the stereotypical division of stories between genders and confirms that she would never write on themes like sports or politics but not because she is a woman but because these are not her fields of interest. She stresses that in culture journalism, men also prevail which is interesting to her mind because she regards culture as a feminine field of journalism. (In Estonia, mostly women work in culture institutions and they are mostly lead by women. Estonia has also a woman as a minister for culture). In work with sources, the sex of the journalist is important according to Ilona.

> Young men get a better contact with middle-aged women and nobody takes a blond young woman seriously. But much depends on the person herself.

> In Estonia, personal relations and family contacts matter: who is whose son or daughter or who is married to somebody.

[Ilona herself is the wife of an outstanding young writer.] Illona believes that this contact network could matter more than the sex of the journalist, and believes this to be a problem typical to small societies.

Ilona thinks that there could be more good women journalists but there are too few women who want to go into the profession. She personally sees that caring for children takes much time from her. "No one asks in a daily how you manage when your children are sick, how much time you spend on these problems. Work should be done and you have to stay late if needed." It is easier for women who do not have children, then you can concentrate on your career and there are some outstanding cases in Estonia (she names her good friend, a well-known Moscow-correspondent Kadri Liik). "Being a journalist takes a lot of energy and one has to be really dedicated to work." Ilona believes salaries are highly personal and she agrees that there have been times when women have earned less than men. Nowadays, she has not heard about such cases. Maybe there is somebody who is feeling offended somewhere, she says, but nobody talks about it. "There is always too little money." Something that she has noticed that Estonian men do not like to let women speak in meetings. And women, therefore, do not even try to say anything because they know that they will not be allowed to speak. But men feel uncomfortable when women start to talk among themselves. Ilonas opinions seem to be quite typical and the gender question is not a specific problem but much depends on the personal choices of women journalists.

Urmet K.

Urmet K. (25 years old) was also asked about gender problems in journalism from the point of view of a young male, an opinion section editor in a major daily in Tallinn, Eesti Päevaleht who is, nontypically, a gender-sensitive person. Urmet thinks that journalist organizations are among the most tolerant and that there are few differences between men and women. According to him, this comes from the notion that in journalism, the stress is on creative work which is not a priori "masculine," and that many of the young people who work in journalism do not follow traditional gender thinking. "When I look at our news department—which is regarded as the nerve center of the paper—there are only women there who write on politics." He names three women. "Men write on human interest." He thinks that this recent phenomenon of young women writing on politics is possibly influenced by the precedent of Kärt Karpa, his colleague and a young, pretty, and assertive woman. "She had very good access to politicians who are mostly men. And male politicians are often vain and prefer to whisper about important matters to pretty female journalists." But he argues that there are also older women journalists writing on politics. And young men can be just as impudent.

Urmet says that tolerance about gender is nothing peculiar to the big Tallinn daily and *Postimees*, which is a major paper in Tartu, has a youngish woman Küllike Roovali as a leading criminal reporter dealing with the difficult issues. Both social and life sections also have male reporters stresses Urmet: *Eesti Päevaleht* has one human interest journalist, Rein Sikk, writing mostly about "ordinary people." Although sports journalism is a purely masculine field with only male reporters, men are also dominating the culture sections—which have long been regarded as a female beat in Estonia. As far as comment and opinion pieces are concerned, there is a slight gender bias, where men are believed to be more competent on economic issues and politics and women are believed to be more competent on social issues. Urmet believes that here one finds the patriarchal attitude which rules in the wider society, but otherwise there is no difference between women and men. He believes that salaries depend on the individual effort of each journalist and how important one's contribution is to the paper. After thinking about these questions for a while, he said to me that gender differences are prominent. "You know where? In themes. The entire paper is organized around a masculine understanding of the world: look at news selection and distinctions and what is important and what is not."

CONCLUSION

The results of this small study confirmed my previous understanding that gender issues are not regarded as the most important problem among journalists but it is possible to achieve some interesting results when asking about possible gender-related distinctions in work or about discrimination. I learned with surprise that Estonian journalists are actually quite open to this kind of questioning about gender in the newsroom. They seem to be more open to gender discussion than some years earlier when any attempt to mention gender issues was understood as an accusation of sexual harrassment (which is not treated as a serious issue in Estonia) and was followed by mocking. There is probably a major cultural change going on but we do not know about it because we have not posed any questions. Maybe the time has now come to carry out research on gender in media organizations?

Researching gender in Estonian media could be especially interesting as discussion on this issue is not very active in society and therefore people do not have any ready "textbook" opinions about the situation nor have ways to label the situation. Journalists seem to analyze their own position and the position of their friends and near colleagues quite genuinely. This gives interesting results although sometimes it seems that people lack the vocabulary to express themselves on gender issues. However, when I explained the purpose of my inquiry—a contribution to an international collection—the journalists were quite open. I do not know what would have been their possible attitudes if a similar survey was carried out in a formal way, publicly and on a large scale, and if the results would even be published in a small country like Estonia. I suppose interviees would have been more careful in giving their opinions because fear of being labeled a feminist discussing irrelevant issues is still strong.

REFERENCES

Jõgeda, T. (1999). *Eesti Ekspress—uue elu sümbool.* [Eesti Ekspress—the symbol of the new life]. Tallinn: Eesti Ekspress.

Joonsaar, A., Jõeorg, M., & Karro, H. (1995). *Estonian women in a changing society* (National Report of Estonia. The Fourth World Conference on Women, Action for Equality Development and Peace). Tallinn: UNDP.

Lauk, E. (1995). *Data from the survey upon Estonian journalists.* Unpublished manuscript, University of Tartu, Tartu.

Lauk, E. (1997). *Historical and sociological perspectives on the development of Estonian journalism.* Tartu: University of Tartu.

Narusk, A. (1994). Töö [Work]. In A. Narusk (Ed.), *Murrangulised 80-ndad ja 90ndad aastad Eestis: Töö, kodu ja vaba aeg* (pp. 25-32). Tallinn-Helsingi: Eesti Teaduste Akadeemia. Filosoofia, Sotsioloogia ja Õiguse Instituut.

Narusk, A. (1996). Gendered outcomes of the transition in Estonia. *Idäntutkimus* [Special Issue: Women and Transition: The Case of Estonia], *3-4,* 12-39.

Pilvre, B. (2000a). *Construction of gender in the cover-column Persoon in the Estonian weekly Eesti Ekspress.* Unpublished master's thesis, Tallinn Pedagogical University, Tallinn.

Pilvre, B. (2000b). Men, women and the media. In P. Maimik, K. Mänd, & Ü.-M-Papp (Eds.), *Towards a balanced society. Women and men in Estonia* (pp. 54-57). Tallinn: Ministry of Social Affairs of Estonia, United Nations Development Programme. Also URL (consulted November, 2001): http://www.undp.ee/gender/)

Pilvre, B. (2000c). Taming the phantom of feminism: Perspectives on women's lives, equal rights and "women's issues" in Estonia. In P. Skelton & M. Tralla (Eds.), *Private views: Space and gender in Estonian and British contemporary art* (pp. 60-71). London: Women's Art Library.

Contributors

Marjan de Bruin is senior lecturer at the University of the West Indies (UWI) in Kingston, Jamaica. Prior to moving to the Caribbean she was a managing editor of a weekly and a monthly in the Netherlands as well as a management consultant. She has published on communication in relation to a range of aspects: gender; HIV/AIDS; adolescents; health and environment; and professional education. This combination of areas reflects her research interests. She is currently Director of the Caribbean Institute of Media and Communication (UWI) and one of the vice presidents of the International Association of Media and Communication (IAMCR). She is a member of the International Editorial Board of Routledge's academic journal *Feminist Media Studies* and a member of the Advisory Board of *Critical Arts*, a publication of Cultural and Media Studies, University of Natal, Durban, South Africa.

Carolyn M. Byerly studies the relationship between popular social movements and the media, with respect to gender, ethnicity and social class. She is the co-editor (with Karen Ross) of *Media and Women: International Perspectives* (Blackwell, 2004), and numerous articles and book chapters, including "Women and Media Concentration" in Rush, Oukrup & Creedon (Eds.), *In Search for Equality in Journalism and Mass Communication* (Erlbaum 2004), and "Gender and the Political Economy of Newsmaking," in Meehan & Riordan (Eds.), *Sex and Money* (U of Minnesota, 2003). Her current research is a cross-cultural study of women's media activism. She teaches in the journalism department at Howard University (USA).

Monika Djerf-Pierre is associate professor at the department of journalism and mass communication, Göteborg, Sweden. Her research fields are environmental journalism, journalism history, political communication, the sociology of journalism, and gender and the media. **Monica Löfgren-Nilsson** is assistant professor and director of studies at the department of journalism and mass communication, Göteborg, Sweden. Her research includes studies on gender and journalism, and the sociology of news production.

Romy Fröhlich is currently a full professor at Ludwig-Maximilians-University Munich (Germany) and president of the German Communication Association (DGPuK). She is also a member of the Associate Editorial Board of the scientific journal *Feminist Media Studies* and head of the educational division of the German Public Relations Association (DPRG).

Her professional experience spans several disciplines: senior consultant at "Kroehl Identity Consultants" (PR-Agency), Frankfurt; research assistant at "GFK-Market Research-Company," Nuernberg; scientific assistant at the"Press and Information Department," Munich Fair and Exhibition Association (MMG). Her major research and teaching interests are public relations, media history, women in mass communication, journalism education, news content/content analysis.

Juana Gallego is Professor of Journalism in the Autonomous University of Barcelona. She has directed and published *La prensa por dentro* (Los Libros de la Frontera, 2002), a study about the production of information and the transmission of gender stereotypes. She is also the author of *Mujeres de Papel* (Women of Paper) (Icaria, 1990). **Elvira Altés** is Associate Professor in the Autonomous University of Barcelona and is the co-author of *Images of Women in the Mass-Media in Europe* (European Commission,1999). **Maria José Cantón** is an Investigative Researcher in the Autonomous University of Barcelona. **Maria Eugenia Melús** is a graduate in history and journalism. **Jaume Soriano** is Associate Professor in the Autonomous University of Barcelona and the Vic University.

Ammu Joseph is a journalist and media-watcher now based in Bangalore, India. Among her books are: *Women in Journalism: Making News* (The Media Foundation/Konark, 2000) and *Whose News? The Media and Women's Issues* (Sage, 1994). She participated in a United Nations Expert Group Meeting on Women and the Media in Beirut (2002) and was on an official panel at the annual meeting of the UN Commission on the Status of Women in New York (2003). Also in 2003 she was awarded the Donna Allen Award for Feminist Advocacy by the Commission on the Status of Women of the Association for Education in Journalism and Mass Communication, USA. Between 2000 and 2003 she was on the visiting faculty of the Asian College of Journalism, Chennai/Madras, teaching on "Covering Gender." She is a founder-member of the Network of Women in Media, India, and co-editor of its Web site (www.nwmindia.org).

Aliza Lavie's doctoral dissertation focused on the influence of gender on Israeli public radio news and current events programming. The thesis specifically explored issues of gender in newscasts and current events programs broadcast on public radio stations in Israel, a society of heavy news consumers. The study was one of the first attempts to apply an integrated qualitative and quantitative perspective to the issue of gender, media products and organizational aspects of media production. She is currently a lecturer and researcher at the Department of Political Studies, Bar-Ilan University (Israel), specializing in gender and mass media in the Public Communications Program. Her efforts, directed to raise public consciousness of the exclusion of women from public discourse, included heading a public research project on this topic.

Wilson Lowrey is assistant professor in the Department of Journalism at The University of Alabama (USA), where he teaches courses in editing, journalism issues, and media and society. He earned his doctorate in mass communication from The University of Georgia after working seven years in the newspaper industry. His research focuses on the sociology of news work and on the impact of new technologies on journalism. Lowrey's research has been published in a number of journals, including *Journalism & Mass Communication Quarterly, Gazette, Mass Communication and Society,* and *Newspaper Research Journal.*

Margareta Melin-Higgins is a senior lecturer and researcher at the School of Arts and Communication, Malmö University, Sweden Her research has mainly been about journalist cultures in Britain and Sweden and has resulted in several international publications. A book summarizing a 10-year research project on British journalist culture will be published in 2005 (Gothenburg University Press). In 2003 she receive the Malmö University Teaching Award. She is presently involved in starting up a research project on feminist pedagogies and media didactics.

Aida Opoku-Mensah is Team Leader for the UN Economic Commission for Africa's (ECA) ICT for Development Programme, based in Addis Ababa, Ethiopia. Formerly program officer for Media, Arts and Culture in the Ford Foundation West Africa office in Lagos, Nigeria. Before she took on responsibilites in Nigeria, she was Regional Director of Panos Southern Africa based in Lusaka, Zambia.

Aida Opoku-Mensah has written extensively on media, ICTs and development in Africa. Her publications include *Signpost on the Superhighway: African Environment, Up in the Air: The State of Broadcasting in Southern Africa, Democratising Access to the Information Society* as well as chapters on ICTs as Tools for Democratisation for African Women, the Future of Community Radio in Southern Africa. Aida Opoku-Mensah did her MA in Communication Policy Studies at City University, London and is currently completing her PhD thesis at University of Leeds.

Barbi Pilvre is a PhD student at Tartu University (Estonia) and University of Tampere (Finland). She also works as editor for arts and is a columnist for an Estonian weekly *Eesti Ekspress*. She is a founding member and a member of the board of the Women´s Studies Centre at the Tallinn Pedagogical University. Her research interests include the construction of gender in different media texts, both press and television. She is currently working on a media training toolkit *Screening Gender* and is a visiting fellow at University College London (2004-2005). Her articles published in English include Taming the Phantom of Feminism: Perspectives on Women's Lives, Equal Rights and "Women's Issues" in Estonia in *Private Views Re/Cognizing the Space in Estonian and British Contemporary Art* (London: Women's Art Library, 2000).

Gertrude J. Robinson is a retired professor and past Director of the Graduate Program in Communications at McGill University, Montreal Canada. She has taught and written extensively on gender, Canadian, European and international communication issues. Her studies include nine books and over 50 artices including a book manuscript on *Gender, Journalism and Equity: Canadian, U.S. and European Perspectives* (Hampton Press, forthcoming); the contributions of feminist theories to media studies (1994); an analysis of Canadian female politicians and their media coverage (1992) and a comparison of women and power: Canadian and German experiences (1990). She was awarded the "Woman of Distinction" award in Communications by the Montreal YWCA; the Dodi Robb award from Media Watch. She is a member of Phi Beta Kappa and Kappa Tau Alpha honorary societies and is listed in the 1998 edition of the Dictionary of International Biography, Cambridge.

Karen Ross is Reader in Mass Communication at Coventry University and is a visiting professor at the School of Politics, Queens University Belfast (2001-2004). She has written extensively on issues of in/equality in communication and culture and her books include: *Women and Media: International Perspectives* (with Carolyn Byerly, 2004); *Media and Audiences* (with Virginia Nightingale, 2003); *Critical Readings: Media and Audiences* (with Virginia Nightingale, 2003); *Mapping the Margins: Identity Politics and Media* (2003); *Women, Politics, Media* (2002); *Women, Politics and Change* (2001); *Black Marks: Minority Ethnic Audiences and Media* (2001); *Managing Equal Opportunities in Higher Education* (with Diana Woodward, 2000); and *Black and White Media* (1996). She is currently researching women politicians in Northern Ireland and is coordinator of a pan-European study of gender and the European Elections 2004.

Author Index

A

Aarons, L., 221, 222, 226, *238*
Abbott, A., 25, 25(*n*6), 28, 29, *38*
Abrahamsson, L, 94, 95, *102*
Abrahamsson, U., 94, 95, *102*
Acker, J., 85, 85(*n*5), *102*, 121, *139*
AGI, 107, *117*
Aldoory, L., 67, 73, *74*
Alfermann, D., 70, 71, 72, *74*
Allan, S., vii, viii, *xiii*, 1, *14*, 136, *139*
Allen, V.L., 138, *142*
Alley, R.S., 155, *159*
Alloo, F., 110, *117*
Aloni, S., 131, *139*
Alvesson, M., 4, *14*, 85, *102*
Alwood, E., 226, *238*
Åmark, K., 84, *103*
American Society of Newspaper
  Editors, 17, *38*
Anderson, W.B., 33, *39*
Aries, E., 67, 70, *74*
Armstead, C., 202, *218*
Armstrong, H., 181, *192*
Armstrong, P., 181, *192*
Ashforth, B., viii, *xiii*, 5, *15*
Asp, K., 202, *220*
Auman, A., 18(*n*2), 26, *39*

Avellan, H., 204(*n*4), *219*
AWMC, 108, *117*

B

Bach, M., 44, *62*
Bachar, S., 121, *140*
Baehr, H., 45, *62*, 204, 215(*n*11), *218*
Bailis, K., 235, *238*
Bakker, I., 224, *238*
Barley, S.R., 25, 26, *42*
Barnhurst, K.G., 19(*n*3), 32, *40*, *41*
Baron, J.N., 29, 33, 36, *39*, 122, *140*
Bartel, C., viii, *xiii*, 3, *14*
Bates, D., 67, *74*
Baude, A., 96, *102*
Baxter, J., 13, *14*
Beasley, M., vii, *xiii*, 122, *139*, 157, *158*,
  204, 215(*n*11), *218*, 224, 228, 231,
  232, 233, *238*
Becker, L.B., 17, 30, 33, *39*. 66, *75*
Bergen, L.A., 132, *139*
Bericat, E., 46, *62*
Bernstein, D., 133, 134, *139*
Berryman-Fink, C., 71, *74*
Bertagna, J., 204(*n*5), 206, 215(*n*11), *218*
Bibble, J., 137(*n*15), *140*
Bielby, W.T., 29, 33, 36, *39*, 122, *140*
Billing, Y., viii, *xiii*, 4, *14*, 85, *102*

Bird, S.E., 155, *158*
Blau, P.M., 34, *39*
Bliss, E., 120, 120(*n*3), *140*
Bloor, G., 25, *39*
Boëthius, G., 95, *102*
Boëtius, M-P., 95, *102*, 198, *219*
Börjesson, B., 202, *220*
Bourdieu, P., 59, *62*, 183, *192*, 195, 197, *218*
Bowman, W., 6, *15*, 187, *192*
Branston, G., vii, viii, *xiii*, 1, *15*
Brants, K., 99(*n*10), *102*
Breed, W., 131, *140*
Brennen, B., 32, *39*
Brewer, M., 2, *15*
Brickson, S., 2, *15*
Bridge, J., 222, *238*
Brinton, M.C., 122, *141*
Brodd, H., 84, *103*
Brown, C.J., 145, *159*
Burns, T., 6, *15*, 208, *218*
Burt, E.V., 233, *238*
Byerly, C.M., 144, 147, 157, *158*, 230, 231, 233, 234, 236, *238*

C

Capek, M.E.S., 67, *74*
Carlsson, J., 94, *103*
Carter, C., vii, viii, *xiii*, 1, *15*
Caspi, D., 68(*n*40), *75*, 122, 132, 135, 136, *140*
Census of India, 162, *178*
Chance, J., 147, 160
Charles, M., 122, *140*
Child, J., 25(*n*6), 29, *39*
Chomsky, N., 132, *140*
Christmas, L., 71, *72*, 156-157, *159*, 203, 204, 215, 215(*n*11), *218*
Claussen, D.A., 33, *39*
Clegg, S., 30, *39*
Cline, C.G., 72, *74*
Cohen, Y., 121(*n*4), *140*
Coit, P., 131, *140*
Collaer, M.L., 70, *74*
Collinson, D., 15, *16*
Connell, R.W., 84, *103*
Cook, J., 202, *218*
Cooley, Z.H., 137, *140*

Cramer, J.A., 135, *140*
Creedon, P.J., vii, *xiii*, 45, *62*, 65, 66, 72, *74*, 81, *103*, 144, *159*, 180, 191, *192*
Crisp, R., 2, *15*
Culbertson, H.M., 19(*n*3), *39*

D

Danner, L., 18(*n*2), 26, 32(*n*8), *42*
Dardenne, R.W., 155, *158*
Das, B., 165, *178*
David, P., 19(*n*3), *39*
Dawson, P., 25, *39*
de Bruin, M., vii, *xiii*, 1, 3, 5, *15*, 131, 132, *140*, 154, *159*, 197, 205, 215(*n*10-11), 216, *218*, 221, *238*
de Certeau, M., 195, 198, 201, *218*
Deaux, K., 2, 3, *15*
Del Rio, O., 45, *63*
Delano, A., 202, 204, 204(*n*5), 205, 206, 210, 217(*n*9), *219*
Demers, D.K., 33, *39*
Denzin, N.K., 47, *62*
Dimmick, J., 131, *140*
Djerf-Pierre, M., 48, 49, *63*, 80, 83(*n*4), 87, 100, *103*, *104*, 148, 150, 155, *159*, 182, 183, 185, 186, *192*, 196, 198, *220*
Donsbach, W., 204(*n*5), 206, *218*, *220*
Dukerich, J., 5, *15*
Dutton, J., viii, *xiii*, 3, 5, *14*

E

Egsmose, L., 83(*n*4), *103*, 199, 200, 203, 204, 208, 209, 211, 212, 215, 215(*n*10-11), 216, *218*
Eide, E., 199, 204, 211, 215(*n*9-10), *218*
Eisenstein, Z., 236, *238*
Eliasoph, N., 155, *159*
Ely, R., 7, 12, 13, *15*
Engblom, L-Å., 93, *103*
England, P., 30, *39*
Epstein, E.J., 34, *39*
Etzioni-Halevy, H., 136, *140*

F

Fagbemi, A.O., 113, *117*
Fagoaga, C., 44, 45, *63*
Farley, J., 45, *63*
Ferree, M., 3, *15*
Fine, M., viii, *xiv*

Fishman, M., 33, *39*
Fiske, S., 4, *14*
Flanders, L., 237, *238*
Fonow, M., 202, *218*
Fontana, A., 8, *15*
Foss, K.A., 67, *74,* 154, *159*
Foss, S.K., 67, *74,* 154, *159*
Frankel, F., 190, *192*
Fraser, N., 223, *238*
Fredin, E.S., 143-144, *160*
Frey, J., 8, *15*
Friedan, B., 231, *238*
Fröhlich, R., 65, 66, 66(*n*3), 68, 69, *74,*
191, *192*
Fulk, J., 25(*n*6), 29, *39*

G

Gallagher, M., vii, *xiv*, 1, *15*, 45, *63*, 65,
68, 69, 71, *75*, 79, 81, *103*, *104*, 108,
117, 122, *140*, 157, *159*, 204, 204(*n*5),
218, 228, 236, *238*
Gallego, J., 44, 45, *63*
Galloway, K., 203, 215, *219*
Galtung, J., 137(*n*14), *140*, 200-201,
219
Gam, A., 121, *140*
Gans, H., 201, *219*
Garcia, M.R., 19(*n*3), 32(*n*8), *39*
Garnham, N., 223, *238*
Gentry, J.K., 18, *40*
Gerald, E.J., 25(*n*6), *40*
Gherardi, S., viii, *xiii*, 85, *103*, 132, *140*
Gibbons, S., 224, 232, 233, *238*
Giffard, A., 19, *42*
Gil, Z., 133, *140*
Gillwald, A., 145-146, *159*
Glick, P., 4, *14*
Godfrey, P., viii, *xiv*, 4, *16*
Golding, P., 132, *140*
Gramsci, A., 123, *140*
Grayson, J.P., 30, *40*
Griffin, C.L., 67, *74*
Griffin, J., 19(*n*3), *42*
Gross, L., 226, *238*
Grunig, L.A., 66, 65, 69, 72, *75*, *76*,
77
Guenin, Z.B., 32, *40*
Gutkind, N., 133, *140*

H

Hagemann, G., 84, *103*
Halford, S., viii, *xiv*
Hall, J.A., 65, 70, *75*, *76*
Hall, R.H., 34, *40*
Hall, S., 2, *15*
Hamilton, S.R., 235, *238*
Hansen, K.A., 19, *40*
Harding, S., 202, *219*
Harquail, C., 5, *15*
Hartley, J., 80, *103*
Hawley, S., Jr., 6, *16*
Haz, H., 121, 123, *141*
Head, J., 37, *41*
Henley, N., 72, *75*
Henningham, J., 202, 204, 204(*n*5), 205,
206, 210, 217(*n*9), *219*
Henry, G., 144, 146, *160*
Herbert, M.S., 30, *39*
Herman, E., 132, *140*
Hermansson, J., 98, *104*
Herzog, H., 134, *140*
Herzog, K., 122, *140*, 147, *160*
Hess, B., 3, *15*
Hewstone, M., 2, *15*
Hilliard, R.D., 26, *40*
Hines, M., 70, *74*
Hirdman, Y., 86(*n*6), *103*, 205, 215, *220*
Hogg, M., 2, 3, *15*
Holland, P., 80, *103*
Hollander, B., 19(*n*3), *41*
Holtz-Bacha, C., 68, *74*
Hon, L.C., 67, *75*
Höök, P., 93, *103*
Hosley, D.H., 120, *140*
Huddy, L., 225, *239*
Hughes, E.C., 25(*n*6), *40*
Huyer, S., 113, *117*

I

Imam, A., 107, *117*
Indian Readership Survey, 162, *178*
Inoue, T., 68, *75*
International Women's Media Foundation
(IWMF), 225, 226, 236, *239*
Iwasaki, C., 68, *75*
Izraeli, D., 122, 123(*n*6), 126, 130, 131,
133, *141*

J

Jamous, H., 29, *40*
Järvinen, M., 197, *219*
Jõeorg, M., 242, *252*
Jõgeda, T., 246, *252*
Johnson, S., viii, *xiii*, 5, *14*
Johnstone, J., 6, *15*, 187, *192*
Jónásdottir, A., 202, 205, 215, *219*
Joonsaar, A., 242, *252*
Joseph, A., 161, 165, 177, *178*

K

Kanter, R.M., 27, *40*, 128, 135, 136, *141*
Kaofman, S., 131, *142*
Karro, H., 242, *252*
Kato, H., 68, *75*
Katz, E., 121, 123, *141*
Kaufman, M., 84, *103*
Kelly, J.D., 19(*n*3), *40*
Keuneke, S., 66, *76*
Kielbowicz, R., 228, *239*
Kilbourne, B.S., 30, *39*
Kimmel, M., 84, *103*
Kirate, M., 5, *15*
Kitzinger, J., vii, *xiv*, 1, *16*
Klaus, E., 183, 184, 186, 190, *192*
Klett, B., 206, *218*
Köcher, R., 201, 202, 203, 206, 215, *219*
Kodama, M., 68, *75*
Kohorst, E., 18, *40*
Kop, Y., 122, *141*
Kosicki, G.M., 17, 30, *39*, 66, *75*
Kvale, S., 203, *219*

L

Lachover, E., 68(*n*4), *75*, 122, *141*
Lafky, S., 65, 66, 66(*n*3), 69, *75*, 145, *159*, 225, *239*
Larsson, LÅ., 203, *219*
Lauk, E., 243, 244, 246, *252*
Lavie, A., 125, *141*
Light, D.W., 25, *40*
Limor, Y., 68(*n*4), *75*, 122, 123, 132, 133, 135, 136, *140*
Lindvert, J., 204(*n*4), *219*
Liran-Alper, S., 122, *141*
Lo, V., 5, *16*
Löffelholz, M., 66, *76*

Löfgren-Nilsson, M., 68(*n*4), 69, *75*, 81, 81(*n*3), 83(*n*4), *103*, *104*, 180, 183, 188, *192*
Lönnroth, A., 198, *219*
Lorber, J., 3, *15*, 121, *141*
Lötgren, M., 202, *220*
Lott, P., 19(*n*3), *40*
Lowery, W., 17, 18, 29, 30, 32(*n*8), 33, *39*, *40*
Lumsden, L., 33, *40*
Lünenborg, M., 45, *63*, 143, *159*, 191, *192*

M

MacKinnon, C., 202, 215, *219*
Made, P., 109, 110, *115*, *117*
Makunike-Sibanda, J., 105, 111, 112, *117*
Maor, A., 131, 134, *141*
Marcelle, G.M., 113, *117*
Marini, M.M., 122, *141*
Markey, R., 135, *141*
Marlane, J., 225, *239*
Marshall, J., 4, *16*
Martin, P., 15, *16*
Maume, D.J., Jr., 30, 33, *40*
Mayfield, W., 30, *39*
McChesney, R.W., 227, *239*
McLeod, J.M., 6, 16, 25(*n*6), *40*
McNair, B., 196, 196(*n*1), *219*
McQuail, D., 206, *219*
Mead, G.H.M., 137, *141*
Megdal, L.M., 30, *39*
Meir-Levy, H., 131, *142*
Melin, M., 196, 202, *219*, *220*
Melin-Higgins, M., 48, 49, 59, *63*, 81, 83(*n*4), *104*, 148, 150, 155, *159*, 182, 183, 185, 186, *192*, 197. 199, 200, 202, 205, 206, 211, 217(*n*10-11), 216, *219*, *220*
Menanteau-Horta, D., 6, *16*
Mendelson, A., 18(*n*1), *41*
Merrill, J., 25(*n*6), *40*
Merten, K., 71, *75*
Meyer, E., 32(*n*8), *40*
Micheletti, M., 98, *104*
Middlestadt, S.E., 19(*n*3), *40*
Miller, P., 37, *40*
Miller, R., 37, *40*

Mills, K., vii, *xiv*, 152, 155, 156, *159*, 234, *239*
Mitchell, C., 132, *141*
Modig, M., 95, *102*
Monczka, R.M., 67, 71, 76
Mörtberg, C., 84, *104*
Moses, M., 18, 32(*n*8), *40*
Muramatsu, Y., 68, *75*
Murdock, G., 132, *140*
Murphy, S., 221, 222, 226, *238*
Nardone, C.A.F., 143-144, *160*

N

Narusk, A., 246, *252*
Nayman, O.B., 25(*n*6), *41*
Nerone, J., 32, *41*
Neuzil, M., 19, *40*
Neveu, E., 68(*n*4), 69, *75*
Newcomb, H., 155, *159*
Newstrom, J.W., 65, 71, 76
Nilson, L.B., 27, *39*
Nordberg, K., 101(*n*11), *104*
Nwanko, N., 107, *117*

O

Ocamb, K., 230, *239*
Ofaz, A., 134, *141*
Ohiri-Aniche, C., 113, *117*
Opoku-Mensah, A., 105, 111, 112, *117*
Oppenheimer, V.K., 122, *141*
Ogan, C.L., 145, *159*
Oring, S., 122, *141*

P

Paechter, C., 37, *41*
Pasternack, S., 19(*n*3), 32(*n*8), *41*, *42*
Peloille, B., 29, *40*
Perkins, A., 217, *220*
Perrow, C., 24, 26, 27, 34, *41*
Peterson, P.V., 66, *75*
Petersson, O., 98, *104*
Pfeffer, J., 26, *41*
Phillips, A., 146, *159*
Pilvre, B., 242, 243, 246, *252*
Pleck, J., 181, 182, *192*
Polachek, S., 29, *41*
Porat, L., 133, *141*

Porter, L.W., 138, *141*
Pozner, J.L., 222, *239*
Pratt, M., 5, *16*
Prine, J., 30, *39*
Pringle, R., 121, *140*
Pritchard, D., 180, *192*
Punathambekar, A., 30, *39*

Q

Quindoza-Santiago, L., vii, *xiv*

R

Raijwan, R., 121, *140*
Rakow, L.F., 67, 69, 76, 121, *141*
Ram, N., 162, 166, 167, 168, *178*
Ramazanoglu, C., 202, *220*
Reese, S.D., 33, *41*, 155, *159*
Reid, L.L., 30, 33, *41*
Reid, T.R., 68, 76
Reif, W.E., 67, 71, 76
Reskin, B., 33, *41*, 122, 130, 130(*n*12), 136, *141*, *142*
Ridgeway, C.L., 137, *142*
Robertson, J., 303, 215, *219*
Robertson, N., 234, *239*
Robins, M.B., 113, *117*
Robinson, G.J., 68(*n*4), 69, 72, 76, 81, *104*, 144, 154, 155, *159*, 179, 192, *193*, 204, 205, 215(*n*10), *220*
Rock, M., 234, *239*
Roos, R.M., 130, 130(*n*12), *142*
Roshco, B., 33, *41*
Ross, K., viii, *xiv*, 183, 191, *193*
Ruge, M., 137(*n*14), *140*, 201, *219*
Rush, R., 6, *16*
Russial, J., 25, 34, *41*
Ryan, B., 19, *41*

S

Saint-Jean, A., 68(*n*4), 76, 81, *104*, 144, 154, 155, *159*, 187, *192*, *193*, 204, 205, 215(*n*10), *220*
Salcetti, M., 25, *41*
Sanders, M., *158*, *159*, 234, *239*
Sandstig, G., 84, *104*
Sarbin, T.R., 138, *142*
Sargent, A.G., 67, 71, 76
Sauvageau, F., 180, *192*

Savage, M., viii, *xiv*
Savolainen, T., 67, 76, 81, *104*
Scherer, C., 228, *239*
Schlesinger, P., 199, 204, 207, 208, 211, *220*
Schneider, B., 65, 68, 69, 76
Scholl, A., 66, 76
Schönbach, K., 65, 68, 69, 76
Schudson, M., 196, 196(*n*1), *220*
Scott, J.W., 121, *142*
Seydegart, K., 79, *104*
Sharma, K., 165, *178*
Shelef, R., 131, *142*
Shilts, R., 234, *239*
Shoemaker, P.J., 33, *41*
Sieghart, M.A., 144, 146, *160*
Sigal, L.V., 33, 34, *41*
Sigelman, L., 7, *16*
Simpson, R.L., 25, 29, *41*
Sines, S., 18, *41*
Singletary, M.W., 25(*n*6), *41*
Sixs, S., 131, *142*
Skidmore, P., vii, *xiv*, 1, *16*, 136, *142*
Slawski, E., 6, *15*
Slawski, W., 187, *192*
Smith, C., 143-144, *160*
Smith, C.Z., 18(*n*1), *41*
Smith, R., 45, *63*, 136, *142*, *143*
Solomon, W.S., 25, *41*
Spears, G., 79, *104*
Spender, D., 202, *220*
Springston, J.K., 66, *77*
Srinivasan, K., 227, *239*
Stamm, K., 19, *42*
Stanley, L., 202, *220*
Stark, P., 19(*n*3), *39*, *41*
Steinberg, R.J., 30, 33, *42*
Steiner, L., vii, *xiv*, 1, *16*, 83(*n*4), 101(*n*11), *104*, 204, *220*, 228, 233, *239*
Stevenson, R., 19(*n*3), *42*
Stier, D.S., 65, 70, 76
Stover, D.L., 30, *42*
Streets, R.M., 138, *141*
Streitmatter, R., 32, *42*, 228, 229, *239*
Stürzebecher, D., 65, 68, 69, 76
Sundin, E., 85, 86, *104*

Suzuki, M., 68, 75

T

Tam, T., 29, 30, 33, *42*
Terry, D., 2, 3, *15*
Thomas, E.J., 137(*n*15), *140*
Toth, E.L., 66, 67, 72, *74*, 75, 76, 77
Trayhurn, D., 30, *39*
Trice, H.M., 25, 25(*n*6), 26, *42*
Tripathi, P.S., 167, *178*
Tuchman, G., 33, *42*, 137, *142*
Tunstall, J., 204, *220*
Turner, G., 135, *142*
Turow, J., 155, *160*

U

Undersood, D.C., 19, *42*
UNECA, 105, *117*
U.S. Department of Commerce, 66, 76
Utt, S.H., 19(*n*3), 32(*n*8), *41*, *42*

V

van Dijk, T., 2, *16*
van Maanen, J., 25, 26, *42*
van Zoonen, L., vii, *xiv*, 1, 4, *16*, 45, 54, 59, 62, *63*, 67, 68(*n*4), 69, 76, 80, 81, 92(*n*9), *103*, *104*, 119, 136, 137, *142*, 151, 153, 156, *160*, 197, 198, 199, 200, 204, 204(*n*5), 205, 205(*n*6), 211, 212, 215(*n*10-11), 216, *219*, *220*
Vinberger, M., 131, *142*
Vivan, J., 135, *142*

W

Wajcman, J., 30, 33, *42*
Wakefield, G., 67, 76
Walsh-Childers, K.J., 122, *142*, 147, *160*
Wanta, W., 18(*n*2), 19(*n*3), 26, 32(*n*8), *42*
Ward, J., 19, *40*
Warren, C.A., 144, 147, 157, *158*, 230, 233, 234, 236, *238*
Weaver, C., 146, *160*
Weaver, D.H., vii, *xiv*, 3, 5, 6, 7, *16*, 17, *42*, 65, 68, 76, 119, 132, *142*, 145, 146, 151, *159*, *160*, 180, 185, 187, 193, 202, 205, 206, *220*, 221, 225, 225(*n*1), *239*

Weibull, L., 80, 87, *103*, 202, *220*
Weick, K., 3, *16*
Weischenberg, S., 66, *76*
Westholm, A., 98, *104*
Westley, M., 25, *42*
Whetten, D., viii, *xiv*, 4, *16*
Wilhoit, G.C., 5, 7, *16*, 17, *42*, 68, *76*, 119, 132, *142*, 180, 185, 187, *193*, 221, *239*
Williams, R., 196, *220*
Wilson, B., 18, *42*
Witz, A., viii, *xiv*
Wright, D.K., 66, *77*

Wright, E., 13, *14*

Y

Yalin, D., 121, 123, *141*
Yamada, G.K., 120, *140*
Yanovzki, Y., 121, 123, *141*

Z

Zang, B., 18, *40*
Zeilizer, B., 32, *42*, 155, *160*, 190, *193*
Zilliacus-Tikkanen, H., vii, *xiv*, 15, *16*, 45, 62, *63*, 65, 68, *76*, 77, 81, *104*, 143, *160*, 196, 197, 199, 200, 201, 204, 211, 215(*n*10-11), 216, *220*

Subject Index

A

Aarens, Leroy, 226
ABC-TV, 48*n*
Acceptance, of "male" values, 59
Access
    to resources, 113-114
    to top management, 27
Activism, consciousness and, 227-230
Advocate, The, 229
African Gender Institute (AGI), 106
African newsrooms, 105-117
    access to resources, 113-114
    gender and media initiative in, 116-117
    gender roles in newsrooms, 111-112
    impact of discrimination on women
      journalists, 114-115
    newsroom culture in, 108-109
    newsrooms as political spaces, 112-113
    sexual harassment, 114
    thoughts and statements of male col-
      leagues, the sociocultural baggage,
      109-110
    women, gender, and the media in
      Africa, constructing a framework, 106
    women in the African media, images,
      voices, and texts, 107-109

African Topics magazine, 109
African Women and Child Feature
    Service, 116
African Women's Media Center (AWMC),
    107
Age variables, and working experience,
    130-131
Agencia EFE, 46, 49-50, 56
Aggression, 199
AGI. *See* African Gender Institute
Aktuellt (SVT1), 80, 86-96
Alfermann, Dorothee, 70
Alpha correlations, for scaled variables,
    21-23
Altés, Elvira, 43-63
Alwood, Edward, 226
America On-Line (AOL), 227
American Copy Editors Society, 18*n*
American Society of Newspaper Editors
    (ASNE), 225-226
Amihere, Blay-Kabral, 110
Antennen, 94
Anthony, Susan B., 228
AOL. *See* America On-Line
*Arbeitsgemeinschaft der öffentlich-
    rechtlichen Rundfunkanstalten
    Deutschlands (ARD)*, 66

ARD. *See Arbeitsgemeinschaft der öffentlich-rechtlichen Rundfunkanstalten Deutschlands*
ASNE. *See* American Society of Newspaper Editors
Assignment book, 52
Assumptions, about the "Free World," 161
Atlanta Constitution, 228, 236
Attitude scales, 202
Attribution, 50
Audiences without gender, 58
Availability, of organizational resources, 24
Avellan, Heidi, 204*n*
Aviva, 229
Avui, 46-50, 54, 56
AWMC. *See* African Women's Media Center

B

Bakker, Isabel, 224
Banter, 183
BBC-TV, 214
Behavior, gender-related differences in, 70-73
Beijing+5, 116
Beijing Women's Conference, 242
Beliefs, 5
Bombay Samachar, 162
Boston Globe, 228
Bourdieu, Pierre, 195, 197
Bowman, Patricia, 234
British journalism, 195, 203-204
Broadcasting Authority Act (Israel), 123
Bush, George W., 237
Byerly, Carolyn M., 221-252

C

Campaigns
  external, 230-232
  internal, 232-235
Canadian newsrooms, 179-193
  gender and narrative form, 189-190
  gendered professional outlooks, 187-189
  gendered work and family expectations, 180-182
  gendered workplace pressures, 185-187

print and broadcast personnel in, 179-182
professional "climate" in the newsroom, 183-187
Cantón, María José, 45-65
Capitalism, 223
Career patterns, 128
Caribbean media, 2, 8
Carlsson, June, 94
Casablanca (movie), 184
"Catch 22," 199
CBS, 161
Center for Integration and Improvement of Journalism, 235
Centrality, degree of, 26
Change, prospects for, 217
Chauvinism, 211
Children, 181
Chronbach's alpha, 21*n*
Circulation, global statistics regarding newspaper, 162
Civil rights movement, 222
Class identity, 14
Clinton, Hillary Rodham, 222
Cohesiveness, within the occupational subgroup, degree of, 26
Coinciding identities, 1-16
Commercial television, placement of categories of news stories in newscasts in, 91
Commercialization, 79
"Commonsense" views, of women's roles, 245-246
Communication professions
  entry level positions in, 72
  gender-based differentiation within, 73
Competition, 183
  versus consistency, 200
Conciliation, 72
Confidentiality, 8
Consciousness, and activism, 227-230
Consistency, *versus* competition, 200
Content. *See* Newspaper content
Contextual mechanisms of gender stereotyping, 58-60
  accepting "male" values, 59
  minority status, 60
Contradicting identities, 1-16

Control
  degree of, 20-23
  quest for, 29
Control over work in the newspaper newsroom, 17-42
  correlations with specialized knowledge, 31
Cooperative behavior, 71-72, 83
Coping with journalism, the tactics of female journalists, 211-215
Copy editing, 25*n*
Corporate culture, ascendance of, 7
Critical mass argument, 148
Culture
  defined, 85
  dominant journalist, 203-205
  dominant newsroom, 13

D

Dagens Eko, 97
Daily Mail (Zambia), 109
Daily Times (Malawi), 111
Dainik Bhaskar, 162
Dainik Jagran, 162
De Bruin, Marjan, 1-16
Derogatory comments, 209
Design directors, gender of, 27, 31-32
Design experts, 18-19, 25*n*
  control over work, 20
Design staffs, influence of, 24, 34
Design work, 36
  gendered perceptions of, 32
Devaluation hypothesis, 31
Dialectical process, within U.S. society, 237
Dil Se (Hindi movie), 168
Discourse, 196
Discrimination, impact on women journalists, 114-115
Distance
  versus involvement, 200
  keeping one's, 10
Djerf-Pierre, Monika, 79-104
Domesticated feminism, 146
Dominant journalist culture, 203-205
Dominant newsroom culture, 13
Dominated marionettes, *versus* women with place and power, 211-212

Double standard, 31
Douglass, Frederick, 228
Doxa, 197, 206-207
"Dual citizenship," 7

E

Editor and Publisher, 20
Editorial meetings, 53, 55-56
Editors, 18. *See also* Copy editing
  by gender and organization, 125
  women as, 244
Eenadu, 162
EEOC. *See* Equal Employment Opportunities Commission
Eesti Ekspress, 244, 246, 249
Eesti Päevaleht, 242, 250-251
EFE Press Agency, 46, 49-50
Ehrenreich, Barbara, 229
El Mundo, 48*n*
El País, 46-50, 52-53, 56
El Periódico de Catalunya, 46-50, 53-54, 56
Emergency period (India), 163-164, 177
Employment, structure of, 134-135
English journalism, 195, 203-204
Entertainment value, of newspapers, 167, 190
Entry level positions, in communication professions, 72
Epistemological issues, feminist, 202
Equal Employment Opportunities Commission (EEOC), 233
Essence, 226
Estonian newsrooms, 241-252
  case studies, 247-251
  on journalist identity, 243-245
  missing research on gender and media, 242-243
  women and change in the Estonian media scene, 245-247
Ethical codes, breaking to get the story, 207
Everyday routines, 208-209
ETV (Estonia), 243
European Union (EU), 241
Expectations, gender based, 73
Experimentation, *versus* formality, 200

Explanations
  at the organizational level, 26-27
  at the subgroup level, 26
Expressen, 87
External campaigns, 230-232

F

Face-to-face interviews, 8
Fairness and Accuracy in Reporting, 237
Faludi, Susan, 228
Family responsibilities, "meshing" work
  with, 181
Federal Communications Commission
  (FCC), 227, 231
Federation of African Media Women, 105
Female ghettos, 199
Female journalists, strategies or tactics of,
  198-200
Feminine and feminist values in communi-
  cation professions, 12, 65-77. *See also*
  Women, stereotypical traits ascribed to
  feminization of communication profes-
    sions, 65, 67-69, 73, 80, 83, 95, 123
  the "friendliness trap," 71-73
  the myth losing its luster, 73
  women as better communicators, 69-71
Feminine Mystique, The, 231
Femininities, multiple, 4, 84-85
Feminism
  domesticated, 146
  liberal, 222
  Swedish, 204*n*
Feminist, gay, and lesbian news activism
  in the U.S., 221-252
  avoiding labeling of, 59
  consciousness and activism, 227-230
  external campaigns, 230-232
  forms of news activism, 230
  internal campaigns, 232-235
  and the political economy of news,
    224-227
  prospects for the future, 235-236
  and the public sphere, 223-224
  terminology, 222-223
Feminist epistemological issues, 202
  reciprocity, 202
  recognition, 202
  reflexivity, 202

Feminist image, 247
Feminist outlook, 148, 185
Feminist Primetime Report, 231
Feminist studies, 45
Feminists, 222
Feminization
  of communication professions, 65, 67-
    69, 73, 80, 83, 95, 123
  defining, 81
  of salaries, 192
Feminization of Swedish television news
  production (1958-2000), 79-104
  gendered practice of news, 81-83
  place of women in the news, 86-100
  stereotypes and dichotomization, 83-86
Fighting for air time (1965-1985), 92-96
Finnish Women Journalists' Organization,
  243
Flanders, Laura, 237
Forbes, 226
Forbes, Malcolm, 226
Ford Foundation, 226
Formality, *versus* the experimental, 200
Fragmentation, systematic, in news gather-
  ing, 56
Fredrick, Pauline, 120
"Free World," assumptions about, 159
Freelancing, 212-213, 215
Friedan, Betty, 231
"Friendliness trap," 71-73
Fröhlich, Romy, 65-77
Future prospects, for feminist, gay, and les-
  bian news activism in the U.S., 235-236

G

Gallego, Juana, 43-63
Gandhi, Indira, 163
Gandy, Oscar, 235
Garrison, William Lloyd, 228
Gatekeepers, a strategy to retain power, 208
Gay and Lesbian Alliance Against
  Defamation (GLAAD), 231-232
Gay and lesbian news activism in the U.S.,
  221-252
Gay rights, 223
Gender
  audiences without, 58
  and career paths, 129-130

and control over work in the newspaper newsroom, 17-42
a (dis)advantage in Indian print media, 161-178
and narrative form, 189-190
and the political economy of news, 224-227
and professionalism, 172-177
Gender and decision making, 126-127
at IDF Radio, 127
role definitions, 127
at The Voice of Israel, 120, 124, 126-129, 131-139
Gender and media
African initiatives, 116-117
missing research on, 242-243
Gender-based differentiation, within communication professions, 73
Gender-based expectations, 73
Gender identity, 3-4, 13
Gender Links, 116
Gender order, in organizations, 86
Gender profiles, of senior positions in three media organizations in Swaziland, 111
Gender-specific differences, 70-73
reading nonverbal signals, 70
verbal behavior, 70
Gender stereotyping in the newsroom, 43-63, 81-83, 111-112, 143-160, 195-220
in Africa, 105-117
in Canada, 179-193
contextual mechanisms of, 58-60
coping with, the tactics of female journalists, 211-215
defining feminization, 82
dominant journalist culture, 203-205
the doxa, 197, 206-207
in Estonia, 241-252
the feminization of Swedish television news production, 1958-2000, 79-104
findings, 47-49
journalism as practice and policy, 149
male and female dimensions in journalism, 82-83
mechanisms of, 55-61
methodology, 201-203

myths and realities of a gendered journalism, 154-158
production process, 49-54
research process, 45-47
sex and money, 152-154
sex and professionalism, 151-152
the sexed newsroom, 143-150
the social field, 203-205
stereotypes and stereotyping, 44-45
strategies to retain power, 208-210
Gendered culture of journalism, 196-201
journalism as a social field, 197-198
journalist culture, 196-197
professional outlooks for, 187-189
strategies and tactics of female journalists, 199-201
Gendered substructures, 1
Gendered workplace pressures, 185-187
and family expectations, 180-182
marriage rates, 181
"masculinist" career notions, 182
number of children, 181
work and family responsibilities, 181-182
German Public Relations Society, 69
GLAAD. *See* Gay and Lesbian Alliance Against Defamation
"Glass ceiling," 130, 139, 233
Global Journalist, The, 206
Globalization, 223
Goodman, Ellen, 228
Graham, Katharine, 225
Grihashobha, 162
Guardian, The, 150
Guerrilla warfare, 199
Gundersen, Etambuyu Anamela, 112
Gyan Appenteng, Kwesi, 112, 115

H

Ha'Aretz, 122
Habitus, 197
Harassment, 9
sexual, 114
Hard news, *versus* soft, 200
Harpies and Quinnes, 213-214
Hill, Anita, 157, 234
Hommikuleht, 245

Homosexuality. *See* Feminist, gay, and lesbian news activism in the U.S.
Homosocial behavior, 27, 37

I

Identification, 2
Identities, 1-16, 13-14
 sharing work in progress, 9-13
 social identities, 2-6, 13
 at work, 7-8
IDF. *See* Israel Defense Forces Radio
In-depth interviews, 8
Incorporation strategy, 148
Independent, The, 150
India Today, 162
Indian print media
 background, 162-163
 gender and professionalism, 172-177
 gender (dis)advantage in, 161-178
 women's experiences and perspectives, 168-172
 women's presence in the Indian press, 163-168
Indian Readership Survey (IRS), 162
Individualism, versus collectivism, 200
Influence, 20
Influence of other media, 57
Information age, creating opportunities for women, 115
Infotainment, 79
Internal campaigns, 232-235
International news editors, 20
International Women's Media Foundation (IWMF), 236
Internet
 news activism on, 235
 training in, 113
InterPress Service (IPS), 112, 116
Interpretive community, of journalists, 155
Intervention, 223
Interviews
 face-to-face, 8
 snowball method, 201
IPS. *See* InterPress Service
IRS. *See* Indian Readership Survey
Isolating facts, versus wholeness, 200
Israel Defense Forces (IDF) Radio, 120, 123, 127-139

gender and decision making at, 127
Israeli Advertisers' Association, 123
Ivins, Molly, 228
IWMF. *See* International Women's Media Foundation

J

Jamaica, class-stratified society like, 14
Jerusalem Post, 122
Jock strap humor, 147
Jögeda, Tiina, 246
Joseph, Ammu, 161-179
Journalism
 convention and tradition in, 44
 coping with gendered newsroom culture, 195-220
 gentrification of, 205
 male and female dimensions in, 82-83
 a man's world, 204
 market-driven, 79-80
 new style of, 79
 process of, 53
 as a social field, 197-199
 soft, 156, 191
 subjective, 213
Journalism as practice and policy, 149
Journalism schools, 29-30, 65-66
Journalist culture, 196-197
Journalist identity, 243-245
Jutterström, Christina, 93

K

Kanal 2 (Estonia), 246
Karpa, Kärt, 250
Knowledge
 occupational, 28
 political nature of, 202
 specialized, 26, 31
Kvale, Steinar, 203

L

La Vanguardia, 46-50, 52-54, 56, 58
Labeling of feminist, gay, and lesbian news activism in the U.S., avoiding, 59
Labor market, for journalists, 243
Ladies Home Journal, 228
Ladies Press Club, 233
Lauk, Epp, 243
Lavie, Aliza, 119-142

Legitimized ideologies, 57-58
Lesbian news activism in the U.S., 221-252
  avoiding labeling of, 59
  consciousness and activism, 227-230
  external campaigns, 230-232
  forms of news activism, 230
  internal campaigns, 232-235
  and the political economy of news,
    224-227
  prospects for the future, 235-236
  and the public sphere, 223-224
  terminology, 222-223
Liberal feminists, 222
Liberator, The, 228
Liik, Kadri, 250
Limor, Yehiel, 133*n*
Liswaniso, Pelekelo, 109-110
Locker room humor, 183
Löfgren-Nilsson, Monica, 79-104
Logic, male *vs.* female, 82
Lönnroth, Ami, 198
Los Angeles Times, 155
Lowrey, Wilson, 17-42

M

Ma'ariv, 122, 133*n*
Made, Patricia, 112
Makunike-Sibanda, Jennifer, 110
Malawi Broadcasting Corporation, 111
Malayala Manorama, 162
"Male" values
  accepting, 59
  thoughts and statements of, 109-111
Management, access to top, 27
Managing editor, 53
Marginalizing, of women, 14
Marionettes, 199
  dominated, *versus* women with place
    and power, 211-212
Marriage rates, 181
Masculine worldview, 59
"Masculinist" career notions, 181-182
Masculinities, multiple, 4, 84-85
McChesney, Robert W., 227
Mechanisms of gender stereotyping
  based on professional culture, 57-58
  contextual, 58-60
  organizational, 55-56

personal-individual, 60-61
Mechanisms of gender stereotyping based
  on professional culture, 57-58
  audience without gender, 58
  classification of news, 57
  influence of other media, 57
  legitimized ideologies, 57-58
Melin-Higgins, Margareta, 195-220
Melús, Marìa Eugenia, 43-63
Methodology, 123-125
Miami Herald, 229
Minority status, 60
Misogyny, 225*n*
"Mission" approach, 185
Money, sex and, 152-154
Mossell, Gertrude Bustill, 228
Ms. (magazine), 229
Mtintso, Thenjiwe, 116
Multicultural advocacy groups, 235
Myth, the, losing its luster, 73
Myths and realities of a gendered journal-
  ism, 154-58

N

Nation (Malawi), 111
National Organization for Women
  (NOW), 231, 233
National Press Photographers Association,
  18*n*
"Natural" differences, between men and
  women, 92
"Naturalistic" culture, 147, 154
Near-equality (from 1985 onward), 96-100
Negotiations, subgroup, 33-34
New York Times, 231, 233
News. *See also* Place of women in the news
  classification of, 57
  forms of activism in, 230
  hard versus soft, 200
  the hunt for, 206
  and the public sphere, 223-224
  soft, 32, 82
  stories covered by female reporters, 95
  "women's," 120*n*
News artists, 18
News gathering, systematic fragmentation
  in, 56
News professionals, *vs.* consumers, 153

News work
    subspecialities within, 17-18, 25
    "visual journalists," 18
    "word journalists," 18
Newscasts in public service and commer-
    cial television, placement of categories
    of news stories in, 91
Newspaper circulation, global statistics
    regarding, 162
Newspaper content
    arguments beyond, 46
    entertainment value of, 167, 190
    gendered, 50-51, 157
Newsroom culture
    in Africa, fighting a mind set, 108-109
    gender roles in, 111-112
    as political space, 112-113
    strategies to retain power in, 209
Newswatch, 235
NGOs. See Nongovernmental organisations
Nickelodeon, 227
Nongovernmental organisations (NGOs),
    217
North Star, 228
NOW. See National Organization for
    Women
Nyheterna (TV4), 80, 86, 88-89, 91, 97-98

O

Oakland Tribune, 226
Occupational knowledge, 28
    and control over work in the newspaper
        newsroom, 17-42
    explanations at the organizational
        level, 26-27
    explanations at the subgroup level, 26
    methodology, 20-23
    organizational influences, gender, and
        control over work, 33-36
    regression results, 27-33
    relationship of gender and control over
        work, 24
    variable measures and alpha correla-
        tions for scaled variables, 21-23
Occupational-level predictors, 22-23
Occupations
    classification of, 121n
    defined, 25n

"Old boys" network, 184, 208
On the Issues, 229
One-of-a-kind (1958-1965), 86-92
One of the boys, or women with attitude,
    212-213
One of the girls, or compassionate journal-
    ism with a mission, 213-214
Opoku-Mensah, Aida, 105-117
Opubor, Alfred, 108
Organizational factors, 119-142
    availability of resources, 26
    constraints, 7
    gender, and control over work, 33-36
    identity, 4-5
    salience of, 131-132
    size, 27
Organizational history, 132-133
Organizational level explanations, 26-27
    access to top management, 27
    availability of organizational resources,
        26
    organizational size, 27
    predictors, 23
Organizational mechanisms of gender
    stereotyping, 55-56
    editorial meetings, 55-56
    systematic fragmentation in news gath-
        ering, 56
    women as decision makers, 56
Organizational structure, 25
    gender order in, 86
Outweek, 226
Overlapping identities, 1-16

P

Page designers, 18-19
Panos Institute, 113
Partnerships, unequal, 111-112
Patriarchal Enlightenment dichotomy, 215
PBS. See Public Broadcasting System
Personal-individual mechanisms of gender
    stereotyping, 60-61
    personal involvement, 60-61
    social beliefs, 61
Photography, 25n
Pilvre, Barbi, 241-252
Place of women in the news, 86-100
    fighting for air (1965-1985), 92-96

near-equality (from 1985 onward), 96-100

news stories covered by female reporters, 95

one of a kind (1958-1965), 86-92

placement of categories of news stories in newscasts in public service and commercial television, 91

topics covered by female and male reporters in public service and commercial newscasts, 88-89

topics in stories covered by female and male reporters in public service and commercial newscasts, 99

Placement of categories of news stories, in newscasts in public service and commercial television, 91

Popularization, 79

Populations of editors, by gender and organization, 125

Postimees, 242, 251

Powell, Michael, 227

Power strategies, 208-210

the gatekeepers, 208

and influence, 128-129

the newsroom culture, 209

the pub, 209-210

the routines, 208-209

symbolic, 197

Presentation work, 18n

Production process, 49-54

topics that affect especially women as a group or men as a group, 51

topics with female presence, 51

topics with gender perspective, 51

topics with male presence, 50-51

topics with mixed presence, 51

topics with no gender references, 50

Professional "climate" in the newsroom, 183-187

Professional ethos, neutral, 183

Professional identity, 6, 13-14

Professional knowledge, 29-33

Professional work, 33

Progressive approach, 62

Promotion, paths of, 135-138

PRSSA. *See* Public Relations Student Society of America

Public Broadcasting Authority (Israel), 123, 132

Public Broadcasting System (PBS), 226

Public Relations Student Society of America (PRSSA), 66

Public service commercial television, placement of categories of news stories in newscasts in, 91

Pubs, and strategies to retain power, 209-210

Q

Questionnaire-based studies, 202

validity issues raised by, 201

Queue Theory, 130n

R

Radical feminists, 222

Radio newsrooms

age variables and working experience, 130-131

background, 121-123

career patterns, 128

findings, 126-132

gender and career paths, 129-130

gender and decision making, 126-127

methodology, 123-125

organizational factors in, 119-142

organizational history, 132-133

paths of promotion, 135-138

patterns of recruitment, 135

power and influence, 128-129

the salience of organization and structure, 131-132

structure of employment, 134-135

study populations of editors by gender and organization, 125

the workplace as a reflection of social structure, 133-134

Radio-Television News Directors Association, 225

Rapport (SVT2), 80, 86, 88-89, 91-95

Recruitment, patterns of, 135

Redgrave, Vanessa, 150

Regression analysis, 25, 34

Regression of degree of control over presentation work

by the design subgroup, 28

by organizational size, 35
results, 27-33
Relationship of gender and control over
work, 24
Reporters and reporting, 18, 25*n*
Reputation, 5
Research processes, 45-47
Resources
access to, 113-114
availability of organizational, 26
Responsibilities, of work and family, 181-
182
Retreating from the newsroom, 148
or getting a place, 214-215
Reuters, 150
Revolution, 228
Rich Media, Poor Democracy, 227
Robinson, Gertrude J., 179-193
Rooväli, Küllike, 251
Routine work, 33
a strategy to retain power, 208-209

S

SADC. *See* Southern Africa Development
Community
Salience, of organization and structure,
131-132
Scaled variables, alpha correlations for,
21-23
Scanning, by readers, 19*n*
Schrewelius, Ingrid, 90
Scottish journalism, 195
Segregation, vertical, 1
Self-esteem, 246
"Self-stereotyping," 3, 14
Sex
distinguished from gender, 119*n*
the primary category, 4
Sex and money, 152-154
Sexed newsrooms, 143-150
Sexist humor, 183
Sexual harassment, 114, 146-147
Sexual minorities, 223
Signorile, Michael, 226
Sikk, Rein, 251
Simpson, Carole, 236
60 Minutes, 161
Smith, William Kennedy, 234

Snowball method, of interviewing, 201
Social beliefs, 61
Social field, 195, 197-198, 203-205, 215
Social identities, 2-6, 13
gender identity, 3-4, 13
organizational identity, 4-5
professional identity, 6, 13-14
Social structure, workplace as a reflection
of, 133-134
Socialization, gendered, 71
Society for News Design, 18*n*, 20, 32*n*
Sociocultural baggage, 109-110
Soft journalism, 156, 191
Soft news, 32, 82
Soriano, Jaume, 43-63
Southern Africa Development Community
(SADC), 105, 116
Spain, women in, 44
Spanish media, 44
Specialized knowledge, 26
correlations with control over work, 31
SR. *See* Sveriges Radio
Stanton, Elizabeth Cady, 228
Statesman, The, 164
Status, 11, 199
Stereotyping, 59-60
and dichotomization, 83-86
and stereotyping, 44-45
Stewart, Maria, 228
Stone, Lucy, 228
Straight News, 226
Strategies of female journalists, 195, 198-
201
competition *versus* consistency, 200
distance *versus* involvement, 200
formal *versus* experimental, 200
hard *versus* soft news, 200
individualism *versus* collectivism, 200
isolating facts *versus* wholeness, 200
work *versus* private life, 200
Strategies to retain power, 208-210
the gatekeepers, 208
the newsroom culture, 209
the pub, 209-210
the routines, 208-209
Structure
of employment, 134-135
salience of, 131-132

Study populations of editors, by gender
and organization, 125
Subgroup level explanations, 26
average years experience of a sub
group, 26
degree of centrality, 26
degree of cohesiveness within the
occupational subgroup, 26
and negotiations, 35-36
specialized knowledge, 26
Subjective journalism, 213
Sveriges Radio (SR), 86
SVT1. *See* Aktuellt
SVT2. *See* Rapport
Swedish Association of Journalists, 81*n*
Swedish feminism, 204*n*
Swedish television news production, feminization of (1958-2000), 79-104
Symbolic power, 197

T

Tabloidization, 79
Tactics of female journalists, 195, 198-
201, 211-215
competition *versus* consistency, 200
distance *versus* involvement, 200
dominated marionettes, or women with
place and power, 211-212
formal *versus* experimental, 200
hard *versus* soft news, 200
individualism *versus* collectivism, 200
isolating facts *versus* wholeness, 200
one of the boys, or women with attitude, 212-213
one of the girls, or compassionate journalism with a mission, 213-214
retreating from the newsroom, or getting a place, 214-215
work versus private life, 200
Tanzania Media Women's Association
(TAMWA), 110
Telecommunications Act of 1996, 227
Telephone surveys, 20
Terminology
capitalism, 223
feminist, 222
feminization, 81
gay rights, 223

globalization, 223
intervention, 223
liberal feminist, 222
radical feminist, 222
sexual minorities, 223
Thomas, Clarence, 157, 234
Time (magazine), 229
Time-Warner, 227
Times of India, The (TOI), 162, 166-167
TOI. See Times of India, The
Top management, access to, 27
Topics
covered by female and male reporters
in public service and commercial
newscasts, 88-89
with female presence, 51
with gender perspective, 51
with male presence, 50-51
with mixed presence, 51
with no gender references, 50
in stories covered by female and male
reporters in public service and commercial newscast, 99
that affect especially women as a group
or men as a group, 51
"Truth," the hunt for, 206-207
Tucker, Cynthia, 228, 236
TV4. *See* Nyheterna
TV1 (Estonia), 246

U

"Underground" strategies, 11
UNDP. *See* United Nations Development
Program
Unequal partnerships, 111-112
UNESCO, 105
Unfemininity, 199
UNICEF, 107
UNIFEM, 107, 116
United Nations Development Program
(UNDP), 107-108, 242
Unity, 235-236

V

Variables, scaled, alpha correlations for,
21-23
Vertical segregation, 1
Viacom, 227

Villarosa, Linda, 226
"Virtual Newsroom," 115
"Visual journalists," 18, 32
Voice of Israel, The, gender and decision
    making at, 120, 124, 126-129, 131-139
Vulnerability, showing, 13

W

Wall Street Journal, 228
'War zone' coverage, 150
Washington Blade, 229
Washington Post, 225
Watchdog role, 188
White Anglo-Saxon Protestants, journal-
    ism the domain of, 204
Will Women Change the News Media,
    236
Williams, Raymond, 196
WINGS. *See* Women's International
    Newsgathering Service
"Woman journalists" (term), 172
Women. *See also* Place of women in the
    news
    in the African media, 107-108
    as better communicators, 69-71
    "commonsense" views of roles of, 245-
        246
    as decision makers, 56
    experiences and perspectives of, 168-
        172
    gender, and the media in Africa, con-
        structing a framework, 106
    information age creating opportunities
        for, 115
    kept in their place, 14
    with place and power, *versus* dominat-
        ed marionettes, 211-212
    presence in the Indian press, 163-168
    in the public sphere, 81
    stereotypical traits ascribed to, 30, 67,
        70-71, 109, 173-177

Women and the Media (conference), 198
Women in Journalism, 144, 217*n*
Women's eNews, 229
Women's International Net Magazine, 229
Women's International Newsgathering
    Service (WINGS), 229
Women's Journal, 228
Women's movement, 86. *See also*
    Feminism
"Women's news," 120*n*
Women's Political Caucus, 233
Women's Studies Centre (Estonia), 243
"Women's work," 30
"Word journalists," 18
Work
    and family responsibilities, 181-182
    versus private life, 200
    "women's," 30
Working experience, age variables and,
    130-131
Workplace, as a reflection of social struc-
    ture, 133-134
Works-in-progress, sharing, 9-13
Writing ability, of journalists, 173

Y

Yediot Aharonot, 122

Z

Zambia National Broadcasting
    Corporation (ZNBC), 112
ZBC. *See* Zimbabwe Broadcasting
    Corporation
ZDF. *See* Zweites Deutsches Fernsehen
Zimbabwe Broadcasting Corporation
    (ZBC), 110
ZNBC. *See* Zambia National Broadcasting
    Corporation
Zweites Deutsches Fernsehen (ZDF), 66

Printed in the United States
26377LVS00004B/202-225

9 781572 735897